DATE DUE

NOV 1 4 2000		
NOV 1 7	2003	
JAN 0 3	2005	

GAYLORD   #3523PI   Printed in USA

Shadows, Fire, Snow

Shadows, Fire, Snow
The Life of Tina Modotti

By Patricia Albers

CLARKSON POTTER / PUBLISHERS
NEW YORK

Published by Clarkson N. Potter, 201 East 50th Street,
New York, New York 10022. Member of the Crown Publishing Group.

Random House, Inc. New York, Toronto, London, Sydney, Auckland
www.randomhouse.com

CLARKSON N. POTTER, POTTER, and colophon are registered trademarks of
Random House, Inc.

Printed in the United States of America

Design by Maggie Hinders

Library of Congress Cataloging-in-Publication Data
Albers, Patricia.
    Shadows, fire, snow : the life of Tina Modotti / Patricia Albers.
    —1st ed.
        Includes bibliographical references and index.
        1. Modotti, Tina, 1896–1942.   2. Women photographers—Italy—Biography.
    3. Women photographers—Mexico—Biography.   4. Photographers—Mexico—
    Biography.   5. Women communists—Italy—Biography.   6. Women communists—
    Mexico—Biography.   7. Communists—Mexico—Biography.   I. Title.
    TR140.M58A43   1999
    770'.92—dc21
        [B]   98-45727

ISBN 0-609-60069-9

10 9 8 7 6 5 4 3 2 1

First Edition

For Benjamin

Acknowledgments

THIS BOOK could not have been written without the unparalleled trust and friendship of Ruth and LaBrie Ritchie, to whom I am deeply grateful. I also owe enormous debts to Christiane Barckhausen-Canale, Gianfranco Ellero, Dainis Karepovs, and Elena Poniatowska, for their expertise and unflagging support. It is in the spirit of Tina Modotti that her biography should be informed by the generosity of individuals in five far-flung countries.

For their memories, insights, and assistance, I also warmly thank Alessandro Baccari, Jr., France Bequette, Beatriz Braniff, John Britton, Pierre Broué, Argentina Ferrau Brunetti, Bob Burchard, Andrew M. Canepa, Gary Carey, Silvano Castano, Laura and John Condax, Mildred Constantine, Bruno Cosolo, Candace Crockett, Robert D'Attilio, Aria DiBiase, Marta Esteverena, Alan C. Freeland, Margaret Gibson, Luciano de Giorgio, Susannah Glusker, Stephanie Gray, Monica and Walter Heilig, Steven Higgins, Livio Jacob, Jesco Köller, Leni Kroul, Marina Kusell, Sarah M. Lowe, Angelo Masutti, Dorothy and Irwin Mayers, Aline Menassé, Loreta Richey Moore, Cathy Perez, Anita Leocadia Prestes, Mimi Quintanilla, Alan Rinzler, Eladia de los Ríos, Cécile Rol-Tanguy, Vincenza Scarpaci, Gerald Schöpfer, Daniel M. Selznick, John H. Stewart, Sam Stourdzé, Riccardo Toffoletti, Edouard Waintrop, Ann Walnum, Cole Weston, Neil Weston, D. Anthony White, Claude Willard, Bill Windberg, and Ella Wolfe.

Many archivists and librarians were helpful to me beyond the call of duty. I wish to thank the Academy of Motion Picture Arts and Sciences, Beverly Hills, California: Scott Curtis, Kristine Krueger, and Faye Thompson; American Film Institute, Louis B. Mayer Library, Los Angeles, California; Amherst College Library, Amherst, Massachusetts: Anne Ostendarp; Archivo General de la Nación, Mexico City; Bancroft Library, University of California, Berkeley, California; Bauhaus Library, Berlin; Biblioteca Comunale, Udine, Italy; Biblioteca Nacional, Mexico City: José Manuel Porras Navarro; Bibliothèque Marxiste, Paris: Catherine Bensadek;

Bibliothèque Nationale, Paris; Boston University Libraries, Department of Special Collections, Boston, Massachusetts: Howard B. Gotlieb and Charles Niles; Brandeis University, Goldfarb Library, Spanish Civil War Archive, Waltham, Massachusetts: Victor Berch; Casa de la Cultura, Tehuantepec, Mexico: Julín Contreras; Center for Creative Photography, University of Arizona, Tucson, Arizona: Amy Rule; Centro de Estudios del Movimiento Obrero y Socialista, Mexico City: María Carmen Ribera; Comitato Tina Modotti, Udine, Italy: Riccardo Toffoletti; Fototeca del INAH, Pachuca, Mexico: Juan Carlos Valdez Marín; The Getty, Research Institute for the History of Art and the Humanities, Los Angeles, California: Brent Sverdloff; Hemeroteca Nacional, Universidad Nacional Autónoma de México, Mexico City; Hoover Institution Library and Archives, Stanford University, Stanford, California; Ibero-Amerikanisches Institut, Berlin; Immigration History Research Center, University of Minnesota, St. Paul: Jennifer M. Guglielmo and Timo Riippa; Istituto Friulano per la Storia del Movimento di Liberazione, Udine, Italy; Kärntner Landesarchiv, Klagenfurt, Austria: Wilhelm Wadl; Archives of *La Prensa,* Mexico City: Graciela Alvarado; Labor Archives and Research Center, San Francisco State University, San Francisco, California: Susan Sherwood; Library of Congress, Washington, D.C.: Rosemary C. Hanes; MacDowell Colony, Peterborough, New Hampshire; Mills College Library, Special Collections, Oakland, California; New York Public Library, Manuscripts Division: Martha Foley; Niebyl-Proctor Marxist Library, Berkeley, California: Aaron Cohen, Edith Laub, Jane Hodes; Palo Alto, California, Public Library; Parrocchia B.V. delle Grazie, Udine, Italy; Parrocchia del S.S. Redentore, Udine, Italy; San Francisco Public Library, San Francisco; San Gabriel Historical Association, San Gabriel, California: Sarah Duncan; Southern California Library for Social Studies and Research, Los Angeles; S.U.S.I., Berlin; U.S. National Archives and Records Administration, Pacific Region, San Bruno, California; University of California, Los Angeles, Arts Library, Special Collections, Los Angeles: Brigitte J. Kueppers; University of California, Riverside, Special Collections, Riverside, California: Sidney E. Berger; University of Maryland at College Park, Special Collections, College Park, Maryland: Beth Alvarez; University of New Hampshire, Special Collections, Durham, New Hampshire: Rebecca M. Ernest; Washington State University, Holland Library, Pullman, Washington: Robert

Matuozzi; and Yale University Library, Beinecke Rare Book and Manuscript Library, New Haven, Connecticut.

My appreciation also goes to those who assisted with the photographs in this book: Doriann Asch; Laura Webb, Baltimore Museum of Art; Dianne Nilsen, Center for Creative Photography; Nancy J. Morris, Charlot Collection, University of Hawai'i at Manoa; Juan Carlos Valdez Marín, Fototeca del INAH; Jacklyn Burns, The J. Paul Getty Museum; Pat Fundom, Hallmark Cards, Inc.; Monica and Walter Heilig; Thomas D. Grischkowsky, The Museum of Modern Art, New York; Jennifer Ickes, New Orleans Museum of Art; Page Imageworks: Tony and Merrily Page; Ruth and LaBrie Ritchie; Malin Barth, Throckmorton Fine Art, Inc.; Library Photographic Service, University of California, Berkeley; and anonymous.

My agent, Laurie Fox, has been extraordinarily supportive from the earliest stages of this project. I also owe special thanks to my editor, Annetta Hanna. It has been a pleasure to work with her and with John Son, Liana Parry Faughnan, Maggie Hinders, Emily Hannon, and Carol Edwards at Clarkson N. Potter.

Finally, I thank the entire Albers and McKendall families, especially my parents, Henry and Marjorie Albers. My son, Sam Spiewak, has been uncommonly patient and wise. To my husband, Benjamin McKendall, who lovingly participated in every aspect of this book, I am immeasurably grateful.

Contents

Preface

"THE MYSTERIOUS VISITOR...Miss Tina Modotti." So reads the caption announcing Tina's entrance in her one starring Hollywood film role. Like that silent five-reeler, her story has a blurred, glamorous, uneven quality. We possess several striking visions of her: Photographer Edward Weston made a celebrated series of portraits and nudes, Mexican painter Diego Rivera depicted Tina in famous frescoes, and the memoirs of Communist agent Vittorio Vidali portray her as a devout revolutionary. However, except for the powerful images that flowed from her camera in the 1920s and a series of vividly expressive letters to Edward Weston, Tina's voice has proved difficult to recover. Her diary and much of her correspondence have been lost, and she never felt compelled to leave an account of herself for posterity.

I became aware of Tina Modotti two decades ago through reproductions of her photographs. As I investigated her life and work (I did not yet know to what end), I grew conscious of her fierce hopefulness, her poetic temperament, her courage in confronting poverty and pain, her nomadism, and her troubling fall from grace. When I spoke with her friends, I was surprised at how often tears welled up in their elderly eyes at decades-old recollections. Then, one Sunday morning—April 24, 1994—I unexpectedly encountered Tina in a wholly different light.

Standard biographical materials note Tina Modotti's marriage to a man with the grand name of Roubaix de l'Abrie Richey, called Robo, an enigmatic artist of French-Canadian origin. I had supposed that, by learning more about Tina's husband, I could bring to light her transformation, during the period the couple was together, from unschooled Italian immigrant to worldly actress poised to take up the camera. I had begun my search for Robo in Quebec, but soon realized that, by birth and upbringing, he was an Oregonian. A series of telephone calls culminated in a journey to the Roseburg, Oregon, home of Robo's first cousin once removed. On that spring morning shortly after 9:00 A.M., my husband and I left the dreary clutter of Interstate 5 for a short drive into the gentle hill country to the west. The sun was out, and the dazzling tender green on all sides and the baby lambs wobbling about the fields gave the scene a feeling of Easter Sunday. Tina never visited Oregon, but I felt a slight shiver of connection to her as we approached a pretty grass-and-clover-seed farm with a sign announcing, in a variant of Robo's middle name, LA BRIE RANCH.

Ruth and LaBrie Ritchie were extraordinarily hospitable, and, after a long and illuminating conversation about their kin, the couple showed us two trunks, which the hired man had carried down from the attic earlier that morning. Battered and blackened with age, these held what remained of the belongings of Robo and his immediate family. One was a massive, once-elegant affair, constructed in wood-ribbed metal, lined with ornate paper, and outfitted with a removable tray for art supplies and a folding easel. The other, a sturdy oak box, looked as if it might have come west on a Conestoga wagon a century earlier. Both were creaky, fragrant with musty wood, and crammed with papers, photographs, periodicals, and mementos. Amid souvenirs of San Francisco's 1915 Panama-Pacific Exposition, crumbling issues of *The Smart Set,* high school pennants, scrapbooks, and bundles of receipts, telegrams, and legal documents, I glimpsed Tina Modotti's handwriting on an envelope.

At the Ritchies' insistence, my husband and I transported the trunks to our California home, where I sat in the living room, poring through their contents, for three days and long into the nights. Leaping out of these boxes, like a genie from a bottle buried for more than seven decades, came Tina's life with Robo Richey: a tangle of high drama and of moments when nothing much seemed to be happening, yet everything was in transition. I turned the well-worn pages of two copies of the *Rubáiyát of Omar Khayyám,* which Robo liked to read aloud to Tina, and, in albums, I found many snapshots of her, some beautiful, some silly, some out of focus, as in any family archive.

Predictably, these documents offered as many questions as answers, and it took years of further research to pry out their meanings. They led me, for example, to discover that Tina's marriage to Robo had been faked, and then to wonder why.

Many have asked if the trunks provide answers to the burning questions about Tina Modotti's life: When and why did she take up photography? Why did she abruptly abandon it? How did she die? I found no direct responses. Yet, the letters to and about Tina, and, especially, some three dozen in her hand, give her a firmer voice, offer insights into how she thought, and explain the meanings she saw in particular events. One series of communications from Tina to Robo's family (whose replies are missing) tells the tale of his tragic death in Mexico and of Tina's introduction to the country where she was to discover herself as a photographer. Between the lines lie clues to her psychological evolution during the dramatic and painful months that carried her to the brink of a new life.

The trunks also contained some one hundred images by Tina Modotti, mostly small contact prints which were gifts to Robo's family. A number of them are reproduced in this book, along with family snapshots and other photographs by and of Tina. Robo had been enamored of Mexico, and, in giving his family these photographs of the indigenous, working-class Mexicans about whom she cared deeply, Tina seemed to be acknowledging a debt to her late companion. Some of the images are well known; others have apparently been lost for decades. Often ragged-edged and hastily captioned, they are nonetheless astonishing in their ability to cut through the years. They reminded me of the empathy that Tina brought to her compelling artistic vision: She puts us in the haunting presence of people distant, perhaps, in time and space yet never strangers.

Writing this book has, of course, meant abstracting into words the jumble of objects and papers in the trunks. In doing so, I have sometimes mulled over Tina's thoughts, penned to Edward Weston a few years after Robo's death, as she sorted through her belongings, some of them no doubt stored in these very trunks. She destroyed many, she said, in hopes of leading her possessions "through a metamorphosis—from the concrete turn them into abstract things—as far as I am concerned—and thus I can go on owning them in my heart forever...."

In portraying her, my endeavor has been, figuratively, to keep one hand upon the tattered objects in the trunks. For I believe that it is her unremitting, sometimes misguided, and occasionally stunningly successful efforts to transcend everyday amorphousness—to "mould life," as she put it, refusing to accept either her own lot or that of others—that set her apart. Sharing her vision of beauty and human dignity is Tina Modotti's distinct gift.

Part I

Tina

Friuli and Austria (1896–1913)

B Y NINE O'CLOCK, Mexico City's Artes Street lies bathed in moonlight and nearly silent. Even a commotion of departures from the shabby little apartment house at number 46 is dying down. It is January 5, 1942, the eve of the Day of the Magi, one last flurry of holiday-making before the onset of what looks to be another hardscrabble and dreary year.

All evening, the war has been on the lips of party guests, who hold forth in German-, Italian-, and Castilian-accented Spanish. Mostly seasoned European Communists exiled by fascism, they exhale streams of words with their long gray curls of cigarette smoke. Caught between rasping laughter and the low moan of the phonograph, voices wrangle over the fate of Hitler's armies, ensnared by the Russian winter, and the tactics of the United States, scrambling to defend its Pacific outposts after Pearl Harbor. In one corner, several women thresh out final preparations for the next afternoon's fiesta where Spanish refugee children will squeal with delight at homemade toys, gifts from the Magi. As the bubbly party babble eases, departing guests pull the door shut with a spate of *hasta mañanas.*

Lights dim in the small flat, modernist and arty, as befits the home of a weaver and a former Bauhaus architect. Four guests, intimate friends, settle in with their hosts for a cozy chat. One couple is Spanish, a distinguished-looking former general and a genial relief worker. The others are Italian. The man, a paunchy, bull-necked sometime journalist from Trieste, dominates the conversation, but his tiny, less voluble companion, María, is easily the more arresting presence.

María had been one of the legendary beauties of her time. Set under quizzically arching brows, her luminescent velvety brown eyes are still stunning. Her teeth, however, are yellowed from years of smoking. Her skin appears mottled and parchmenty, and her mouth is drawn.

As always, she has groomed herself carefully and rather severely. Parted in the middle and pulled to the sides of a low forehead, her dark hair, dulled with gray, is twisted back into a complicated chignon. She wears no jewelry. Dressed in a black suit and white blouse, impeccably tailored, if slightly frayed, she might be mistaken—at a distance—for a soulful Mexican *abuelita,* a grandmother perpetually in mourning. Yet she is only forty-five years old.

Warm and attentive to her companions, she talks and smiles, but the sacred fire that once danced inside her has been squelched. Instead, says a poet friend, so muffled is María, that thinking of her is like "trying to scoop up a handful of mist." Her hush is less an estrangement from the living, however, than strained attention to the low clamoring of the dead. María has loved many who have not survived the savagery of the century. Submerged deeply within her memory are their faces and stories, too complex and painful to discuss. In years gone by, she was eager to talk out important issues. Now she feels less North American, more Latin, more austere.

Chitchat bounces from Soviet general Simeone Tomoshenko to anti-tank trenches to Dimitri Shostakovich's Quintet op. 57. Pleading a late-night editorial meeting, the journalist takes his leave. Someone begins fantasizing about a postwar journey to Madrid, Genoa, and María's hometown of Udine, Italy. There would be feasts of *panettone* and Chianti, and she would roam the old streets for the first time in twenty-nine years.

Feeling fatigued and queasy—perhaps from the heavy meal and the wine—María departs after midnight. She is accompanied to the street by a neighbor who stuck his head into the gathering on his way upstairs. As they step onto the pavement and walk two long blocks to Ramón Guzmán Street, María feels a night chill wrapping itself around her. On the busy thoroughfare, an outstretched arm easily stops a cab, whose fare she automatically bargains down from two pesos to one. Stepping up on the running board, she then nestles her wispy body into a corner of the ample backseat.

"*Hasta luego,*" she murmurs.

"*Hasta luego.*"

According to her habit, María gives the driver the name of the General Hospital, a landmark across the street from her apartment. The vehicle rumbles over the uneven pavement of central Mexico City, the light of a full moon quivering and darting among its lugubrious buildings. During the window-rattling ten-minute ride, the only sound from the backseat is a bout of wheezing. After the driver pulls up in front of the hospital, he swivels to collect the fare, only to discover his passenger slumped over. Dashing into the admitting room after she barely responds to his questions, he is instructed to rush her to the Green Cross emergency facility. María's last flickering perceptions are of darkness, solitude, and drift. By the time the cab reaches the hospital, she sprawls lifeless across the smooth cold leather.

Though many knew her as María Ruíz or María Jiménez, the woman's true name was Tina Modotti. Never a flamboyant personality, she was nonetheless pursued, even after death, by a glaring spotlight of publicity and controversy. Her burial, in a fifth-class tomb, drew many of the grand old warriors of international communism. Meanwhile, Mexico City's modern art gallery readied a retrospective of her photographs, and journalists dredged up yellowing scandal sheets shrieking of romance, violence, deceit, and Tina Modotti. In the obituaries, old rumors mingled with new: Tina died drunk, she had a heart attack, or she was eliminated because she knew too much. "The dramatic circumstances surrounding [her death] measured up to those of her agitated, subterranean and adventurous life," typed one eager reporter. "Bees, shadows, fire, snow," intoned Chilean poet Pablo Neruda in his elegy, "silence and foam combining with steel and wire and pollen...."

Fittingly, Tina Modotti died en route. Though she reveled in being of a place, a people, a profession, all proved slippery to her touch. No sooner did she plant one foot on firm ground than the earth eroded under the other, leaving her geographically and emotionally homeless. Acknowledging a "tragic conflict between life which continually changes and form which fixes it immutable," she responded by improvising, with all the grace she could muster, a series of remarkable lives.

In the first, the one that seemed her destiny, Tina Modotti was the flesh and blood of impoverished Italian workers. Not yet two years old when political and economic turbulence cast her family from its homeland, Tina would grow up to cling tenaciously to her Italianness, all the more precious because precarious. Her early childhood was spent in Austria, and when she finally learned Italian, at age nine, she spoke with a faint German accent. Often labeled the "tempestuous Italian" or "*bellissima italiana*," Tina was barely familiar with the country. *Her* Italy was no more than one provincial town. "Of Italy," she once wrote, "[I know] only Udine...."

Tina Modotti's hometown is the capital of the northeasternmost Italian region, officially named Friuli-Venezia Giulia but usually called simply Friuli. Fabled cities lie within easy range—Venice and the mottled neoclassical seaport of Trieste—but Tina's is a modest bourg set on a yawning plain of maize fields, vineyards, and orchards. From the pine-bristling slopes of the Carnic Alps, to the north, a lush carpet of wild hawthorn, clover, and shaggy grasses tumbles down Friuli's village-dotted valleys, running out at the sand-rimmed sea. Drab in winter, then suddenly sodden with alpine runoff, the region turns dazzlingly verdant in spring.

Friuli might have been nothing more than a bucolic agricultural hinterland had it not the misfortune of a strategic location at the head of the Adriatic. As chaotic as its name implies, Friuli-Venezia Giulia has a history that abounds in annexations, invasions, sieges, and overswarming armies. In ancient times, the Romans imposed a sprawling port city at Aquileia; during the Dark Ages, Central Europe's landlocked suzerains made Friuli's mountain passes their bloodied corridors to the sea. For nearly four centuries, Venetians chiseled the winged lion of San Marco on public buildings as a seal of ownership, never quite secure from raiding Turks. It was ultimately Napoléon who, in 1797, quickstepped in to wrest the territory from Venice, then trade it to the detested Austrians, thus earning for himself an enduring role as a buffoon in Udinese street theater. In 1866, the region was partitioned, with Udine swept into the new nation of Italy. Flush with the patriotism of the risorgimento, the town doted no less upon its legacies of raisin-studded Slovenian pastries, plumed Tyrolean hats, and Venetian-style *carnevale*.

By the late 1860s, when it enjoyed a respite from military turmoil, Udine was a conservative textile manufacturing center of nearly 37,000 inhabitants. On Sunday afternoons, townspeople took the air in its charming central piazza, graced with a candy-striped loggia, and wended their way up its *castello*-crested hill. Udine's prevailing atmosphere was unostentatious and countrified. Errant cobbled or dusty streets strung together the once-medieval burgs of Poscolle, Grazzano, and Cussignacco, behind whose animated commercial districts clotted narrow, shuttered houses. They bore their years gracefully, faded frescoes appearing out of patchy umber, sienna, or saffron facades, and window ledges bright with coquettish tumbles of geraniums. Here and there, stone walls hid neat rows of tomato, pepper, onion, and radicchio, and church bells steadily chimed out the hours of the day. With its gentle light, utterly unlike the hard glint of southern Italy, Udine was cluttered with pleasant corners tempting one to while away the afternoon. Some lingered in its market square cafés, others on footbridges arching canals sputtering with trout. Unlike the grand waterways of Venice, these were narrow, prosaic streams whose reflections danced across the facades of overhanging houses. To their embankments, womenfolk eternally lugged big stiff-handled baskets of laundry, bending low at scrubbing and rinsing as tongues wagged with gossip.

Among the washerwomen at the old moat near Gemona Gate was Tina Modotti's paternal grandmother, the only grandparent the girl ever knew. A flinty, rather shriveled matron by the age of thirty, her hair stuck into a tight knot, Domenica Bertoni Saltarini Modotti was, more often than not, heavy with child. One scarcely noticed, however, for she rustled about in layered Friulian peasant dress—an aproned ankle-length dirndl, fringed capelet, and head scarf tied low behind the neck—fashioned from dark patterned fabrics.

Like Tina's parentage on all sides, the Bertonis had been entrenched in Friuli for as long as anyone could remember. Born in the mill town of Molin Nuovo, Domenica had managed to snare for herself a fine Udinese husband. The widower Domenico Saltarini Modotti, a parishioner at the Church of Redentore, knew how to read and write, and, more consequentially, owned a small acreage just outside town. As a Friulian peasant, he would have been hardworking, frugal, and undemonstrative by temperament, judicious in his words and actions.

Domenico's dual loyalties to Italy and Friuli were mirrored by his composite surname. The Italianized plural of Modotto, Modotti was a name common enough that the family distinguished itself by retaining the Friulian appellation Saltarini. The reference was probably to ancestors once inhabiting the hamlet of Salt or employed as forest guards, *saltarîn* in the Friulian language. Both Domenico and Domenica had been subjects of Austrian emperor Francis Joseph I and now owed allegiance to Italy's king, but their deeper identification lay close to home. Between themselves, they spoke Friulian—very like Switzerland's Romansh—and this regional language, less lyrical and more raucous than Italian, would be Tina Modotti's native tongue.

With her marriage, Domenica had inherited three children, and from the union with Domenico issued Giuseppe, Francesco, Vittorio Emanuele, Anna, Pietro, Lucia, Angelo, and Andreas Leonardo. As the new generation came of age, the future boded ill, owing to Italy's plunge into severe and prolonged economic depression. The girls set to work on dowries, and the boys, a slapdash education under their belts, briefly took up scythes in their father's fields. But one small tract of land could never be stretched to support the Saltarini Modotti progeny. Andreas Leonardo departed for Gorizia, Giuseppe and Francesco apprenticed as mechanics, and Pietro became a pork butcher.

Curly-haired, with bright, hard eyes and a soup-strainer mustache, Giuseppe Modotti was a quick-witted, easygoing young man, who showed himself to be thoroughly modern by discarding the name Saltarini. Passionate about opera and endowed with what his daughter Tina described as "a pleasant, jolly voice," he was given to intemperate outbursts of aria. Rarely did he appear without a newspaper, which he could read fluently, though he never felt confident enough to claim that he could write. At twenty, Giuseppe was declared unfit for military service because of severe phlebitis; at twenty-four, he hied himself to the bustling Mediterranean port of Genoa to search for work.

Larger and more industrialized than Udine, the city opened Giuseppe's eyes to the disjointed welter of disparate factions that was Italian radicalism. One set of quarrels opposed Mikhail Bakunin's anarchist followers—romantic, antireformist, and bent on mangling the bourgeoisie with acts of violence—to adherents of "scientific" socialism, loosely based on the tenets of Engels and Marx. From two years in Genoa, Giuseppe carried home a newly sophisticated political awareness, which he channeled to his brothers, some of whom enrolled with him in the nascent Italian Socialist party.

Agitating for universal male suffrage, Socialists endeavored to coalesce the visceral hostility of Italy's masses into political activism. Giuseppe's circle took a moderate anarcho-syndicalist line, militating for shorter working hours, holidays off, and safer conditions in the mills, but its overarching concern was with advancing class consciousness and the knowledge that the masses were the creators of society's wealth. In the absence of working-class solidarity, Socialists fumed, there was no hope that Udinese laborers could pull off a decent strike, for "the capitalists would be chuckling under their mustaches because they knew they could easily find other workers...."

Back in Udine, a stint as an orphanage handyman brought Giuseppe to Via Tomadini and twenty-six-year-old Assunta Rosa Catterina Mondini, who lived around the corner. Of the youthful Assunta, we know that she was short and lovely to behold, with narrow, lively eyes and waves of mahogany brown hair. A serious and composed woman, she was also a great talker, who may have made it her business to become acquainted with the good-looking mechanic.

The Mondinis constituted a veritable guild of clothiers. Assunta's maternal grandmother had been a silk embroiderer. The girl's mother, Adelaide Zuliani, a dressmaker, married Giuseppe Mondini, a hatmaker, and their brood of nine counted several garment makers, three hatmakers, and a cobbler. Needles flying over lengths of linen or silk, Assunta and her sisters expertly whipped out piecework in the small apartment where they all lived on top of one another. Rarely finding enough employment to absorb their industriousness, the Mondinis made ends meet one month at a time. Yet, money or no, to be a Mondini woman, or, like Tina, the daughter of a Mondini, was to be impeccably dressed and to sew like an angel.

The family inhabited the upper floor of an undistinguished two-story house on Via Pracchiuso. Renters rather than owners, the Mondinis nonetheless felt deeply at home in their neighborhood, called San Valentino, after its tiny church. Fate seemed to confirm their belonging with the birth of Assunta's brother Valentino, on February 14, and Assunta's own birthday on November 25, Saint Catherine's Day, feted since the Middle Ages on the neighborhood green. By the time Giuseppe came courting, however, marriage and emigration were plucking apart the Mondini clan.

In the spring of 1892, Assunta discovered she was pregnant. The news did not unduly shock or shame her family, for Assunta's eldest brother had been born out of wedlock. A month later, however, his parents had hastened to tie the knot, ostensibly because of the stigma attached to the misbegotten child. Identification papers, even school lists, would otherwise carry the mention "child of unknown father," and epithets on the street were considerably less polite.

Halfway through Assunta's pregnancy, the Mondinis were stunned by the deaths, probably from infectious disease, of their patriarch, Giuseppe Mondini, and, the very next day, of Assunta's sister Leonzia. With two fewer breadwinners, soon another mouth to feed, and a heightening economic crisis, the family's tattered Via Pracchiuso remains—old Adelaide, three adult children, and a niece—faced a bleak future.

In her eighth month, Assunta resolved, or at least ameliorated, the situation by marrying Giuseppe Modotti in the grand Basilica delle Grazie. The bride, in mourning, would have had a kind word and gracious smile for each of her guests, while the groom masked with bonhomie his chagrin at being married by a priest. The church was hand in glove with the possessing classes, yet Catholicism permeated Udinese culture, and, Socialist that he was, Giuseppe was also an eminently pragmatic man.

Unfortunately, we are not privy to relatives' gossip about why Assunta and Giuseppe Modotti chose to plight their troth, nor do we have a single wedding picture to scrutinize. What kept the couple hesitating about marriage, one wonders, until the last weeks before the birth? Did the union have its basis in emotional trauma and obligation? Was theirs, at bottom, a vital relationship invested with passionate love, or was the pair ceding to what seemed an inevitability for burdened, uneducated, struggling folk?

Given Tina's dismissive attitude toward marriage and the tumult of her relationships with men, it would also be fascinating to know more than we do about the emotional texture and tone of her parents' thirty years of connubial life (interrupted for half that time by Giuseppe's fortune-seeking in the United States). The marriage no doubt saw few stormy scenes but was shot through with strains and misapprehensions. Implicit in her children's frequent references to Assunta as "a saint" and "our blessed mother" may be the thought of Giuseppe's distraction or infidelities. The notion that the relationship was disturbed is borne out by the observation that the couple's six children who reached adulthood lacked the capacity for long-term, stable, intimate bonds. Instead, their affective lives were confused sagas of brief happiness, dashed hopes, squabbles, separations, and divorces.

Whatever disenchantment the Modottis' marriage held, it was leavened by mutual devotion to their offspring. Tina spoke affectionately of her father, although the two were not well acquainted until the last years of his life, for Giuseppe was inevitably toiling or chasing down another dreary factory job somewhere. But she admired his entrepreneurial spirit and the gutsy way he labeled himself, as circumstances dictated, mechanic, machinist, mechanical engineer, bicycle repairman, inventor, marble cutter, or photographer. He was, she boasted, "a true fighter, an untiring worker," and he never grew sour or taciturn, instead remaining "younger in spirit than [his own sons]—how much I [admire] him always!" She inherited his resourcefulness, his faculty for hard work, and his undying faith in the millennium.

An old soul, stoic, sweet, and indomitable, Assunta played a larger role in the lives of her children, whom she cosseted and cared for as best she could. Her possibilities constricted from childhood by lack of education and the dreary lot of poor *friulane* (including those married to Socialists, who typically recognized no specific oppression of women), Assunta displayed inextinguishable selflessness and serenity. Having witnessed her mother's considerable suffering, Tina felt unwavering tenderness toward her. One side of Tina, more pronounced as she grew older, was the very image of Assunta.

The Modottis' firstborn, Mercedes Margherita, would arrive four weeks after the wedding, and their second, Ernesto Renato (sometimes called Carlo), twenty-two months later. Both births took place in the Mondini home, Giuseppe having disregarded convention by moving in with his bride's kin, rather than the other way around. Picked from neither branch of the family tree, the babies' names were perhaps of their father's invention.

With the baby born on August 16, 1896, Assunta put her foot down. The newborn's namesakes, all Mondinis, were Assunta herself (the mother), Adelaide (the grandmother), and Luigia (a maternal aunt). The first name also brought to notice the child's Catholic heritage and her birthday's near miss of the August 15 Festival of Our Lady of the Assumption, Assunta in Italian. Probably following the Friulian custom of altering offsprings' names to confound malevolent spirits who would do them harm, the baby's parents used the diminutive, Assuntina, then simply Tina.

It was five months before they proceeded to christen her. A sweeping glance around the drafty basilica's baptismal font on January 27, 1897, would have revealed, besides more Modottis and Mondinis than anyone could keep straight, a barber named Antonio Bianchi—the baby's godfather—and her two sponsors. One was Assunta's sister Lucia, whom Giuseppe grandiosely listed on the baptismal act as his daughter's governess, and the other a shoemaker named Demetrio Canal. A well-known figure in the history of Udinese radicalism, Canal no doubt had to be coaxed into his role, since he routinely lambasted Catholicism—"that religion"—for its oppression of the working masses.

Canal was a moving spirit of the Via Cicogna circle, a Socialist fellowship that Giuseppe Modotti attended on Thursday evenings. The group discussed the meanings of radicalism, devised and carried out militant actions, and, briefly, published a weekly called *L'Operaio*. The paper took to task Udinese bakery owners for forcing youngsters to toil through the night, then deliver bread at dawn, and silk tycoons for levying fines on young workers who paused to rest. For Giuseppe, the struggle against local oligarchs, who wielded power as their God-given right, was no armchair gambit. His three children could look forward to only the briefest of childhoods, with perhaps a year or two of schooling, before wading into decades of dreary factory grind. Marriage to a steady, hardworking man seemed his daughters' brightest hope.

That spring, Udine plunged into turbulent social unrest fueled by the free-floating anger of jobless workers and hungry peasants pried from the land. Factory employees improvised a round of strikes, repressed with increasing violence. For acts of solidarity with a spinners' walkout, potentially crippling to the vital textile industry, the Via Cicogna circle was banned.

Under scrutiny by Udinese police and probably unemployed, Giuseppe Modotti bid farewell to the family and joined a rowdy, ragtag caravan of Italian job seekers bound for the southern Austrian province of

Carinthia. His train heaved itself over the Alps to the cow town of St. Ruprecht where it disgorged its load of brawn for forests and factories. In a cycle of economic recovery, Carinthia was reaping the benefit of new rail links to convert itself into a regional supplier of heavy construction materials. Employment generally lasted as long as the mild season, and, by November, with winter closing in about the village, most Italians had returned home. Hired for an indoor job, Giuseppe, in contrast, convened the entire family in St. Ruprecht. Then fifteen months old, Tina would call Austria home for the next seven-and-a-half years.

Tidy and picturesque, St. Ruprecht nestled among low mountains, a kilometer or two from a popular villa-lined lake resort. Sprawling rail yards delimited the hamlet's northern boundary; massive stone-and-wood edifices petered out in pastures to the south. The only thoroughfare sliced the little settlement in half, then continued on to nearby Klagenfurt, the prosperous burgher town of which the village was a workers' ghetto.

The Modottis were assigned to a dormitory, called Building No. 74, hard by the railroad tracks. Their lodgings provided lumpy straw mattresses, a primitive kitchen without running water, and only a fireplace for heat. Biting cold filtered in around windows and doors, and soot scooted into every cranny. In the evenings, the intermittent, earsplitting roar and screech of trains would drown out distant bursts of beery shouting. Intended for seventy people but meagerly inhabited in winter, their abode would be invaded come spring by a stream of Slovenian and Italian new arrivals as St. Ruprecht's population swelled to three thousand.

Giuseppe's mechanical skills earned him a good job as a maintenance man for steam-powered equipment at the crate, beam, and building materials mill of magnate Friedrich Brodnig. Meanwhile, Assunta—one eye trailing the trio of little Modottis—knuckled down to housekeeping and piecework for someone such as Anna Pagura, the Italian who sold clothing from her home on the Klagenfurt road.

Just as the family established itself, tragedy struck. Seized by high fever and convulsions, three-year-old Ernesto suddenly expired, the causes of death listed as tuberculosis and meningoencephalitis (possibly linked to drinking unpasteurized milk). This older brother may have quickly faded from Tina's memory, and even Ernesto's parents had scant opportunity to express their grief, for, by May, Assunta was in the morning-sickness phase of another pregnancy, and Giuseppe was hospitalized for unknown reasons in Budapest, where he was doubtless attending a union meeting for Italian migrant workers.

Baptized Valentina Maddalena (but called Gioconda), the baby was born after the Modottis had quit St. Ruprecht for the misty hamlet of Ferlach, two hours to the south by creaking horse-drawn carriage. Secluded by the wide Drau River valley and walls of jagged peaks, Ferlach lay under an oppressive winter silence, pierced from time to time by volleys of church bells, ice chunks crashing from the roofs, and the crack of its famous hand-built rifles. The family took rooms in a building shadowed by the church, where Mercedes learned the German Christmas carols she remembered her entire life. As spring stirred, she and little Tina streaked through boggy meadows glorious with wildflowers, their boisterous laughter met with terrifying sternness from leathery-faced, loden-hatted burghers. Italian loggers arrived en masse, and, in the evenings, they kindled up small fires and cooked their polenta outdoors.

It was southern Austria's bicycling mania that put Giuseppe in Ferlach. Klagenfurt's Grundner & Lemisch bicycle works, renting space from a local arsenal, had engaged him as a mechanic, and family lore has it that he invented a lightweight bamboo mountain bike successfully manufactured by the firm. But something soured, and, some two years later, the Modottis resumed their vagrancy. Tina's third sister, Yolanda Luisa, was born in 1901 in St. Ruprecht's Building No. 105, and, in 1903, Assunta gave birth to Pasquale Benvenuto, called Ben, in Building No. 129.

At four, Tina was chubby and hoydenish, with brown eyes and dark unruly hair. Dolled up with an intricate embroidered collar, she appears, in the only surviving photograph from her girlhood, most friendly with the camera. Just emerging as a self-aware person heedful of the outside world, Tina experienced a cultural identity subject to constant renegotiation. To Austrians, she was an Italian child, though she spoke scarcely a word of the language. At home, she made herself understood in Friulian, but on jaunts with her mother around the village, conversations were interlarded with Italian, German, and Slovenian. At primary school, Tina would discover that pupils were required to use German and not one word of other languages, on pain of punishment, a policy that so enraged the Slovenian community that it published a long tract of protest. Whatever else Tina's memory retained of the Austrian years, it absorbed foggy, troublesome impressions of nationality, cultural identity, and marginalization, issues that would stack up as significant in her life.

Ethnicity took on other dimensions in the adult world, where discrimination and festering animosity were taken for granted. Austrian employers pitted the interests of one set of workers against another by locking out strikers and replacing them with newer, cheaper immigrants. Attempting to organize across ethnic lines, Giuseppe Modotti and his cohorts found music in words such as those spoken by a Triestine immigrant before three hundred construction workers at a Klagenfurt rally: "Your friends, your colleagues, are German and Slovenian workers. Your own compatriots, Italians with money, are totally indifferent to your well-being." One of Tina's earliest memories, told to her sister Yolanda, was of a similar gathering, a clamorous May Day parade through the streets of Klagenfurt, where she bounced along on Giuseppe's shoulders as he explained the significance of the hard-won holiday. The story has been singled out and emphasized by those who would make of Tina a working-class heroine, and, while true, it does have the ring of official biography.

The year she turned nine, Tina's life was transformed by a chain of events beginning with a letter postmarked "Turtle Creek, Penn., U.S.," and signed by Giuseppe's brother Francesco. For thirteen years, Francesco had moved between Italy and the United States, but now he must have discerned particularly bright opportunity in the steel mills and mining zones of western Pennsylvania. Returning to Udine, where he deposited his family and settled his affairs, Giuseppe caught a train in the direction of Le Havre, France, to embark for New York and then join Francesco. At forty-two, Giuseppe would make a fresh start, summoning his offspring one by one as he amassed enough savings for their passages. Two months after his departure, the Modottis' last child, Giuseppe Pietro Maria, called Beppo, came into the world.

The family had settled back into Udine's San Valentino district, renting a room or two in a house where the children had the run of a cobbled courtyard and its clutter of brooms, birdcages, potted plants, and stray cats. The siblings lived in frenzied expectation of tidings from Giuseppe, but letters rarely reached them, money almost never, and he sank from the little ones' memories. "For long periods of many months, we had no news of him, and he didn't send money because of lack of work," Tina remembered. "That meant that we practically lived on charity." Despite helping hands from the Modotti and Mondini clans, the family's fortunes deteriorated rapidly. In the little pool of light around a coal stove and a candle, they dined frugally on the eternal polenta of Friuli's poor, smothered with vegetables and cheese when times were good and thinned with extra water when they were bad. Afterward, chattering with cold, the children would pile into bed together, snuggling to keep warm.

"In Udine," a friend paraphrased Tina's anecdote decades later, "there was a fine house, and, something strange, this man's daughter, an aristocrat's daughter, invited her for dinner and, later, Tina's mother told her to invite the girl back. 'But Mamma,' she wailed, 'we only eat polenta!'"

Tina's dinner guest (polenta or no, Assunta insisted) was her classmate at the Dante Alighieri Elementary School, whose two long wings and train station–style clock seemed grandiose to nine-year-old eyes accustomed to a village schoolhouse. Assunta had enrolled Tina with the expectation that she would be assigned, at her age level, to the third grade. She failed the placement examination, however, and a note was made in her record: "does not know the Italian language." Humiliated, she was sent to the first grade along with her little sister Gioconda.

The event made a profound impression upon Tina, installing in her an irrational and indelible self-image as intellectually inferior. A quarter century later, while offering a journalist a thumbnail sketch of her life, she zoomed in on this incident. "[S]he went to the educational establishment and was sent back to the lower grades," her interviewer reported; "in sum she considers herself untutored." Dogged by a sense that she was insufficiently bookish, Tina sporadically struggled to compensate by diligent reading and study. One friend (an artist) would describe Tina, in her late twenties, as "the most cultivated person," while another (a librarian) asserted that she was intelligent and sensitive but an out-and-out "mediocrity" in terms of erudition. Her formal education probably totaled four years. Later, overcome by feelings of inadequacy in the presence of literati, Tina would mask them with silence. In the remembering and telling of her youthful mortification, she seems to have nearly forgotten that, by spring, she was fluent in Italian and was promoted to the second grade with an almost perfect score of fifty-nine out of sixty. That Tina was resilient and quick-minded, no one doubted.

For years, Tina had listened to uncounted tales of Udine, but now she drank in its sights, sounds, and smells for the first time, and she was smitten. A friend remembered the adult Tina speaking "of Udine with such fervor, such force, despite the fact that she had departed, I won't say in a stampede, but, well, the way so many Italians did, under very difficult circumstances...." But she left little testimony about her hometown. At best, we have intimations of childish amusements such as a school holiday declared so all could attend Buffalo Bill's Wild West Show, its big top pitched at the end of Via Pracchiuso. Every November, for the Saint Catherine's Day Fair, Bläser's traveling Gigantic Cinema would roll onto the green at the other end of Via Pracchiuso, and, despite the family's dismal fortunes, the young Modottis must have found ways to be among goggling and shrieking audiences as Bläser's screens flickered with such epics as *Ali Baba* and *Grandpa Chases the Cat for His Grandchildren*. More memorable to Tina was an excursion to Venice, which flooded into her mind's eye years later as she read Theodore Dreiser's travel essays. "Think of these old stone steps," Dreiser had written, "white marble stained green, loved by the waters of the sea these hundreds of years...."

There were also casual visits to Pietro Modotti's photographic studio. In his early forties, Giuseppe's younger brother—a dynamo with piercing brown eyes and a mustache of the exuberant style favored by the Modotti brothers—had abandoned the butcher's trade and become one of Udine's preeminent photographers. Pietro championed crisp landscapes and architectural studies, although, for portraiture, he preferred what he termed the "intense soft focus," achieved by a method of candlelight photography, which he tirelessly promoted in photographic journals. Flattering and proficient, his sepia- and gold-toned portraits of men in fashionable otter-skin hats, women in off-the-shoulder gowns, and children stiff in summer linens adorned the town's finest overfurnished bourgeois parlors.

It is hard to say what effect the existence of a photographer uncle had on Tina Modotti. At the Studio fotografico Modotti, Tina experienced a first pungent whiff of sodium hyposulfite up her nostrils and her first glance at a print magically "coming up." Besides making material contact with the métier, she might have observed the passion with which her uncle stopped short—pipe clenched between his teeth, jacket pockets sagging with tools—to expound upon the fine points of optics, lighting, or composition. Like radical politics, photography was part of the Modotti family repertoire and thus within Tina's mental range of possibility. In view of the financial support Pietro provided his brother's family, photography's strongest connection, in the child's mind, may have been to comfort and security such as she seemed unlikely ever to enjoy.

In 1909, Pietro closed shop temporarily, traveling to Paris, where he learned the Lumière brothers' novel autochrome color process (which he later introduced in Italy) and to the United States for a reunion with his brothers Giuseppe, Francesco, and Angelo. With little to show for two years in the East, Giuseppe had struck out for San Francisco, which was rebuilding after its devastating 1906 earthquake and advertising excellent machinists' wages of $3.75 a day. However, a series of fortuities propelled him instead into opening a photography studio with a compatriot named Augustino Zante. Using skills (and perhaps venture capital) picked up from Pietro and Americanizing his name to Joseph, Giuseppe did business from a second-floor shop in the city's thriving Italian quarter. "MODOTTI JOSEPH & CO. (J. Modotti and A. Zante)," read his boldfaced advertisement in the 1908 City Directory. "Artistic photographers and all kinds of view work." But the district boasted a fraternity of photographers, and the affair failed within the year. Ever sanguine, Giuseppe offered his services as "machine shop, marble working, machinery made and repaired" and astutely listed a telephone number.

In contrast to her husband, Assunta could only have been disheartened by their situation four years after his precipitous departure. Even with Mercedes on a factory production line, the family barely kept bodies and souls together. Tina, too, was obliged to drop out of school and take a series of odd jobs, culminating in stints at a silk-reeling mill, where she worked ten-hour days for a pittance.

Udinese sweatshops were typically unembellished high-beamed wooden-floored cracker boxes, chilly or sweltering, according to the season.

As a beginner, Tina was put to work scooping up silk cocoons that bobbed in basins of hot, foul-smelling water. Hers was the tedious task of peeling off their netlike coverings and groping, as it was phrased, for their filament ends. A few days on the job turned her hands swollen and raw, and her thumbs throbbed from rubbing against the strands of silk, so fine that they were nearly invisible, yet as durable as steel. With experience, she was promoted to a spot in the chain of steam-powered skein winders that twisted gossamer spun thread quickly and evenly into silk bricks. Arranged in long ranks, ten-, twelve-, or thirteen-year-old girls, pale and hollow-eyed, their pinned-back hair sprouting tendrils limp with perspiration, operated the machinery with such alacrity that arms and hands were a flying blur.

At their backs paced the overseers, middle-aged men in ill-fitting suits who scrutinized the bricks for irregularities or breaks. If a worker's output was deficient, she had to answer a dreaded summons to the "big table," but if skeins were piling up lustrous and regular, silk reelers were sometimes allowed to sing as they toiled. At first pianissimo and barely audible over the whirring of machinery, the juvenile voices would soar into the popular "They Call Me Mimi" from *La Bohème* or "Vês dôi vôi che son dôs stelis," a Friulian love song they had all been humming since childhood. Tina was one of the rare Modottis unblessed with an enchanting voice, but she adored music and would have perceived how it lifted the workers above the stink of silk gum, chapped hands, aching feet, and dreariness.

After six years, Giuseppe scraped up the cash to summon Mercedes to San Francisco as Tina graduated to a weaver's position, almost certainly at Domenico Raiser e Figlio's velvet, damask, and silk establishment near her home. It was more highly skilled labor, slightly more lucrative, but no less frazzling or unstable. As hands shifted and shunted at breakneck speeds, Tina's heart was absorbing and memorizing the wretchedness walled up in Udine's factories. Her own hardship transmuted into perceptiveness and sympathy, it would one day inform her photographs of underage Mexican workers, their wistful faces, coarse and shapeless garments, and resolute gaits.

She would understand hunger as well, for the Modottis' diet had grown ever leaner. As an indigent student, Tina had been given free lunches—unvaryingly a chunk of white bread, some Emmental cheese, and a hunk of salami—but now she fended for herself at midday. Sometimes the family went dinnerless as well, which set six-year-old Beppo into jeremiads. Yolanda told this tale:

> Our fire and candles had gone out, as often happened. My mother and I were waiting for Tina, hugging each other to keep warm. We were sad and dejected because there was no light and nothing to eat. When there was food, I went to meet Tina, anxious to give her the good news....
>
> That night we finally heard the sound of her footsteps. She was running, an unusual occurrence since she was usually so tired that she walked slowly despite the chill.
>
> Opening the door, she cheerfully said: "Guess what I have brought you?" Approaching us, who could not see, she put a package on my mother's knees, saying, "Bread, cheese, salami! Enough to last until tomorrow!"
>
> "How did you get them?" asked my mother. Hesitant, but trying to present the fact as normal, she told us that she had never really liked the blue scarf that Aunt Maria had given her and that the factory girls, on the other hand, had admired so much that she had decided to raffle it off. Wasn't that a good idea?
>
> When I was older, I understood why my mother began to cry while Tina, crouched on her knees, repeated that she did not like the scarf. It was strange because she had shouted with joy when they gave it to her, and it was, in fact, the only item of quality in her scanty winter wardrobe. When I realized how brave the little liar was...I admired her a great deal and felt a great respect for her.

Tina was too modest to include the anecdote in her own repertoire except by aphorism. "Misery and hunger unite a family more than riches and comfort," she once told a companion.

Her summons to America did not arrive until a year and a half after Mercedes's. To please Assunta, Tina took catechism lessons that spring at the Catholic Church of Saint Anthony, and, with Aunt Anna as her sponsor, was confirmed by the archbishop of Udine. At no time in her life did Tina evince religious faith, and, a few years later, she would declare outright that she had "[no] belief or religion." Taking a page from her father's book, she acquiesced to the sacramental ceremony, but precious few friends would ever be privy to the secret.

On June 22, with a big send-off and many maternal admonitions, Tina departed Udine by rail for Mestre, Milan, and Genoa. On the eve of her seventeenth birthday, she must have been suffused by two mental images of herself in the world. One was her mother's outlook, by which everything had its beginning, ending, and meaning in the Mondini and Modotti clans, in *campanilismo,* that which lies within earshot of one's campanile. Family connections were bedrock; emigration, even if it lasted a lifetime, was by definition temporary. Such nineteenth-century notions held an appeal for Tina and would prompt her, at the startlingly young age of twenty-six, to avow that she had "always expressed the desire to be buried in Italy." Simultaneously, she was seduced by her father's joy in rolling with the punches and by his incessant reinvention of self. Leaving Udine overturned her presumed destiny as the daughter, granddaughter, and great-granddaughter of Friulians. The psychic voyage proved inseparable from the physical voyage and, from now on, her journeys would be frequent and almost always one-way.

Tripping up the gangplank of the German steamship SS *Moltke,* Tina affected one of the dashing homemade ensembles of which Mondini women had the knack. On her head sat what she later realized was a "ridiculous" hat decorated with artificial flowers and fruit. Barely clearing five feet, soft-spoken, with big, watchful, shining eyes, Tina had a doll-like quality about her. The *Moltke* docked briefly at Naples, where more emigrants crowded aboard, over a thousand in all. As the ship weighed anchor, a shimmering Neapolitan skyline was to be Tina's last glimpse of Italy.

Chapter 2

San Francisco (1913–1918)

TINA FIRST TASTED American-style coffee and bread aboard the meandering, dingy-windowed transcontinental immigrant train carrying her to Oakland, California. From there, travelers were embarked by ferry across San Francisco Bay, its glorious theater of water, clouds, and distant shores awakening all but the most insensitive to the poetic spectacle of their new home. Gulls quivered and danced as she bounced through waters ruffled by the passages of fishing boats, steamer tugs, and the occasional ocean-bound freighter. In one direction, summer fog languidly draped itself over silver ridges; in another, a range of warehouses and docks poked fingerlike into the bay. Someone would have pointed out the Italian shantytown atop Telegraph Hill and the Ferry Building bearing down ahead. For generations, the edifice's distinctive pseudo-Moorish clock tower had witnessed San Franciscans' tearful farewells and reunions, and, now, as the boat slowed and cartwheels of sea spray dropped from its sides, Tina's eyes scanned the confluence of figures before her for the half-familiar faces of her sister and father.

A bit portly at fifty, though more ebullient than ever, Giuseppe Modotti was the self-satisfied proprietor of a thriving repair shop where, at odd moments, he tinkered with inventions. Around the Italian colony, he enjoyed a reputation as an upstanding citizen, a dilettante of musical entertainments, and a faithful contributor to mutual-aid societies. Giuseppe's political convictions had survived the transition from factory worker to businessman, though most of his crusading now took place around the dinner table while pulling on a good cigar.

The Modottis lived at 1952 Taylor Street, on the steep northern slope of Russian Hill, crowded with newly constructed homes that replaced casualties of the 1906 earthquake and fire. A Tuscan and Friulian enclave, the area was less pricey than the gardened mansion district on the hill's crest, but more so than bustling Little Italy at its foot. From the Modottis' front steps, the bay was a dazzling, dizzying drop below.

Cheerful but modest, the flat boasted an ornate fireplace, a bow window, and two bedrooms. Tina would have been struck, above all, by the jarring contrast between her father's creature comforts and her mother's still brutally impoverished existence. Presumably, Giuseppe Modotti was regularly subsidizing the family in Udine while he saved for five additional passages to the United States, but his payments could only have been paltry. Having long been strapped for amenities, did he now set such store by the good things of life that he could not bring himself to relinquish the cash his wife badly needed? Or have tales of Assunta's poverty been exaggerated? If not, it is difficult to fathom the situation, for in other circumstances, Giuseppe showed himself to be generous and kindhearted. In any event, with three family members drawing paychecks in San Francisco, there was every reason to believe that the Modottis would soon be reunited.

The most practical and dependable of Tina's siblings, twenty-year-old Mercedes could be relied upon for her contribution. After two years in California, she was bringing home a decent salary as a seamstress for I. Magnin, a downtown emporium catering to white-gloved ladies from exclusive Pacific Heights. An intelligent, sympathetic, and style-conscious brunette, Mercedes was a conventional soul who adored roses and sentimental songs. Having a domestic turn of mind, she kept the household purring while nursing a rankling regret that family demands were siphoning off the best years of her life. Her impatience to shake loose notwithstanding, Mercedes burned with a desire to marry. She carried the torch for a succession of men, which had Ben Modotti commenting, with brotherly vulgarity, that she "reasons with her uterus." Tina, in contrast, was uncensorious with Mercedes, and though the two sisters were very different women, they remained close throughout their lives, owing in part to the five impressionable years together in San Francisco.

With Mercedes to show her the ropes, Tina quickly secured a place in the production line at a shirt factory where she would be employed for two years. Stints as an I. Magnin seamstress, mannequin, artist's model, actress, and hatmaker were to earn Tina's livelihood in San Francisco. After she became fluent in English, the fabulously chic Alice Rohrer took Tina under her wing as an employee of Du Barry Hats, renowned for its one-of-a-kind creations designed on clients' heads. Tina went into the job—delivering, clerking, fabricating, and modeling—believing that she was apprenticing for her future profession, and, for a time, shopkeepers' hours pleased her. She waxed poetic for that moment of transition "when night comes and one by one the folks come home from work just as of old...." But, unlike many immigrants who burdened themselves with two or three jobs in dreams of a triumphant return to Italy, Tina held dear her leisure hours. Shaking the Friulian dust from her shoes, she ventured into Little Italy, known as North Beach.

It was a short walk to picket-fenced Washington Square, drowsy with idlers, harmonica buffs, and wiry young ballplayers, until holidays transformed it into the Italian colony's brassy, sentimental heart. Slicing through one corner of the park was Columbus Avenue, lined with prominent business establishments, the Banca Populare Fugazi, Fontana's Jewelers, the Guerrini Accordion Factory, and Molinari's grocery, stacked high with tins of olive oil, perfumed with garlic, and festooned with sausages and cheeses. Sidewalk vendors hawked fruit, vegetables, and pumpkinseeds, and housewives leaned over windowsills to gab. Not all of North Beach's denizens were Italian, however. The neighborhood's rowdy saloons and trattorias, where customers dined like kings for thirty-five cents, lured artists, writers, and bohemian hangers-on from around the city. One took midnight supper at Gianduja on Stockton Street or crowded into Buon Gusto for pasta al pesto washed down with wine. "[North Beach] is appealing, enticing and hypnotizing," gushed the 1914 guide *Bohemian San Francisco*. "Go there, and you will learn why San Francisco is a Bohemian city. You will find out that so many things you thought important are not at all worth while."

The neighborhood also wore a face of hardship and poverty, salved by the good offices of mutual-aid societies. Childhood experiences fresh in her mind, Tina volunteered for the Italian Aid Committee and, after World War I erupted, for the Italian Red Cross. Considered a seemly activity for young women, such charity work consisted mostly in elaborating benefit concerts, dances, and variety shows at Green Street's Casa Coloniale Fugazi. Cheerfully and conscientiously, Tina occupied herself with reception and introduction committees, buttonholed merchants for door prizes, and organized donations of Christmas gifts for the poor. Often she was among the nubile beauties selected to pass the hat. She quickly discovered a flair for scheduling, planning, fund-raising, and a miscellany of organizing tasks that she would undertake for Italian charities throughout her San Francisco years, and for causes artistic and political over the course of a lifetime.

Another indication of things to come was Tina's simultaneous enthusiasm for social work and art. On February 20, 1915, the splendid Panama-Pacific International Exposition opened its doors not far from Taylor Street, and an unsuspected world was revealed to her.

Officially, the exposition celebrated the inauguration of the Panama Canal, but its spirit was imbued with overweening pride in San Francisco's heroic response to the 1906 catastrophe. A magnificent dreamscape fronted the bay between Van Ness Avenue and the Golden Gate: dozens of national and state pavilions; the Tower of Jewels, encrusted with fifty thousand bits of colored glass; an amusing carnival midway; and the neoclassical rotunda and lagoon of the Palace of Fine Arts. More jaded eyes than Tina's were wonderstruck. Poet Edwin Markham came away from the exposition staggered by "the greatest revelation of beauty that has ever been seen on the earth."

To Tina, the ten-month Panama-Pacific International Exposition seemed miraculous. Hungering for learning, at Ellis Island she had wistfully declared herself to be a student. Suddenly, the world was depositing at her feet an encyclopedia of history, geography, literature, anthropology, industry, and art, realms ordinarily sealed off from the life of a factory girl. Taking a hand in her own education, Tina haunted the fair, most assiduously its exhibitions comprising eleven thousand works of art. She brought with her an inchoate appreciation and an avid eye, but Uncle Pietro's pictures and Udinese ecclesiastical art were the *A* to *Z* of her experience. Now she studied allegorical representations of the American West, Oriental tea services, puzzling Cubist canvases by Picasso, colorful California Impressionist landscapes, Italian Futurists' radical explosions of paint, Marcel Duchamp's much-reviled *Nude Descending a Staircase,* mawkish photographs of sylphs and satyrs, and the unblushing *Stella,* "the nude painting that breathed." They fired her ambitions to do something very artistic and very grand.

Tina's enthusiasm for the exposition was an exemplar of what photographer and family friend Alessandro Baccari saw as the young Modottis' hunger for "new-world activities." His observation recognizes the alacrity with which the siblings assimilated another language and culture. Tina, in particular, found freedom wafting in the Pacific air and something magically empowering about a city where streetcar lines begin in the workaday world and dead-end in windswept ocean dunes.

Tina turned nineteen the year of the fair, though a snapshot taken around that time seems to depict a schoolgirl, skittish, unsophisticated, and astonishingly beautiful in her shapeless middy blouse. Framed by an opulence of dark wavy hair, her face is pale, with a low forehead, full lips, flawless skin, and sensuous, deep brown eyes. She wears a grave, inquisitive expression, devoid of silliness or mirth. It isn't difficult to suppose that she was already developing a richly contradictory personality: an introvert finely attuned to people's feelings and emotions, a levelheaded person whose mind swarmed with idealistic notions, a circumspect young woman pouncing on life like a tiger.

Tina's eagerness for experience had her in a breathless bustle, and, around the Italian colony, one opinion held the "young immigrant girl" Tina Modotti to be "beautiful though eccentric, possessing a number of striking talents." Dabbling in poetry, delving into theater and clothing design, she had embarked upon what would prove a tortuous search for self-identity. At first, it seemed that life could be picked up as deliberately as a length of silk and fashioned into a splendid garment to be pulled over her head in an act of transformation.

Amateur theatricals abounded in the city's garment industry, which suggests that Tina came to acting through an Italian-language workers' ensemble. Bereft of a professional company since 1912, North Beach teemed with would-be thespians whose ragged fare was the quarter's amusement of choice. Avid theatergoers, the district's inhabitants flocked to see hodgepodges of comedy, tragedy, opera, and recitation that enlivened the back rooms of cafés and clogged sidewalks around Washington Square. Lack of scenery or flubbed lines were ignored if actors displayed charisma, spontaneity, and an ability to enter into the spirit of a character—in a word, brio.

In the summer of 1916, a wondrous opportunity came Tina's way. On July 15, both of the city's Italian-language dailies mock-seriously announced a performance of *Stenterello the Slob*, a "most amusing spectacle" starring the well-known actor Arturo Godi and booked into the old Liberty Theater on Broadway. "Mr. Arturo Godi," they reported, "has received a long Marconigram [wireless radio message] sent by his oh so intimate friend Stenterello the Slob, in which the Florentine wit informs him that, due to invidious German submarines, he will not commit himself to an ocean crossing but has instead hired a hovercraft in which...the artists of his company are taking their places...." Buried in the list of players was the name of the novice Tina Modotti, cast as the impish Sofia.

Troupes such as Godi's were short-lived ventures whose actors joined fortunes under the name of the *capo comico*, or chief comic, for the duration of a series of performances. Typically, a shock of theater folk would sweep into town from New York or Chicago, audition locals to flesh out the cast, run a round of rehearsals, and ring up the curtain. Tina's was a minor part in an unsubtle farcical entertainment, but she had speaking lines, and the star was Arturo Godi, renowned around the Italian theater circuit as a master Stenterello.

An inveterate scene-stealer, Stenterello was a popular stock character, the Florentine cousin of Charlie Chaplin's Little Tramp. Confused, garrulous, excitable, and naïve, Stenterello stumbled through an inexhaustible store of comedies. Often digressing from prepared patter, he lampooned current events and local notables, which set audiences wild. Godi's version sported a bowl haircut, heavy inverted **V** eyebrows, an ill-fitting waistcoat, and spats. Most of Tina's early stage roles were in Stenterello comedies, and the skirts the old mischief-maker chased, to great tittering, were frequently hers.

As rehearsals for *Stenterello the Slob* progressed in untypically sweltering July weather, the performance was upstaged when a bomb exploded at a patriotic parade, killing ten people and injuring forty. San Franciscans could speak of nothing else, and amid a frenzy of hysteria and paranoia, the radical unionist Tom Mooney was charged with the crime and imprisoned, in a case that was to become a cause célèbre among radicals worldwide. Stenterello nonetheless packed the house, and the Italian papers wedged in brief notices, both of which got Tina's name wrong. "We are not going to forget Misses Ida Modotti, Antonietta Ceccanti and Elvira Bocci who recited with ease and brio," bubbled *L'Italia* (which published only two types of reviews, wildly enthusiastic and slightly less so). A role in *Stenterello in Paris* followed, with Tina presumably touring in Los Angeles, where the troupe repeated its dual successes. By now, she was bitten hard by the theater bug, and her "promising career as a *modiste* was terminated by the call of the more glamorous stage."

Godi's productions were curtain-raisers for a revival of professional theater in San Francisco, which would center on the Liberty. A Neapolitan entrepreneur purchased the building and began negotiating contracts for a menu of entertainments. It was a moment to be seized. Scrambling to put together a portfolio, Tina went to see the highly regarded German immigrant photographer Arnold Schröder. Ruddy-faced and ham-handed, the gregarious Schröder was as disorganized in business management as he was fastidious in photographic method. He lived and worked at a rambling artists' colony at 1625 California Street, where he threw bacchanalian parties.

The glamorous and immaculate Tina Modotti who appears before Arnold Schröder's lens is strikingly different from the adolescent we saw only two or three years earlier. She has shed all provincialism, her movements are graceful and self-aware, and her carriage is elegant. Clearly, she is conscious of her loveliness and skilled in projecting it to the camera. Already, Tina resembles Cuban writer Lolo de la Torriente's description of several years later: "Not very tall, her body lithe and well-formed, soft curves, an expressive face, fiery dark eyes, a sensuous mouth, plum-colored hair, a broad forehead, and expressive, slim hands. Her movements were slow and harmonious, her voice soft, and her gaze tender and lively."

In Schröder's profile shot, Tina is arch and swanlike, pulling delicately at the neckline of her dress. In the full-faced composition, her dramatically lit head appears against an artistic haze, as one hand disappears behind her hip, the other floats across her knee, and her look is lost in reverie. The images take their places among a dozen artists' portraits of

Tina Modotti, some obscure and others celebrated works of art that have powerfully shaped our understanding of her. Yet the flesh-and-blood Tina, uncertain about her identity, also peered into them, as into so many mirrors, eager to read in their play of light and surface a revelation of selfhood. A few years later, she would write briefly and revealingly of how portraiture and self-awareness entwined in her mind. Her words were to another photographer: "Just the fact that you have made such immortal portraits of me shows your capacity to bring out the best in me."

Schröder's photographs in hand, Tina auditioned and was accepted into Alfredo Aratoli's City of Florence Company, which made its San Francisco debut in April 1917, and her theatrical career began in earnest. After a taste of Stenterello, the North Beach public couldn't get enough of the Florentine buffoon. Tina performed in the outlandish *Twenty Years in the Life of a Cadaver,* followed by *Stenterello Under the Bed, Stenterello Deserter in Time of Peace,* and *Stenterello in the Insane Asylum of Stockton.* The Aratoli company was dominated by two veteran actors. One was its director, Alfredo Aratoli, a zany Stenterello and putty-faced striker of poses. The other, old barnstormer Oreste Seragnoli, was renouncing the international circuit to settle in San Francisco. A hulking man with raccoon eyes and a symmetrical hairdo, he was a father figure, widely admired for his generosity and compassion as well as for his prodigious playacting.

The pair coached their ingenue for her weekly performances. From the beginning, Tina displayed a remarkable stage presence and a gift for recitation, memorizing her lines easily and enunciating them with crispness and impetuosity. She learned to breathe, project her soft, husky voice into the farthest corners of the auditorium, and add larger-than-life gestures to her repertoire. Tina's gift was for drama and tragedy, and she could not have found the Stenterello comedies easy fare. Besides, Italian audiences were a hard school, for they expected belly laughs and didn't bother to mask lukewarm reactions with polite applause. Lacking her colleagues' aptitude for uninhibited horseplay and their ability to chew up the scenery, Tina worked at vamping, sashaying, and well-timed repartee. Rehearsing scrupulously and hearkening to her mentors' counsels, she made rapid progress.

There were the usual shenanigans and mishaps. In the comic opera *Fra Diavolo* (known in English as *The Inn at Terracine*), Tina performed with

Luigi Poggi, a middle-aged actor renowned as a star tenor on the lowbrow nickelodeon opera circuit. Romantically involved for a time with Mercedes, Luigi was to live with the Modotti family, and Giuseppe hailed him as son-in-law. Poggi was cast as a bandit who is to be shot by a carabiniere. Unfortunately, the soldier's gun refused to fire. The crowd sneered, and, cursing under his breath, the unlucky carabiniere tried again. Keeping his wits about him, Luigi yelled out, "Boom!" and collapsed on the floor as a cheering audience leapt to its feet.

From Alessandro Baccari's son comes an anecdote about prompter Gennaro Dorso, ensconced in the pit at City of Florence productions. The prompter was a crucial element in Italian-American theater, where productions were launched with such frequency that even conscientious players like Tina were unable to get lines letter-perfect. According to Baccari, Dorso had a great weakness for Tina's ankles, and, at the jests that inevitably followed mention of his predilection, he would make a shrugging, supplicating gesture to the heavens and rejoin, "*Eh,* I'm on the floor!"

September was to bring the ensemble's disbanding, after five months, though Aratoli pledged to resurrect it the following year. One of the Aratoli company's final offerings was the musical comedy *Out of the Shadow, Into the Sun,* a performance dedicated to Tina Modotti. An honor normally reserved for the most prominent actors, actresses, and directors, a celebratory "evening" was rarely bestowed upon neophytes.

Assigned the demanding role of Lisetta, Tina rose to the occasion "all fire, vivacity and seduction," managing to pull off even the vocals. Her curtain calls brought showers of bouquets and crescendos of foot-stomping applause. Colleagues reappeared before the curtain to offer her an exquisite toilette set and a pair of diamond earrings, whose brilliance, Seragnoli must have rhapsodized, was outshone only by its lovely recipient. The next day, *L'Italia* gilded the lily:

> Tina Modotti, the gracious signorina we have so often admired and applauded in our city's small amateur theaters, could not have made her professional debut with a comedy more appropriate to her vocal and emotional capabilities, stirring appreciation for her innate artistic sentiment and promising the glory of a brilliant and enviable career.

The years will pass, and the times will change, but yesterday evening's performance will always leave in her all the freshness of a soul in love with her art.

For instructing and launching her, Alfredo Aratoli and Oreste Seragnoli were saluted with "a heartfelt bravo."

The public's surge of enthusiasm for Tina Modotti rewarded her hard work but was disproportionate to her modest artistic achievement. She owed the triumph, in part, to the public's enchantment with her Cinderella quality. A plucky, kindhearted young woman, fresh from the factory, is one of only two local amateurs accepted into the respected Aratoli company, where she becomes a protégée of the brightest lights in Italian theater. The heartwarming tale made Tina a recognized personality around North Beach. "And truly, her passage from amateurism to professionalism could not begin more auspiciously," *L'Italia* assured its readers.

On top of it all came Tina's captivating presence. Audiences were enchanted by the manner in which she floated across the stage. Her mere appearance could hush a restless, murmurous multitude. Remembering "a magnificence and a nobility" uncommon in one so young and humble, old-timers of the Depression era would still wax nostalgic over her brief career. She was a dazzling jewel of the North Beach stage, ever "the fabulous Tina Modotti."

Aratoli's departure left Tina bereft of theatrical opportunities. After five fast months of performances, rehearsals, and costuming sessions, combined with part-time modeling and sewing jobs, the breathing space was welcome, yet Tina missed the theater's sweet camaraderie. She volunteered to collect prizes for the Red Cross Christmas benefit ball and sought other kinds of work, since acting—a financially unreliable profit-sharing venture—had probably left her short of cash.

Everything else dimmed, however, next to the catastrophe in Italy. The outbreak of European hostilities in 1914 had confined Assunta and the adolescent Modottis to Udine and intermittently interrupted the flow of news and funds from San Francisco. After two years of savage combat and wholesale carnage in eastern Friuli, the Italians had failed to break through Austro-Hungarian lines. In October 1917, as French and British units rushed to brace the Italians, Udine was evacuated in anticipation of enemy occupation. North Beach cafés and kitchens were robbed of joy that fall by low, urgent-toned talk of the enemy sweep, a cholera epidemic, and deaths under fire of brothers and cousins.

Meanwhile, the military debacle had cut off communication with the family in Italy, leaving Tina, Mercedes, and Giuseppe frantic with anxiety. Was Tina also experiencing guilt that she had been absorbed in playacting as her loved ones suffered? If so, it was not the last time she would anguish over the thought of art making in the face of human affliction.

In early December, a bulletin in the childish hand of fourteen-year-old Benvenuto reached 1952 Taylor Street, easing the trio's dread. It bore a postmark from central Italy, where the family was camping in a drafty castle:

> The sad emotions of today are such that I barely find the strength to recount the changes which we have come up against. I will only say that from our Udine we have had to come as refugees to a small village in Abruzzi among people who are absolute strangers, though they are very hospitable. We had to leave in great haste, without thinking about our clothing or anything else.... We journeyed three days and three nights. We arrived safe and sound, but our thoughts keep returning to our Udine and to you who seem so far away.

As the family fled Udine, eighteen-year-old Gioconda was six months pregnant by a soldier she had known fleetingly, and in January, she gave birth to a son called Tullio. Assunta pampered and adored the infant, but, at fifty-four, she could not have found it easy to be responsible for one more human being.

While Gioconda's early romances were informed by the realities of war, Tina was experimenting with lighthearted romantic intrigue. The identities of her first suitors are unknown, save that of Bruno Pagliai, a short, coal-eyed Sicilian who clerked for the Bank of Italy by day and waited tables by night. But she gently spurned the young man, who was to become a billionaire financier and, for a time, the husband of actress Merle Oberon. By late 1917, Tina was being wooed by someone more fascinating to her and just beginning a relationship that would transform her life.

Twenty-seven-year-old Roubaix de l'Abrie Richey was a painter, writer, and aristocrat manqué as well as a longtime bellhop at the fancy St. Francis Hotel on Union Square. A gentle man and a curious mix of provincialism and sophistication, Robo—as he was universally called—reveled in the bohemian life. He grew his hair and fingernails long, affected Prince Albert jackets and smocks with flowing ties, and distributed calling cards bearing the name Xavier de Zyzannes. An esthete who lived for beauty, he nonetheless surrounded himself with "tumbled beds, [a] table heaped high with dirty tea cups, scraps torn from magazines, books, cigar ashes and clothes...."

Born in Pleasant Valley, Oregon, south of Portland, Robo Richey issued from a prosperous farm family. His maternal grandfather had mule-trekked out from Quebec; the rest of his ancestors were of sturdy midwestern stock. At twelve, Robo had been the ringleader of a prank alarming enough to warrant cancellation of his school's Class Day and the convening of a family palaver at which it was decided that the lad should live with a Catholic priest. Dispatched to tiny, desolate Brooks, Oregon, Robo passed his adolescence with the amiable and worldly Father Paul Datin. His mentor taught Robo scant religion but peppered him with citations from Saint Augustine and Mallarmé and polished the crude French picked up from his Québecois great-uncles. Privately, the two rolled their eyes at "Brooks and its aborigines." At eighteen, Robo started high school at Grants Pass, where he devoted himself to romantic dalliances and caricature.

September 1912 saw him enrolled at San Francisco's Mark Hopkins School of Art. Within weeks, he was at the head of a pack of rebels bolting from the institution ("very backward and unprogressive," he wrote home, "...in the hands of a lot of fogies") to establish the California Art League, which, he boasted, would "make us the art leaders of California." His somber, phantasmagoric paintings of temptresses and snake goddesses found little success, but he took a Romantic stance and feigned indifference: "I work day after day here, only to scrape out all that I have done at the end of the week. I do not care whether anyone likes my pictures or not. It is only a means unto an end—the preliminaries—the ladder by which I hope to reach the far, fair shores of those Ultimate Islands which float so high above us in the skies of sunset."

Robo cut a wider swath with his short stories, which were published by the venerable *Overland Monthly* and *The Saturday Evening Post.* By 1917, he had become a contributing editor to *Bohemia,* which featured his popular "Wanderer's Song" ("I have slept me a sleep/ And dreamed me a dream/ And tramped me a tramp/ With the heart of a rover..."). He fraternized with the *Bohemia* crowd that year, cultivating the friendship of fellow editor George Sterling, the writer who tagged San Francisco a "cool, grey city of love." Sterling had been a protégé of Ambrose Bierce, whose witty, bitter epigrams Robo emulated. Not long after 1913, when Bierce left for the Mexican revolution where he joined Pancho Villa's army and then vanished, the Oregonian enrolled in Spanish classes at the YMCA. He had taken a fancy to the idea of a sojourn in Mexico or Argentina, as a prelude to Paris, "the heart, the brain, the soul of the world!"

In the interim, his best energies were lost in a wilderness of affairs with artists' models, acrobats, silk stockings, and showgirls. On a swing through Grants Pass in 1914, he had made the acquaintance of Viola McClain, a petulant, precocious fourteen-year-old whose parents had left her to her own devices. Finding Robo both baffling and seductive, Viola capped his visit with the announcement that she was coming to live with him in San Francisco. "For goodness sake don't fail to meet me at the station," she instructed, "as I don't know one street from another in Frisco and would probably get lost, then the bogey man might get me sure." Nonchalant and casually affectionate, Robo put no obstacles in her path. A slow-witted, moon-faced young woman with powder white skin and a crimp of dark hair, Viola chose, as her *nom d'artiste,* Vola Dorée. She took cracks at modeling, dancing, and acting, but her heart's true desire was to reel in Robo Richey, and the couple was wed in October 1915. "He was the best man in the world to me," she later remembered, "for we all have our faults, but Robo was ever good at heart." Yet he endlessly two-timed her, receiving billets-doux at the St. Francis and hatching complicated schemes, all the while exhorting her to be faithful to him. "Never give any other the pleasure of my love, my own true virtuous little wife!" he told her.

In the spring of 1917, Robo fled the confusion of his life and traveled to New York, where he studied at the Art Students League. Feeling betrayed, Vola fired off letters both furious and sloppily sentimental but received scant reply. Meanwhile, in San Francisco, Robo's sister, Marionne Richey, a Mills College student, paid a visit one day to the studio of the

Richeys' close friend Arnold Schröder. There she happened upon Tina Modotti, and the two women, both twenty, struck a friendly chord. Marionne quickly appointed herself intermediary between Tina and Robo, who she sensed would fancy the Italian beauty. When her brother pressed for details, Marionne teased, "I am glad I don't know Tina very well. I'll not have to bother to tell you about her. That is one less responsibility!"

Robo prolonged his travels and could not have looked up Tina before the autumn of 1917. Nothing is known of their early meetings or mutual impressions. In surviving Richey family correspondence, the first mention of Tina is a story of patching up two lovers' quarrels. On March 28, 1918, Robo wrote to Marionne, now living in Los Angeles:

> Nothing seems to change here but I am as contented as I ever can be I suppose. I feel that I am making some artistic progress. Poor little Volee! Sunday evening about quitting time two big trays of coffee pots fell on her [Vola had taken a job as a waitress] and hurt her back so she had to be helped home.... Things go rather well with us now apart. You cannot imagine me being chained up. V. found out all about Tina during my absence so that there was nothing much to tell her but the truth. Tina and I made up—V. saw Tina and liked her looks. Now there is an understanding and I hope there will be no further trouble about it.

Curiously, the true story of Tina and Robo's meeting was to be concealed from virtually everyone, including Tina's younger siblings. The couple invented its own version, which has been repeated in every account of Tina Modotti's life. First published as part of *L'Italia's* reporting of their nuptials, it was probably written by Robo, translated by Tina, and delivered to the newspaper by Mercedes. The tale romantically situated the encounter at the Panama-Pacific International Exposition, where "the two young people often met each other in the Palace of Fine Arts and their shared ideals and admiration for art were transformed into mutual love...." It was a prettier, less complicated, more satisfying story than the truth. "Facts are not always beautiful," Robo liked to say, "and I wish only to be beautiful."

Tina was also in the habit of stretching and rearranging reality to serve a friendship or a cause. A case in point was the eyebrow-raising Pezza-Portanova scandal, good for café gossip in war-weary North Beach.

The affair pitted painter Stefania Pezza against her live-in companion, sculptor Giovanni Battista Portanova. In December, Pezza had instigated legal proceedings against Portanova, demanding that the San Francisco Superior Court enforce their business contract and award her the substantial sum of $25,000 in damages. Back in Italy, she alleged, the Pezza family jewels and real estate holdings had been sold off to subsidize Portanova and underwrite the cost of the couple's move to San Francisco. In consequence, a bargain was struck to divide equally all subsequent earnings by both. When it turned out that Portanova's sculpture sales were brisk, continued Pezza, he had violated the agreement, and, on top of that, had proposed marriage, then stood her up at City Hall.

As the Pezza-Portanova trial got under way, the Italian-American art world anticipated juicy revelations. One of the first was that Tina Modotti had modeled for Portanova's allegorical portrait bust *Regeneration,* recently commissioned by the Fairmont Hotel, and claimed by *L'Italia* to be "one of the most beautiful works of sculpture ever executed in the United States." Portanova's attorney acknowledged that his client had been "inspired by the classic face of this gracious young woman in the execution of...*Regeneration,* and the beautiful lines of the woman Portanova sculpted were none other than the features of Miss Tina." Both Tina and the woman who had served as the sculptor's nude model would testify on his client's behalf and shed light upon the workings of the Pezza-Portanova household.

One of the trial's contentious issues was whether or not Pezza had kept faith by continuing to produce and sell paintings, and Tina testified that she had never seen Stefania Pezza at the easel. Further interrogation drew Tina's statement that cash payments for her modeling had come from Portanova's pocket, whereas Pezza had handled disbursements by check. After coverage of her testimony appeared in *L'Italia,* Tina rushed a carefully worded letter to the editor:

> Some newspapers, including your own, speaking of the Pezza-Portanova trial, have referred to the undersigned as a model. I beg you to correct this affirmation because I have not served as a model for the sculptor, Portanova, but rather, being a friend of both par-

ties, I consented out of pure courtesy to permit the above-mentioned artist to sketch the outline of my head as he put the finishing touches on *Regeneration.*

Though the details of the matter are murky, Tina's use of the expression "out of pure courtesy" seems to contradict her own testimony that she was a paid model. Moreover, the letter hints at a session or two at the sculptor's studio, whereas in court, she had alluded to regular modeling. Perhaps most laden with significance is the phrase "of my head," for *L'Italia* did not rule out the possibility that Tina had, in truth, been Portanova's nude model. That she was modeling unclothed was a distinct possibility, for Alessandro Baccari, Jr., remembers his father's nude photographs of Tina from this period. If so, she must have feared that revelations would damage her career. In any event, she escaped with reputation unscathed, while Stefania Pezza walked away from the imbroglio $25,000 richer.

We can surmise that Tina implored Robo's counsel on the Pezza-Portanova situation. The two saw a good deal of each other that spring, with their social life revolving around the all-night Columbus Avenue trattoria of Rosina and Raffaele Alessandrelli. For some years, the Modottis and the Alessandrellis had been fast friends. Rosina mothered the Modotti sisters, and both families were fond of long drives through Golden Gate Park in the Alessandrellis' roadster, one of the first in the Italian colony.

Officially, the couple's eatery was called the Bologna after Raffaele's hometown, but, on most lips, it went by his nickname, "Bigin's." Bigin cheerfully accepted art in lieu of cash and fed painters free pasta, wine, and cigarettes as they decorated his establishment. Dubbed "the *famiglia,*" habitués were "an irresponsible flack of artist folk such as rarely gather in one place." The *San Francisco Examiner* listed the habits of the restaurateur's odd brood:

> They come nightly. They dine. They go from table to table. There is excited talk. The merits of Cézanne, of Picasso, of Boggione are discussed, warmly. Nothing at Bigin's is perfunctory.
>
> There is sketching on the table cloths and serviettes, and many a bit of Bigin's linen has gone away never to return because it was the improvised canvas for some sketch. Bigin's linen bills are high....

"Yes, have they money, they will pay. Have they not, well, what of it. They are my friends, my guests." So [Bigin] philosophizes.

As they mingled with Bigin's flock of bon vivants, Tina and Robo must have marveled that they had not become acquainted sooner. Not only did the two share a friendship with gregarious man-about–North Beach, journalist Ottorini "Caesar" Ronchi, but also Robo had a place in Bigin's inner circle of artist decorators:

> A truly futuristic thing in a style not beyond the realm of easy understanding is "The Snake Woman," a nude figure with snakes for arms, by Ramboise la Brie Kickey.... Below it sit Heine, with his friends, Otto Ronchi, an Italian writer, and Mahlon Blaine, a young American artist who "did" the decorations of Bigin's menu. About them, many a night, are A. Borghesi and C. Vergellini, who did the "nursery" room, sacred to "regulars"; George Sterling, when he is here...and a host of other artist-folk.

Among Robo's closest friends were illustrator Mahlon Blaine and rakish Belgian-born Harry Heine, a former roommate and the "oddest genius that ever sat before an easel." Heine picturesquely earned his living as a lamplighter on Van Ness Avenue and loved to bend Tina's ear with grandiose plans to establish a "little theater" with a cast of singing Italian fishermen.

At Bigin's, as at various art openings and soirées, Tina and Robo were an arresting presence. Six years older and a foot taller than his companion, Robo was a lanky man with a strong nose, jaunty mustache, and slender, elegant hands. In public, his dark eyes struck a world-weary look, but in private, they often lapsed into a tender or startled gaze. Though not handsome, he was vain about his appearance and cut a charming aristocratic figure that many found irresistible. Tina could never be certain which Robo would appear for their assignations, for occasionally his black curls were snipped short and the Beau Brummell attire discarded for a pinstriped suit, white shirt, dark tie, and spats.

Adoring well-dressed women, Robo found Tina's wardrobe to be part and parcel of the spell she cast. Like her father, Tina now ascribed great importance to that which had long remained beyond her means. Her closet overflowed with pretty, well-cut garments, mostly homemade, fashioned from good-quality fabrics in rich hues. For late afternoon, she might choose her ivory dress with Peter Pan collar, satin tie, and jacket, or her ankle-length suit, with a self-belt and collar in a contrasting shade, and matching cape. She was rarely without a hat.

But, for Robo, Tina's appeal did not stop at her appearance, enchanting accent, or European manners. She shared his disregard for convention and middle-class values, as well as his fine social delicacy. Tina was shocked by vulgarities at which Vola batted nary an eyelash. Perhaps most important to Robo, who babbled incessantly of his dreams and grandiloquent plans, she hung upon every word. "If Tina cared," a friend observed, "her attitude was: I'm with you now. Nobody else exists. We live for this moment." Smitten with Robo's "simple charm and gentle manners," with what seemed his vast knowledge of art and literature, and with his sterling idealism, she gave him her undivided attention.

The couple's peregrinations frequently took them beyond North Beach to bohemian *hauts-lieux,* whose doors Robo opened for Tina. Among them were those of the Verdier mansion, atop Russian Hill, where the self-proclaimed King of Bohemia, Sadakichi Hartmann, was holding court that season. No doubt it was through George Sterling that Robo knew the eminent fifty-one-year-old writer, critic, gadfly, and stylish freeloader on the smart sets of half a dozen cities. Tall and thin as a reed, with a shock of shaggy gray hair, Sadakichi served guests green tea, scenes from Ibsen, and a "perfume concert" as they chuckled over the story, no doubt apocryphal, that their host had been booted out of the high-society Bohemian Club for being too bohemian.

From Sadakichi's digs, Tina and Robo might wander downtown to Paul Elder's Arts and Crafts–style bookshop, which displayed antiquarian volumes and decorative art in an atmosphere of quiet reserve. They may have attended Elder's spring lecture series by visionary British socialist writer John Cowper Powys, with whose appearance, said one observer, "all that was beautiful, intelligent and worthwhile contemplating in the way of thought and spirit suddenly swept into the room." Such lofty-minded, dreamy-souled luminaries made deep impressions upon Tina. In Robo's world of platonic idealism, art and poetry hovered above the mundane, and beauty was the only worthy subject. Hours with Robo set Tina's mind spinning and roused notions that the theater, her whole education in recent years, might be insufficient, and her own artistic circle of histrionic troupers tinny and unsatisfying next to this intelligentsia.

Yet, she had thrilled to be cast as the godchild Amelia in Oreste Seragnoli's staging of the highly touted drama *Papa Martin's Basket*. The Saint Valentine's eve performance benefiting the Italian Red Cross turned out a big crowd at the thousand-seat Washington Square Theater, recently renovated after five years of darkness. Tina's first entrance under Italian and American bunting drew extra whistles and applause for the "kind and passionate daughter of heroic Friuli," and, from that moment on, there were few dry eyes in the house. The curtain dropped to thunderous applause. Along with Oreste and actress Elvira de Ricci, Tina was honored with a gold medal and an artistic parchment in a ceremony so moving that Oreste was nearly overcome with emotion as he rendered thanks. The evening netted $556 for war-relief efforts, with Giuseppe Modotti grandly topping the donor list at five dollars.

As promised, actor and director Alfredo Aratoli reappeared that spring, and Tina's stage career was swiftly resurrected. She sailed through *Don Francesco, Silent Waters, Nobody's Children,* and *La Mòrte Civile,* a Zolaesque drama whose notices praised her diction and scenic action. Professional theater had returned to North Beach in a big way, and by midsummer, the Italian colony buzzed with news that Seragnoli and actress Amalia Bruno were assembling a resident company for the Washington Square Theater. The two raided Aratoli of his talent, including Tina Modotti, and heralded an influx of East Coast stars in September.

The summer of 1918 confirmed Tina's reputation as a rising Italian-American actress. *Love in the Time of War* brought exit applause for her beautiful scene. In *Tosca,* she was a Gennarino "full of brio," and she played leading lady in *The Misplaced Letter* and *The Urchins of Paris. L'Italia* pronounced her "most gracious, exquisite" as Madame de Fornaris in *The Dishonest Ones,* and Seragnoli staged a reprise of her earlier triumph in *Out of the Shadow, Into the Sun.* The culminating moment of Tina Modotti's theatrical career came on August 21, a few days after her twenty-second birthday. Oreste Seragnoli directed a cast of dozens in the sellout U.S. debut of *The Enemy,* a drama set in World War I Italy. This tale of a man compelled to denounce his own mother set spectators on tenterhooks and had *L'Italia* swooning over the performance of

> Tina Modotti, whom all in our colony have so often admired and whom…we all love as much for her goodness as for her brilliant artistic qualities. She is still at the beginning of her career and yet demonstrates enormous progress day by day, yesterday surprising even her warmest admirers by the dramatic intensity of her acting, especially in the great final scene of the first act…. Always careful, dedicated, and conscientious…Signora Modotti has already obtained—if we may so phrase it—her diploma as an artist and, continuing to study as she does, her career is assured.

Absent since May on a camping trip in Oregon and Yosemite National Park, Robo missed the ascendancy of Tina's star. But a steady stream of long blue envelopes addressed in his ornate hand was flowing to 1952 Taylor Street. They commenced "Dear Little One" or "Dear Tinella." Intrigued by the sounds and colors of words, Robo took great pains to invent inspired terms of affection for his friends. Tinella: The name evoked a remote tintinnabulation, something airy and exotic that lingers in the mind. Understanding its importance to Robo, Tina pondered carefully before choosing, as her pet name for him, Robetu.

August found Robo back in San Francisco in an uncharacteristic mood of resolution. On the eighth, he filed for divorce from Vola, citing an unsavory scene before friends and alleging that her faultfinding had caused him, as a "person of refinement and delicacy of sentiment," to "suffer extreme mental pain and anguish, made him feel humiliated and mortified, outraged his sensibilities, destroyed his peace of mind…and impair[ed] his health." Then he turned his attention to enticing Tina to quit the theater and run away on a mad escapade.

It was a moment when cards were being reshuffled at the Washington Square Theater. After only six weeks of existence, the Bruno Seragnoli Company was breaking up, to be replaced by La Moderna, well stocked with star performers from around the Italian-American circuit. Honored with an invitation to join the new troupe, Tina had already posed for a publicity cameo to be used on the playbill for September's "colossal debut."

In contrast to the future laid out for her in North Beach, Robo proposed a leap into another world, where they would go castle building and recast life's dross into something visionary and fine. The old desire for education swept over Tina, and Robo seemed complicitous with her aspirations to fine art and idealism. As she entertained his proposal, she may have realized that life with Robo held prospects of freedom and time such as she had not known in a decade of grinding labor. Empty-pocketed though he usually was, Robo was heir, through his mother, to assets substantial enough to allow him to dodge paid work. Characteristically, Tina mulled over the situation before plunging ahead intuitively. Given Robo's bouts of traveling, her time with him could not have totaled more than five months. In many ways, he was an unknown quantity.

The couple remained in San Francisco until August 28, when a superior court order granted Roubaix de l'Abrie Richey an interlocutory, or provisional, decree of divorce from Vola de l'Abrie Richey, with the dissolution of marriage to become final in one year. In a manner worthy of Italian-American melodrama, Tina allowed herself to be spirited off just as her skill and success reached their zenith, leaving the public, primed for her appearance with La Moderna, puzzled and unhappy. The whereabouts of Tina and Robo that cool, rainy September are an abiding mystery.

Part II

Madame de Richey

Lompoc and Los Angeles (1918–1921)

O
NE DAY IN EARLY OCTOBER, an attractive couple stepped out of the oceanside rail depot at Lompoc Junction (now Surf), California, in the sleepy backcountry south of San Luis Obispo. The sky was a cloudless blue, and white sands, spreading in all directions, served as a palette for immense blobs of brilliant yellow lupine and fuchsia sand verbena. Intoxicated with color and wind, the pair climbed into a horse cart driven by an elderly woman. Three or four miles through the dazzling, unpeopled landscape and a jaunt up a eucalyptus-lined, washboard canyon road took Tina and Robo to the gloriously solitary ranch of Clarinda and Vernon La Salle.

Affable septuagenarians, Robo's great-aunt and -uncle were kindly, hardworking, self-reliant folk. Their homestead was a spread of animal pens and sheds, longhaired sheep, chickens and roosters, spiky sisal plants, ramshackle picket fences, and an apiary. In its midst stood the rambling rose-bowered cottage crowded by nasturtiums where Tina and Robo would dawdle away the month, their "honeymoon" and Tina's first vacation.

Two other houseguests were motoring up from Los Angeles. One was Robo's sister, Marionne, and the other, his fifty-eight-year-old mother, Rose Richey, burning with curiosity about Tina. Aristocratic in bearing and folksy in manner, Rose was tall and slender, with a sharp nose, hooded and bespectacled gray eyes, prominent teeth, and a mound of silvery hair. A conventional woman, she was generally untroubled by nonconformity; financially well fixed, she was both penny-wise and generous. Rose's days were given over to cooking, sewing, visiting, and other garden-variety concerns, but her psychic energies poured into the well-being of her two grown children. In a crabbed hand, she penciled to the relatives in Oregon hour-by-hour accounts of the family's comings and goings, a practice that earned her Robo's nickname "Vocio," meaning "chatterbox" in Italian.

Born Rose Salina LaBrie, Vocio had grown up in Roseburg, Oregon, and married a farmer named James Akin Richey, a quiet man whose beard hung around his mouth like an overgrown vine. For twenty years, Vocio lived uneventfully as a Pleasant Valley farm wife until "Papa" succumbed to tuberculosis in 1914. By then, Robo and Marionne were established in San Francisco, and she followed them south. Novel sights and sounds, along with an inheritance from her stepfather, Judge John O. Booth—a prominent businessman, hotel owner, mining executive, and county magistrate—put fresh sparkle into her eyes and wanderlust into her heart. When Marionne hankered for an automobile, Vocio bought a Model T Ford, and within days the two women were sputtering and lurching out of San Francisco. Vocio aimed to visit all of California's twenty-one Franciscan missions, strung from Sonoma to San Diego, and she became an intrepid sightseer. She drew the line, however, when Robo proposed that the three of them move to Argentina. "I have been looking in [stepsister] Amy's Atlas in regard to South America," she informed her son. "Argentina is six thousand miles from New York. That seems a long way off...not knowing...something about the country and if living is expensive there."

In Lompoc, Marionne recorded the household's outings with her Kodak as Tina got acquainted with the family she was soon calling "the folks." The band of holidaymakers picnicked at the Old Wharf, where Tina sampled abalone, nibbled on grapes, and savored potato salad. They ambled along crumbling walls, all that remained of La Purísima Mission, and wandered through sun-soaked brushwood as Tina looped sweet-smelling eucalyptus around her straw hat. Uncle Vern explained bee lore to the visitor, and Aunt Clarinda taught her how to milk a goat. The older woman wore a poke bonnet and apron for the lesson, but Tina, in the barnyard, affected a pale ruffled gown, Japanese sandals, and thin white socks, the height of bohemian fashion. Now and then, she donned practical doughboy-style knickers, tall boots, and khaki shirts, but then discarded them again in favor of the extravagant Japanese silk kimonos and flowing voile blouses Robo adored. The other women puttered around in old cotton housedresses. Imagine Vocio, slightly starstruck by the actress and straining her attention to the details of such unusual finery, yet discerning in Tina someone genuine and unassuming.

Marionne, too, peered quizzically at their guest, for the pair's San Francisco friendship had been brief and casual. Gangly and angular, Marionne had a clump of sandy brown hair and hooded blue eyes, shyly dropped under the gaze of strangers. At home, however, she was transformed into an irrepressible, tart-tongued creature, unbridled in her enthusiasm for fishing, hiking, and all things mechanical. Unlike her brother, she had not an artistic or bookish bone in her body, yet the two were exceptionally close. She was a roughhouse and sisterly tease, and he garnished her with waggish nicknames: "Mutt," "Medion," "Old Sheep," and "Czepe," meaning "sister" in Ziziquiyana, a language he had invented and which only they spoke fluently. With Tina, however, Marionne scraped along on lukewarm friendship. The two women had fundamentally different mindsets, Marionne's straight-thinking prosiness looking askance at Tina's shape-shifting quest. In later years, when Tina's life had become a scroll of dramas, Marionne would simply refuse to discuss her, fending off conversations by saying, "Oh, she got mixed up with Pancho Villa."

Snapshots in the Richey family album throw light on Tina's mood of high spirits and tingling sensuality during the month in Lompoc. Beaming and complicitous, she and Robo pose, collapsed in a tussock of grass with a bouquet of black-eyed Susans so large that they hold it with four hands. When midday somnolence drifted over the canyon, the twosome lolled in a secluded spot, intoxicated by the dry perfume of eucalyptus and shaded by a canopy of leaves perfectly still until the late-afternoon breeze commenced its rustle. Robo was wont to pull out a sheaf of poetry or his tiny, well-thumbed volume of the *Rubáiyát of Omar Khayyám*, a paean to hedonism and a bohemian handbook of sorts. "In his periods of buoyant enthusiasm," Tina remembered, "he would talk by the hour about the plots of his books and the characters in them, which were more real to him than real people." A multitude of dreams possessed them in those halcyon days. Immersing themselves in each other, they made love, she calling him *"dolce cuore,*" literally "sweetheart," and he whispering that she was the only girl in the world for him.

All the while, they were elaborately cloaking from nearly everyone the truth of their legal bond, or rather, lack thereof. On October 16, under the caption "Tina Modotti Weds," along with a photograph of the young woman looking more the model than the bride, *L'Italia* published an explanation for those waiting "in vain for several weeks for the appearance of this young, kind, intelligent actress." Tina Modotti had "decided to become part of a love poem of two persons. A few days ago she married signor R. De L'Abrie Richey, an excellent and notable young Canadian American and member of a distinguished family and passionate devotee of painting." On the heels of the Santa Barbara wedding, continued the article, would come "several weeks hosted by the De L'Abrie Richey family which is staying precisely in the vicinity of that city." This tale of a Santa Barbara wedding was also fed to the couple's San Francisco entourage. Meanwhile, the two cooked up for the Richeys a story of nuptials at the San Mateo County Courthouse in Redwood City, south of San Francisco, and another of Robo's finalized divorce from Vola Dorée.

As far as we know, Tina avowed the fabrication only to her later companion Edward Weston, her father (who told a 1920 census taker that both Tina and Robo were single, but qualified Robo as his son-in-law), and probably her sister Mercedes. In time, the possibility of a falsehood dawned on Marionne Richey. While settling some financial affairs in 1932, she inquired of the San Mateo County clerk, "Will you please tell me if you have a record there of a marriage between Roubaix Richey and Tina Modotti, in either September or October of 1918?" and was told, "We haven't any record of the above mentioned matter."

All her life, out of loyalty to Robo, Tina was steadfastly untruthful about the marriage. Even her sister Yolanda believed the bond was legal and said so to Tina's chroniclers as well as to the Richey family genealogist. (The family tree records a wedding in San Francisco in 1918.) By the mid-1930s, years after Robo's death, Tina's deep commitment to communism made the union with an apolitical, self-indulgent artist rather embarrassing. As a result, she mischaracterized the relationship but did not unburden herself of the fictional wedding. According to a friend and comrade, Tina then professed that it was art that united her with Robo. He was a sick man; he had problems with his lungs. As she always had a particular compassion for other people, she pitied this young man incapable of enjoying life. She knew that he would not have a long life and she could not refuse his proposition of marriage. She told me that Robo always pretended to hate life, but that she understood how much he suffered at the idea of death. From all that she told me, I would say it was a marriage of compassion. What united the two of them, above all, was tenderness. She was, more than anything else, a loving and understanding mother and less a wife, and I believe that the two of them had a very harmonious relationship.

As to the baffling question of why Tina and Robo trumped up the nuptials, the answer probably lies in the relationship between Robo and his mother. Knowing full well that Vocio expected her offspring to be forthright and loyal in matters of love, Robo had long concealed his tangled romances. But she found out about the fiasco with Vola. "I tell you to let the women alone if you expect to get any place," she scolded at the very time he was falling in love with Tina. "You will never get any place for long if you have a woman hanging to you. She will squeeze every cent out of you she can get.... I think and worry about you a great deal." Devoted to his mother, burdened with debt, and not yet self-supporting at age twenty-eight, Robo depended on her monthly dole. The least contentious way to introduce an inamorata was no doubt to present Vocio with the fait accompli of a marriage.

Young, in love, and raised on opera, Tina must have enjoyed the situation's stageworthy qualities. Hints are that her actions found a sympathetic response at home, for the word *marriage* was used loosely in the Modotti household. Mercedes and Luigi Poggi (married to a different woman but, again, labeled a son-in-law) cohabited under Giuseppe's roof, and, later, Mercedes would refer to a man named Marchese as her husband, though their union does not appear in official marriage rolls. By the same token, Tina's brother Beppo was to live for one year with a certain Clara Modotti, another mystery to the state of California (though such records are notoriously unreliable). Their casualness about matrimony is unsurprising, for the Modottis were a progressive family, and, in the 1920s, many radicals and bohemians were rejecting convention and seeking love in forms that did not impinge upon personal freedom.

Tina's actions, however, were more purely spontaneous and less intentional. Were she and Robo assuming a commitment to observe a moral code of marriage, or was each free to engage in relationships with others? Had Robo implicitly renounced the kind of double life he had led with Vola? Did Tina take for granted the option of sexual experimentation and self-expression? They may have been too sanguine to discuss such matters.

Meanwhile, the two were circulating a second set of fictions. These were intended to parlay Robo's French-Canadian heritage into a widespread impression that the Richeys were Gallic blue bloods. Perhaps they believed it to be true, though family genealogies do not make mention of aristocratic French antecedents, nor are relatives aware of such. *L'Italia's* account of the wedding described "an excellent and notable young Canadian American and member of a distinguished family," and Tina once cited an "ancestor, of generations ago, sent out to the Louisianas from France by one of the Louises...." A Los Angeles journalist typically would refer to Robo as "a French artist," and a friend of Tina's was to write that "she had married a French aristocrat." Astonishingly, Giuseppe Modotti believed Robo to be a French-speaking Canadian, the son of a French father and British mother. Occasionally, Tina retreated into coyness about the matter, as when she wrote an introduction to an anthology of Robo's poetry and prose: "When, where and under what circumstances, Roubaix de l'Abrie Richey...was born, will be of little importance to the reader...."

It isn't difficult to suppose that Robo had been occasionally fudging his origins all along in order to lend himself an aura and advance his career as an artist. As time went on, nearly every published mention Frenchified him. He viewed the deception as part and parcel of his art. "We are often ashamed of, and take great pains to conceal the truth concerning our most trivial and innocent things of life; our name, our relatives, our environments and our sincere thoughts," he mused. "At the same time we often admit—nay, boast, even, of disgraceful scenes, crimes and petty meannesses—all depending on their harmony with the character-part which we decided to play in the world. What is out of key we reject. That is man's primal instinct for art."

With Robo's encouragement, Tina began using the nobiliary particle *de* with her name. She became Tina de Richey, Tina Modotti de Richey, Madame de Richey, and, alternately, Tina Modotti-Richey. Few ever addressed her as plain Mrs. Richey. The name certainly did not chime with Robo's vision of his muse, whose presence would give him a fresh start and bring to him the artistic success so long overdue.

In the early days of November, the four Richeys drove south to Los Angeles, where Tina and Robo camped at Vocio and Marionne's charmless 3055½ Harrington Avenue abode, in an unfashionable section of the Wilshire district. They hit town just as three-inch headlines shrieked the end of World War I, shops closed "for the Kaiser's funeral," and streets churned with flag waving, bell ringing, and snake dancing. The paroxysm of celebration gradually subsided into a string of pleasant sunny days, which the quartet devoted to playing tourist at public gardens and Mission San Juan Capistrano. When the Richeys' relatives came to visit, they all returned to Capistrano, where the young people buried Cousin Eva up to her neck in sand and held a mock funeral, Robo feigning prayer and Tina boo-hooing into a kerchief. Afterward, looking plump, she sunbathed in a swimming costume that hit her at midthigh and scampishly thumbed her nose at Robo when he grabbed a shot with the Kodak.

Tireless gadabouts, the Richeys piled into the Model T convertible to tour Tina around Los Angeles and the nearby towns of Santa Monica, Beverly Hills, Sawtelle, and Glendale. In 1918, the basin was still checkered with fields and groves, and air streamed across their faces dusty and desert-dry. Flaming bougainvillea, pepper trees, and metallic green citruses protruded from undergrowth on misshapen homesteads where folks sat out after dinner to catch a breeze and watch the world go flat against the sky.

Yet, at war's end, Los Angeles was full of incident and change. Inside the city limits, two thousand oil rigs were twitching day and night, and film studios, from Goldwyn in Culver City to Mack Sennett in Edendale, cranked out two-reeler pie-in-the-face slapstick, sappy romances, and standard cowboy-and-Indian fare. Bungalow-seekers swarmed into once-small towns, now deliriously dividing and subdividing themselves, filling in and pushing out, inaugurating housing tracts with stunt flying and Spanish dancing. Real estate agents, fortune-tellers, vacuum-cleaner salesmen, gogetters, and evangelist Sister Aimee Semple McPherson struck rich veins. Palm trees and ersatz haciendas made their appearances, and automobile traffic hummed alongside the clang of electric red cars linking Los Angeles to its surrounding sprawl.

The ideas of beauty that Tina and Robo brought to Los Angeles vouchsafed no dreary middle-class existence, however. Leaving Vocio and Marionne behind, they planted themselves in the palatial, marble-staircased Bryson Apartment Building, a white stucco extravaganza across the street from Lafayette Park. Vaunted by the *Los Angeles Times* as the "finest structure devoted exclusively to apartment-house purposes west of New York City," the Bryson was home to many silent-film players. "Blue Ali Baba oil jars...big enough to keep tigers in" and potted date palms decorated the elegant lobby, from which a birdcage elevator ascended, six flights to the Richeys' apartment, and nine to the grand ballroom.

Robo had tasteful calling cards printed up—"Roubaix de l'Abrie-Richey, ARTIST, Studio 615 Bryson Bldg."—and Tina envisaged acting lessons leading to engagements on the English-language stage. But it wouldn't be surprising to discover that Robo rarely stood before his easel and Tina never enrolled in classes. Instead, they frittered away their days with long talks, outings, and exhibitions. In due time, they began experimenting with batik.

Not only was Tina fascinated with clothing design but also, for years, Robo had been keeping a clipped newspaper feature about Léon Bakst's ornately patterned, lushly colored Orientalist costumes for Diaghilev's Ballets Russes. The pair's interest may have been piqued further by the Los Angeles Museum's annual batik exhibition, on view as they arrived in the city. They found inspiration for a medley of peacock-shimmery fabrics, stained deep indigo blue, salmon pink, arsenic green, and canary yellow and ornamented with quasi-Buddhist, Islamic, and Chinese arabesques and lyrical floral motifs.

Derived from Javanese practices, their process was complex and tedious. Reaping the benefit of years in the garment trades, Tina expertly selected lengths of silk and cotton, which Robo painted with a liquid dye resist, a mixture of hot beeswax and resins. Daubed with whorls, waves, and curlicues, the fabric was immersed in a cool dye bath, three times a day over the course of ten days, until it was imbued with a rich hue. The two then scraped off the resist, and Robo applied another design set, a process repeated as many times as there were to be colors in the completed batik. Finally, they soaked the cloth in lime and water to set the dyes, then suspended it to dry.

It was Robo who signed their creations, with Tina taking the role of assistant and occupying herself with tie dye projects. Some of the batiks were created as wall hangings, and these garnered the first sales, exhibitions, and laudatory reviews of Robo Richey's artistic career. The *Los Angeles Times* praised them as "notable batiks, beautiful in design and color," and a popular Mexican weekly would gush over their "exotic qualities of a colorful thousand and one nights. They are tapestries of illusions, miraculous cloths that you believe to have already seen far away in some mysterious and marvelous castle." Robo's satisfaction in his achievement was clouded only by a belief in an artistic hierarchy in which the "masculine" medium of painting towered over "feminine" arts such as batiking. Yet waxes and resins flowed from his brushes with a sure-handed fluidity he never achieved in oils, and the new mode of expression briefly infused his art making with energy and purpose.

Tina fashioned other batiks into dresses and blouses, and the sight of her loveliness in such exotic raiments turned Robo febrile with emotion. The Bryson was a stage setting, and Tina's finery a costume for the art of living beautifully. She was content to allow Robo to mediate her relationship with the world and guide her choice of clothing, activities, and books. In their first years together, he was the maker of meaning, and she its bearer. He played the role of Pygmalion, she that of an eager Galatea. "Robo was a tremendous influence on her," maintains Alessandro Baccari, Jr., whose father saw the couple frequently. Tina corroborated the observation, speaking of Robo's "wonderful love, sympathy and influence" and perceiving herself to be "filled with his wonderful love and influence."

To beguile him, and thereby please herself, she slipped into flouncy tutus and ballet shoes, harem skirts, batiked sarongs, bandeaux, baubled headbands, bodices, and lacy black mantillas. Realizing her powerful aura and ability to spellbind with costume—in real life as in the theater—Tina formed a lifelong habit of using dress symbolically. Certain occasions called for selecting attire as if fitting herself out for the stage, and her style of dress was to shift along with her ideas about the part she wanted to play in the world. This mannerism merged with Tina's inability to accept life's rawness and confusion, and a need to process what came to her into orderliness, abstraction, and symbol—in short, a quest for form and meaning.

The spring of 1919 found Tina dolled up in picturesque garb for a minor role in *The Mission Play,* a popular annual pageant at the Mission San Gabriel, east of Los Angeles. Though unlisted in the program notes, she was probably among a bevy of castanet-clacking "Spanish girls" flouncing and swaying through act two's rollicking fiesta scene.

Equal parts Oberammergau Passion play and Disneyland, *The Mission Play* was an amalgam of "music, mime, drama, pageant, choral singing, and dance," which dreamed up for Southern California a florid Spanish yesteryear, thus infusing lackluster suburbs with a boosterized version of culture, attractive to potential homebuyers. Later, Tina must have cringed at the memory of the spectacle's aesthetics—of the "lo! hark! school," noted one observer—and at its thesis that the greatest accomplishment of the missions' Franciscan padres was employing the idle race of California Indians. Yet, for the moment, she saw the extravaganza through Robo's eyes, as an escape from commonplace realities into the "vague and terrible beauty" of the past.

So popular was *The Mission Play* that special trains were run from Los Angeles to accommodate the throngs. Among its enthusiasts was photographer Jane Reece, a high-strung, birdlike woman in wire-rimmed spectacles, vacationing from the demands of her Dayton, Ohio, portrait studio. Reece somehow crossed paths with Tina and Robo, whom she used as models in a series of gauzy and self-consciously arty *tableaux vivants,* replete with mysterious hooded figures, crumbling mission walls, emotive gestures, and foggy medievalist atmosphere. For Reece's portrait *Madame de Richey,* Tina applied a stagy mole to one cheek and donned peasanty garb not unlike that of her Friulian grandmothers. Most spectacular of the series is *Have Drowned My Glory in a Shallow Cup,* an interpretation of a quatrain from the *Rubáiyát:* "Indeed the Idols I have loved so long/ Have done my credit in this World much Wrong/ Have drown'd my Glory in a shallow Cup/ And sold my Reputation for a Song." Enveloped in vaguely Oriental finery, Tina is a rare blossom, the embodiment of reverie and refinement. Panels of a batiked gown swirling at her sides, and bracelets, anklets, and rings lustering, she stares with kohl-blackened eyes from beneath a jeweled Juliet cap.

Reece was happy enough with the picture to submit it to the London Salon of Photography, and it appeared in a newspaper story with the mention "posed by Mme. de L'Abrie of Los Angeles. A French actress…"

The Ohioan was a devotee of pictorialism, a movement that inscribed photography within the realm of fine art by downplaying its mechanical qualities and mimicking paintings and etchings in appearance and choice of subject. Years later, the photographer Tina Modotti would roundly reject pictorialism, as typified by Reece's moody, sentimentalized images. Seeing a Mexican photograph of the "head of an old man with a long beard" was to bring to mind Reece's 1919 chiaroscuro picture of Robo as a Christ figure. A "terrible thing," Tina gasped of the mawkish portrait, "the sort of thing Jane Reece might have done and called 'Son of Man.'" But Tina must also have felt grudging respect for the older woman, who enjoyed financial success while upholding her artistic ideals, which by then was Tina's enterprise as well.

With his love of high-flown beauty and his disdain for the industrial age, Robo adored Jane Reece's photographs. His literary tastes were similarly belletristic. In a letter to Marionne, he had reeled off his favorite works, among them *Bel-Ami, A Ladies' Man* by Maupassant; Turgenev's *Rudin*—the tale of a Russian aristocrat paralyzed by his lack of will—and *A Nest of Gentlefolk*; John Masefield's *Salt-Water Ballads*; "Ashes of the Beacon" by Ambrose Bierce; and fin de siècle English writer Richard Le Gallienne's *October Vagabonds*. "I have not finished many books," Robo admitted to his sister, "but have dabbled in them." Nonetheless, he set great store by literature, and, under his intellectual mentorship, Tina began to read steadily. Besides books, their home was strewn with magazines—Robo subscribed to *The Little Review*, and he religiously perused *The Smart Set*, "A Magazine of Cleverness," whose best stories he marked with an *X*—as well as art publications such as Tina's lavishly illustrated catalog of the Uffizi Gallery's sculpture collection.

Whether it was painting, poetry, or American cooking, whatever the young Tina deemed worthy of attention, she absorbed with a single-minded focus. Her struggle to make sense of her life was quiet but intense, and her curiosity, receptivity, and capacity for intellectual and emotional growth was astounding. As much as Jane Reece's mise-en-scènes, the representative image of this period is an ordinary snapshot catching Tina seated at her desk and engrossed in a volume spread across her knees. Her English became fluid and felicitous, and Robo taught her tolerably good French and a smattering of Spanish. Meanwhile, she polished the Italian he must have picked up from Father Datin, for Robo was as remarkably gifted with languages as she.

The pair went on to explore an undigested mix of contemporary thinkers, skimming Freud, Oscar Wilde, Daniel De Leon's essays on socialism, and the meditative poetry of Indian nobelist Rabindranath Tagore. Most significantly, Tina steeped herself in the work of Friedrich Nietzsche, especially *Beyond Good and Evil.* She read:

> ...today the concept of "greatness" entails being noble, wanting to be by oneself, being capable of being different, standing alone, and having to live independently; and the philosopher will betray something of his own ideal when he posits: "He shall be the greatest who can be the loneliest, the most hidden, the most deviating, the human being beyond good and evil, the master of his virtues, he that is overrich in will."

Nietzsche was fashionable in 1920s bohemia, but Tina was more profoundly marked than most by her reading of him. She accepted his ideas about the vital importance of making art. She also retained the notions that one must, at all costs, avoid a herd mentality, live on one's own terms, and decide for one's self what constitutes happiness.

In February 1920, happiness took the form of a giddy, emotionally overwhelming reunion in San Francisco with her mother and siblings, who had reached the United States at long last. Such a strange and joyful occasion! Assunta and Giuseppe embraced after fifteen years, fourteen-year-old Beppo set eyes upon his father for the first time, Yolanda turned out to be a stylish, dimpled signorina, and Ben, nothing at all like the ten-year-old Tina remembered. Missing were Tina's two-year-old nephew, Tullio, and his mother, Gioconda, whose attempts to secure a passport for her son had probably delayed them all long after the war's end, and finally come to naught. Anticipating the reunion, Giuseppe and Mercedes had taken a more spacious, light-filled apartment, perched half a block higher on Russian Hill. The newcomers met Robo, and charmed by his gentle manner and fluid Italian, Tina's brothers and sisters made plans for visits with the hospitable Richey clan.

Tina's younger siblings never knew the Bryson Building, for that folly was long past. After four or five months, Tina and Robo had taken up residence in a modest downtown studio at 342 North Main Street. By November, they were again under Vocio's roof, in a house on Eleventh Street, and, only two months later, the quartet set up housekeeping at 271 South Lake in the Westlake district (near what is now MacArthur Park). Toward the end of 1920, they finally settled down at nearby 313 South Lake.

Clinging to a steep lot shaggy with grasses, stands of bamboo, and untended fruit trees, the Richey homestead, surrounded by a forest of oil derricks, appeared more rural than urban. It comprised a wooden cottage, shared by Vocio and Marionne, and a large, rough-planked, vine-covered shed, home and studio to Tina and Robo. Rain dribbled through the ceiling, they had to trek next door to cook, and their lair was unheated except for a fireplace, but it was marvelously spacious and high-ceilinged. With tasteful artistry, the pair created an uncluttered workshop atmosphere "recall[ing] medieval Florence." Two high north windows, propped open to chase the heavy odor of molten wax, were hung with batiks, filtering the sun's dazzle and lending the studio area a "soft amber duskiness." Low divans were garnished with a pillow or two, arranged just so. A few rustic sticks of furniture were scattered about, and a long table was laden with art supplies, but the feeling was orderly and well disposed. Photographs and oils dotted the jute-covered walls along with Robo's batiks, a gloomy piece entitled *The Pirate* and the expressionistic *Hysteria*.

Gone their separate ways during the day, the foursome usually dined together—on Vocio's brown beans or fried ham and potatoes with apple pie—often setting extra places for Mercedes, Yolanda, Robo's elderly grandmother, dubbed "Grand Vocio," or any one of a dozen friends dropping by. Afterward, they would pile into the Model T to see the latest picture at the De Luxe, or play "My ship is coming in laden with," or huddle around a fire in the studio. Robo read poetry aloud as Vocio pieced quilts, Marionne braided silk rag rugs, and Tina sewed new collars on Robo's shirts or fashioned self-image dolls from scraps in the household's bulging ragbags. Whimsically, Tina baptized them "nuns of the perpetual adoration," perhaps a nod to the lavishly dressed effigies of saints displayed in

Italian churches. It was curious that she represented herself as a Catholic sister, but the idea must have seemed wicked and funny. She dispatched one of the figures to a friend, dancer Betty Brandner, with a note: "May [the nuns] protect you and may all their blessings be for you—I had no time to make another one—therefore I send the one I had with no 'Tina' on it— You see—the signature should be waxed on the first thing. The little ribbon keeps the cloth from stretching. If it was some brighter color—purple perhaps—it would be more decorative, but this is all I had—"

Though the Richey household showed little strain or discord, Tina and Robo doubtless yearned for a more independent life, bankrolled by their own earnings. Robo got a job as an attendant and checker at a Hollywood cabaret, a pseudo-château with tar-paper roof, where he sported a uniform of pantaloons and curly-toed slippers. He also took a fling at political cartooning for *Gale's Magazine,* a radical English-language monthly published in Mexico City, which found favor in Californian leftist circles.

A venture of Linn Able Eaton Gale, a crankish red-bearded draft evader, the magazine preached Communist insurrection as it proselytized for Gale's Church of the New Civilization and ballyhooed his real estate offerings. Robo produced two roughcast cover drawings, one of a predatory, serape-swathed "Wall Street" tiptoeing around Mexico, and the other depicting a banker, suddenly sweat-drenched as he stumbles upon a Bolshevist demonstration. Progressive in his sympathies, Robo was inattentive to politics and disinclined to activism. His motives for contributing to *Gale's* were doubtless financial rather than political, and nothing suggests that Tina felt differently at the time. Yet the pair relished the bravado of seeing Robo's signature on the cover of a Communist magazine during the period of the so-called Red scare, when U.S. Attorney General A. Mitchell Palmer was unleashing raids on suspected radicals, a campaign that took more than six thousand into custody.

The association with *Gale's* lasted no more than a few months, however, leaving Robo no less dependent on Vocio's largesse. Was he thinking of this or of his impotence before the easel and blank page when he lamented to a friend, "Then the failures, the wrecks I meet on the street, seem to stare at me as if to convince me of the uselessness of all my efforts. Ah, if only we could reach up to the sky and tear away the smothering canopy of blue! But we only quietly put on our clothes every morning so that we can take them off again when night comes!"?

Tina, meanwhile, was bringing in some income from minor film roles, but she sought a broader channel for her creative urges. Given her background, beauty, and proximity to Hollywood, the obvious step was to find meatier work in motion pictures. She turned to her best friend, the celebrated film star Myrtle Stedman, nicknamed "Myrto."

We are in the dark about how the two women met around 1919. Myrto's first career had been as a child star in Chicago light opera, and her second as a leading lady in silent pictures for the Windy City's Selig Polyscope Company. She had led the tenor Marshall Stedman to the altar, but Marshall was exceedingly fond of the bottle, and they parted company when she went to Hollywood in 1913. On contract to Morosco, and later Bosworth, Myrto made twenty-two films before stopping to catch her breath. Winsome, with round blue eyes, honey blond curls, and a retroussé nose, she was a talented comedienne and a bighearted woman, magnanimous with gifts and favors. A superb equestrian, Myrto had a voice that charmed birds out of the trees, and she lied shamelessly about her age. "Myrto is red, wine red," Robo mused, "and someone who passes a thin silk, cloudy-like cloth over a cloudy glass as if to polish it." She is a "dear, precious friend—how much I owe her...," Tina once blurted out to Vocio of her close relationship with Myrto, one of several with women that belie Tina's reputation for being interested only in men.

By 1920, Myrto's constant companion was Canadian painter and photographer Walter Frederick Seely, in *Variety's* words, "a pioneer Hollywood portrait photographer" who worked with "virtually every silent picture personality" and enjoyed a vast network of connections in the film colony. Under contract to various studios, Seely generally shot his pictures on film sets, but he developed and printed at the darkroom that occupied a portion of Tina and Robo's studio, loaned or sublet by Vocio. He solicitously made virtuoso portraits of the Richey family, who thrilled to have their pictures taken, especially under circumstances smacking of Hollywoodian glamour. Vocio sat for Seely in her rocking chair and Robo struck dramatic poses, but most sensational of the portraits was an asymmetrical, fashionably *japoniste* study of Tina, sensual in a silk kimono, its folds suffused with light.

Through Myrto and Seely, Tina met film goddess Anita Stewart, Myrto's costar in the 1920 *Harriet and the Piper.* Tina no doubt figured as a bit player in Anita Stewart Productions pictures. Six were released in 1919, and three more in 1920, improbable tales of gold diggers, imposters, black-mail, and love affairs between painters and their models. (Tina's screen efforts included one role in which she wore nothing more than a sheer veil, according to a Mexican friend's memory, substantiated by a publicity still.) But she went on Anita's payroll in another capacity as well, most likely as the fashion-plate actress's personal assistant for handling correspondence, running errands, and helping with fittings. She did not have an easy time of it, for Anita Stewart was given to tantrums and full of the devil.

The star had hazel eyes, a prominent nose, reddish brown curls "bunched against her neck like tokay grapes," and a voice leaving no doubts that her hometown was Brooklyn, New York. She had made her screen debut, as a high school student, in a film directed by her brother-in-law, Ralph Ince, and went on to become the hottest property of New York's Vitagraph Studios, which signed her to a multiyear contract. In 1917, how-ever, the brash up-and-coming producer Louis B. Mayer, angling for a star of his own, lured Anita away from Vitagraph with promises of a hefty annual salary of $127,000, a roadster, and the prestige of her own produc-tion company. A famously ugly court battle ensued, but, by 1919, Mayer and Stewart were in Hollywood shooting *In Old Kentucky* (the *National Velvet* of its day), and both were major Hollywood players.

In truth, the actress's success owed as much to fans' fascination with her fabled wardrobe as to her thespian skills, and, for a time, Anita Stewart paper dolls were all the rage. She indulged in ten-day shopping binges, making the rounds of the film capital's finest dressmakers and boutiques, her limousine crammed with the extravagant velvet capes, tall leather boots, and smartly tailored walking suits she favored by day. For evening occasions, she glittered in flowing gowns fashioned from the Richeys' batiks. One of the wealthiest women in Hollywood, Anita loaned Tina and Robo the money for silk and supplies and sometimes handed down to Tina her discarded frocks.

Anita Stewart operated out of a dainty pink dressing room at the Louis B. Mayer studio on Mission Road. Called "the Selig Zoo," the prop-erty—a maze of village sets, offices, carpenter shops, and prop rooms—was leased from Myrto's former boss, William N. Selig, on forty acres (later the Lincoln Park Zoo) that also housed lions, elephants, leopards, bears, hyenas, anteaters, parrots, and other animal actors. Though credited in each of Anita's pictures, Anita Stewart Productions amounted to little more than Mayer's consultations with the actress on his choice of scripts, directors, and supporting cast. It boasted, however, an attractive blue letterhead— "Anita Stewart Productions, Inc., 3800 Mission Road, Los Angeles, California, Telephone East 33"—stacks of which found their way to the Richey household, presumably so that Tina could handle correspondence from home. Saving themselves the trouble of stationery purchases and tingling at the glamour of it all, the Richeys penned much of their voluminous correspondence on Anita Stewart's paper.

In 1920, as Anita summered at her Long Island estate, Tina and Myrto were hard at work at Melrose Avenue's Robert Brunton Studios. Myrto had almost certainly pulled strings to secure for Tina her first and only major role, in the five-reel silent picture *The Tiger's Coat*. Revolving around a Mexican servant named María ("The mysterious visitor...Miss Tina Modotti"), the film's plot is slight. It opens with María knocking at the door of the La Classe, California, home of Alexander MacAllister, who believes her to be Jean Ogilvie, a long-lost MacAllister family friend and María's recently deceased Scottish employer. The tweedy, pipe-smoking Alexander adopts the strangely exotic young woman, whom he stows away from neighborhood gossips with a high-strung artist and his wife, played by a saucy, sympathetic Myrto. Having fallen in love with María, Alexander asks her hand in marriage, but then, as La Classe high society makes merry over the engagement, comes word that she is not Scottish after all but, rather, a "low-born greaser peon girl." The betrothal is broken, and María flees, later prancing back into town at the head of an artistic dance troupe. By this time, Alexander is pining for her and regretting the hasty rupture. Lights and music fade on a de rigueur kiss of reconciliation.

Variety turned up its nose, calling the plot thin, the directing bad, and the montage uneven, and the film magazine *Harrison's Reports* agreed in spades: "A bad film. Provokes neither interest nor sympathy." The film's mediocrity was relieved only by its message of love besting racial and class prejudice and by Tina's astounding wardrobe. Actors were under obligation at that time to provide their own costumes, and Tina outdid herself with a garish plaid travel ensemble, satin cloak, bejeweled brassiere, feathered beret, harem pants, tie-dyed shawl, and batiked gown. As for the eponymous tiger's coat, meant to signal foreignness and treachery, it appeared on her shoulders in come-hither publicity images of the "sleek and sinuous and softly sweet—and as dangerous as a tiger" actress.

With the swoon of Rudolph Valentino and sultriness of Pola Negri packing houses across America, a foreign-born starlet such as Tina could expect no more than roles in the mold of exotic, tempestuous, chest-heaving vamp. Seeing one of her films a few years later, she "had a good laugh over the villainous character she portrayed. The brains and imaginations of our movie directors cannot picture an Italian girl except with a knife in her teeth and blood in her eye." After *The Tiger's Coat*, which she could only have found disappointing and rather degrading, Tina was ready to turn her back on Hollywood. Still, there were moments when she indulged the pleasure of being a minor goddess of the cinematic temples, autographing stills for the family and viewing *The Tiger's Coat* at least three times.

As Tina labored at the Brunton Studios, Robo was engrossed in illustrating a thin volume of verse entitled *Satires and Loves*. Written by a close friend, the Mexican Ricardo Gómez Robelo, the poems stewed with eroticism and suffering, themes dear to Robo Richey's heart. The artist penned clumsy, sinuous drawings, among them a death's-head, a beseeching self-portrait, and the nude specter-haunted Vola. An icy Tinaesque figure also appears. A lacy mantilla grazing her head and shoulders, a rose at her crotch, she is labeled *Temptation* and seems to embody "Life's unconscious cruelty and indifference."

Thirty-six-year-old Ricardo Gómez Robelo was a man of letters, lawyer, journalist, pre-Columbianist, and politician in exile. In 1913, Gen. Victoriano Huerta's coup had brought him a brief tenure as Mexico's attorney general; a countercoup swiftly drove him abroad. Six years had passed, and still the Robelo ménage, which included his wife—an unhappy woman nicknamed "La China"—and an adolescent son, waited out the Mexican revolution in Los Angeles. An indefatigable reader with a passion for Shakespeare, Nietzsche, Mallarmé, Wilde, and Edgar Allan Poe, Robelo dazzled the Richeys with his erudition. In after-dinner conversations, he would outspeak everyone, possessed not only by fervor for his literary heroes but also by strange visions roused by malaria and heavy drinking. Yet he was the soul of courtliness and impeccable manners. "These Mexicans are surely the most gallant men I have ever known," Tina was to marvel, and she, like the others, was oddly mesmerized by the ugliness of Robelo's thick lips, aquiline nose, and smooth face, and by the slender, natty figure that he cut.

With Robo, Robelo shared a mournful, overwrought sensibility and a tendency toward psychological torment. The Mexican took his nickname, "Rodion," from an incident in a Mexico City whorehouse where he had knelt before a prostitute, excitedly caressing her feet and shouting, in the words of Rodion Romanovitch Raskolnikov, Dostoyevsky's *Crime and Punishment* protagonist, "I am kissing not you but all of suffering humanity!" A decade had passed, and his tumult of passion now settled upon Tina de Richey. Soulfully, he gazed upon her and, before the publicity still with veil, "pour[ed] out tears of sensual tenderness." One wonders, Was Tina only flattered by Robelo's adoration, or was something in her relationship with Robo loosened and thrown out of kilter, thus made more susceptible to breakdown in the future?

In the eclectic atmosphere of 313 South Lake Street, gusts of Dostoyevskian passion mingled with decidedly lowbrow episodes. In January 1921, Marionne Richey's beau, Emile Scolari—an Italian-Swiss contractor and self-described bootlegger—dashed off a note to his sweetheart, in Santa Barbara for a few days:

> Last night I went over to the house on the chance that you might have changed your mind [about driving to Santa Barbara] on account of the rain and lo! Tina said after a pause: Marionne is in the kitchen! Of course I had to find out right then and there—then Mercedes remembered that you had to go down to Mrs. Brather (or Brader or Braither) and you would be back presently—meanwhile Tina and the other bluffers told me how disgusted you were with the weather and the road and the flivver and everything. It appear[ed] that you went away early, in spite of the rain in Santa Barbara. Owing to tire mischief, spark plug perversity and skidding trouble, like a good girlie you turned around and came back the same day.

Naturally, since the kitchen episode, my trust was badly shaken—but I turned to your brother—he should have felt flattered to be picked among the crowd as the *truthful one*—and solemnly, on his honor, you might say, asked him for the truth:

Oh, yes—he cheerfully lied—she had to go there—but she'll be back—wouldn't go down there if I were you—you'll get your shoes all muddy—She has rubber boots on—this last from Tina who, by the way, I'll tell the world belongs on the stage alright.

Put on a loud record—Marionne will hear the music—she will know you are here and will come over—said Robelo—he was there also.

I could see them enjoying the situation enormously so I told them that I knew very well they were fooling me—since there was no flivver outside…but to show them I could enter the spirit of the joke I would pitch a coin: head, I would go after you—tail, I would wait till you came.

Well, head won! Then they finally told me the truth!

The most enduring memories of 313 South Lake Street are of boisterous parties in the studio, mobilizing Los Angeles's small bohemia, a provincial avant-garde striving for effect. "[I]ntense, dreamy and vibrant," in Robelo's recollection, evenings throbbed "with the magic of art and congenial, exquisite friends and Saki!" Photographer Edward Weston noted of his fellow revelers: They were "well-read, worldly wise, clever in conversation,—could garnish with a smattering of French: they were parlor radicals, could sing I.W.W. songs, quote Emma Goldman on freelove: they drank, smoked, had affairs.…"

The screen door slapping open and shut, Tina greeted her guests wearing something flowing and distinctive, her tie-dyed tunic perhaps, over a long skirt. She adored silk stockings and stacked jangling bracelets on her arm. Her eyes were rimmed in black, mouth painted into a ripe cherry, hands smoothed with her favorite honey-and-almond cream. Dashing in suits or the loose shirts and ties of the artiste, the Italian sculptors Humberto Pedretti and Francesco Cantello, known for his bust of actress Eleanora Duse, buzzed over to Tina like bees near nectar. The lithe, raven-haired Betty Brandner glided into the room, and Miriam Lerner, a handsome, intense-looking woman, both a socialist and secretary to oil baron Edward Doheny, arrived to plant tender kisses upon Tina's cheeks. Murmuring "dear" in the cultivated manner she now affected, Tina would compare toilettes with her female friends and chitchat about the exhibitions they attended together at Exposition Park.

As the evening heated up, the gregarious, streetwise Wobbly Roy Rosen might set the room on a roar with tales of the scoundrels he confronted as a "tough, tough baby" bill collector. Rosen hailed from New York, but many guests were refugees from San Francisco art circles: the painter Clarence Hinkle and his wife, Mabel, and the curly-haired Mexican Francisco Cornejo, who had created costumes and décor for *Xochiquetzal,* the "Toltec ballet" staged by the Denishawn modern dance troupe. An unruly sexual charge swept around the room, sending tall, tousled ex-barmaid Dorothea Childs reeling into somebody's arms as the lecherous and amusing old satyr Sadakichi Hartmann pranced from one woman to another. Jazz or Japanese music spinning on the Victrola, the studio dissolved into a smoky, incense-fragrant maelstrom dotted with pools of colored lights from Tina's homemade Japanese lanterns. The crowd wrangled over aesthetics, got drunk on bootleg sake, and sucked on cigarette holders as they quoted Nietzsche and Wilde. Eyelids drooping, Robelo recited Swinburne while couples drifted out to the porch in a fever of kissing and groping.

Among the Richeys' guests was Ramiel McGehee, a baby-faced man with one glass eye and a pinched, disapproving mouth. Once a dancer who had toured Asia and was obsessed with Eastern mysticism, Ramiel metamorphosed into an undulating contortionist at the first sound of a sitar or daibyoshi. "I yearn so eagerly for a glimpse of oriental places—their color—their flamboyancy call me, a starved soul," Ramiel would lilt. He had entered their circle through Weston, whom Tina and Robo befriended around 1919 and invited to two or three of their all-night parties. Edward was a short, wiry man with a soft, dry voice, probing brown eyes, and a large forehead dusted with freckles and framed with rusty brown hair. "I, at Tina's and Robo's," Edward would later reminisce, "—when Robelo lived, and I was first enamoured of Tina: Robelo was too, and God knows, many others."

Tina leaves no record of the dizzy all-night entertainments, nor do we know what thoughts preyed upon her by day. The comforts for which she had once yearned—a lovely wardrobe, access to art and books, time to dispose of as she pleased—were hers, and Robo cosseted and worshiped her. Yet she longed to give rein to a half-seen artistic impulse. Restiveness was growing within her, and her spirit drifted as if out to sea.

Los Angeles and Mexico City (1921–1922)

A WINDY MORNING in late August 1921 saw the Richeys' Ford convertible thread its way through the San Francisco streets toward the Valley Road, stretching south to Los Angeles. In the backseat, Robo towered over Tina while Vocio prattled away in the front, and Marionne (the family's only driver) played chauffeur. An aura of good humor hung about the foursome as they wrapped up a two-week vacation, "such a happy, pleasant trip!" Tina later bubbled to Vocio. Marionne calculated a lunch stop in Salinas, and Robo burst out in waggish parody: "The Ford is my Auto; I shall not want. It maketh me to lie under it in green pastures...." When they reached the highway and picked up speed, wind snapped voraciously at the American flag hood ornament and muscled their words to the side, offering a pretext for each to retreat into thought.

Houseguests at the Union Street apartment shared by Giuseppe, Assunta, and four of their offspring, the vacationers had filled their days with visits, shopping, dinners with old friends, and spins in Golden Gate Park. In its green leafy crannies, they posed by twos and threes before Marionne's camera, and, for a group portrait, all eleven Modottis and Richeys lined up by order of height, from long-limbed Robo to tiny Yolanda. In this emblem of the families' insolubility, Tina rests hand on hip and fixes the camera with a bold and self-confident gaze, masking the turbulence inside her.

For several months, she had been posing professionally (though probably free of charge) for photographer Edward Weston in the two-room shack that served as his Glendale studio. One spring afternoon, daylight was fading from the burlap walls and dark pine floors, and the violin strains of Sarasate's "Romance" poured from the phonograph. Sake was spilled on Tina's hand, and the two became lovers. Illicit affairs were frequent in their milieu, and Tina knew that Edward had a reputation for seducing his models, but, from the beginning, theirs was an uncommon intimacy. For both Tina and Edward, it would deepen into an essential love, eclipsing everyday considerations and touching upon the eternal.

From Tina to her lover had flown rapturous reveries mingling thoughts of flesh and spirit:

> Once more I have been reading your letter and as at every other time my eyes are full of tears—I never realized before that a letter—a mere sheet of paper could be such a spiritual thing—could emanate so much feeling—you gave a soul to it! Oh! If I could be with you now at this hour I love so much, I would try to tell you how much beauty has been added to my life lately! When may I come over? I am waiting for your call.

She continued in her astonishingly articulate and lyrical prose:

> One night after—all day I have been intoxicated with the memory of last night and overwhelmed with the beauty and madness of it—I need but to close my eyes to find myself not once more but still near you in that beloved darkness—with the flavor of wine yet on my lips and the impression of your mouth on mine. Oh how wonderful to recall every moment of our hours together—fondle them and gently carry them in me like frail and precious dreams—and now while I write to you—from my still quivering senses rises an ardent desire to again kiss your eyes and mouth—my lips burn and my whole being quivers from the intensity of my desire—How can I wait till we meet again?

Since the beginning of her intimacy with Edward, Tina had been living at a high pitch of emotional susceptibility in which every sensation was heightened. She felt longings for novel experience. A week after her arrival in San Francisco, she had taken the unusual step of making advances to a stranger and jotted a note to photographer Johan Hagemeyer, one of Edward's closest friends:

> Before everything else, please excuse if I have misspelled your name as I fear I have.
>
> Mr. Weston gave me your address before leaving (or rather I asked him for it) as I was looking forward to see[ing] you. He also told me of the good books and music you have (therefore my impertinence).
>
> I am only going to be here one week more, so any time it is convenient for you, please call me on the phone and I will come over. My number is: Franklin 9566—about 9 o'clock in the morning is the best time.
>
> Tina de Richéy

Tina spent one "precious afternoon" at the photographer's Webster Street flat. A brooding, scraggy-featured Dutchman with hooded eyes, a strong nose, long frame, and a thatch of ash brown hair, Johan Hagemeyer had the mien of a seafaring man. Yet he was something of a neurasthenic, prone to illness and shifting moods. Women often came apart under his languorous gaze, and Tina was not immune to his charms. Slouching in a velvet smoking jacket and wreathed in clouds of pipe smoke, he must have told her of his life as the reprobate son of a working-class family, of the tramp steamers and bookshops where he took odd jobs, of avant-garde galleries he prowled, and of his anarchist convictions. His personal photographs included dramatically lit studies of the urban environment, sometimes viewed from offbeat angles. But these were less fascinating to Tina than his knowledge of Tolstoy, Ibsen, Jung, and Upton Sinclair, his adoration of Monteverdi, Palestrina, and Bach, and his companionship with Edward.

Johan had learned of Tina four months earlier in a note from his friend. "Life has been very full for me—perhaps too full for my good," the Angeleno had written. "I not only have done some of the best things yet—but also have had an exquisite affair...the pictures I believe to be especially good are of one Tina de Richey—a lovely Italian girl." Although that communication stopped short of revelation, Edward had subsequently confided in Johan about the madcap liaison.

The presence of her lover's confidant that August afternoon in San Francisco revived Tina's fluster of expectation. Johan put several records on the Victrola, but not until he dropped the needle on a recording of "Nina," Giovanni Battista Pergolesi's sublime *canzonetta,* did she feel a troubling surge of emotion. The song is a lover's soul-stirring supplication, not to his beloved but, rather, to forces that would rouse her. "For three long days my Nina, my Nina, my Nina upon her bed has lain, upon her bed has lain," it began. As the music swelled and billowed—"Louder and louder, ye players all!"—she listened intently to lyrics that seemed to refer to her own yearning for transcendent experience and the obligations that thwarted that possibility. Filled with incoherent emotion and utterly disconcerted, she nonetheless held back her tears as the tenor implored, at first piano, "Awaken my Ninetta, awaken my Ninetta, that she may sleep no more... that she may," then pianissimo, "sleep no more."

A week later, bouncing along in the Richeys' automobile on the way back to Los Angeles, Tina perhaps attempted to order her chaotic thoughts by composing a letter to Johan. The words she would eventually send reveal not only her powerful response to the romantic "Nina" but also a tingling reaction to the Dutchman's presence:

> I have written you about a dozen letters in my mind...the impressions left to me since the afternoon I spent with you were so many and deep they overwhelmed my mind...not even to myself can I clearly answer why I suppressed the great desire I had to call on you once more. Was it will of power? Or was it cowardice?... I left without satisfying my desire of listening once more to Pergolesi's "Nina" in your company. Since then I have played it twice—only twice—for I fear to play it oftener—and besides I must be alone when I listen to it—all alone—in order to give myself the illusion that I am not alone, nor here, but at 2616 Webster Street [Hagemeyer's address]. Whether I will ever see you again or not, the brief but rich hours spent with you are most precious to me and I will live them over with the same beauty and sad-

ness of that day. Thanking you for the joy your books and music together with your sympathetic company have procured me.

Despite Tina's expression of doubt over whether she would see Johan again, the two were to continue their friendship during his later visits to Los Angeles and hers to San Francisco. But she wrote in a brooding, apprehensive frame of mind, for coming weeks held the dismaying prospect of an abrupt end to the flight of passion with Edward.

As Tina's thoughts tarried in San Francisco, Robo contemplated their move to Mexico City. With the decade-long revolution at an end, Robelo had been summoned by an ambitious new administration to head the Mexican Ministry of Public Education's Department of Fine Arts. No sooner was he settled than he offered Robo a teaching position, a studio, and an exhibition. All four of the Richeys must come to Mexico, Robelo urged, where they would be comfortably lodged for several months.

Robo needed no prodding, for, the batiks' success notwithstanding, he had made little artistic headway in Los Angeles. Still vacillating between painting and writing, and hindered by a psychological block, he had confided in a friend:

> There are innumerable ideas haunting me and crying for birth—my brain is throbbing to give life to those images—vague, bright-colored images. I wish to run home and seize my palette and brushes, to hammer away on the typewriter, but suddenly all becomes dim and unreal—a fear, a doubt, takes hold of me, and I stand abashed before my canvas—the paper on my machine is blank, wide and pitiless as the desert—my dreams have become intangible. A moment ago they were right here within reach, breathing with life—I stretch out my hand, and they are gone!

Envisioning "the beauty and the charm of the past still lingering" in Mexico, Robo swiftly resolved to take up the brush once more. Having been disappointed first by San Francisco and then by Los Angeles, he would migrate to an even more luminous and southerly city in an attempt to throw off "the curse of shadowy, dreaming, hesitating souls!" The Richey family's departure for Mexico was imminent.

Back in Los Angeles, they plunged into frenzied preparations. Trunks and clothing were purchased, art supplies readied, and Vocio and Marionne obtained Mexico-only passports valid for one year. Meanwhile, Johan heard from Edward that "T goes to Mexico very shortly" and from Tina that Edward had invited her to pose one last time. She accepted, and something occurred at that session, the lovers' first in over a month, to change her attitude from resignation to deft resistance. She cast around for reasons why she could not accompany Robo to Mexico and must linger in Los Angeles.

The object of Tina's passion, a decade older than she, was distinguished by his coffee brown eyes, which rarely ceased their restless scouting. Unsophisticated, except behind the camera, Edward Weston was unstinting in his devotion to photography. He was "a modest, provincial, beautiful soul," observed a friend. "His whole life was wrapped up in photography. He wanted to be a great man."

Most knew Edward as gentle, intuitive, and sparing of conversation, except with a few intimate friends, yet parties turned him into a cutup and outrageous flirt. He relished icy baths, naked wrestling, and sporadic vegetarianism, but he smoked heavily and drank his share of the wine that flowed at artists' gatherings. He sought the company of dancers, painters, writers, and photographers and still struggled, at thirty-five, to shed the vestiges of his midwestern middle-class upbringing.

The son of a suburban Chicago doctor, young Eddie had been a freckled-faced Tom Sawyer, playing hooky and escaping to vacant lots or fishing holes. His mother died when he was five, and, after his father remarried a woman the child disliked, he was raised mostly by a doting older sister named May. In 1902, his father presented him with a Kodak Bull's-Eye no. 2 camera, and, from then on, his enthusiasm for picture taking never abated. The following year, Edward dropped out of school to become an errand boy at the Marshall Field department store. He saved up to buy a view camera ("And then what joy! I needed no friends now—I was always alone with my love") and then a developing tank.

After May married and moved to Tropico (later Glendale), she coaxed her little brother to California, where he essentially remained for the rest of his life. She also picked a wife for him, her own friend Flora Chandler, whom she had met at a dance. Slender, blond, and attractive, Flora was a daughter of the powerful Chandler family, whose wealth derived from vast real estate holdings and who later owned the *Los Angeles Times*. Edward simple-mindedly fell in love, the couple wed, and they had four sons, whom both adored. Flora, however, proved to be not the little woman he had bargained for, but, rather, "tough, 'insufferable,' fundamentally brave, and superficially hysterical," someone who "gave you her heart when all you wanted was a cup of coffee." Edward's philandering, begun not long after they wed, raised Flora's hackles. She loved him deeply, while his affection for her dimmed. He found her both infuriating and indispensably generous with money.

In 1911, Edward had opened a commercial studio in Tropico, where he "boiled the pot" with slick, flattering portraits and baby pictures. It was not long afterward, at the Los Angeles Camera Club, that he met photographer Margrethe Mather, a tiny, pretty woman with periwinkle blue eyes and high cheekbones, who was to rank as "the first important person in [his] life." Margrethe was "sophisticated, magnificent, well-read, well-lived," recollected a friend, and Robelo considered her "the most terrible spiritual genius." She nurtured Edward artistically and intellectually, challenging all that he assumed about photography. She became his colleague, model, and maddeningly capricious business partner in the portrait studio. Edward was enamoured of her, and she with him, although she was a lesbian. Much passionate embracing and sexual teasing went on between the two, but, for a decade, she fended off his attempts to consummate the relationship. Instead, she showered him with tender notes and "drift[s] of jonquils," when such was her fancy.

Besides Margrethe, Edward's models included Violet Romer, whose portrait brings to mind a hoop-skirted porcelain figurine plucking roses in a vaporous garden, and the kimono-clad dancer Ruth St. Denis, spun of light and air. Self-consciously arty, his photographs were infused with shimmer and dewy-eyed sweetness. Edward sent them off to the national and international salons that were forums for pictorialist photography, and they returned rewarded with prizes, medals, and ribbons. In 1916, *Camera* magazine devoted an issue to his work, and, the following year, he was accorded the high distinction of election to the London Salon of Photography. Yet, by the time he met Tina and Robo around 1919, Edward was questioning the pictorialist formulas he employed and pondering the essential nature of the photographic medium. He had begun to discard cos-

tumes, flowery settings, and allegory in favor of sharper focus, bolder composition, and an acknowledgment of the contemporary world. "Feeling his
way toward modernism," he explored different approaches to picture making, among them a series of Cubist-influenced portrait heads set amid the
odd, angular corners and interlocking shadows of attics.

What was it about Edward Weston that gripped Tina Modotti's heart?
Though such fervor as she felt for him is essentially inexplicable, her desire was fueled by the authority of his creative accomplishment. Edward's
single-minded preoccupation with photography stood in sharp contrast to
Robo's distracted fumbling, in which Tina glimpsed something frightening
about herself. For the rest of her life, her most significant love relationships
were to be with men such as Edward, who dedicated themselves with crusading zeal to high-minded vocations.

Tina was awed not only by Edward's fixation on making photographs
but also by the prodigious power of his vision. Whereas Edward, like Robo,
had once searched for Beauty in flights of illusion, only Robo clung tenaciously to "an intentional disregard for the modern spirit of this age."
Edward, in contrast, had rejected what Tina now saw as maudlin masquerade in order to seek Truth. As his favorite model—Edward made at least a
dozen portraits of her that year—she found herself enmeshed in a
grandiose undertaking. "Oh, I hope he does something very great again!"
she had written to Johan of her upcoming modeling session with Edward.
"For his sake—as for me I cannot desire anything greater than what he has
already done of me."

Craving meaningfulness and endeavoring to make sense of her place
in the world, Tina discovered in Edward's portraits a new scaffolding for
her identity. Still young, she fell in love with what she saw of herself in his
eyes as much as with the human being before her. Composed around Tina's
tremulous gesture of inhaling a blossom's splayed petals, the seminude
White Iris evokes the intoxicating stir of her senses. In *Tina, Los Angeles,* perhaps even more revealing to its model, Edward blocked the dark tones of
kimono, hair, and background so that her neck and face emerged, clear-
eyed, disarming, and wistful. She kept a print of this image to the end of her
life (precious few of her possessions survived so long), and it was to grace
her funeral bier.

The couple's assignations were rare, and thus all the more thrilling.

Exercising great caution that an imprudent utterance or action not expose the affair, they exchanged letters through a friend or the post office box Tina rented. Long before she set her hand to political undercover work, secrecy and subterfuge were familiar ingredients in Tina Modotti's life.

She was wise enough to realize that the affair was probably destined to be short-lived. Her communications to Edward are infused with a sense of time passing, suggesting the fervor with which she must have attempted to forestall her departure. Tina's disillusionment with Hollywood notwithstanding, she pursued film roles that would retain her in Los Angeles. Almost immediately, she set to work on *Riding with Death*, a melodramatic Western shot at the Triangle Film Company in Culver City.

In this rough-hewn vehicle for cowboy actor Charles "Buck" Jones, Tina took a trifling part as another exotic Mexican. (Marionne's snapshots of the Triangle Ranch, as well as of Vocio posing in ruffled calico and sunbonnet and Robo sporting a uniform, kepi, and rifle, hint that the project may have turned into a family affair.) *Variety* judged the picture dreadful, and its distributor, Fox, misspelled Tina's name on the press release, so that her scant publicity fell to Tina Medotti, but she was indifferent. On the heels of *Riding with Death* came a five-reel romantic imbroglio titled *I Can Explain*. Impersonating another Mexican, the kohl-eyed, spit-curled Tina throws herself at the picture's leading man, Gareth Hughes, in scenes filmed in San Diego's Balboa Park, intended to pass as South America.

Tina's barrage of reasons why she should stay in Los Angeles included a passport predicament. Although she could have traveled on Italian papers, she would not, perhaps telling Robo that, as the daughter of a socialist, she feared being caught in Mexico at a time when fascists might be asked to form an Italian government. It is also plausible that the couple feared to rouse the suspicions of Vocio, who believed that Tina's marriage to Robo had entailed U.S. citizenship and thus entitled her to a U.S. passport. For reasons impossible to sort out, Tina and Robo schemed that he should travel first to Mexico City, where he would persuade the American embassy to issue her the passport she could use to join him.

In the interim, Vocio had had second thoughts about the trip, ultimately deciding that she and Marionne would forgo Mexico to purchase a house. Robo, too, hung back from departure, owing to the batiks' inclusion (along with photographs by Edward Weston and Margrethe Mather) in an

October exhibition at the prestigious MacDowell Club downtown. The show brought enthusiastic mention in the *Los Angeles Times,* topped by a glowing feature in the November issue of *California Southland.* Readers were transported to a romanticized "small, lone studio" where a "French artist and his Italian wife [make] batiks much superior to those of the Javanese themselves."

The article was illustrated with a photograph by their friend and studio mate Walter Seely, who depicts Robo applying designs to a fabric panel while Tina stitches a nearly completed garment. As the image suggests, they seemed a harmonious couple whose relationship was cemented by creative collaboration. Robo had not gotten wind of the affair, and no breach was apparent between them.

With Robo in mind, Tina quoted Oscar Wilde in a letter to Johan. She wrote, "There are only two tragedies in this world: one consists in not obtaining that which you desire; the other consists in obtaining it. The last one is the worst—the last is a real tragedy." Paradoxically, as an unmarried woman, she was technically free to do as she pleased, yet she was acutely aware that Robo's love for her was the glue that held him together. By another paradox, his bond with her had transformed him from unrepentant philanderer unable to resist the coquettish bat of an eyelash to impeccably faithful husband. But, tender and playful though they were, Tina's couplings with Robo—"our happy awakenings," in their private language— paled beside the ardent eroticism of lovemaking with Edward.

Robo's perception of Tina's building discontent cast a pall over a departure bright with promise. On an otherwise blank piece of paper, Robo typed, "O slow and sad, the slow sad years go by." He also wrote, "Tina is wine red, and something very precious that one puts gently down to become more precious as they carefully put it down."

Robo finally struck out for Mexico City on December 6 as gray curtains of gloom dropped around Los Angeles. Big cold raindrops pushed in on the wind, and the studio sprung leaks everywhere. "Tina has to run around with cans and catch it," Marionne reported to her brother. No matter how many blankets Tina piled on, she shivered in bed at night, and, on stormy afternoons spent hemming silk handkerchiefs she planned to offer as Christmas gifts, she hugged the edges of the hearth. Seely came and went, lavishing her with firewood and finishing up a big batch of family pictures, among them his recent double portraits of Tina and Robo. The artist Mahlon Blaine barged in for a few days on his way home from Mexico City, where he, too, had enjoyed Robelo's hospitality. The young man's dirty laundry kept Tina and Marionne busy for an entire Sunday morning while he entertained them with anecdotes and sketches of Mexico. With Vocio and Marionne, Tina caught *The Affairs of Anatol* at the De Luxe, and Tina invited Vocio to a special showing of *The Tiger's Coat*. Fat letters from Vocio kept Robo apprised of everybody's occupations.

Christmas Eve's mail delivery brought Tina her first word from Robo. "We had been looking for several days for letters from you and Tina was just tickled to death to hear from you," Vocio advised her son. "She was all excitement when she read them aloud to us." In low, breathless tones, she captured his sense of surprise at how well he blended into the Mexican crowd ("Everyone carries a cane, wears spats—mustaches. No one notices *me* here") and of his longing for her. "Oh, just to see you would be the most wonderful thing I can think of. It may be all right to run off and be a bachelor, but I'm cured. No more! Would like to see you in the pajamas...."

After supper, the three women devoted a pleasant hour to unwrapping Christmas gifts. From Sadakichi Hartmann (to whom Tina had presented a silk handkerchief) came an incense burner, and, from Seely, a blessed electric heater for the studio. Myrto's package to Tina revealed "a silver bracelet, one of those real fine ones." "She wears three on one wrist now," Vocio reported to Robo. A box from San Francisco contained a little tray made by Mercedes and, from Yolanda, a powder puff and "two pairs of real flashy garters." "Tina says she will just have to show them to someone," Vocio related to her son. "She does not know who it will be. She says it will not be you."

Rain tattooed on the studio roof all Christmas Day, and continued the next evening as friends dropped by for a gathering. "Rosen has just come and all are having a big laughing time," continued Vocio's chronicle. "At the supper table Myrto put on your old green sweater and sat in your chair by the side of Tina and kept kissing her and trying to make believe she were you. She said to tell you she could not eat as much as you did." Tina created a cozy atmosphere in the studio with a roaring fire, and, when a foxtrot began to play on the phonograph, Scolari and Marionne jumped up to dance. As the clock chimed ten, Vocio pulled out stationery for another letter to her son while the others braved the downpour to collect Beppo Modotti, arriving by train for a monthlong visit with his sister.

Meanwhile, from Mexico City, Robo was swamping the family with descriptions of sights in a "wonderful and beautiful city. Every street every house every door way is a picture." Some of his images bear an uncanny resemblance to Tina's later photographs:

> Boys driving turkeys—men carrying huge baskets on their heads—coffins—merchandise—jugs—all on the head. Women and children sitting asleep in the very gutter or making tortillas— a beggar crawling on hands and knees—One man carrying another in a chair on his back...One sees men carrying almost unbelievable loads—even away out into the country—they go jogging along at a trot in bare feet or leather sandals.

Robo had arrived in Mexico as revolution's end was unleashing vast energies and firing the people's will to cure their society's ills and forge a new destiny. In July 1921, the reform-minded strongman President Alvaro Obregón had established a Ministry of Public Education as the nucleus of his government. He appointed an ingenious and hardworking Oaxacan lawyer and philosopher named José Vasconcelos to the key position of minister. A strange breed of traditionalist, messiah, and bureaucrat, Vasconcelos launched a massive crusade to combat the scourge of illiteracy and inspirit the Mexican people. Underpinning the program was his concept of Mexico's vanguard "cosmic race," a people of mixed blood, Indian in soul, and Spanish in language and civilization. By the end of 1921, a wealth of experiments was in progress. Cheap editions of the classics—Plato, Dante, Cervantes, Homer, and Tolstoy—were flying off government presses to be distributed to the people. Free workshops and concerts abounded, public libraries opened their doors, and hastily trained teachers were departing to remedy illiteracy in the hinterlands.

Robelo's position at the right hand of Vasconcelos, a childhood friend, put him at the center of the capital's artistic and cultural effervescence. And, as Robelo's houseguest, Robo was a privileged observer of experiments in progress. He had traveled south of the border in quest of the romance of colorful old Mexico yet demonstrated unflagging enthusiasm for the new society on the rise. Robo's letters brim with talk of places and ideas later dear to Tina's heart, presaging her own great love affair with Mexico and its people.

Among Robo's closest Mexican friends was photographer and film-maker Roberto Turnbull, a short, pugnacious man who sported jockey caps and liked to shoot the breeze with stories of his bloodcurdling adventures during the revolution. Roberto arranged for Robo to accompany him on documentary shoots for the Pathé News Service, one of which took them to the ancient Indian site of Teotihuacán, north of Mexico City. As the filmmaker cranked out footage of the Pyramid of the Sun and the Pyramid of the Moon, Robo and a knot of friends walked the site with Dr. Manuel Gamio, who was simultaneously excavating the ruins and conducting an anthropological study of surrounding villages, whose inhabitants he believed to be descendants of Teotihuacán's builders. A seminal figure in social anthropology and a tireless crusader for Mexico's Indians, Gamio so mesmerized his visitors with ideas about bringing Indians into full partici-pation in society that the excursion was prolonged with a convivial dinner at his home. Longing to share this marvelous adventure with Tina, Robo bought up a stack of postcards of Teotihuacán and requested more pictures from Turnbull. "I thought of you darling so many times and wished you and the folks could be there to see that wonderful pyramid and the ruins for it is an impressive sight," he rhapsodized. She briefly caught his enthu-siasm. "Tina received a letter from you today, the one with the postcards of the pyramids..." Vocio signaled. "Tina just raved when she read in your let-ter about your climbing to the top of the pyramid and she thought that must be wonderful."

With equally rapt attention, Robo took in painter Alfredo Ramos Martínez's open-air art school in Coyoacán, south of Mexico City. "It is the greatest school of its kind I have ever seen," he wrote. "They have taken an old 'hacienda' or ranch house and made a school of it. For models they use various inhabitants of the town, Indians, beggars, Aztec girls. Board, room and paint are free for all who wish to study." After his tour of the school, Robo was invited to the "palatial mansion" of Ramos Martínez. There he sampled frothy Mexican chocolate and berries from the artist's garden, and he raved that he had "never tasted anything better than these things."

Robo also caught a glimpse of a more brutal Mexico, its face turned toward the wall. Without commentary, he sketched for Tina "a dirty, crumbling, forgotten old town full of Indians. The church is big and gloomy and set back at the end of a long avenue of trees. An odor of rottenness rises from the green and stagnant canals. The air is filled with sun and dust. The black ribbon of death floats over many door ways, showing that some occupant has just died there. Flies swarm—dirty children play in the nearby fields among the shocks of dry corn."

Robo's constant companion on his expeditions was painter Francisco Cornejo, a fun-loving bohemian whose parents had made a fortune in Baja California's pearl-diving enterprise. In years past, Robo had mixed with Francisco in San Francisco and Los Angeles, and now he met his friend's sisters, Laura and Beatriz, who put Tina to mind with their soft brown eyes, wavy hair, and interest in things artistic. Many mornings, Robo pitched his easel at the Quinta California, the Cornejos' big cattle and corn ranch in Coyoacán, where, by some magic, he was painting the most inspired canvases of his career.

A fascination with Mexico's picturesque characters, colonial churches, and gold-dusted landscapes drove the doubts and dark obsessions from his mind, and his style—exemplified by a fluid pencil sketch of a campesino—had grown looser and more confident. Believing that he stood on the threshold of his best work, Robo informed Marionne, "I am planning to do a lot of work here in the painting line and have a big exhibit in L.A. and S.F." He would "remain [in Mexico] long enough to come away richer artistically and financially—and I will do so— Then Paris!"

Robo's finances were also showing promise. The director of the National Preparatory School, Vicente Lombardo Toledano (whom Tina was to befriend nearly two decades later), had commissioned Robo's drawings for Spanish-language editions of Upton Sinclair's *The Cry for Justice* and Karl Marx's *Das Kapital,* and the Academy of Fine Arts had engaged the artist as a drawing teacher at a monthly salary of sixty-six pesos. Slated for January was an exhibition and sale of Robo's batiks, along with friends' drawings and photographs that Robelo had brought with him from California. Robo planned to "take orders for photographs," he explained to Tina, "so that, if there are enough, Weston or any of them could come and do the work, which would pay [for] the trip."

Robo had also cooked up a deal-making scheme for Hollywood star

Pauline Frederick, the famous "girl with the topaz eyes," whom he had met through Seely. Once queen of Broadway, Frederick had known a smash hit with the 1915 *Eternal City*, but now her career had slumped badly. *Variety* was trumpeting her "comeback in motion pictures," however, probably linked to the film Robo was pitching to the education ministry on behalf of a mogul named Boone. The idea found favor with Vasconcelos, and Robo let Tina know that "they are willing to offer any assistance to bring her here to make a picture. [Vasconcelos] will write me their offer and I will forward it to Mr. Boone with my own letter." Robo's commission would go toward repaying Anita Stewart's loan for the batik silk, so that he and Tina could begin saving in earnest for life in Paris.

The only cloud on Robo's horizon was Tina, who was writing him no more than once a week. Letters took eight or ten days to arrive and were delivered in batches. With each communication, he took heart; when several days passed without word, he was assaulted by anxieties and doubts. On December 22, he chirped, "I am always thinking of you and wishing to be with you. Have seen many Mexican 'doddles' but so far I give the grand prize to Italia! *But I may be partial!*" The following day, he repeated himself in Italian: "I am always thinking about you, you know, little one, and I am as cheerful as possible—here among the Mexican dolls! But you know that you have my heart—*all of it*—and *forever*! Oh! How I love you…I send you kisses for every part of your adored body!"

On New Year's Day, his hunger for her intensified:

And how are all the animals I love? What do they think about receiving no more kisses from me? Are the doves sad? And the white crow—what does it think? Oh, to be near that crow in the mornings and to give it kisses! And my little darling—the black, black kitten—so flirtatious and pretty—born between your beautiful white legs—does it think that I have gone away never to return? Tell it that I am faithful to it and that I will soon return to give kisses, caresses and so much pleasure…that I long so much to smell your maddeningly wonderful scent because nowhere in the world is there any other like that. Oh! To be near it in the mornings and find it waiting for me!… Am I crazy? Perhaps. My love for you, Tinella, my little girl, I feel—is such a spiritual and physical thing that every time I think of it, it is a form of insanity. But it is a divine thing to have such a great love and to know that you love me in the same way. I always look into your eyes in the photograph and I send prayers that I will soon be with you in your...tender arms. Write me, darling, because your letters are life to me.

Although Robo received three more letters from Tina in the days that followed, he was dismayed there were not more and enlisted Vocio in his cause:

It has been nearly four weeks since I left home and I have had only *four* letters from Tina— One a week— Really, you should not be surprised if *I* did not write for I am busy seeing things and going places and sometimes it is hard to crowd in time for a letter but I've missed very few days. You folks are at home with plenty else to think about and do not need the letters I do— While letters are an event here for me—far away among strangers....I figure that to date I have at least twelve letters coming from Tina—but they do not arrive.

After a week, another turned up, and, in a letter to Tina, he brightened:

A letter from you this A.M. which made the day a *real* day!...Your letter of New Year's Eve— How much I too, thought of the past year when we were together....What makes me the most happy is that you seriously are thinking of coming here— Like you I believe that it is better to come the last of this or the first of next month... by that time the exhibit will have been given—and I hope—the batiks sold.... *You must see Mexico sweetheart!* You'll appreciate it as much as anything in your life.

Still unwilling to wrench herself away from Los Angeles, Tina put off scheduling her departure, and a shadow flitted over Robo's happiness. He wrote to Vocio, "Tell Tina I shall expect her any time now. She ought to leave not later than Feb. 1st." To Tina, he dispatched the U.S. passport and travel instructions by registered mail: "So great you have decided coming…" he enthused. "Sun is shining bright."

Before Christmas, in a friendly, collegial letter, Robo had shared with Edward his impressions of Mexico, an "artists' paradise" where "one becomes drunk with subject matter." To Edward, the idea of traveling to Mexico had become freighted with notions of personal and artistic freedom, and Robo's words may have sent him into a fierce, quiet rage against the middle-class life to which he seemed condemned. On New Year's Day, Tina told Vocio, and she relayed to her son, that "[Tina and Edward] were thinking of going to Mexico, I don't know when, and Mr. Weston called up Friday Evening and said he had a letter from you." Fearful for Tina's safety, Vocio was urging Edward to accompany her to Mexico City, and Robo had broached the idea that the two men share a studio. Edward "is anxious too [to go to Mexico]," Marionne chimed in, "and was inquiring about passports, fare there, etc." It appears that Tina and Edward ultimately decided, however, that she should travel alone, and he follow within days. They said nothing of the plan to the Richeys.

Tina's impending visit threw the Robelo household into a state of commotion. Only days earlier, Robelo and his wife, La China, had separated, and Robo moved with his friend, and a beauteous cousin who was the Mexican's mistress, to a mansion in the fashionable Santa María la Ribera district. There Robo lodged in a servant's room, reached by a steep antique staircase from the roof. By cutting a window into one wall, he transformed an airless den into a sunny refuge overlooking the garden and tennis courts. Robelo ordered one hundred pots of brightly hued flowers to decorate the courtyard as Robo set about furnishing the retreat in anticipation of Tina's arrival. "All day I was busy working at this little room and have been doing the same today," he told Marionne. "I put up shelves, a big place to hang clothes, a little dressing table, etc. The window was to be ready today but did not come yet. Then I will get two *'petates'* (mats of straw) for the floor, a wide couch and mattress, and we shall have a dandy little room." He strained with impatience to have Tina with him: "How much I have missed her—I shall be a different person with her here. It is just as if half of me were not here." To his mother, he wrote, "Of course I shall be so happy to have Tina with me. I feel as if I were only half here without her." He told Marionne, "I can hardly wait for Tina to come."

Since Christmas, sixteen-year-old Beppo Modotti had occupied much of his sister's attention. A strapping blue-eyed lad, a head taller than she, Beppo had overcome the wartime traumas that had left him a constantly fearful and fleetingly dumbstruck child. Tina escorted him around the Selig studios and zoo and to a citrus grove, where he swiped lemons as souvenirs, and, amid staccato bursts of music and laughter, she taught him to dance. Seely and Myrto, who was between films, dropped by every afternoon, sometimes staying on for the polenta or spaghetti dinners that Tina and Vocio whipped up so that Beppo would not feel too homesick. Leaving her brother to spade the garden for Vocio, Tina shopped for her Mexican wardrobe, coming home with a spectacular two-textured black coat embroidered in gold. She also consulted an optometrist, who diagnosed her as farsighted and prescribed glasses, which she apparently never purchased. As Beppo's visit drew to a close, the boy wrote to Robo, using his best English: "I intend to go to San Francisco by machine [automobile], so I will wear your over coat, and your cap, so that I will be one second Robo." On the twenty-fifth, the Richeys waved him off, and, the next day, very different scenes played themselves out simultaneously in two love nests at twilight.

In Mexico City, Robo's eyes found satisfaction in roaming his little room, charming and in perfect readiness for Tina. Plucking a pen from its holder, he settled in at the writing table beneath her photograph to jot a note to his sister: "Tina will no doubt have gone ere this reaches you. She must have gotten the passport today.... I expect her to leave Feb. 1st and arrive Sunday Feb. 5th."

At the same time, in Glendale, Tina was slipping into Edward's studio, past its trailing ivy and morning glories. The preceding weeks had offered few opportunities for trysts, leaving her suspended between heaven and earth. Perhaps it was as she arrived, collar rolled up against the cutting cold, that Edward turned his camera upon her for a portrait. One wrist encircled by Myrto's silver bracelet, Tina clutches at the fastenings of her coat as if gathering herself up in a flush of breathless timidity before the self-forgetful ardor of the coming moments. On such stardust occasions, Edward remembered, he "used to laugh at Tina," out of sheer emotion, "and she would look at me surprised and wondering."

Tina would write twenty-four hours later:

Edward: with tenderness I repeat your name over and over to myself—in a way that brings you nearer to me tonight as I sit here alone remembering—.

Last night—at this hour you were reading to me from an exquisite volume—or were we sipping wine and smoking?—or had darkness enveloped us and were you—oh, the memory of this thrills me to the point of swooning!—tell me, were you at this hour—kissing my left breast?

Oh! The beauty of it all! Wine—books—pictures—music—candle light—eyes to look into—and then darkness—and kisses—.

At times it seems I cannot endure so much beauty—it overwhelms me—and then tears come—and sadness—but that sadness comes as a blessing and as a new form of beauty—.

Oh Edward—how much beauty you have added to my life!...

How vividly I can recall each episode— Each one stands before me strong and life like yet with all the vagueness of a dream and irreality—.

Your last letter laid under my head till morning— Was it its faint fragrance that awoke me? or the spirit of your desires and mine—that seemed to emanate from it?

Yes—to be drunk with desires to crave their attainment—and yet to fear it—to delay it—*that* is the supreme form of love.

It is very late now—and I am exhausted from the intensity of my feelings— My eyelids are heavy with sleep but in my heart there is a hidden joy for the hours that will still be ours—.

Three days later, anxiety welled up inside Robo, who addressed his sister with false jocularity: "Spank little Tina if she has not left yet—."

It was not until the morning of February 3 that Tina climbed aboard the Golden State Limited, bound for El Paso. Just beyond Los Angeles, as she was wiping away crumbs of the glazed fruitcake sent along by Vocio, she was handed two telegrams dispatched earlier that day from Mexico City to Western Union in Los Angeles and forwarded to the train. "HAVE SMALLPOX LIGHT FORM RETURN HOME FROM EL PASO ROBO," she read, and then ripped open the second: "HAVE LIGHT FORM SMALLPOX—DO NOT

COME—DETAILS LATER ROBO." Without warning, the drama of romantic intrigue and desire shifted into something more ominous and somber. As the train lunged into the desert, blinding light spit through the windows, and her compartment grew stuffy and oppressive. Tina was struck by a throbbing headache and longed to open a window, but the dust-laden winds made it impossible.

At dusk came a long halt at Yuma, Arizona, and Tina rushed into the depot to wire 313 South Lake Street: "RECEIVED TELEGRAM FROM ROBO HE HAS LIGHT SMALLPOX WANTS ME TO RETURN BUT WONT WILL LEAVE AS PLANNED TINA." Into a nearby mailbox, she dropped a note scribbled on the train. "By now you will have received my telegram with the terrible news..." she had written. "I got [Robo's telegrams] about 10 o'clock. You can imagine how I felt. He wants me to return but *I wouldn't think of it!* I know he must need me terribly—only he is afraid that I might get sick too. *Nothing could stop me however!*"

Tina's misery was compounded during the days of uncertainty that lay ahead. In El Paso, she missed a connection to the Mexico City train and was delayed by twenty-four hours. Customs, baggage, and ticket complications left her on Sunday morning in the waiting room of the Ciudad Juárez station. From the pen of a woman who would make the plight of Mexico's dispossessed her own flowed a surprising paragraph: "I am sitting in the waiting room and am surrounded by Mexicans," she said. "How picturesque Juarez is but I am too nervous to enjoy anything. Some of the faces here make me shiver—they always look at your purse when you open it."

At midnight on Tuesday, Tina finally descended from the train in Mexico City, to be greeted by Robelo's embrace. The next morning, moving as if in a nightmare, she went to the British Cowdray Hospital with Robelo's son Enrique. The danger of contagion precluded a bedside visit, but Robo was told of her presence and sent word, through a nurse, not to worry. "You can imagine what I felt to be so near him and not be able to see him," Tina lamented to the Richeys. From Robelo's brother, a medical doctor participating in Robo's care, she learned what had happened. Robo had been feeling poorly for three or four days before symptoms of smallpox appeared, on the very morning Tina had departed Los Angeles. The illness had probably been transmitted by the candy he purchased from street vendors, and it could have been prevented, Tina seemed surprised to learn, by vaccination. His recovery would require forty days, but the disease would leave him horribly disfigured. "The sickness in itself is nothing compared to the consequences. Think Vocio and Marionne dear how terrible it will be for our dear Robo to have his face marked by that terrible disease. And that will be the case with him, the doctor said, just because he wasn't vaccinated. And to think that Robo didn't want to be vaccinated just for the reason that it left a small mark," she exclaimed. "The tragic irony of it all!"

As she wrote from Robelo's guest room, she paused from time to time to turn the situation over in her mind. She thought it important to be brave, and the best way, she sensed, was to let her feelings go numb. One matter vexed her, however: how to get word to Edward. Too distressed to write him directly or fearing that her letter would fall into Flora Weston's hands, Tina grabbed at a lame excuse to ask that Vocio contact him. "Please let Mr. Weston know about this," she requested. "Call him up and maybe he can come over and you could read him this letter. He should know about Robo's state as the exhibit is needless to say delayed again on account of it. Call him up and tell him I asked him to come over and read this letter as otherwise I should write the same to him to inform of things and I cannot do it. He must excuse me—but surely he will understand."

The next day, in Robelo's absence, Tina wandered aimlessly around his home. She prepared a note for Robo (enclosing a sealed letter that had just arrived from Edward), hung her clothes to air on the patio, and waited in vain for her host's brother to arrive with a bulletin from the hospital. With no news to report, her late-afternoon letter to Vocio and Marionne was desultory, though she again pressed the pair about contacting Edward: "I hope you telephoned Mr. Weston by now for I am very anxious for him to know of the present condition here. Tell him to excuse me if I don't write to him, but I cannot do it now. I simply cannot."

Even before Tina wrote the Richeys, however, Robelo had dashed off a telegram at 1:09 P.M. to inform the two women that Robo was dying. With the strain and his attempts at delicacy, Robelo's English became so incoherent that the Richeys did not clearly grasp his meaning and saw hope where none existed. By the time another telegram clarified Robo's condition to his sister and mother, he lay in extremis, and, that evening, Robelo gently told Tina of his death.

On Friday, she sequestered herself, shattered, bereaved, remorseful, and unable even to pick up a pen to write Vocio and Marionne. The next morning, as she dressed for the small memorial service arranged by Robelo, she began a letter:

> My poor dear Vocio and Marionne,
>
> There is nothing I can say to you in this terrible and tragical hour—there is nothing you can say to me for my grief is above all consolation—I still wonder whether it is all a bad dream. I can hardly write for my eyes are full of tears. It seems that all is dead in me also—and oh Vocio and Marionne dear—not to have a baby by Robo—how terrible that seems now—never have I wanted one so much by him as now that it is no more possible....
>
> Oh—what a sad sad life—I feel that I cannot go on through it without my poor beloved Robo—Oh and not to have seen him— not to have heard his last words—that must have been for us all.

At Robo's funeral, held in the American Cemetery, Tina was a tiny, unsteady figure in black, moving among a handful of sympathetic friends. Afterward, she took to bed, shaken and distraught. "*My very dear Vocio and Marionne,*" she wrote,

> I am going through the greatest tragedy of my life—indeed as I look ahead and get a glimpse of myself going through life without my beloved Robo I ask myself if it is all worth while. But then I think of you two and of the great sorrow that draws us closer together and I say to myself that I must live so that Robo can live in our memory. Truly, I feel that Robo goes on living in me. I am filled with his wonderful love and influence— How happy our life has been together and how he has enriched it!
>
> And I think of all our wonderful plans for the future and the baby we were going to have! You don't know how often we spoke of that. And it seemed to us that the time had come for that and we were looking forward to our reunion with such impatience because of that and instead such a terrible fate awaited us!
>
> But I must not—I cannot go on torturing myself and you this way—nothing can be changed now and he is resting, I hope peace-

fully, under this beautiful sky and amid all kinds of trees and flowers.

Yes, I insisted to be present at the burial—a few faithful friends and I accompanied him and now he is sleeping....

Now—I ask nothing more than to die and be buried near our dear and beloved Robo!

Chapter 5

Mexico City and Los Angeles (1922–1923)

SEIZED BY BONE-DEEP WRETCHEDNESS, Tina sequestered herself in the Robelo home. On Monday morning, she ascended to the retreat Robo had lovingly prepared for her, where, ignoring Robelo's urging that servants be summoned to do the work, she dusted and swept in slow motion. "I thought my heart would break," she lamented to the Richeys. She gazed dolefully at Robo's palette hanging on the wall, ran her fingers around the knobbed surfaces of his watch and rings, and caught his scent and touch in his favorite hat, his old sweater, his blue sport coat, and his walking stick. Stumbling upon a cache of earthenware pottery, she imagined Robo's joy in selecting each plate and cup, and she requested that her meals be served on this set of dishes.

The next morning, Tina gave words to her impressions:

> I am up here in the little room so filled with Robo's spirit and so loved by him. Everything here speaks of him—all the work he has done for our comfort—and all his dear and precious things are up here—I put them all in his trunk now and am waiting to hear from you about them....
>
> I slept here for the first time last night. Robelo tried to dissuade me but I insisted—yesterday I fixed the little room up just as I thought he would like it and his pictures are all around the room—

do you know at times—I seem to forget the terrible reality and I almost imagine he is out some place and that he will be back any time—and in bed—oh, then it is when I suffer the most, for I remember our happy awakenings in our beloved studio in L.A. and all the other details of our happy life together—for you Vocio and Marionne know how much we loved each other and how well we got along—never was there a more congenial and sympathetic couple!

Having replaced her own portrait, tacked up over the writing table, with that of Robo, Tina found herself staring him in the eyes each time she paused from her task.

"I have no desire to go any place—to see anything—nor anybody—and yet I must get out—I need to exercise," she continued. By midweek, she had roused herself sufficiently to run errands, always with a family member, for the prospect of negotiating Mexico City's streets alone intimidated her. Accompanied by Robelo's mistress, she called at the stationer's where Robo used to make provision and was assailed by grief as she wandered the aisles and purchased envelopes matching those that had once enclosed Robo's letters to her.

The two women also strolled from the Robelo home to the Alameda de Santa María, a pleasant square canopied with ancient shade trees. Here they sought out the bench where Robo had often lingered to eat fruit, admire the splendidly ornate Moorish-style bandstand, and watch neighborhood children cavort. His spirit seemed to hover about, and, although Tina took pains to conceal her heartache in public, she found it impossible not to weep. In the park, as elsewhere, Robo was both acutely present and acutely absent. Writing to their friend Roy Rosen, she wailed, "I walk the streets and go places he used to go to—recalling his beloved figure and I torture myself imagining him at my side...."

Unsurprisingly, the thoughts of clothes-conscious Tina flew to the lovely coat that had been her major purchase for Mexico. "Is it not strange that my overcoat should be black?" she asked incredulously. "Oh, when I think of how anxious I was to show it to Robo and my poor little dress that I made just before coming here! How he would have loved it! Everything I had enjoyed just because he liked and admired my things so!"

Judging mourning clothes to be "useless and unnecessary," she nonetheless busied herself with assembling a proper widow's wardrobe. Her brown dress, white sport shirt, and pink blouse were sent to the dyer, while a shiny black silk gown could simply be turned inside out, as the reverse of the fabric was dull. Because she found Mexican prices too steep, it fell to the Richeys to purchase and mail two yard-long black veils and a pair of black gloves. In the matter of the gloves, however, Tina's impatience prevailed over her thriftiness, and she invested eight pesos in buying a pair. The coat proved of service after she laboriously snipped and swept away its network of glittery stitches, transforming dazzling finery into widow's weeds. Although she did not realize it at the time, her action was symbolic of the end of Madame de Richey, the Tina who had existed as an approving reflection in Robo's eyes. For the better part of a year, Tina remained in mourning, and, when she took up everyday attire once more, she chose simple, pretty dresses and suits. Gone forever were the batiked gowns, lacy mantillas, and tie-dyed sarongs.

Tina's change of wardrobe bespoke a realization that her relationship with Robo had been something essential and transformative. This was her first close encounter with death, and she shielded herself from the void with a notion that Robo still existed inside her. "Truly, I feel that Robo goes on living in me," she avowed. Three weeks after his death, she claimed it "impossible for me to realize it yet—that is all there is to it! And when I do—when the truth takes hold of me—it seems every time that it is the first time I really realize it: Oh—how will I ever, ever get over?...the only consolation I derive is in the thought that he goes on living in us—that his wonderful love and ideals will always give us strength and influence our life!"

She idealized Robo, pointing up his sagacious observations about Mexico and overstating the regard in which he had been held. A flurry of condolence letters and telegrams descended upon her, "many from S[an] F[rancisco]—from people whom I hardly knew—that shows in what consideration and esteem our beloved Robetu was kept." Her gush of admiration extended to Vocio and Marionne, whom she assured of Robelo's profound respect and her own unwavering devotion. "I worry so for you both and think of you constantly," she wrote, "that is when I don't think and dream about my poor beloved Robetu."

By exaggerating Robo's goodness (and that of his family), Tina may have quieted a subliminal and irrational anxiety that he had abandoned her in death as retribution for the liaison with Edward. With no confidante at hand, she must have dragged around many discomfiting thoughts. Would her earlier arrival have changed the course of events or somehow mitigated the loneliness of Robo's death? She was troubled to learn from Francisco Cornejo that Robo had appeared frail and unwell throughout his stay in Mexico. Had pining for her so weakened his defenses that he was unable to resist the disease when it attacked? By a different turn of the lens, Tina's guilt was assuaged by the realization that Robo's death had relieved him of what would have been the supreme agony of permanent disfigurement. Yet it was some time before she salvaged from the situation a sense of her own worthiness and integrity.

Ironically, Robo's promiscuous past would have endowed him with a singular understanding about Tina's affair. A month after Robo's death, on what would have been his thirty-second birthday, his much-deceived former wife, Vola, penned words that might have been Robo's to Tina, had life taken them in another direction. She wrote, "I have never been really happy since we parted, but I realized it was for the best.... I was consoled in the thought that it was possible to hear from him and see him once in a while. Now life seems dreary, but he wrote me that, regardless of the past, he would always love me, and so I am glad he was happy, for that is everything."

From the day of Robo's death, Tina was filled with thoughts of carrying out the exhibition he had long planned with Robelo. Despite Robo's two months of efforts to breathe life into the project, it had stagnated, and in his last letter, which now read like a testament, he threw in the towel: "Perhaps [Tina] can get this exhibit started—I cannot." The idea for the show had sprung up when Robelo carried to Mexico City a portfolio of artwork by California friends and a desire to pay homage to the artists who had been warmly hospitable to him and other Mexican intellectuals during their long exiles. These friendships had flourished against the background of hostile Mexican-U.S. relations, thus demonstrating once more to Robelo the superiority of creative community. Besides Robo's batiks, the exhibition was to include drawings by Mahlon Blaine and photographs by Edward Weston, Margrethe Mather, Jane Reece, Arnold Schröder, Walter Seely, and Seely's friend, J. W. Horwitz. At issue was not only artistic glory but also monetary rewards, since all the pieces would be for sale. Tina had arrived in Mexico with more pictures and the intention of nudging things along, but now the project carried the additional weight of informing Robo's death with a cultural significance.

His obituary in *El Universal Gráfico* announced an upcoming exhibition in Robo's honor, and Tina quickly floated the idea to Vocio and Marionne, assuming they would be delighted: "...don't you feel that exhibiting Robo's works will be a satisfaction? A sad one indeed—but knowing how he lived for his art, I feel that this tribute to his talent and aspirations would please him." On the contrary, the pair adamantly opposed the idea. Sequestered at home with no opportunity to come to terms with the death through a memorial service or a good graveside cry, they were terribly eager to hear Tina's account of events and have Robo's possessions in hand. On February 22, Tina was awakened by the delivery of Marionne's telegram instructing her to depart Mexico City immediately, taking care to bring all of Robo's belongings, or else Marionne would come to fetch her. Tina dashed off a response—"SHALL KEEP EVERYTHING BUT WHY THE HURRY MUST WAIT FOR EXHIBIT ALL ARRANGED"—then set her bafflement on paper:

> Your telegram took me by surprise and I must confess I don't know what to think of it—*I am just puzzled!* For really I cannot understand why you want me to return immediately.... You must have received my letter where I say that I will remain for the exhibit—well. I thought that would please you. *I am sure it would have pleased and hope it will still please our dear Robo!...* The exhibit is all arranged and will open in a few days—I couldn't possibly leave now— You must realize that—*it is my duty to stay!* It will last three weeks—so shall return soon after it closes. Believe that I am just as anxious to be with you dear ones as you are to see me!

The tiff continued as Marionne countered Tina's letter with demands that the batiks be exhibited in Los Angeles or retrieved as family remembrances. Tina's rejoinder revealed that most of Robo Richey's works shown that spring in Mexico City were actually her own tie-dyed pieces: "Well—

in the first place the exhibit is all arranged, and then do you realize they are almost all tied and dyed pieces and those I made? Of the batiks there are three panels—one Robo has given to Robelo and the other two have been promised to people who want to buy them by Robo himself. Then there are two waists [blouses] and one dress." Tina's next letter stated soothingly, "Now I know why you sent that last telegram—you feared I wasn't telling you the truth [about my health]—but really—I am well." Later, she wearily concluded the exchange: "It is useless to discuss the exhibit any more as I hope by now you received my precedent letters when I explained everything."

Having settled exhibition dates with the National Academy of Fine Arts, Robelo put all practicalities into the hands of Tina, Robo's friend Francisco Cornejo, and the school's director, the soft-spoken and elegantly turned-out Alfredo Ramos Martínez, whom Robo had so admired. Francisco good-naturedly tutored Tina in exhibition installation, and she wondered how she "could have gotten on without him—he has so much experience in that line…very artistic and always among exhibits and things of that sort." The trio made a last-minute decision to cover the walls in burlap, setting off the artworks to perfection but, to Tina's chagrin, again pushing back the opening. "[Y]ou surely know without my telling you that the delay was through no fault of mine," she made clear to the Richeys. "You have no idea how discouraged and impatient and worried I have been over it. Yet as our dear one said: 'One cannot move faster than the country!'" By coincidence, the exhibition's inauguration came on Robo's birthday, and, the next morning, Tina triumphantly wired Los Angeles: "EXHIBIT OPENED YESTERDAY GREAT SUCCESS SEND MONEY FOR RETURN."

For fourteen days, from 10:00 A.M. to 1:30 P.M., Tina staffed the gallery, greeting visitors, explaining the works of art, chatting with reporters, and ringing up sales, all tasks she found to her liking. The exhibition was proving a phenomenal success, less on the basis of the batiks' novelty—as Tina had predicted to the Richeys—than on that of photography as a medium of personal expression. Edward's photographs of Tina were the show's runaway best-sellers. As viewers entered the gallery, they blinked at the double vision of the "slim, elegant, refined, and very pretty" widow, demure at the information table, and the seductive, slow-burning beauty on the walls. The myth of Tina Modotti, exotic and imperturbable femme fatale, was brewing.

At its origin, one can discern the infatuation of Ricardo Gómez Robelo. With enormous gallantry and tact, Robelo had shouldered the burdensome dealings with hospital, mortuary, cemetery, and press that attended the death of his guest. To illustrate Robo's obituary in *El Universal Ilustrado,* the nation's most widely circulated cultural supplement, he had selected, among others, the artist's drawing *Temptation,* in which Tina wears little more than a mantilla and a thorny rose between her legs. Moreover, for weeks, he had been privately showing photographs of Tina by Weston, Seely, Schröder, and Reece to the male artists, reporters, and tastemakers who shared his world of refined machismo and gentlemanly indolence. One newspaperman noted that Robelo "trembl[ed] with emotion" on viewing the images, in what measure owing to lovesickness for their model is impossible to say.

Robelo's attitudes found amplification in those of Minister of Public Education José Vasconcelos, his employer and friend. A dapper black-suited figure with sad brown eyes and a stand of dark hair, Vasconcelos appeared at the exhibition one day to purchase from Tina three photographs (it is not known which ones). The pair met several times during Tina's stay, and the minister's later words suggest that he, too, was smitten with her. Always thin-skinned, Vasconcelos was, by the time he published his memoirs in the 1930s, a man deeply embittered by the course his political career had taken. His chronicle of Tina must be read not only in the context of romantic rejection but also as a settling of accounts between an increasingly conservative politician and the Communist Tina had become:

La Perlotti, let us call her thus, practiced the profession of vampire, but without commercialism *à la* Hollywood and by temperament insatiable and untroubled. She was seeking, perhaps, notoriety, but not money. Out of pride, perhaps, she had not been able to derive economic advantages from her figure, almost perfectly and eminently sensual. We all knew her body because she served as a gratuitous model for the photographer, and her bewitching nudes were fought over. Her legend was a dark one. One husband she had liquidated in California, kept in a lunatic asylum because of venereal excess, and at the time of which I am writing, she kept two strong men pallid and gently rivals: the famed photographer [Edward Weston] and our friend Rodión [Ricardo Gómez Robelo]....

I met her for the last time in the official auto in which she was to accompany us with a friend of hers on a visit to an abandoned convent in Coyoacán. Her voluptuous silhouette was a powerful magnet in the afternoon full of sun. The car raised clouds and she said: "A splendor of gold envelops us." Sure gift of art it was to find beauty where others found only inconvenience. A glance awakened swift temptation, but then I felt pain in my spine: I remembered her victims sucked dry of their marrow. I never saw her again....

If Mexico glimpsed Tina through Robelo's eyes, so, too, did she first behold Mexico. As he chivalrously escorted her to places that had impressed Robo, she began to pay attention to the city that so far had been only a backdrop to her personal drama. "Robelo rented a machine [automobile] and we with his cousin rode to several little towns near here," she reported to the Richeys. "Also to that art school Robo wrote so much about. Oh—how beautiful everything was and how sad! All the time I kept thinking how Robo passed through and saw the very same things I did and how it would have been with him along! I just can't enjoy anything."

Another day, Robelo squired her around Chapultepec Park, a landscape of verdant grassy slopes, thick shrubbery, and giant *ahueheute* trees. On the park's winding drives, Mexico City society took its daily late-afternoon paseo, with motorcars creeping along in processionals slow enough for their occupants to exchange elaborate sets of greetings. Tina described this to the Richeys:

> Yesterday—Sunday—Robelo rented a machine and we went riding for several hours through the most beautiful places here. The day was beautiful—not too hot—but balmy and mild—just at twilight we rode through the wood of Chapultepec where the castle is which you know Robo has visited. That is the hour all the people go there for a ride or walk. It is the fashionable thing to do and a very old custom. One also sees a few carriages—very elegant and aristocratic they are—then there are several cafés scattered around playing wonderfully well all kinds of music—they all have

outdoor tables and it is indeed very enjoyable to sit there sipping something and watching the crowd go by—it reminded me of Europe very much.

Other outings were surely afoot, but Tina's communications with Vocio and Marionne underplayed her leisure activities lest the pair get the impression that she was holidaying on their time and money. She saw little of workaday Mexico, however, commenting, "I hardly ever go out among the people."

Conventionally, Tina thought the country's climate to be one of its primary attractions:

> So it is still raining in L.A.! Really, aren't you just disgusted with the weather? What do they want to talk about sunny California for? Oh—I wish you could have this climate! I never in my life thought it possible that such a wonderful climate could exist! Such a sun and sky and the nights balmy and peaceful! I could never describe it well enough! It has showered two or three times while I am here. Those showers are very good however as they eliminate the dust and purify everything and believe me many things need purifying! I don't think you two could *ever* get used to [living] here. There are many many things one misses here in the way of comforts in the home.... But, as Robo said, one cannot have everything and there are wonderful things here which [the] U.S. will never and never can have.

One letter suggests that the thought of living in Mexico had already tumbled through her mind:

> People here surely take things easily—they do everything so slowly—one notices it more coming from the U.S. Here at Robelo's home for instance it never takes less than an hour or an hour and a half at the dining table—that is just the common every day dinner—and so is everything else. Time passes just doing nothing. Of course now I have nothing to do—but I wonder how I could ever get along if I had to do something. Everything is so impractical and slow—at times it gets on my nerves—it may be that [the] U.S. and

its efficiency has spoiled me. They still put everything off till "mañana" here.

Tina's emotional state remained wobbly, and she frequently fell into anxious pining. One sunset found her feeling particularly bereft:

> I have felt as sad as I could feel this late afternoon ever since Robelo left—about 4 o'clock. The sunset and twilight have been wonderful today—never have I seen a more beautiful sky—I was sitting out on the roof up here and one of the servants was with me—the oldest one—she was so fond of Robo and whenever she has a chance she talks about him—today she was repeating to me all the things he used to say to her especially about us. She says he was always talking about us to them. She comes from Strawberry town and Robo had told her that he wanted to take me there when I came and her too. It just breaks my heart to listen to those things. Yet, I like to hear everything concerning him. I seem to feel the loss more and more as time goes on—really I wonder how I can go through life this way. Oh—my heart—how it hurts me!

February turned to March, and Tina grew fatigued, depressed, and tongue-tied in the presence of her host's brilliant dinner guests. She shed weight (as she would throughout her life in unhappy or stressful situations), and Robelo's physician brother pronounced her anemic. Now flowing more sluggishly to the Richeys, her missives were rife with complaints over Mexico's high cost of living and with ill-concealed irritation at Vocio's incessant admonitions to fumigate everything. Then a second calamity dropped from the clouds, and tearful suffering swept away her doldrums.

On March 17, Tina opened a message from her sister Mercedes, to learn that their father was gravely ill with stomach cancer. Only hours later came Robelo's knock on her door, in hand a telegram bearing news of Giuseppe Modotti's death. "No doubt you know all about my poor father's death!" Tina blurted to the Richeys.

> I just can hardly believe it! You can imagine what a shock it has been for me—although—I must admit—my sorrow and pity is not

so strong for my father as it has been for Robo—one thing is that at his age one is sooner reconciled with death. What makes me feel very bitter is not to have seen him once more. Poor dear father! To think that I came here too late to see Robo and then besides be so far from home—just when they needed me so badly! Is it not a cruel fate that follows us this year? I thought the loss of our dear boy would put a stop to our misfortunes—but just a little [more] than a month after comes this other terrible loss.... Pardon my terrible scribbling. I am too nervous to do better. Am going to the Academy now—going there is also a distraction—otherwise I would go crazy.

After pulling shut the gallery's doors on March 23, Tina unhooked the remaining artworks, which would nestle at the bottom of Robo's trunk during the journey to California. Her final day in Mexico was devoted to overseeing the installation of a simple tombstone. It read: ROUBAIX DE L'ABRIE RICHEY, 9 MARCH 1890, 9 FEBRUARY 1922, SU ESPOSA [HIS WIFE]. Landscaped with geraniums, marguerites, violets, and shrubs planted earlier by Tina and La China Robelo, Robo's final resting place was deemed worthy of his discriminating taste.

Tina's rail trip north was a thread of impressions: the desolate aridity of the desert, Vocio's uncontrollable weeping during their brief encounter in Los Angeles, an impulse of happiness as she looked up from a dining car breakfast of toast and grapefruit to a lush sea of greenery, and twinges of a backache and sore throat as the train pulled into San Francisco. Within hours, she succumbed to the flu and was ensconced on a couch in Giuseppe's old room, hastily refurbished, where her mother and siblings danced attendance upon her. To strengthen her blood, she began daily rations of a hard-boiled egg and a glass of sherry, supplied by her friend Rosina Alessandrelli.

Tina reported to Vocio and Marionne:

> I found my family better than I expected—I mean their spirit—and I am glad of it. I think that *even they* felt Robo's death more than they did my father's. Yet—it is very sad for us....
>
> [M]y dear mother and I talk about you so much—her poor heart goes out to you—I guess none can come as near to your sor-

row and understand it as a mother can—her eyes are full of tears whenever Robo and you come into our thoughts.

It is very sad here for me—this place is so full of memories for me and to think that I never will get [Robo's] blue letters anymore as of old—it just breaks my heart.

Her words notwithstanding, Tina had begun to lift above feelings of helplessness. She personified the powerfully unsettling events that had blindsided her in recent weeks as a malevolent Nature, against which she felt a healthy surge of resistance. "Oh! How bitter I feel against life and nature!" she exclaimed to Roy Rosen. "But I must defy it and smiling ask to it: What next? I must look at nature as an enemy not as a conqueror."

Although she had decided to avoid friends during her two weeks at home, Tina nonetheless abruptly pulled out a pen one day to dash off a note to Johan. "I feel that only by living in the past can we revenge ourselves on nature—I wonder how you feel about all this—perhaps we can talk it over." But the emotional impulse behind her gesture was a longing to recapture the sublimity she had once experienced in hearing "Nina" in his company:

> ...the other day—finding myself alone—an uncontrollable desire came upon me to hear "Nina" again. And so I did—and as I listened to it the agitated life of these past few months became dimmer and dimmer while the memory of a certain afternoon came back to me with all the illusion of reality—a certain afternoon when for the first time that soul-torturing music took hold of me and left me a little sadder, perhaps, but with a richer soul. And because of all this I feel the desire to spend another afternoon with you—can the first ever be duplicated? I fear not—but "Nina" at least will be the same.

Tina remained in San Francisco for the Easter holiday, then traveled to Lompoc for a two-week reunion with Vocio and Marionne. The trio returned to Los Angeles together, and Tina's sorrow-clouded odyssey was ended.

Late April brought Tina and Edward face-to-face at last. At the time of Robo's death, Edward's condolence note to Marionne Richey—penned in his bold upright hand—had relegated to the past his friendships with both Robo and Tina, as if to acknowledge fundamental and inescapable change. "—[T]enderness—pity and tears for you and your mother," he had written, "—from one who loved Robo and Tina deeply—Edward Weston." Simultaneously, he wired Tina, who responded via the Richeys: "Thank Myrto for her kind words and Mr. Weston also for his sympathy."

Letters postmarked Glendale had quickly merged into the flow of sympathy notes to Mexico City. "Mr. Weston has written such wonderful letters to Robetu and me," Tina commented glowingly to Vocio and Marionne; "his words have been real blessings to us!" Tina's responses brought Edward news of the overwhelming success of his photographs. "[A]lready many of your prints have been sold," she wrote shortly after the exhibition opened. Edward claimed to have sold previously a total of two artistic photographs, and the tidy sum Tina carried to him from Mexico seemed little short of miraculous. Back in Los Angeles, the pair's delight at the success of their photographic collaboration dominated the continuing affair, which, for a time, must have been informed by a new sobriety and sapped of its breathless sexuality.

No sooner was Tina settled into life at 313 South Lake Street than Vocio and Marionne were pressing her to accompany them on a long summer holiday in Oregon. Pleading exhaustion and a need for calm, she burrowed into the studio instead. After the pair left, Seely, Myrto, and Scolari turned up regularly to keep Tina company, while spells of solitude meant opportunity to sift through her thoughts. Edward, too, visited her at the studio, where he made a photographic study very unlike his previous portraits of her. With hair piled carelessly atop her head and a smoldering cigarette fixed in one hand, Tina balanced upon a hatbox stool for an appealingly straightforward and earthbound image bearing no traces of sentimentality. When the Modotti family came to visit, Edward pulled out his camera again for a double portrait of the two somber and beautiful widows, in which Tina's seemingly disembodied head floats above the stalwart, luminous face of Assunta.

"How can I ever live again there," Tina had wondered of the studio, "where so many memories will haunt me?" Summer must have brought moments when home seemed a sad, musty place, and Robo's figure flitted through the spaces they had shared. From Emmeline Brady, an artist friend, Tina received a letter describing an experience that echoed her own:

> Sunday night I had the most vivid and beautiful dream.... I went into your studio. The place was very quiet.... While I was standing near the divan, uncertain what to do, Robo came toward me, quiet and restful, just as he always came. He said:
>
> "I am glad you came, Mrs. Brady. I have something I want to show you."
>
> He opened a magazine and pointed to a line, I can see it very distinctly, it was: "But not all loves have been as beautiful as Robo's and Tina's." Then he said:
>
> "My friend in San Francisco wrote that after I went away, and I have wanted you to see it."
>
> I began to cry, sitting on the end of the divan, and he looked down at me questioningly, as though he were surprised that I should cry. I too seemed to be sorry that I was crying and tried to dry my tears, but before I succeeded he was gone, and I was left in the studio alone.

Perhaps it was fitting that Robo sometimes peered over Tina's shoulder, since uppermost in her intentions was to acquit honorably the sum of her debts to him. In so doing, she not only purged her own remorse but also demonstrated an enormous capacity for emotional generosity. She aimed at nothing less than realizing the dreams that had been his raison d'être and heaviest burden. The first was an exhibition of batiks and paintings, which was, by all evidence, the only solo show of Robo's career. Collecting oils from the studio and batiks unsold in Mexico City, Tina used her newly acquired skills to produce a two-week exhibition at the MacDowell Club on the fifth floor of the Tajo Building downtown. "Rain on the low studio roof played a mournful accompaniment to Tina Modotti's story of her husband's death," commenced a publicity piece in the *Los Angeles Examiner,* the first of many, over the course of Tina's career, in which a reporter's bedazzlement by her beauty would eclipse discussion of the artwork at hand. "The light from the high north window fell coldly across her white brow and face heightening the contrast of her dark eyes and hair and her trim black gown," the article continued. After she sketched the story of Robo's death, "Tina Modotti's lustrous eyes lowered. There was a momentary quiver of the lids and a quick little paroxysm of the throat. 'I am thinking of him—dying alone, with no member of his family near him. It was terrible.' A pathetic shrug of the shoulders.... There was nothing else to say. So Tina Modotti, young and beautiful, held out her hand."

That fall, Tina undertook the more ambitious project of a sixty-page published anthology of Robo's writing, to be entitled *The Book of Robo*. From his papers, she culled two dozen poems, scraps of verse and prose, a series of sardonic aphorisms, fragments of a novel, and a sprinkling of vocabulary words in his invented language. The distinguished and perpetually cash-strapped British writer John Cowper Powys, then living in San Francisco, was hired to write an introduction, and Tina penned a lyrical preface. With sensitivity and candor, she evoked her companion's lonely boyhood, delicacy and irresoluteness, love of beauty, craving for affection, and obsessive, ineffectual attempts at art making, concluding with a question derived from a Nietzschean precept. "And one wonders!" she wrote. "Did this tireless pursuer of beauty and romance, this ardent lover of beautiful sounding words and luxurious colors—did 'this weaver of thin dreams,' which were to him both his life and his burden, die at the right time?"

Covered in exquisite turquoise-and-brown-striped Japanese paper, *The Book of Robo* was meticulously fabricated, using sewn binding, handset type, and tipped-in photographs. As moving as Tina's text is the care she lavished upon the volume's production, for she meant to imbue it with Robo's spirit, thus making it truly the realization of his elusive dream of publishing a book. Two hundred copies were offered to subscribers, while the family set aside ten for themselves, one of which Tina inscribed to Vocio: "'To Rose Richey, The Mother of my beloved Robo—For his memory—' Tina M. Richey 1923."

Ironically, shortly after *The Book of Robo* rolled from the presses, Tina also became a published poet. For a decade, she had been quietly writing verse (the lot probably later fed to a fire), and now, "at a moment of mysticism," the poem "Plenipotentiary" entered her head. Its vibrant, lapidary style could not have been more different from Robo's tortuous odes:

I like to swing from the sky
And drop down on Europe,
Bounce up again like a rubber ball,
Reach a hand down on the roof of the Kremlin,
Steal a tile
And throw it to the kaiser.
Be good;
I will divide the moon in three parts,
The biggest will be yours.
Don't eat it too fast.

Tina submitted the poem to *The Dial,* a prestigious New York journal whose contributors' list is a directory of the decade's literati, and it was accepted. Though poetry was not a form of expression she would long pursue, recognition by *The Dial* must have provided a swift infusion of self-confidence at a time when she was flooded with uncertainties about her aptitudes and direction. Tina shared the pages of the May 1923 issue with writers Katherine Mansfield, D. H. Lawrence, Paul Rosenfeld, Roger Fry, and Edmund Wilson, Jr., and readers were informed that Tina Modotti de Richey "is now living in the West, and is engaged in the study of photography."

The statement's simplicity belies her season of bewilderment over the future. Living on cash from the batik sales and Vocio's largesse (which the older woman would have happily continued indefinitely), Tina must nonetheless have felt intense pressure to decide upon a means of livelihood. Given her yearning for creative accomplishment, Seely's daily example, and memories of Uncle Pietro's business, photographic portraiture was clearly an option. Yet hers was not an easy decision. On the practical side, photography required only modest training, and it was considered a "suitable" occupation for women, whose "intuition" and abilities with children were believed to stand them in good stead. But, although Tina was in many ways a pragmatic woman, prosaic considerations alone could never have brought her to such a crucial decision. In long conversations with Edward, she spoke of life's chaos, and he of photography's purity, and it was probably at this moment that he proposed solving "the problem of life by losing [herself] in the problem of art." Five years later, Tina would gratefully tell him, "You don't know how often the thought comes to me of all I owe to you for having been *the one important* being, at a certain time of my life, when I did not know which way to turn, the one and only vital guidance and influence that initiated me in this work that is not only a means of livelihood but a work that I have come to love with real passion and that offers such possibilities of expression...."

The opportunity to become a photographer had naturally existed all along, but it seemed as if some ineffable obstacle now dissolved into an expanse of clear sky. Tina had responded to the demise of Robo and her father by doing what Freud termed "the grief work," mentally processing her losses until their rawness disappeared and her pain was relinquished. Death's intimate touch ultimately refocused Tina's vital energies, bolstered her sturdiness and resiliency, and propelled her into unparalleled creativity and joy. She emerged from mourning with the insight that life derives its piquancy from death and its beauty, in part, from fragility, an idea not surprising to viewers of her photographs.

Tina's decision to become a photographer coincided with Edward's critical reappraisal of his creative practice. He was spurred, in part, by a Paul Rosenfeld article in which the critic argued that photographer Alfred Stieglitz alone took full advantage of the medium's intrinsic qualities, while his colleagues abused photography by their insistence upon making art. Tina caught Edward's febrile enthusiasm over the idea of "[realizing] more fully the fineness of my medium of expression—to feel that I have only scratched its possibilities—that it has only the limitations of the brain and vision behind the ground glass." While retaining the concept of photography as fine art, he no longer borrowed effects from other media and sought a more direct relationship with the object and with the medium itself.

We are in the dark about when or where Tina made her first pictures and if these attempts predated an October journey to San Francisco to investigate the possibility of opening a portrait studio there. One might assume that her determination to pursue photography implied a continuing liaison, or at least a friendship, with Edward. By the time she traveled north, however, their relationship seemed a thing of the past. From San Francisco, she posted a melancholy letter of farewell:

I looked out [from the train] at the black night—at the houses lit from within—at the trees shadowy and mysterious—I thought of you—of your trip—of your dear letters to me and the desire to draw near you was so intense—I suffered—the best in me goes out to you my dear one—Good-bye—good-bye Edward—may you attain all you deserve—but is that possible—you give so much— how can "Life" ever pay you back? I can only send a few rose petals and a kiss—

Edward, meanwhile, was en route to Ohio, to say good-bye to his sister and brother-in-law before setting off for Mexico. The stupendous success of the Mexico City exhibition, organized by Tina, had left him exultant. Not only had sales been brisk but she brimmed with stories of Mexico's enthusiastic embrace of the work, reinforcing his impression of an artists' paradise. In Ohio, at the American Rolling Mill factory, Edward made bold, unsentimental photographs of smokestacks, images that marked a point of no return on his journey toward modernism. A cash gift from May and her husband drove him on to New York City, where he found validation in Alfred Stieglitz's response to his work and inspiration in Charles Sheeler's sharp-edged photographic studies of New York skyscrapers.

"Have you heard from Edward since he arrived at his sister's?" Tina inquired in a note to Johan Hagemeyer. "I hope the best of luck follows him." But the casualness of her remark belied her undiminished affection. She dispatched, to Edward's New York address, two "specials," each enclosing twenty dollars, because he would surely need more cash, and because he *must* see Nikita Balieff's popular vaudeville review *Chauve-Souris.*

Perhaps the separate journeys led Tina and Edward to realize that something precious was slipping through their fingers. In any case, back in Los Angeles in November, they not only swiftly resumed the intimacy but also laid plans to move together to Mexico City and establish a portrait studio. If San Francisco had once brought to life Tina the stage actress, and Los Angeles had seen the Hollywood starlet, Mexico City, Tina felt, could nourish and sustain the photographer. Firmly putting her uncertainties aside, she prepared to abandon the security of the Richey household and make another of the tremendous transformations her personality would accommodate.

As if to encourage their undertaking, the much-anticipated exhibition "Arts and Crafts of Mexico," opened in Los Angeles on November 10. Initially curated by a team of artists and scholars for the centennial celebration of Mexican independence, the exhibition had now been repackaged for export to the United States. Coming at a time when Washington was denying Mexico diplomatic recognition, pending the settlement of property and commercial feuds triggered during the revolution, the U.S. tour was both a nationalistic and artistic gesture. Either for lack of financial guarantees or because the exhibition was deemed political propaganda, the U.S. Customs Bureau had detained its thousands of objects at the border, shunting boxcarsful of art onto a rail siding, where they moldered for several weeks. The impasse over their status was finally resolved by selling the works as commercial goods to a dealer who then displayed a selection at the MacDowell Club. On some days, three or four thousand people filed through for a look at polychrome trees of life, green-glazed figurines, lacquered boxes, watercolors by artist Diego Rivera, an enormous stone *chac-mool* warrior, and artworks by children taught with an innovative method based upon an alphabet of seven Mayan motifs.

The catalog boasted writer Katherine Anne Porter's enthusiastic essay idealizing Mexican popular art and photographs by Robo's friend Roberto Turnbull, who had accompanied the show to Los Angeles. Probably through Roberto, Tina secured a minor administrative position and met the show's artistic director, twenty-six-year-old painter Xavier Guerrero, a small, handsome man with high cheekbones and a bow tie, with whom she would later fall deeply in love.

When the Mexican exhibition closed after two weeks, Tina turned to work as Edward's studio assistant. The atmosphere at the Westons' 1315 South Brand Boulevard homestead remained fraught with unhappiness and tension. As a gesture of defiance in one of his countless disputes with Flora, Edward left the house to live in the tiny studio. Meanwhile, petulant, resentful of Tina, and intermittently engaged in bouts of heavy drinking, Margrethe plagued him with emotional demands as his four boisterous sons swarmed everywhere. Under the circumstances, Tina's steadiness and reliability more than compensated for her lack of photographic expertise.

"What would I do without you and Tina these days," Edward rhetorically asked his dear friend Ramiel, "—I fear the whirlwind is upon me...."

In January, Johan was told, "We leave for Mexico in March...this seems quite definite at this writing," but April found the couple lingering in Los Angeles. Delayed repeatedly, usually by opportunities to earn additional cash, the Mexican adventure became "a joke to our friends and a source of mortification to us."

While Tina and Edward spoke plainly of their plans for Mexico, the sexual relationship supposedly remained a closely guarded secret from the Richeys and Flora Weston, whom Edward would assure that a "fine friendship exists between Tina and myself—nothing else." A year after Robo's death, Tina would have judged a new affair ill-timed and uncomfortably demanding of explanations. Yet she had taken to heart the way in which the ambiguity of her understanding with Robo played into his tragic demise. Almost certainly at Tina's instigation, the couple entered into a verbal contract concerning their professional and personal lives. In exchange for photography lessons, Tina was to assist Edward in the darkroom and, at the business end of the studio, purchase supplies, keep records, and bill clients. In addition, she would manage the household—becoming, in effect, a "wife" for the first time, as well as surrogate mother to Edward's thirteen-year-old son, Chandler, who was to accompany the pair as "a hostage to [Edward's] past." On the personal level, they conceived of the arrangement as a "trial marriage," albeit both were free to engage in sexual affairs with whomever they pleased.

Tina's new interest in free love derived, in part, from a timely and momentous discovery that she was to be childless. By one plausible scenario, she consulted a medical doctor in preparation for the journey and learned that she suffered from what she called an infantile uterus, later diagnosed, in more sophisticated terms, as fibroid tumors, a condition that permanently prevented her from bearing children. Tina was deeply shocked and saddened, for she adored little ones and had always assumed she would have a brood of her own. Witness the thought that rushed into her mind upon Robo's death: "not to have a baby by Robo."

Never did Tina fully overcome her distress. At one time, she would take a Mexican orphan under her wing, and, later, at what was a difficult moment for her sister Gioconda, Tina tried unsuccessfully to arrange a long visit from her nephew Tullio. At another moment, staring skyward, she was to blurt out, "I would like to have had as many children as there are stars!" And when she and Edward later disembarked in Mexico, she came upon a tiny, sleepy, ragged pumpkinseed vendor. "Will you come with me, Carmen, to Mexico [City]?" she asked with an impracticality that speaks volumes. "You shall be my little sister." But Carmen's mother demurred.

Rueful awareness that a certain ordinary happiness was to be denied her inspired Tina's decision to pursue unions based solely on love and desire. With biological offspring never to be her means of besting fate, she sought what Nietzsche called "hidden love and the splendor and trembling and overflowing of [her] soul" and plunged into a swirl of creativity.

Dawdling in Los Angeles that spring, Tina and Edward struck up a friendship with Gjura Stojana, a painter, sculptor, and irresistible poseur, who recounted a dozen versions of youthful adventures in Italy, Austria, Serbia, and the Far East. With Edward, Johan, Ramiel, and Margrethe as her companions, Tina "spent many vivid hours—at Stojana's—the Philharmonic—once an evening with Buhlig listening to his reading of that amazing poem [*The*] *Waste Land* by T.S. Eliot...." Absorbed in discussions of photography, poetry, and dance, the little group sipped wine and savored long drags on their cigarettes, setting themselves apart from the self-promoting complacency of Los Angeles, exemplified by the enormous HOLLYWOODLAND sign that now disfigured once-lovely hills.

In April, the visiting Johan made tiny, cryptic notations in his diary:

> April 14: Stojana and Tina...out at studio. Great great day—red tulip—night at the house.
> April 15: T[ina]—M[argrethe]—E[dward] and I working at the tile factory (am). Later all at Stojana—What a day!!! Oh—T—drunken with pictures—wine—rose petals—.
> April 16: T and I developing—out with [T]...willow—confessions.

For two days, Johan and Tina labored over photographic reproductions in Stojana's studio, pausing once for a traipse through hills rippling with wild mustard. It was probably during this visit that Johan made portraits of Tina looking pensive and self-composed. Whether she gave rein to her new sexual freedom is impossible to say, though we know that, around the same time, Edward disappeared for several days with Margrethe, who was desperate enough to sleep with him at last.

On Sunday morning, July 29, 1923, Tina awoke to oppressive heat, but, anticipating ocean breezes, she dressed in a long-sleeved two-piece outfit with white collar and cuffs and a brimmed hat with a wide band. After pulling the door shut on the studio, she gave a last hug to the tabby, then climbed with Vocio, Marionne, and Scolari into the Richeys' convertible for a ride to the industrial port of San Pedro. Meanwhile, Edward's neighbors Peter and Rose Krasnow had collected the Weston clan, and, from his home in Redondo Beach, Edward's friend Ramiel also converged upon the freighter docks. After good-byes both emotional and awkward, Tina, Edward, and Chandler tripped down the gangplank of the rust bucket SS *Colima*. Peering upward shortly before they weighed anchor, Tina's eyes roamed the familiar figures of Vocio, Marionne, and Rose Krasnow, pretty in loose-fitting summer frocks and wreathed in smiles; Ramiel, resting a steadying, avuncular hand upon the shoulder of Edward's uncharacteristically quiet son Brett; and Flora, mustering a half-pleasant grimace. Ten years and one month had passed since Tina set sail from Genoa, Italy. The Mexican freighter reeked of the animal hides it transported, and its pitch and toss made her seasick, but the wind smelled thrillingly of distant, uncharted territory.

Tina (top) *at age four with* (clockwise) *Mercedes, Gioconda, Beppo, Yolanda, Ben, and their mother, Assunta* (center).

Publicity for La Moderna's *"colossal debut."*

Snapshots of Tina and Robo at Lompoc.

Tina as Robo's "Spanish girl."

TOP, LEFT: *Robo Richey,* Tentación. TOP, RIGHT: *The soul mates Robo Richey and Ricardo Gómez Robelo.*
ABOVE: *An Arnold Schröder photograph of the starlet Tina Modotti in a batiked gown.*

A publicity shot autographed by Tina Modotti de Richey.

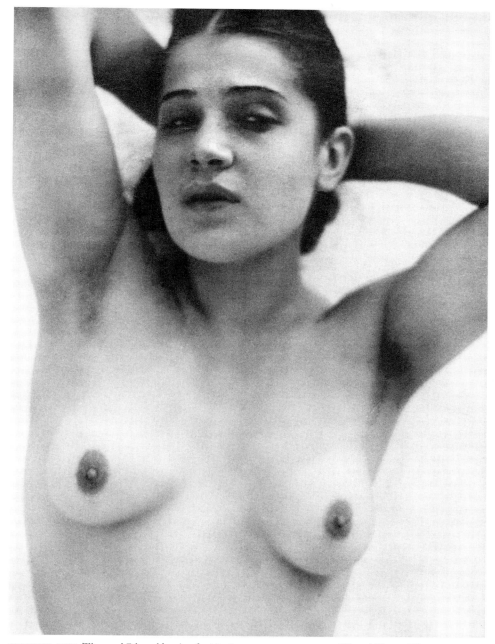

OPPOSITE, TOP: *Tina and Edward leaving for Mexico.* OPPOSITE, BOTTOM: *Edward Weston,* Tina, 1923.
ABOVE: *Edward Weston,* Tina, 1924.

Tina Modotti, Portrait of Edward Weston with a Camera, *c. 1923–1924; gelatin silver print.*

Edward Weston, "Caught in the act of going upstairs to my little room on the 'azotea.'"

Tlalpam - Nov. 1924 -

Tina Modotti   Jean Charlot

OPPOSITE, TOP: *Rafael Sala, Monna Alfau, Tina, Felipe Teixidor, and Edward at the* pulquería *[bar]* *"La Gloria en Triunfo."* BOTTOM, LEFT: *Edward Weston,* Tina, Reciting, 1924. BOTTOM, RIGHT: *Jean Charlot,* Tina Modotti, 1924. ABOVE: *Tina Modotti,* Calla Lilies, 1925; platinum print.

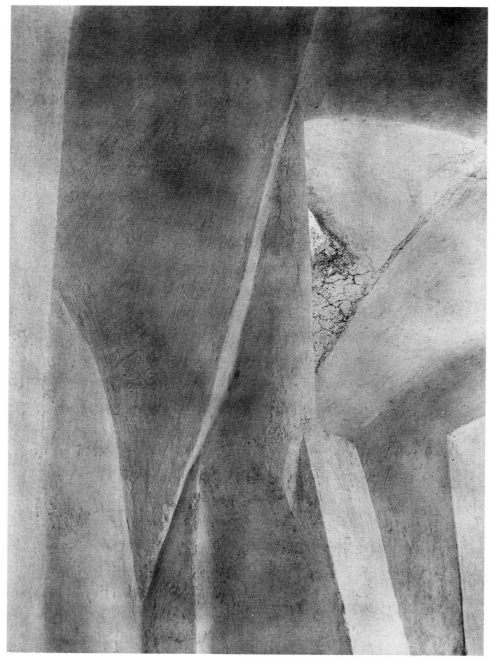

ABOVE: *Tina Modotti,* Interior of Church, *1924; platinum print.* OPPOSITE, TOP: *Tina Modotti,* "Xochimilco—Mexico—Nov. 1925—The little girl is the daughter of the boatman—I am not in the picture because I took it," *1925; gelatin silver print.* From left, *Brett Weston, boatman's daughter, Mercedes Modotti, Edward Weston.* OPPOSITE, BOTTOM: *Tina Modotti,* Roses, *1924; platinum print.*

TOP (clockwise): *Beppo, Ben, Mercedes, Assunta, Yolanda, and Yolanda's husband, Guido Gabrielli, photographed by Tina in San Francisco, 1926.* BOTTOM: *A day in the country: Rafael Sala, Monna Alfau, Brett Weston* (with butterfly net), *Carleton Beals, Tina, and Edward.*

Tina Modotti, Telephone Wires, Mexico, *1925; platinum print.*

Tina Modotti, Campesinos (Workers Parade), *1926; gelatin silver print.*

Part III

Tinísima

Mexico City (1923–1924)

IN 1923, Mexico City teemed with fanatics, bohemians, idealists, radicals, and visionaries. Intellectuals who had once looked to Europe for cultural revelation now turned their backs upon the old continent, embracing instead the genius of peasants and indigenous peoples whose inclusion in the Mexican community promised to bring forth the "regeneration and exaltation of the national spirit." Military chieftains had retreated to their ranches or ensconced themselves in plush ministries. Artists and writers were unfurling the blueprints of a more authentic culture, forging new values, and constructing a modern utopia.

Lured by such vibrancy and ferment, anticipating inspiration, and titillated by skirmishes between marauding guerrilla bands, foreign pilgrims shook off their own tired affairs to board trains and boats bound for Mexico. Some came as intellectual sightseers; others seized the opportunity to embroil themselves in the artistic, social, and political experimentation, the nation-building, and the fiestas.

Early one August morning, feeling clammy after wobbling through the rain-drenched night in a leaky train compartment, Tina and Edward steamed into the bustle and grime of Mexico City's rail station. Their destination was the first-class Princess Hotel, advertised as the "Hotel where Americans feel at Home." Across Hidalgo Avenue beckoned leafy Alameda Park, a haven of splashing fountains, whitewashed trees, shoeshine stands, and strips of grass where old-timers snoozed away the morning. To their left gleamed the white marble National Theater, skirted in scaffolding. On the right, two grandiose baroque churches, sinking irregularly into the city's old lakebed, heaved and pitched as if on waves, their towers tilting madly in several directions. With great peals of bells, the likes of which Tina had not heard since leaving Udine, they summoned the faithful to Mass.

By midday, the couple again stood before their hotel, talking over the idea of a slow trot around the city in an old-fashioned hackney coach, when one wheeled up as if by magic. Edward wrote in his journal:

> A moment of preliminary bargaining in which the driver dis-
> covered that though we were tourists we knew "the ropes," and
> Tina stepped up into the cab, happy over the anticipated ride. Now
> Tina is not thin—neither is she fat—but as she stepped in, she also
> went down, for the cab floor gave way and there she straddled, one
> leg on the step, the other passing through a hole in the cab floor!
> Pedestrians and loungers had a good laugh...we regained our lost
> dignity and bravely hailed another cab, while the first driver, mum-
> bling oaths and apologies, stood contemplating his wreck.

As their mirth subsided, the pair was overwhelmed by the din and tur-
moil of this metropolis of more than 1 million people. The carriage crawled by massed walls and domes of ancient churches, colonial palaces, red stone office buildings and stores—their windows crammed with vulgar, showy goods—then burst into the immense open-skied Zócalo, Mexico City's main square. At the foot of its marble and granite cathedral, torrents of rat-tletrap Ford jitneys converged, their boy conductors barking out, "Zócalo! Zócalo!"

Squeezing back into narrow streets, the couple beheld colorful, naively painted *pulquerías,* crowded to the doors with men, women, and children gulping out of big earthen pots the sour milky-white intoxicant distilled from the maguey plant. Well-heeled passersby gingerly side-stepped the heaps of flesh and rags who had staggered out to the sidewalk "like so many poisoned flies."

Farther along, vendors blared the marvels of sticky yellow sweets, pyramids of pistachios, or enormous sheaves of gladioli, their buds like flames about to ignite. Behind streams of acrid smoke, women patted out tortillas or grilled ears of corn while colossal loads of chairs, coffins, or bags of charcoal zigzagged across plazas on their porters' backs. Curled up against the walls, enveloped with their infants in striped rebozos, Indian women extended cocoa brown hands and raised pleading eyes that swiftly brought Tina to tears.

From the moment of her arrival, Tina was claimed by Mexico, whose spirit resonated with childhood memories. The limpid blue overhead, she marveled, resembled the sky of Udine, and elegant sprays of calla lilies graced Mexican markets as they did the Friulian countryside. Responding to her impressions of a vaguely Italianate culture, Tina professed to "feel Mexican [when I am in Mexico], unlike in the United States where I feel as if I am in a foreign country." Indeed, many mistook her for a compatriot, "until I open my mouth," she said, laughing, and out tumbled charmingly botched Spanish, colored by an Italian lilt and a North American accent.

As Mexico emerged "humane [and]...genuine," California suddenly seemed stale and staid. Unlike their northern neighbors, Mexicans nurtured the emotions and the spirit: To walk down a Mexico City street was to experience farce, tragedy, beauty, and raucous bittersweet humor. Tina absorbed each day, "her eyes full of wonder at the life around her."

Topping the list of sights she wished to see were Diego Rivera's murals in progress at the Ministry of Public Education. Tina brought with her vague childhood memories of theatrical Tiepolos beaming from the ceilings of Udine's churches. More vivid were recollections of the exuberance of wall paintings inside Mexico City's National Preparatory School, which she had almost certainly visited with Robelo some seventeen months earlier. Believing art to be superior to rational knowledge and, indeed, the most eloquent expression of the human spirit, Minister of Public Education Vasconcelos was offering artists public walls on which to teach and uplift the Mexican people. Some lauded the revival of the ancient art of Chichén Itzá and Teotihuacán and spoke of a renaissance, but reporters sneered and students found sport in bombarding the art and artists with tomatoes, eggs, and garbage. Tina's experience at the school, however, had left her unprepared for what she beheld in the arcaded patios of the Ministry of Public Education.

Loading his brushes with yellow, ocher, Venetian red, cobalt blue, and vine black pigments, Rivera was choreographing a luminous, dreamlike dance of humanity. Elaborating upon the theme of work in different regions of Mexico, he pictured ordinary people toiling in fine comradeship. From tropical Mexico came weavers, dyers, sugar refiners, and the splendid Indian women of Tehuantepec, balancing fruit- and flower-filled gourds upon their heads. Coal miners, pottery makers, and peasants labored mightily in panels representing the central region, and, in the north, smelters, ranchers, and iron miners fell to their tasks. To Tina, the mural must have seemed a magical window onto Mexico's soul.

After they strolled the Court of Labor, the artist amiably lumbered over to chat with Tina as Edward rued his inability to speak Spanish. A three-hundred-pound pear-shaped phenomenon, in overalls and clodhoppers speckled with paint, Diego gazed at the pair with protruding eyes swimming in "a sort of sweet-oil…as if they had been toasted in butter and floating, [suggesting] a vast and sensuous romanticism." At thirty-seven, he had behind him a decade and a half of study in Europe, a period as a Cubist, and friendships with Picasso and Modigliani. Since returning to Mexico in 1921, Diego had rarely devoted less than ten or twelve hours a day to painting, which he considered a biological necessity. His voracious appetite for making art was rivaled only by his lust for beautiful women and a zealous, if idiosyncratic, attachment to communism. At parties, he delivered grotesque tall tales in superb deadpan or, a little brandy under his belt, whipped out a six-shooter to plug bullets into lightbulbs.

Tina's admiration for Diego and his enchantment with her would ripen into a solid friendship. Over the next five years, Tina would sporadically haunt the ministry as peasants, Indians, and workers proliferated on its walls. She was overwhelmed by certain faces and gestures and by the fresco's idealizing, profoundly respectful attitude toward the common people. Rivera's vision of a lyrical Mexico was to echo in Modotti's photography, and hers in his painting. In time, she would undertake the daunting task of documenting the murals. At the moment, however, pressed the more mundane chore of organizing a household.

Tina and Edward had signed a six-month lease on a fusty hacienda plopped down in an untilled field in Tacubaya, forty minutes by streetcar from central Mexico City. El Buen Retiro—the Good Retreat—was poorly situated for a portrait studio, yet, the pair rationalized, appointments could be scheduled by telephone and an appreciative clientele might not mind the detour. From outside, fifteen-inch-thick walls and a row of heavily shuttered windows gave the place an institutional look, but, inside, ten wonderfully cavernous rooms, strung around a patio, promised the space and privacy required for a business and household of four. Besides Edward's son, Chandler, a good-natured swaggerer in knickers, they had in their temporary charge the adolescent stepson of *Los Angeles Times* literary editor Paul Jordan-Smith. German shepherd and piano in tow, Llewellyn Bixby-Smith had followed Edward to Mexico for photography lessons.

El Buen Retiro's greatest attraction was its sun-drenched patio, part swept earth, part tumble of vines, shrubs, and musk roses. In one corner, stone steps scrambled to a cowshed roof, where Tina and Edward drank in an unimpeded view of the heavens and the daily drama of the rainy-season sky. It would begin after lunch when a metallic glint dissolved into watercolor softness, issuing in a swiftly swimming stream of billowy white clouds. Midafternoon brought a frenzy of shuddering and swaying in the trees, followed by the first big wet splatters. Huddled on their perch, the two watched lightning illuminate the distant city as the storm swept toward them, sheathing everything in rain, then easing off and dying with the light. When the showers abated, they sometimes lingered to inhale the aroma of a wet field sinking deep into the blue of twilight.

Such ceaseless brewing was to make the Mexican sky irresistible to Edward's eye. References to photographing clouds dot his *Daybooks:* "…[C]louds!" he marveled. "They alone are sufficient to work with for many months and never tire." When Tina unpacked her camera, she, too, would briefly turn it heavenward. On the back of one print, she was to jot, "The clouds are almost every day so wonderful— This picture I took from our 'azotea' [roof] looking toward Chapultepec. You can see the outline of the castle."

El Buen Retiro's charms notwithstanding, furbishing it for home and business was a laborious undertaking. Hideous wallpaper had to be steamed and peeled, plumbing repaired, furniture purchased and painted, and armies of fleas counterattacked. Ever competent and shrewd in domestic matters, Tina outdid herself, as if to demonstrate to them both that they had been right to gamble on the Mexican adventure.

For small items, she nosed out bargains among the stands raveled into a sprawling thieves' market not far from the Zócalo. Good-naturedly haggling over prices (as she would on virtually every purchase she made in Mexico), Tina heaped into Edward's arms newspaper-wrapped polychrome Talavera dishes, brass candlesticks, an inlaid chest, brilliantly hued woolen fabrics, and "eighteen amber beads...half-hidden in the clutter of an old Italian's stall...." Frustrated only in her quest for a decent teapot, she finally asked Vocio to ship one from Los Angeles.

Disheveled but pleased, Tina saw the plaster dust settle, revealing a sparsely modernistic décor: pale gray walls, floors lacquered a darker gray, simple furniture draped with colorful fabrics, and an enormous Moresque vase anchoring the branches of a tree. Yet, only days after the project's completion came disastrous news that a telephone line, as crucial to the portrait business as a camera, was impossible. Not only money but also much time and energy had been wasted. Edward's first solo Mexico City exhibition, arranged by the whirlwind Tina, was to open in five weeks, and they were still without a darkroom.

Reluctantly breaking the lease on El Buen Retiro, they scoured the city until they found 12 Lucerna, oversized and costly but equipped with a phone. Best of all, perhaps, it was situated in the Colonia Juaréz, a smart asphalt-paved subdivision not far from the city's center. Through the wrought-iron gates and leaded windows of its ostentatious gingerbread mansions, one glimpsed nannies cooing to chubby infants as young matrons in organdy and pearls came and went on the arms of dark-suited, spat-wearing gentlemen. It was the ideal clientele for the soon-to-be-fashionable Weston-Modotti studio.

Tina undertook little redecorating, quietly closing the door on rooms disfigured by eyesore wallpaper and ugly fixtures. She and Edward did not share a bedroom (nor would they ever), and the foursome vied for the small unheated servants' rooms. Tina ended up with the plum, reached by a steep wooden staircase from the roof. On the back of a snapshot, she scribbled to the Richeys: "Caught in the act of going upstairs to my little room on the 'azotea' (roof garden). I am isolated there and have the best view of the house—I can see all the roofs of Mexico...." Her lair was undistinguished except by its view of the city cradled into a harsh ring of volcanoes glistening with snow. Perhaps Tina had been marked in childhood by the experience of putting her face to the wind atop Udine's central hill with its sweep of streets, canals, orchards, and icy blue mountain tips etched on the sky. In any case, among the half a dozen Mexico City apartments she would occupy over a lifetime, her favorites commanded such vistas, which unfailingly steadied and sustained her.

The household was complete when they hired as their maid Elisa Ortiz, an inquisitive, gaunt-faced Guadalajaran. Wide-eyed over such gringo habits as cold baths and toothbrushing, Elisa met Tina's gentle campaigning for dental hygiene with the comment: "O, that is only for rich people!" One morning, however, Tina hollered up to Edward's bedroom, "I have gained a real triumph, Elisa is brushing her teeth! I don't know whether she is using your brush, or my brush, or a new one of her own, but she is actually brushing them!"

Still preoccupied with her side of the bargain with Edward—and happily so—Tina switched hats in October to organize and staff his exhibition at Aztec Land, a Madero Avenue tourist shop and tea salon. Installed in the mezzanine gallery, she greeted visitors and presided over the guest register, whose first entry was her own: "Long life to your work—The only thing which never fails you—Tina Modotti-R, Mexico 1923."

On the invitation, the pair displayed the words of Marius de Zayas, a Mexican critic and art dealer in New York. "Photography begins to be Photography for until now it has only been art," de Zayas had proclaimed. Much to the point, in their thinking, the reference was to images that eschewed fussy special effects in favor of the medium's unique ability to render "the very substance and quintessence of the *thing itself,* whether it be polished steel or palpitating flesh." Pictorialism, in its heyday in Mexico as in the United States, upheld a radically different point of view. "The business of a work of art is to make an effect, not to report a fact," judged a well-known pictorialist. "Otherwise…the camera has no more artistic potentiality than a gas-meter."

Nearly one thousand people flocked to Aztec Land, many of them men uninterested in artistic theorizing but eager to peek at nudes that would never make it into an exhibition by a respectable Mexican photographer. For the avant-garde, however, Weston's work was a dazzling eye-opener of another sort, since modernist photography had not gained currency in Mexico and few had thought beyond the categories of portraiture, documentation, and journalism. Though Edward and Tina earned little (eight photographs sold, six of them pictures of the clothesless Margrethe Mather), they considered the exhibition a triumph because of the number of visitors and the intensity of their reactions.

Several of Tina's old acquaintances put in appearances. Beatriz Cornejo turned up without her straitlaced millionaire husband, Oscar Braniff, and Robelo, seriously ill and looking like a ghost of himself, strode in and clasped Tina and Edward in his trembling arms. (Within the year, he would succumb to either malaria or tuberculosis, though Vasconcelos gave some to understand that Robelo had been ravaged by his passion for Tina.) New friends also attended, Diego Rivera clambering up the stairs behind his wife, the barbarically beautiful Guadalupe Marín. Lupe was an imposing woman—six feet tall, with sea green eyes, olive skin, and coarse black hair dripping off her head. A torrent of opinion and emotion, she mesmerized any gathering by simply strutting into the room and held her own against the womanizing muralist with sweet talk and finely calibrated acts of revenge.

Stay-at-homes during the idyll at Tacubaya, Tina and Edward suddenly found themselves bombarded with invitations. One evening, they dined with sometime painter Nahui Olín and her lover, the quirky artistic prophet Dr. Atl. In symbolic rejection of Hispanic culture, Atl had shed his real name, Gerardo Murillo, in favor of the Aztec moniker for "water is the source of all life." He communed with Mexico's volcanoes and made paintings that Edward judged "full of half-baked metaphysical striving." The other member of this legendary couple was the daughter of a famous general. A brazen, pouty woman and renowned beauty, Nahui trailed a whiff of scandal. She had married a painter and run away to Paris, where their baby was smothered to death under controversial circumstances. Back in Mexico, she had branded her husband a homosexual and commenced, with Atl, the torrid affair and bohemian existence that often brought them face-to-face with Tina and Edward.

The next round of invitations delivered to 12 Lucerna was to the radical chic artistic salons hosted by Beatriz's brother-in-law, Tomás Braniff, and his wife, Luisa Dandini, in their splendid tile-encrusted Majolica red mansion. A stiff-backed tycoon like his brother, Tomás didn't give a damn about the arts but liked to see himself reflected in their glory. A proper salon, in Tomás Braniff's lexicon, required speakers on philosophical and artistic matters, and such were regularly brought out to drone after dinner. Nonetheless, the evenings were enchanting affairs where guests bunched up at tables under the spreading star-hung branches of jacarandas, pepper trees, and palms in a fountain-splashed garden. Tina and Edward arrived for the first time, to find Nahui and Lupe tilting at each other with outrageous anecdotes, and Robelo, cocktail in hand, holding forth on the historical import of Mexican pyramids. From a wrought-iron balcony erupted a gleeful thumping of guitars and crooning of ballads while, downstairs, grubby painters busied themselves replacing their usual repasts of tortillas and beans with caviar, roast beef, cognac, and French pastries.

It was at the Braniffs' that Tina and Edward made the acquaintance of Jean Charlot, their most consistent, if not closest, friend. A French artist, with two Mexican grandparents, Jean was a sensitive, rather owlish young man, at once devoutly Catholic and fervently antielitist. Uninterested in playing the role of temperamental artist, he kept "a strictly normal face outside to the world, while all the adventure took place in his studio." Jean had painted epic frescoes at the National Preparatory School and the ministry, but as jealousies festered among the muralists, he turned to oils, gouaches, woodcuts, and drawings. His sure-handed likeness of Tina captures her characteristic look of rapt attention, while her photographic portraits of him conjure up an intelligent, mild-mannered, thoughtful man. He teased her like a brother and once playfully drew on her back; she called him "dear boy."

Like most of their circle, Jean lived modestly, money and self-aggrandizement being less to the point than conviviality and artistic synergy. "[W]e were looking for more or less for the same things, we worked along the same lines," mused one. "And it wasn't like the social friendship of today: It was a revolutionary atmosphere, almost like the atmosphere of a workshop." Over pulque or hot chocolate and whatever could be scrounged in the kitchen, they gossiped, laughed, and shared their work. Painter Carlos Orozco Romero evoked a typical evening in somebody's walk-up: "[We] were all poor, but it didn't matter...all there began to chat, jokes and more jokes...ten o'clock would strike, ay, such hunger!...Nothing more than a pot in the kitchen, a dingy kitchen, a pot of black beans. Well, finally we would sit ourselves in the kitchen at the kitchen table, in dim light, then tortillas and black beans. [We would leave] at seven with the dawn."

As Tina had once stepped briskly into San Francisco theater circles, she now entered into the whirl of Mexico's decade of high-spirited possibility, knowing that she would thrive. Denizens of Mexican bohemia adored the vibrant, earthy, and ethereal Tina Modotti, and friends praised her generosity and impulse to be helpful. Tina was "capable of great friendships because of her complete unselfishness.... She was marvelous," one observed. "And she had a great sense of humor, she liked to laugh, she knew how to enjoy life. There was much goodness in her...."

She remained extraordinarily lovely and had no qualms about reaping the advantages of her good looks. Shiny blue-black hair, uncut for five years, cascaded down her back or, more often, was parted in the middle and pinned into a loose arrangement. Lightly flecked and polished, like a delicate stone, her face had the plasticity and dramatic affect of the actress. Among its expressions, two were pure Tina: the old listening look caught in Jean's drawing—sooty-lashed lids half drawn over her eyes and mouth slightly ajar—and her new photographing look—face "really screw[ed] up ...she was concentrating so hard." She dressed with cheerful simplicity: flowered sundresses, embroidered Mexican blouses, straightish skirts, and comfortable low-heeled shoes. Her once-favorite silver bangles were put away, but she kept out the earrings. It is part of her legend that she was the first woman in Mexico to wear blue jeans.

Tina had no intention of being mere ornament. She gave rebirth to herself not only as "Mexican" but also as a photographer of Mexico. A state of creativity was summoned up and sustained in her, to wither not long after she left the country. In an emotionally expansive mood, she set about making pictures.

A few months into their stay, Tina began regularly to cloister herself in the darkroom. Probably already competent in developing and printing, she tackled a batch of Edward's snapshot negatives. Using his basic technique, she inserted the negative, emulsion side up, into a glass printing frame, added a sheet of paper, and secured the apparatus before turning it over for exposure to a lamp. Development yielded a contact print, identical in size to the negative. To make an enlarged print, she created an interpositive of the desired size, exposed and developed another negative, and, finally, took a print. Inexpertly or out of curiosity, she sometimes cut the paper wildly off angle or flipped the negative so that the image printed backward.

Jotting captions on the reverse ("Mazatlán—agosto—1923," "Exterior of our house in Tacubaya—but maybe I already sent you one"), she dispatched them to family and eagerly undertook photographs of her own.

Though Tina's technique was still imperfect, she found a visual language seemingly without hesitation. Her long apprenticeship in the arts—picture taking in Los Angeles, her gravitation toward photographers and painters, her careers as model and actress, assiduous gallery going—helped to precipitate a startlingly mature body of work. Among her early photographs are some of Tina Modotti's most enduring images.

Working with a large-format camera and tripod on the *azotea,* she made a series of mock-serious portraits of Edward, very much the stiff-collared, pipe-clenching master, attending to his camera as if to a large, faithful dog. Fastidiously composed, the images reveal an ironic sense of humor, as does her print of a big-hatted papier-mâché cowboy, which she dispatched to Johan Hagemeyer. "See? What I have for a lover today?" she quipped in a note. "I send you his image...."

Around the house, various corners and vistas slowly penetrated her photographic consciousness. These could be studied on the camera's ground glass at different times of day and put on film when every light and angle was in place. Tina pointed her lens down a zigzag of stairs, finding an intricate arrangement of tightly interlocking diagonals like the plaiting of a Mexican mat, and out the window, toward the dovetailed rooftops of neighboring buildings. Bathed in a pale, clear light, with subtle gradations of tones and visually compelling patterns, the images have a contemplative, atemporal quality. Yet, like empty stage sets, they are informed with a sense of latent drama, stirring a desire to peer around a corner or strain for a telling sound.

When a Russian circus pitched its tent on nearby Bucareli Street, Tina and Edward wandered over with his Graflex camera. Both were fascinated by the big top's light-filtering fabric panels, of which they made utterly different photographs. Edward's resembled the detail of a stained-glass window, graphically bold, abstract, and giving the viewer no clues about its dimensions. Tina's image was more visually complex, playing off the volumetric effect of the tent's seams against a flattening shadow and establishing scale and a human context by including shadowy figures of four spectators absorbed in action outside our field of view.

A favorite subject was flowers, which Tina's camera found elegant, poetic, and bittersweet. She photographed cacti, Easter lilies, and a scrawny, struggling geranium, which she sprinkled with water to give a sheen to its leaves. The long, dramatically lit stalks of two calla lilies elegantly slice up one image, making viewers acutely aware of the shape and texture of the wall seen around and between them. The photograph would be starkly abstract were it not for the sudden burst of trumpetlike blooms, slightly wilted around the edges yet exquisitely sensual.

As the towering calla lilies derive much of their impact from a markedly vertical format, so Tina's study of a crush of pale roses is inseparable from its blocky, slightly horizontal shape. She photographed heaped blossoms lying on their side, one of her first attempts at the innovative visual strategy of filling her viewfinder with an accumulation of a particular object. Besides roses, she would use hats, palm trees, sugarcane, and cornstalks as quasi-abstract overall patterns.

In the overlapping folds of Tina's rose petals, many discerned eroticism, specifically female genitalia, though one critic wrote of the flowers' "white massed purity." The attribute of Venus, the rose represents love and the eternal mysteries of life, as well as silence and secrecy, as in the expression sub rosa, literally "under the rose." Tina again chose imperfect blooms whose languid wither hints of encroaching loss. Art historian Sarah M. Lowe has written perceptively of *Roses* as a memento mori, a still life representing mortality, and, more generally, of Modotti's flower photographs as prompting "a projection of human suffering onto the flowers, while reminding the viewer that death and decay are evident in even the most beautiful objects."

One is also tempted to see, in Tina's roses, a self-portrait of sorts, an allusion to the photographer's vulnerabilities, and, in retrospect, a poignant metaphor for the incipient tragedy of her life. The idea of the rose was to hover around Tina Modotti, whose elegy by Pablo Neruda evokes "the last rose" and "the new rose." "They will pass one day by your little tomb," Neruda would write, "before yesterday's roses are withered...."

Much of Tina's darkroom time was devoted not to personal work but rather to developing and printing for the Weston-Modotti studio, which hobbled along in feast or, more often, famine. Though Tina cut expenses to the bone, the pair routinely finished the month with only a stack of tortillas and handful of pesos to their names, and nothing resembling rent money. Sometimes a big order materialized, once they dipped into Elisa's savings, and, if they were lucky, Flora Weston wired cash. At the end of 1923, an attempted putsch left them nearly insolvent.

Revolution notwithstanding, the Mexican government still functioned more or less as a military dictatorship, and strongmen kept their own private militias. When it emerged that Gen. Plutarco Elías Calles would succeed Obregón in the presidency, politician Adolfo de la Huerta made his bid for the office by hurtling fifteen thousand irregulars against the Mexican army. From Tacubaya sounded the rat-a-tat-tat of gunfire, tin soldiers marched and bugled through the streets, and Edward bought a pistol to defend the homestead. The pinch came when food prices skyrocketed, and well-heeled citizens, who might otherwise be sitting for their portraits, rushed to purchase steamship tickets.

Edward spelled out the situation in a letter to Johan: "Tina and I sit here smoking our respective pipes—sounds complacent?—we are not— the revolution nearly finished us—fortunately frijoles are still obtainable— though sittings are not—but the former depend on the latter as do film and chemicals...." The ruckus had another repercussion. It gave Tomás Braniff the jitters, and he halted the artistic salons "because of grave conditions resulting from the revolution."

New Year's Eve found the kitchen at 12 Lucerna in an uproar as Lupe Marín whipped up a spread of firecracker Mexican dishes, for which she had shopped, thus enabling a couple unable to scrape up January rent to throw a lavish party. Guests fox-trotted their way into 1924, pausing to quaff rum punch and smack their lips over the delicacies. So successful was the *tertulia* that Tina and Edward made it a weekly event, to be underwritten by passing the hat. "Because of grave conditions resulting from the revolution," the pair chortled, they kindled up the fabled Saturday nights, turning the Modotti-Weston household into the most dazzling light on the vanguard social circuit.

Virtually every well-known writer and artist in Mexico participated. Mexican-born, Texas-educated journalist Anita Brenner described how "workers in paints drank tea and played the phonograph with union and non-union technical labour—scribes, musicians, architects, doctors, archaeologists, cabinet-ministers, generals, stenographers, deputies, and occasional sombreroed peasants." Edward agreed that it was "an amusing contrast, the refined Madame Charlot along with Mexican generals comparing bullet holes in their respective anatomies...."

Anita was a mainstay of their parties, along with Jean Charlot (and his mother); Lupe's comely brother, Federico Marín; a feisty Californian named Frances Toor; and Lupe and Diego, a one-person tourist attraction for the inevitable contingent of visiting gringos. A hand-kissing German whose persistent attentions to Tina roused Edward's ire and provoked hilarity in Federico and Jean, Dr. Leo Matthias would cast about for the object of his affection. The leathery-faced, guitar-toting Gen. Manuel Hernández Galván also strode in with Tina on his mind. Most likely, the two had an intense affair, cut short when Manuel departed for the front.

Dubbing themselves "the family," the cohorts grew "accustomed to certain things and certain attitudes," as Jean observed to Anita, "simplicity and naivete, a certain infantile directness.... We even have our own language and certainly an etiquette that is original and unmatched.... Scorn for sentimentals, humanitarians, reformers, moralists, and authorities...." Invariably hungry, they dug into Tina's spaghetti with butter and cheese, Anita's version of *chongo*, a traditional syrupy curd, which she served with cinnamon toast and tea, and a delicious curry and sweet rice prepared by an Indian revolutionist named Gupta. After dinner, the men heaped Colts on a table as tangos and the wicked Cuban rumba scratched their way out of the phonograph. On one memorable occasion, a guest stumbled upon her lover entwined with another woman and holloed him from room to room, popping at his feet with a small pistol. On another, Tina and Edward exchanged clothes, mimicking each other so convincingly that revelers were perplexed until Edward kicked up his pink-gartered legs and vamped outrageously.

Edward loved to prance, but Tina, clumsy and uncomfortable on the dance floor, caught her breath on the parties' less frenetic edges, where talk gravitated to revolutionary art and politics. Habitués of the Saturday nights, the muralists in the crowd would have been filled with news of the Syndicate of Revolutionary Painters, Sculptors and Technical Workers, a guild of "citizen artists working for a revolutionary state." Bourgeois individualism had been jettisoned in favor of collective labor, indigenous values trumpeted, and art made accessible to the people. The syndicate repudiated easel painting and all other forms of elitist art. Its president, painter David Alfaro Siqueiros, had presented to Vasconcelos the group's demands that painters, masons, and assistants be paid equally and by the square meter of wall surface covered, and the minister was amused.

Painter Xavier Guerrero had been dispatched to buy guns so members could do their part against the insurrectionary de la Huerta, but he lugged back a cache of weapons so dilapidated that they were more likely to harm the trigger puller than his target. The syndicate's political engagement also entailed an application for membership in the Communist International, the winning vote taken with an understanding that, as Comintern members, their first responsibility would be to get drunk with the masses at a *pulquería*.

"We certainly have been plunged into a swirl of communism here," Edward avouched to Flora. "Almost all our acquaintances are active participants in revolutionary activities.... A new revolutionary newspaper is being published, 'El Machete.' I know personally nearly every one among the contributors and editors, most of them appear at our Saturday nights, and most of them are artists."

Launched by the syndicate, the weekly was one of the biggest newspapers ever published, "a veritable bed sheet." On its masthead, a fist brandished the machete, the tool and weapon of the Mexican peasant. Underscoring the message of solidarity with oppressed peoples was a poem by folklorist and revolutionary Graciela Amador, a driving spirit of the publication: "The machete serves to harvest cane/To open paths through wild forests/To kill snakes and mow down weeds/And to humble the arrogance of the godless rich."

Peddled for five centavos an issue, *El Machete* was also slapped up around town by brash militants wielding glue buckets and fat brushes. Thus the masses, those who were literate, could read upon the city's walls the syndicate's ever-more-ferocious attacks upon the government. Dismayed by forces he had unleashed with the mural commissions and embroiled in bitter political feuding, Vasconcelos resigned as Minister of Public Education. His successor, José M. Puig Casauranc, cautioned the artists about their attacks and threatened to whitewash "those horrible frescoes." The pages of *El Machete*, retorted Siqueiros, were their "new walls."

Another frequent Saturday guest, the Berlin economist Alfons Goldschmidt, a popular professor at the University of Mexico, had signed a lead article in *El Machete*'s inaugural issue. An avuncular and dumpling-faced man, Herr Goldschmidt would bustle in with "his hearty embrace…his tickling of the ribs, his infectious laugh." In Germany, Alfons had been a key player in the establishment of a workers' aid society, a task that had taken him to the Soviet Union. He was a capable, energetic Marxist, one of many Tina would know in Mexico. The Goldschmidts reciprocated Tina and Edward's hospitality with invitations to teas in their bric-a-brac- and doily-cluttered home, where busybodies noted that, for Reds, they lived high off the hog. Lina Goldschmidt played the grand piano for her guests, and the professor, on one occasion, stumped to recruit members for a nascent Communist group. Edward shook his head no, but we don't know Tina's response.

The Saturday nights also brought to 12 Lucerna the newlyweds Monna Alfau and Rafael Sala, a Catalonian couple whom Tina and Edward had met at Aztec Land. A saucy librarian with prettily mussed chestnut hair, Monna took an interest in all things artistic. Rafael, a rumpled, elegant string bean of a man, was a painter of odd biomorphic canvases. Edward once remarked that he considered the Salas not a couple but, rather, a threesome, since Monna and Rafael were inseparable from Felipe Teixidor, a clumsy and attractive bibliophile. The presence of Felipe, Rafael's closest friend since childhood, had lured the two to Mexico for an interminable honeymoon.

"The three Salas" saw "the Westons" almost daily, and the Sunday excursions of which they were all unwavering devotees took them to the Basilica of Guadalupe, the village of San Cristóbal, and the sun-parched pyramids of Teotihuacán. Such expeditions were ritualized affairs, their high moment the uncovering of baskets bulging with bread, cheese, fruit, Tina's famous potato salad, and bottles of red wine. After lunch, the five-some lounged in the shade, idly talking or taking siestas until Monna and Rafael drifted toward the shops or the hills, inevitably returning with a trove or two. Finally, hats snared on a giant maguey, they would pose in a clump of blond grasses or around the doorway of some amusing tavern for the souvenir snapshot. The men sported jodhpurs, boots, and vests, and the women wore trousers or long khaki skirts with mannishly attractive ties.

At Easter, the little band spent a week in the colonial town of Tepotzotlán, north of Mexico City. By special permission, they lodged in the former monastery of San Francisco Javier, its cloister choked with overgrown, insect-buzzing gardens. In a damp monk's cell, they feasted on succulent roast pigeons, howling with laughter over their candleholder, fabricated from a tripod and a toilet paper roll and quickly disassembled when anyone bolted for what passed as the bathroom. Sleeping in an open-air mirador, Tina and Edward thrilled to the sight of a full moon slipping into the horizon to the west as the sun sponged up morning mist to the east.

After coffee, they were off to stalk photographs. Ignoring a Baroque church dripping ornamentation, Tina strayed into the disused monastery, planting her big wooden tripod before its ponderous archways and splotchy walls to make photographs of intriguingly empty spaces, lit from the wings and approached as if at a hushed, anticipatory moment. The scenes before her camera involved surfaces at various distances and a range of brightness from deep shadow to white glare, yet—presumably following Edward's practice of working without a light meter—she managed exposures that allowed her to keep nearly everything in sharp focus and preserve details in her prints.

Tina's favorite Tepotzotlán photograph was of a spatially disorienting chapel interior. Here a convergence of adobe walls, recesses, and arches defies logic and, like clouds, becomes a catalyst for free association. The resulting image is a sensual dream about light, shadow, and form. Back in Mexico City, Tina printed it on sumptuous Willis & Clement platinum paper specially ordered from England. With platinum salts embedded in its very fiber (unlike the silver salts used in gelatin silver prints, which remain on the surface), this paper yields exquisitely soft, dusty, and luminous images. Tina adored the effect, which she found worth the tedious printing procedure. Because platinum salts require exposure to ultraviolet rays, present in sunshine but not in artificial light, making prints meant scurrying between the *azotea*, where they were exposed, and the darkroom, where they were developed.

Unlike Edward (who believed that the creative moment occurred at the clicking of the shutter, not in the laboratory), Tina had no objection to darkroom manipulation. She pulled both positive and negative prints of *Interior of Church*, and exhibited it upside down, thus reinforcing the image's abstract qualities. Her first published photograph, it appeared that summer in a Mexico City newspaper, which labeled it "cubist" and credited Edna Modotti. "She is very happy over it and well she may be," noted Edward in his journal. "I, myself, would be pleased to have done it."

In the darkroom, on traipses with the Salas, or in homegrown amusements—such as a game of naked roof tag one drizzly evening—the couple exuded harmony. On the anniversary of their arrival in Mexico, after a much-anticipated lunch-counter breakfast of eggs, hotcakes, and syrup, Tina and Edward climbed the stairs to a commercial photography studio chosen for its hackneyed props and display case cluttered with faded prints and dead flies.

"We have been married just a year today," purred Tina to the bustling, self-important owner. "We wish a photo to commemorate our anniversary. El Señor is very religious, perhaps you can put a church in the background; and I should like to hold these lovely flowers. But you will have better ideas than we—your pictures are so artistic!"

A ponderous tome was thrust at Edward as Tina clutched the dusty paper blooms. Demure in a dark skirt and frilly blouse, she solemnly held Edward's hand, and they exchanged adoring looks as the cameraman clicked away.

"Your light is very good."

"Yes, I study the latest lighting effects from the U.S."

Back on the street, splitting with laughter, Tina gasped, "How did we keep a straight face?"

But such moments of connivance gave ground to bouts of disaffection, and at times the relationship turned as storm-tossed as the Mexican sky. The sore point was Tina's other suitors. Despite the pair's pact on sexual freedom, the mere thought of other men around Tina turned Edward sour and wrathful. "Next time I'll pick a mistress homely as hell!" he growled. Though he had confided to his *Daybook* that he looked upon her less hungrily than before, he remained deeply and possessively in love.

She, too, had experienced a cooling of the quivering hothouse sensuality that had once informed the relationship. As with Robo, she sought to replace it with a different kind of union, beyond sex, based on genuine friendship and mutual respect. On Edward's birthday, she gave utterance to her abiding love, presenting him with a two-word note (accompanied by a sprig of his favorite purple hyacinth buds): "Edward! Edward!" Yet Tina underreckoned the agony of his jealousy, for she was of a generally unpossessive nature and felt no lingering resentment over his dalliances and liaisons. When one of his California lovers was considering a Mexico City visit, Tina would write from out of town, "...in case she arrives while I am there: Are we not good pals dear? I assure you that I will help you and make it easy for you—really I would even welcome a chance to give my 'ego' a lesson...." She made no secret that she claimed for herself the same sexual emancipation. Felipe Teixidor later remembered a parlor game in which each player recorded something personal on a scrap of paper. When Tina's turn came, she coquettishly submitted the words "Tina Modotti—profession—men!"

According to Edward's biographer, it was "not infrequent...that Tina's lover would stay the night in her room while Weston lay sleepless in his own." Ardent though they were, none of these trysts evolved into a lasting intimate union, and they were no more numerous than those enjoyed by men and certain women (Nahui Olín comes to mind) of their milieu. Edward told himself he did not want the burden of a woman fixated upon him alone, yet everything about Tina's admirers stirred up a mental hornet's nest. For a time, it was a crucifix:

> For weeks it hung across her bed, a plaster Christ on a varnished cross, a present of unpardonable taste. How well I remember the night he brought it to her, and how I secretly stuck up my nose. But my position precluded an opinion—might be considered "catty." So I suffered silently, writhing in anguish as it hung there week after week mocking my memories—a Christ symbolizing disillusion. She has removed the cheap vulgar thing and it rests on the floor, dust-covered in another room.

With his camera, however, Edward possessed Tina as no other man could. His photographic creed held nudes to be no more erotic than clouds or vegetables, and his images of women (or their backs or legs) are frequently bloodless. "[S]heer aesthetic form," he insisted. Yet many views of Tina on the *azotea* not only brim with desire but also convey a whole human being. The trust between the two was still enormous. Unselfconsciously posing on an old serape or directly on the sun-warmed stone,

Tina gave up every pore, undulation, and crease of her body to Edward's camera.

Although Tina was keeping a diary at the time, it has been lost or destroyed. But her companion's *Daybooks* offer an anecdote (later heavily edited) revealing how he saw desire, distress, and photography coalescing in their conjugal life:

> She called me to her room and our lips met for the first time since New Year's Eve—she threw herself upon my prone body pressing hard—hard—exquisite possibilities—then the doorbell rang, Chandler and a friend—our mood was gone—a restless night—unfulfilled desires—morning came clear and brilliant.
>
> "I will do some heads of you today, Zinnia"— The Mexican sun—I thought—will reveal everything—something of the tragedy of our present life may be captured—nothing can be hidden under this cloudless cruel sky—and so it was that she leaned against a white-washed wall—lips quivering—nostrils dilating—eyes heavy with the gloom of unspent rain clouds—I drew close to her—whispered something and kissed her—a tear rolled down her cheek—and then I captured forever the moment—let me see, f.8— 1/10 sec K1 filter—panchromatic film—how brutally calculated it all sounds—yet really how spontaneous and genuine...the moment of our mutual emotion was recorded on the silver film—the release of those emotions followed—we passed from the glare of the sun on white walls into Tina's darkened room—her olive skin and somber nipples were revealed beneath a black mantilla—I drew the lace aside....

Six years later, we hear from Tina a comment about the effect of Edward's nudes, which sealed her reputation as a sexual adventuress. "The scandal exploded when they saw the nudes of Weston, particularly my nudes," she recalled. "It was too much even for the Mexicans. The stern remarks of our friends also intimidated me."

Their life at 12 Lucerna came to end that spring when the couple moved to a cheaper house. They left at 5:30 one morning to avoid paying a fee owed the landlord, but Tina was caught and threatened with a lawsuit if the money was not handed over in two days. Their new home stood at 42 Veracruz, in a pleasant district near Chapultepec Park. Sunny and boasting a delightful *azotea*, it was wedged into a triangle at a bustling six-way intersection rife with sputtering Fords and picturesque hurdy-gurdy men.

One late afternoon around the same time, the couple wormed its way through the vernissage crowd at a hole-in-the-wall dubbed Nobody's Café. Half a dozen Westons hung on the walls, along with a medley of paintings and masks, artworks that had found favor with a clique of intellectuals known as Estridentistas, meaning "the strident ones." Billed as "the first exhibition of Estridentism," the gathering was less a traditional art opening than what the Estridentistas gleefully called an "irruption." Through a musical whine and clouds of cigarette smoke, madcap poets pulsed out their phrases—"We perfume ourselves with benzene!" "We throw stones at houses filled with furniture grown old in silence!"—to a raucous bohemian crowd.

Edward shrugged his shoulders, but Tina was drawn to Estridentism, an essentially literary movement, whose members' antics aspired to shock out of existence the swooning señoritas and chivalrous swains of Mexican poetic tradition. Politically astute utopists, its adherents published staccato odes to urban and industrial civilization, admitted no barriers between art and life, and admired the dynamism of the machine. "To a motorcycle," Tina once declared, sounding like a burgeoning Estridentista, "it is possible to dedicate a poem." The group had affinities with the Italian Futurists, though the Mexicans generally distanced themselves from Futurism and abhorred its benevolent regard for fascism.

Finding bold, repetitive pattern in urban subjects, Tina made a number of photographs partaking of the Estridentista aesthetic. Among them are *Stadium, Mexico City,* a study of the austere geometry of empty bleachers, and *Telephone Wires, Mexico,* an elegant web of crosshatching seen against a heaving sky. Created by sandwiching together two negatives, *Experiment in Related Form* is a quasi-cinematographic composition of wineglasses, glinting and almost audibly clinking as if jostling down an assembly line. Although the work of many European and U.S. artists celebrated progress through technology in the 1920s, virtually no one but Tina was making artistic photographs of industrial Mexico. It was a subject she would pursue.

Among Tina's Estridentista cohorts were the poet Germán List Arzubide, his crest of dark curls and ear-to-ear grin visible across a crowd, and Luis Quintanilla, an up-and-coming diplomat (himself an ambassador's son) who mingled in avant-garde circles. Luis was a sophisticated, congenial man who signed books of poetry bearing titles such as *Radio* and *Aviation* with the homophonic pseudonym Kin Taniya. Godfather to the *Mexican Theater of the Bat*—a pastiche of drama, burlesque, and folklore loosely based on the Broadway hit Edward had seen two years before—Luis briefly lured Tina onstage for a role in the short-lived venture.

Their collaboration came as she was in the throes of a love affair with his younger brother José Quintanilla, nicknamed "Pepe." Nineteen years old to Tina's twenty-eight, a mathematician by training and a mystic by inclination, Pepe was a smooth-skinned man with beautiful, sad deep brown eyes. He appears with her in a double portrait, probably clicked off by Tina herself, who wears a rapturous expression as she snuggles into Pepe's bare chest.

Only months after the affair began, Tina's emotions slackened, and she no doubt tried to recast it as friendship. She viewed Pepe as "a gentle abstract presence," but he never considered her as anything less than the love of his life. From the point of view of the Quintanilla family, to whom Pepe had showed her off, Tina Modotti gave men everything or nothing.

Afflicted with tuberculosis, Pepe lived seven years more. As he lay dying, at age twenty-six, in a Davos, Switzerland, sanatorium, his final gesture would be toasts with bubbly French champagne, and a last conversation with his mother would bring the words "Send a telegram to Tina Modotti."

Even before Tina's distressful affair with Pepe, Edward stood on the brink of leaving Mexico. Pushed by emotional and financial turmoil, Flora's drumbeating for his return, and guilt over the long absence from his three younger children, he had set a tentative date for his departure. Farewell dinners had been digested and gifts opened when, to Tina's enormous relief, he abruptly canceled the plan, realizing that his photography had more to gain if he stayed.

In the weeks that followed, the couple shared professional triumphs. Tina organized some seventy prints into Edward's second Aztec Land exhibition, again garnering high acclaim, and submitted her works to a government-sponsored group show at the Palacio de Minería, her first exhibition. The photographs lost "nothing by comparison with mine—they are her own expression," Edward wrote in his *Daybook*.

Coming after a year of work in Mexico, the exhibition must have been an occasion for Tina to take stock of her photography. Like Edward, she strove to "[accept] all the limitations inherent in photographic technique and take advantage of the possibilities and characteristics the medium offers." A keen eye for the sensual materiality of life, its textures and tones, is one hallmark of Modotti photographs. Paradoxically, it has led to the critical undervaluation of her work by those who have not viewed the exquisite nuance of originals but only mediocre reproductions.

If Tina's images resemble Edward's in their modernist approach and powerfully graphic qualities, the two oeuvres diverge sharply from other points of view. Seeking to capture the quintessence of his subjects, Edward made photographs he believed to be devoid of allusion or sentimentality. Tina's work, on the other hand, admits a rich web of connotation and finds symbolic import, rational or irrational, private or collective, conspicuous or half-sensed. Her early works discern, in various objects and settings, a wondrous presence that intensifies and clarifies the life experience.

Though eminently compatible as colleagues, the pair knew a checkered relationship that fall, and designs for their future took many shapes. In October, Edward wrote Johan: "Tina and I cast our lots together deciding to work here another year and then make for New Y.—well plans have not changed...." Three weeks later, however, he was impatient to pack his bags and catch the next boat to Los Angeles.

Sensing the impossibility of untangling their skein of emotions, Tina and Edward nonetheless embarked upon marathon discussions of what lay ahead. Many factors weighed in: finances, Edward's children, the portrait studio, Flora and her money, their artistic aspirations, their alienation from each other, and their abiding mutual affection. That Edward would travel to California was a given. Although Tina had no desire to leave the matter in abeyance, she nonetheless unselfishly shunted her feelings aside to urge that he postpone a decision about his return to Mexico. With loyalty she reserved for those who had figured importantly in her life, she offered to move to any mutually agreed-upon place, and they toyed with the idea of a portrait studio in New York City. Adding to the stew of Tina's emotions was a fear that Edward's swift and irrevocable disappearance, like those of Robo and her father, would leave her a lonely survivor in Mexico City.

"[Modotti was], in a way, clearer about where she was going...than Weston," observed Anita Brenner. Certainly, she was less encumbered by family obligations, and she was determined to pursue photography. Ironically, having set her course for financial and creative independence, she lingered in Edward's long artistic shadow. Later, Diego would write that Tina's work was "more abstract, more aerial, even more intellectual [than Edward's], as is natural for an Italian temperament. Her work flowers perfectly in Mexico and harmonizes exactly with our passion." Yet a shaky self-confidence about her photographic abilities was undermined by partnership with a single-minded "genius," and her modesty reinforced by voices that dubbed him "the Emperor of Photography," and her, "the *bellissima italiana.*" She had no other role models. Among local photographers, only a sprinkling were women, and, in any case, the artistic work of Weston and Modotti broke all Mexican molds.

Unable to "pierce the future," Tina and Edward could only circle around basic understandings. "I shall write quite frankly," Edward told Johan in mid-November:

> After a rather stormy year together which presented many diffi-culties—a kind of a "trial marriage" as it were—Tina and I have decided to cast our lots together for the future—so you will see that my *intention* is to return to Mexico—besides this reason—I have no money to start life anew elsewhere nor the energy nor desire to begin another studio.... *But!—there are my children* and they are my *first consideration....* Tina understands exactly my position and agrees—so you see I may arrive in California to unforeseen— or may I say half-sensed complications—now this much *is sure* that I shall not in any event return to Mexico for about three months....

On the morning of Saturday, December 27, Tina deposited Chandler and Edward at the train station, tearfully kissing them good-bye without being certain that Edward would return, then wending her way home with the sympathetic Jean Charlot. Dazed, she indulged in a spasm of cleaning and moved into Edward's bedroom, where she hung his portrait next to pictures of Robo and her mother. Light falling from that strange, lonely day, she settled into a corner of the studio to write Edward as their black cat skidded onto her lap. She had baptized the creature Scaramouche for the bodice-ripping swashbuckler film that had crowds flocking to Mexico City cinemas.

That delightful film was far from Tina's mind, however, as she gave vent to utterly unhappy and self-chastising thoughts:

> …Edward Edward—for your peace I should not perhaps—and yet—for my outlet I must tell you that I am lonesome—lonesome—and that I am overwhelmed by tenderness as I think of you—of your precious being—.
>
> Dear one—surely I have always appreciated and have *before tonight* realized *how much* you mean to me and yet why is it that since you left I have been suffering and accusing myself of not having been worthy of all the wonders of you— Dear one—send me a word about this—tell me—please—that perhaps I have not been as bad as I imagine for really Edward I am suffering too much tonight—and I miss you—I miss you—.

Uncharacteristically childish and saccharine, she prattled, "…as I promised to be a good and obedient girl while you are gone I will not open the window below—so no 'generals' can get to me…. Boo—boo—dear one." By Sunday, she was valiantly printing and retouching for the Weston-Modotti studio, and, on Monday, she called at Kodak for a "grave" talk about photographic papers. It was her firm intention, during Edward's absence, to produce photographs that would make him proud and speed the time along.

C h a p t e r   7

Mexico City (1925–1926)

F OR EIGHT MONTHS, the couple's letters flew furiously back and forth across the Rio Grande. On New Year's Day 1925, Tina, Monna, Rafael, Felipe, and Nahui Olín dispatched giddy pages of "kisses," "come soons," and doodles penned at the Salas' festive shrimp and Chartreuse supper, and Edward shot back dispirited descriptions of the old Glendale homestead and studio. As if to settle the score with Tina, he jumped into an affair with their friend Miriam Lerner before traveling on to San Francisco, where he was buoyed by a reunion with the Modottis:

> such a night!... Of course we got beautifully borrachito [a little drunk]—no—I should not have added the diminutive—at least in regard to the condition of Johan, Benvenuto [Tina's brother] and myself—and if Mamacita was not, she didn't need to be, for she was quite the gayest person in the room. I made love to her and then to Mercedes [Tina's sister] with intense fervor and shocking indiscrimination. O she is lovely! Tina mia! I am quite crazy over her. With a few drinks, Johan is always a scream. Last night was no exception. Benvenuto was superb—gave us Grand Opera in the kitchen and acted all over the place. We jazzed—sang—did mock bull-fights.... And the dinner!—what a feast—with little pigeons so

tender one ate bones and all—fresh mushrooms too—and then for emphasis I repeat—the wine!—the Wine!

On the heels of the joyfully febrile evening atop Russian Hill came troubled days in a rented Cow Hollow studio. Lonely at times in San Francisco, Edward chafed over family obligations and constant penury. "The fog sweeps by like smoke," he wrote, adrift in malaise "The sirens shriek dismally. I am alone in this great room—no, you are with me, but only your counterpart on the wall, forming a kiss I never got. I read a bit, walk the floor, smoke nervously, try to write but cannot...."

Rattling around the oppressively quiet house, organ-grinders' tunes drifting up from time to time, Tina was haunted by equally unsettled thoughts. At once pleased and nervous about running the studio, she contended with rounds of sittings, processing, retouching, deliveries, and billing. "How relieved I will be when the order is off and the money in our pockets," she wrote of one job. "I am rather proud of the prints—I am sure you would find not many faults with them—oh Edward—how 'stuck up' I feel and how important printing platinums...."

Among Mexico City personalities who appeared at the studio for portraits was petite raven-haired Dolores Del Rio. Wed at sixteen to a wealthy socialite who had smoothed her path to Hollywood, Del Rio was on the eve of making *Joanna,* the picture that would set in motion a glittering five-decade acting career. Probably the aspiring starlet and the disillusioned show business dropout spoke of the film world as Del Rio perfected her Cupid's-bow mouth and Modotti adjusted the lighting and angle of the bulky Korona. Tina's portraits were skillful asymmetric compositions playing the dark shape of Dolores's hair against her glittery beaded dress and the whites of her eyes, whose brilliance the photographer achieved with a shot of potassium bichromate into the developer.

Clients such as Del Rio were few, however, and, deprived of Flora Weston's bailouts, the business merely limped along. By April, Tina found herself in such dire financial straits that she accepted a $250-a-month full-time position in the San Juan de Letrán Street bookshop of her genial Italian friend Ettore Guastaroba. From the first moment, she was miserable, and on her lunch hour she rushed home, consumed by the idea of disentangling herself. Feeling foolish but oddly thrilled, she hastily phoned in

her resignation to Guastaroba ("darn decent" about the whole thing).
"Edward," Tina wrote Weston the next morning:

> I may be ridiculous absurd—a coward anything you want but I
> just had to quit—I have no other reasons in my defense only that
> during the first morning of work I felt *a protest of my whole being*...
> the moment I got out—I knew that I was free free and that I would
> never go back— Oh, my dear one, it was good to have had this
> trial—this morning of suffering—for now I appreciate so much
> more my freedom—my time—my life—everything. I am as drunk
> with this wonderful sense of being free....

Shunning inauthentic, just-for-the-money work (as she would ever
after, even if poverty proved the alternative), Tina reclaimed photography
as her métier: "Now then what is there left for me? This: a new ardour—a
new enthusiasm to take up photography again....Exult with me dear—and
do not fear for me—I am not afraid—nor worried—."

Yet when she took personal inventory three months later, Tina had to
face an enormously disturbing fact: Despite her resolve, despite freedom
from domestic tasks, despite a keenly appreciative circle of friends, her creative output had slowed to a trickle. One of the few noncommercial images
to exit her darkroom that spring—a still life of the cactuslike *flor de manita*,
resembling a desperately clutching claw—reads like an emblem of her distress. Struggling to understand the powerful undertow carrying her away
from the artistic ground she had gained, Tina yoked the problem to
woman's essential nature:

> I have not been very "creative" Edward as you can see—less
> than a print a month. That is terrible! And yet it is not lack of inter-
> est as much as lack of discipline and power of execution. I am con-
> vinced *now* that as far as creation is concerned (outside the creation
> of species) women are negative— They are too petty and lack
> power of concentration and the faculty to be wholly absorbed by
> *one thing.*
>
> Is this too rash a statement? Perhaps it is, if so I humbly beg
> women's pardon—I have the unpardonable habit of always gener-

alizing an opinion obtained mainly from an analization of *just* my personal self—And speaking of my "personal self": I cannot—as you once proposed to me "solve the problem of life by losing myself in the problem of art"— Not only I cannot do that but I even feel that the problem of life hinders my problem of art.

Now what is this "my problem of life?" It is chiefly: an effort to detach myself from life so as to be able to devote myself completely to art—.

And here I know exactly that you will answer: "*Art* cannot exist without *life*"—Yes—I admit but there should be an even balance of both elements while in my case life is always struggling to predominate and art naturally suffers—.

By art I mean creation of any sort— You might say to me then that since the element of life is stronger in me than the element of art I should just resign to it and make the best of it— But I cannot accept life as it is—it is too chaotic—too unconscious—therefore my resistance to it—my combat with it—I am forever struggling to mould life according to my temperament and needs—in other words *I put too much art in my life*—too much energy—and consequently I have not much left to give to art—.

She no doubt had in mind the way she expended her energies on trivialities and the ineptness with which she fended off both friends and strangers who would consume her darkroom hours. She thought of the continual ebb and flow of important relationships and of her protean pattern of embracing and then rejecting communities and ways of life. All wreaked havoc upon her capacity for sustained creativity.

More insidiously, Tina's inability to "solve the problem of life" by "losing [herself] in the problem of art" was perhaps indeed tied to gender. As a man, Edward assumed the right to the sacred fire of creative work, while Tina, during the years when one powerful and exquisite photograph after another issued from her darkroom, wrote self-deprecatingly of being "impotent" and "distracted," of her "wasted" and "futile" efforts, of having "the nerve" to take pictures of the same building Edward had once photographed, of her failure to make "full use" of the medium's potential for expression. Vowing to lock photography into her life and calling it "this precious work," she nonetheless doubted her worthiness for a vocation she so greatly esteemed. Gauging her own artistic practice by Edward's and judging herself inadequate, she demonstrated to what extent she had internalized the attitudes of a society whose artistic models were masculine and which assigned to the male Prometheus the role of audacious usurper of the sacred fire. Tina Modotti the artist was, of necessity, shaped and limited by the spaces that Tina Modotti the woman was made to occupy.

Tina struggled mightily against photography's friability in her hands, and her imagery itself was to give primacy to the theme of work. Rarely did she portray people at leisure, concentrating instead on grinding, scrubbing, hawking, and hauling wage earners and sometimes artists and intellectuals setting hands to their tasks. Edward Weston checks his camera, folklorist Frances Toor peers over a typewriter, and muralist José Clemente Orozco pushes pigment into wet plaster.

To make matters more perplexing, Tina had begun to act upon her staunch antifascism, and political work became another obstacle planted before her darkroom door. Compelled by moral obligation, nagged by childhood memories, and intuiting that not to respond to events in Italy would be tantamount to relinquishing some part of her Italianness, Tina plunged into a lifelong battle to rescue the land of the freedom fighter Garibaldi from the despot Mussolini. She had a hand in translating, from Italian, *El Machete*'s sudden crop of antifascist articles and helped plan a fall protest against the Mexican port call of the goodwill ship *Italia*. Most significant, she pulled together a handful of progressive Italian expatriates to form the Anti-Fascist League of Mexico.

"[I am an antifascist] because I am an enemy of tyrannies," she would declare. "But especially of the one which reigns in my country where the humble people are experiencing deplorable conditions. I believe that one should work for the progress of that humble class and its attainment of a better place in life." The thought of the triumphant trample of Benito Mussolini's Blackshirts installed itself within her like a tumor. In the mid-1930s, after a decade of doing battle with her intractable enemy, Tina was to assert, "My life is practically destroyed by fascism. I have no country...." She never saw the demise of Mussolini, who would cruelly outlive her by three years.

An intriguer and ex-socialist, the inventor of Italian fascism had exploited his country's postwar tensions to lash ragtag malcontents into a frenetically patriotic party a quarter of a million strong. In their 1922 march on Rome, the Fascisti had muscled past Italy's weak-willed king to hoist Mussolini into the prime minister's chair. Heads swollen with power and pockets bulging with lire easily swapped for bombs and machine guns, squads of black-shirted thugs embarked upon bloody leftist-bashing sprees. Communists, socialists, and anarchists grabbed arms of their own, and violent street skirmishes erupted. A narrow victor in Italy's 1924 election, Mussolini bent the nation's institutions to his will. Thank God, Tina must have been thinking, Giuseppe Modotti had not lived to see such dogs swagger through the streets of Udine.

While the Right settled into power in Italy, Mexico City, by contrast, buzzed with the promise of revolution from the radical Left. The next in the nation's string of political and social convulsions was hastened, many believed, by the Obregón administration's diplomatic recognition of the Soviet Union. "The lungs of Russia/ breathe in our direction/ the wind of social revolution," enthused Estridentista poet Manuel Maples Arce.

Taking up residence at the new Rhin Street embassy, Soviet envoy Stanislav Pestkovsky shunned stuffy receiving-line receptions in favor of lively soirees where tuxedoed diplomats rubbed elbows with workers in overalls. Quickly an habitué of these parties, Tina commemorated them with clubby group portraits. She portrayed the jaunty, unconventional ambassador in a Vandyke beard, Stetson hat, and look of crinkly-eyed amusement.

Tina had already befriended Pestkovsky's decoding clerk and trusted woman Friday, Ella Wolfe. Russian-born and Brooklyn-raised, Ella was no dour apparatchik, but, rather, breezy, charming, and opinionated. While still an adolescent, she had married lank, push broom–mustached Bertram Wolfe, and the pair became stalwarts of the U.S. Communist party. The Red scare roundup had sent them underground in Boston, but they resurfaced in Mexico City, where Bert worked with the Mexican Communist party on the Comintern's behalf. Meanwhile, they had become regulars at the Saturday nights, where Ella once served borscht and both raved about Soviet Russia.

With Pestkovsky, the Wolfes boosted Mexican communism, Bert cajoling fractious comrades into mending their ways while the ambassador brokered connections and put up the pesos. On May Day 1925, *El Machete* was designated the official Communist organ. Around the same time, with Ella handling behind-the-scenes arrangements, International Red Aid set up shop in Mexico.

A worldwide organization launched by the Communist International, Red Aid was sometimes glibly tagged the "Communist Red Cross," though it took no hand in natural disasters. Instead, the group ministered to victims of "bourgeois injustice," or "white terror," in its favorite catchphrase. Legal, political, material, and moral support were in Red Aid's purview, everything from establishing orphanages, to deploying lawyers in prisons, to doling out tortillas, beans, and next month's rent to striking workers. In its heyday, the organization would boast that 14 million people carried its slim red membership book, to which a stamp was pasted each month as dues were paid. Sixty-seven national chapters and hundreds of local circles tended to the unfortunate in grim factory towns from Kraków to Paysandú. Around the world, Red Aid was known by an alphabet soup of acronyms, but the rich Soviet mother chapter, MOPR, so dominated the operation that the terms MOPR and Red Aid were used interchangeably. Though in the mid-1920s Red Aid still seemed a guild of like-minded groups, it was moving swiftly under Soviet control and ever more stridently defended Moscow's interests.

Tina eagerly took out membership in both Red Aid—her most enduring commitment over the next thirteen years—and another Comintern-spawned group, the Anti-Imperialist League of the Americas. Tilting swords with the many-headed monster of U.S. hegemony as well as with the League of Nations, which it branded colonialist, the Anti-Imperialist League attracted a wide swath of intellectuals, artists, syndicalists, socialists, and liberals as well as national liberation leaders of the stature of Jawaharlal Nehru, Léopold Senghor, Socrates Sandino, and Madame Sun Yat-Sen. Probably by virtue of Tina's short speech to the group, the Mexican chapter endorsed the Anti-Fascist League of Mexico.

Tina got busy with political spadework, often toiling shoulder-to-shoulder with Ella. Only weeks later, however, the Mexican government packed off the "pernicious foreigner" Bertram Wolfe, and Ella followed. From "Yanquilandia," the pair kept current on the Mexican situation in a brisk correspondence with Rafael Carrillo, an affable assembly-line worker whose meteoric political career put him in the seat of Communist secretary-general at age twenty-one. As Tina and Rafael developed a fine friendship, he joined in the chorus of males extolling her "truly extraordinary graciousness, so that lots of men, including me, were in love with her, and not because of any flirtatiousness or because she led them on, her graciousness was just a natural thing...."

August found Tina in Guadalajara, a balmy provincial capital stretched out on a high plain northwest of Mexico City. After incoming Minister of Public Education Puig Casauranc nullified most Mexico City mural contracts, a contingent of painters—among them David Alfaro Siqueiros and Xavier Guerrero—had made its way to Guadalajara, where artist-turned-cacique José Guadalupe Zuno was fostering a public-art renaissance. His own contract secure, Diego Rivera had placidly continued painting, refusing to make common cause with outraged colleagues. Already undermined by long-festering feuds, the Syndicate of Revolutionary Painters, Sculptors and Technical Workers collapsed, though its concepts about the role of artists in society survived and flourished.

Guadalajara's sympathetic climate for the arts boded well for the Weston-Modotti exhibition that brought Tina to the city. Thanks to her old friend, artist Carlos Orozco Romero, it had been booked into the Jalisco State Museum and scheduled to coincide with Edward's arrival from California in early September. Dashing from her hotel room to the museum and then to the printer's to iron out problems, Tina nonetheless found spare moments for Siqueiros and Guerrero.

Both beguilingly handsome Communists with revolutionary fire in their bellies, the two men had utterly different personalities. Stony-faced as an idol, Xavier appeared all the more impassive beside the intemperately snapping coil of energy that was David Alfaro Siqueiros. Long of face, with milky skin, curly-lashed emerald eyes, and dark tendrils spilling onto his forehead, David had the look of a lusty, overgrown baby. All his life, he would swing like a pendulum between art making and revolution mongering, and the summer of 1925 was no exception. With the painter Amado de la Cueva, Siqueiros had just decorated a workers' assembly hall with a set of dynamic, ideologically charged compositions of muscular and emphatically Mexican figures. Without bothering to change his paint-smeared overalls and tattered cardigan, he now jumped each morning on a bicycle to charge around exhorting miners and peasants to throw over the sub-servient CROM union for the radical Left's CGT.

One can picture Tina, David, and Xavier in a noisy working-class cantina where the photographer drank in, along with her red wine, the men's accounts of the local proletariat. Miners sweated away their short, disease-blighted lives in dank foreign-owned shafts. Barefoot dirt farmers scratched out a squalid existence as they awaited long-promised land redis-tribution, and workers' assemblies, as often as not, were smashed by federal troops. The bourgeois revolution had done little to dismantle Mexico's feu-dal system, Tina's companions agreed, and the people had yet to throw off their chains.

A week before the museum's doors opened to the Weston-Modotti exhibition, Tina dressed in "a silk blouse with high collar, a wholly mascu-line tie and a narrow skirt of a North American cut" for a hotel-room inter-view with a set of local reporters. Puffing on a Buen Tono cigarette, she offered a miscellany of opinions, ranging from her fondness for Mexican products to her distaste for retouching photographs. Out of frustration with the snail's pace of exhibition preparations, she launched into praise of Mexico's neighbor to the north. "Life in the United States pleases me because I find it perfectly organized. There everyone walks quickly and I don't know how to walk any other way. This is not to say that I don't admire and love the Mexican. You have naturally enchanting things."

Days later, North America arrived in the persons of Edward and his son Brett, tousle-headed, uninhibited, and by his own description, "a darn good looking kid." Brett's exuberance contraposed the chariness Edward and Tina must have felt at resuming their relationship after a separation stretching over the better part of a year. But if their talks lasted far into the night, daylight hours were absorbed by events surrounding the exhibition.

The artists were often on hand in the cheerful stone-floored gallery, natural light percolating through its windows, where, matted but unframed, their photographs hung in tight double rows. Visitors plied them with ques-tions and critics sang their praises, but, except for Zuno's purchase of half a dozen prints, not a sale materialized, and the pair badly needed cash. Feel-ing churlish, they were restored one evening by dinner with Lupe Marín's large, vivacious family, and, another, by María and Carlos Orozco Romero's masquerade party, where they stylishly pulled off their usual stunt of exchanging clothes, and Brett minced around as a golden-curled California beauty queen.

After ten days, the trio continued to Mexico City, where Edward indulged in an orgy of journal writing. Two entries read like red flags waving. One, clearly heavily edited before the *Daybooks'* later publication, evokes Edward idling in the darkroom, his berry brown eyes foggy and distant, at a time when Tina was preoccupied with the *Italia* protest. "I have been sitting on the 'hypo' barrel in the dim green light of my dark-room, reflecting upon the past, pondering over the future..." he wrote. "However, I willed myself in Mexico again—and here I am!"

The second recounts the train trip from Guadalajara to Mexico City:

> Tina insisted on riding second class the journey to Mexico [City]. Brett and I had our first class tickets straight through from L.A., so I bought a berth for Brett,—too cruel to make such a sleepy head sit up all night, I thought, and I spent the night alternating between a watch over my cameras in first class and Tina in second, in the dim light among the Indians, sprawled over each other on the hard seats, dozing or drunken or garrulous.

Tina's act of class solidarity rankled Edward. Repelled by Mexican militants' quasi-religious zeal and believing individualism the stance best suited to the artist, he took a dim view of his companion's newfound activism. She was not the same person to whom he had bid farewell in December, and, if her insistence on sexual freedom was a barrier then, politics put a nearly insurmountable wall between them now. They talked over the matter, but discussions proved pointless and stale. Edward's heart shriveled, yet he was not so emotionally aloof as to be indifferent to Tina's "parade of suitors [who] marched in and out, until my last day in Mexico, keeping me in hot water." He consoled himself by sexually "romping" with their Indian servants.

The couple still collaborated in the darkroom, sometimes sipped morning coffee together, and showed up arm in arm at parties. But Edward no longer photographed Tina, and we can infer that they stopped being lovers. Though she steadfastly offered him friendship and collegiality, he frequently turned snide. Long, leaden silences fell over the relationship, which Tina regarded "with sadness but without drama."

Both turned to photography. Not only strangers but also friends were eagerly stepping in front of Tina's Korona for portraits. Unlike contemporary 35-mm cameras, which lend themselves to spontaneous clicking away, the view camera imposes slow, careful picture taking and fewer opportunities to capture a revealing look or stance. Generally, Tina placed her subjects against plain backgrounds in a soft, even light. She brought to the work not only the eye of a photographer, attentive to the shape and texture of a collar, a wave of hair, a draped scarf, but also that of an actress, finding expression in gesture. Her subjects frequently look away from the camera. For the Estridentista poet Germán List Arzubide, she chose an audacious, dramatic angle. His head is lowered, as if reading, so that the viewer encounters not List Arzubide's eyes but, rather, his whorl of hair and wide forehead, the site of a feverish intelligence. A portrait of Anita Brenner accentuates the contour and torque of the writer's neck and jaw, thus managing to convey her roguish personality. Another Modotti photograph shows a fashionable, well-groomed Anita, eyes shadowed by a felt chapeau and bow tie tilting rakishly.

The deliberateness required by studio assignments suited Tina's photographic temperament. She had no desire to wade into fast-changing situations and capture them on film, and she did not like working with people peering over her shoulder. Requiring a tripod and sheet film, the big Korona lent itself to unhurried composition. But Tina frequently borrowed Edward's three-and-a-quarter-by-four-and-a-quarter-inch Graflex, which could be handheld, and, for various reasons, she was to do a fair amount of work on the street in the course of her photographic career.

She kept the Graflex on hand during rambles with her husky blond Irish-American friend Pablo O'Higgins. At the bustling San Lázaro bus station and in the rutted serape-weaving village of Chiconcuac, she discovered material for her lens. In Alameda Park, the pair would thread its way among open-air stands, a jumble of hand-carved toys, baskets, cotton candy, and masks hawked to the accompaniment of waltzes floating over from Hidalgo Avenue carousels. Tina photographed unflinching urchin vendors, trestle tables bristling with fanciful whittled creatures, and a gaggle of dangling piñata Charlie Chaplins and potbellied cowboys with huge mustaches, but she sometimes judged the results messy and ill-composed.

Tina and Pablo had met one afternoon, months earlier, as Tina squinted through her viewfinder at the Ministry of Public Education. From his scaffolding, Diego did the honors: "Here is Tina, a magnificent photographer." That afternoon, the young man walked Tina home, where he admired her portfolio, made Edward's acquaintance, and discovered, over cups of café con leche, a sympathetic camaraderie.

Born Paul Higgins in Salt Lake City, Pablo was a former child-prodigy pianist, lured to Mexico by Diego Rivera's unexpected reply to a fan letter. Donning sandals and serapes, he refashioned himself as Pablo O'Higgins, Mexican painter and, within a couple of years, creed-bound Communist. He quickly fell in love with Tina, saying "she impressed me immediately as a beautiful woman. I mean beautiful—not trying to be beautiful—but born beautiful." Pablo was "crazy about Tina," confirmed María Jesús O'Higgins, the artist's wife in later years. Yes, said a mutual acquaintance, Pablo "knew [Tina] intimately for many years (they were very much in love)." But there is scant evidence of Tina's romantic feelings, if such existed, about Pablo.

We know that, in their long walks and over cups of tea on the roof of Pablo's shabby colonial-era building near the Zócalo, the two forged an enduring friendship based in art, politics, and music. Perhaps they were intermittent lifelong lovers, more tender than passionate. Lacking machismo, steadfast yet intense, Pablo was to reappear in Tina's life at various times, and, so mutually trusting were they, she invariably found solace in his arms.

The artistic education of Pablo O'Higgins came from working as Diego's assistant for frescoes at Chapingo, the National Agricultural School occupying a bucolic seventeenth-century hacienda east of the capital. Commissioned to decorate the chapel (transformed into an assembly hall), Rivera composed a sensual and awe-inspiring "hymn to the earth," whose theme is the liberation of the land, conceived as a dialectic between natural phenomena and social forces. Dominating the mural program are monumental nudes of *Virgin Earth* and *Liberated Earth*, whose models were Tina and Lupe, respectively.

Posing at Chapingo proved another distraction from photography, but one Tina never regretted. Artist, masons, models, and assistants—dubbed the "Dieguitos," meaning "the little Diegos"—would hop aboard the dilapidated 7:00 A.M. Mexico City-to-Puebla train that rattled to a stop before the school's wrought-iron gates. A pleasant walk took them down a light-splashed cobblestone road, past gurgling fountains and byways with such names as Street of Labor or Avenue of Production, to the Spanish Baroque rectory enclosing the ex-chapel. At dusk, the return train's whistle-stop in nearby Texcoco signaled the moment to grab their belongings and make haste to the front gate.

Chapingo was a hopeful place, enrolling zealous brown-skinned young men from Yecapixtla and Tlacochahuaya, their souls filled with an "immense longing for justice and truth." Graduating as agricultural technicians, they sweated and toiled alongside campesinos, fellow sons of the earth, to coax Mexico's all-important corn from a rugged, sun-baked, cactus-studded soil. The school's spirit of "strict and silent devotion" is captured in Tina's portrait of her friend Pandurang Khankhoje, an Indian agronomist and teacher. Head reverently bowed, he runs his fingers over an ear of corn, the sacred staff of life, catching its sheen from a nearby window.

In Diego's painting *Virgin Earth*, Tina is all pale, voluptuous languor. Her hair trailing across her eyes and gently writhing, rootlike, into the ground, she wraps her hand and body around a tiny phallic plant. She appears again as an anthropomorphic tree, as the embodiment of subterranean forces, and as Earth monopolized by capitalists, priests, and soldiers. Across a sea of wooden pews and down the barrel vault—a Joseph's coat of oxblood red, cream, and cerulean blue—reclines *Liberated Earth*, represented by Lupe, still full-figured in the weeks following the birth of the Riveras' first child.

Tina's stints at Chapingo continued sporadically for more than a year. The project was overwhelmingly ambitious, yet not all was grinding work. Throwing down charcoal, brushes, and sacks of marble dust, letting freshly troweled plaster dry unpainted, the gang occasionally took off for Texcoco or Cuautlalpan to join in fiestas and peasants' assemblies where Tina and Pablo got political edification at Diego's hands.

Tina was in the thick of the Chapingo project as her older sister, Mercedes, arrived from San Francisco for a six-week Mexican holiday. Sweetly smiling, exuding charm and self-control, never less than perfectly put together, Mercedes had steadily risen in the ranks of I. Magnin's sewing workshop. Fifteen years of fitting gowns to society matrons had left her restless, however. Despite numerous affairs, she remained single at thirty-three, and middle age brought hollow hunger for a good marriage. Despite their differing interests—Mercedes cared little for art and ignored politics—the sisters remained easy confidantes.

In Mercedes's honor, Tina arranged outings, dinners, and a party that gave 42 Veracruz Avenue a semblance of the old days and filled two floors with animated babble. One could pick out the familiar voices of Pablo, Jean, Anita, Pepe, Frances, Diego, Lupe, Monna, Rafael, Felipe, Guastaroba, the guitar-strumming Manuel Hernández Galván, and journalist Carleton Beals. Carleton reappeared one raw morning, pulling up in a finagled government limousine, and the foursome visited Chapingo, which Edward deemed "worthy of anyone's pilgrimage and homage" and Carleton christened "the Sistine Chapel of the Americas."

Tina's flattering portrait of Carleton Beals reveals a fresh-faced man, clean-shaven and neatly trimmed (when it suited his purposes), with eyes like searchlights for a keen, excitable intelligence. A radical leftist viscerally opposed to dogma, Carleton was possessed of a magnetic personality that kept him well stocked with contacts, cronies, and women. After college, he had done time behind bars for draft evasion, then meandered down to Mexico and on to Italy, where he made his journalistic reputation by taking the wraps off the growing fascist movement. Back in Mexico City, Carleton functioned like a one-man press service and still found time for madly sowing wild oats.

As a murky late November chill permeated Mexico City, Edward, Carleton, and the Modotti sisters took refuge in the soothing warmth of Cuernavaca, in that day five hours away by slow-chugging train. Mexico City art dealer and businessman Fred Davis had loaned the quartet his villa, its luxuriant pink-walled garden dripping in coral and scarlet bougainvillea. Fred's estate also enclosed an immense palm tree, which, like a prop in some silly bedroom farce, witnessed both Edward's attempts at a perfect nocturnal shot of its smokestacklike trunk and the moonlit trysts of Mercedes and Carleton. "In memory of the warm shadow of a certain palm-tree in the warm south night of Cuernavaca—*notte d'Italia*," Carleton would write in Mercedes's travel diary, and she once reminded him of "an immense palm...a clear and beautiful stream.... And then a night of love and kisses, kisses, kisses."

Though Tina jocularly addressed Carleton as *cognato,* Italian for brother-in-law, she understood him better than did Mercedes and must have tried gently to caution her beloved sibling about what lay ahead. "Dear sister," read Tina's dulcet inscription in the travel diary, "I feel that I love Mexico more now that you have left your memories here." For months after her departure, Mercedes penned cloying, love-struck letters, but she apparently never again saw Carleton, and within weeks, he was also posting billets-doux to Anita Brenner.

After Mercedes's departure, Tina quickly settled down to work, only to be stopped short by a telegram bearing alarming news that her mother was seriously ill. On December 9, she boarded a northbound train for the grueling five-day journey to San Francisco. Arriving in the densest fog of the season, she sought her way through familiar streets to Russian Hill.

Apart from her mother's bad health, Tina found the family doing passably well, though straitened circumstances had pushed them from the bright, airy crow's nest at 901 Union Street to a nondescript building across the intersection. Ben and Beppo were working stiffs with a handsome sulk about them, but the resemblance stopped at that. An upholsterer's apprentice, the retiring Beppo pined for a middle-class American way of life, while Ben, a machinist, embroiled himself ever more deeply in militant politics. That winter's cables from San Francisco's Italian consulate to authorities in Rome branded Ben a member of the antifascist ring Revendication.

Down Union Street lived Tina's dimpled and flirtatious youngest sister, Yolanda, now wed to Guido Gabrielli, a Triestine immigrant. The couple had met after a performance by Guido's sister, a popular Italian-American cantatrice, at the San Francisco Opera. "Girls," advised a local newspaper's account of their nuptials, "always go back stage and meet the stars when you attend grand opera! Because sometimes there's a romance a-lurking in the wings." The marriage, however, was proving joyless, and Tina heard an earful.

Her ten-week visit to California seemed a muddled, irksome episode. Yet the disconcerting self-image it reflected to Tina compelled the photographer to define herself artistically. After Assunta's health was reestablished, Tina made rounds of visits to friends, and these jolted her into realizing how she hungered to be recognized for her images. "You know what they say about a prophet in one's own country," she wrote, venting her frustration to Edward, "well—in a way it works for me too: you see—this might be called my home town—well of all the old friends and acquaintances not *one* takes me seriously as a photographer—not one has asked me to show my work...." Ex-Californian Frances Toor was also visiting from Mexico City, and the pair socialized over dinners in San Francisco and Berkeley. Frances had never known Tina as anything but a photographer, and the contrast between her attitudes and those of Tina's San Francisco friends gave rise to Tina's insight that her roots in California were shallower, and those in Mexico deeper, than she had assumed.

Most gratifying were Tina's encounters with a seemingly charmed circle of photographers to whom she had connections through Edward. "No detailed comments now on all these lovely people whose acquaintance I owe to you," she wrote him; "when we get together we will talk of them—." One was Dorothea Lange, later famous for her searing portrayals of victims of the Great Depression, but, in the mid-1920s, a shrewd commercial photographer making lovely, if prescriptive, portraits of wealthy San Franciscans. At Dorothea's flower-covered Russian Hill cottage, not far from the Modotti home, the two photographers talked and shared their work. Lange took a fancy to the visitor, apparently dropping the usual fee for use of her Union Street studio and darkroom. Little but frustration ensued from Tina's use of the facility, however. Her sitter, the youngest sister of milliner Alice Rohrer, dragged in an hour late to plop herself in front of the camera, wearing a "wooden expression...spoiled and conceited," while another photographer chum of Dorothea's monopolized the darkroom. "[T]he other photographer was there—*all day long*—developing, printing, spotting," Tina confided to Edward, "—you know how nervous I get working with people around."

The lively redheaded photographer Imogen Cunningham and her husband, printmaker Roi Partridge, were also dear friends of Edward's. But, with "things...very chaotic and difficult," Tina may have renounced the idea of a trek to their Oakland home. She nonetheless arranged for Partridge to collect from Lange her photograph of wineglasses as a donation to the Mills College art gallery, which he directed.

Closer to home lived Consuelo Kanaga, a master printer who earned her livelihood from portraiture and photojournalism. Kanaga's recent work caught the effect of her encounters with denizens of San Francisco's richly ethnic neighborhoods. Belying her timidity and professional uncertainties, she generously organized for collectors and colleagues an evening viewing of Modotti's images at her 1371 Post Street studio. Meanwhile, a photographer named Dan was helping Tina comb camera shops for the Graflex she now considered vital to the evolution of her vision. "I am going to work hard when I return to M[exico] and differently—if I can get a Graflex," Tina vowed to Edward in a rare written comment about her image-making practices. "I have always been too restrained in my work *as you well know*— but I feel now that with a Graflex I will be able to loosen up...."

Financially strapped as usual, Tina reluctantly traded in her four-by-five-inch Korona to pay for a single-lens reflex Graflex outfitted with a tall black plush viewfinder and holder for three-and-a-quarter-by-four-and-a-quarter-inch sheet film. Though unwieldy to contemporary hands and sorely lacking a neck strap, the Graflex allowed Tina to dispense with a tripod, and, in this difference from the Korona, she saw possibilities of more free-spirited work. She tried out the new camera with a clutch of family portraits taken on the roof of 890 Union Street, then departed San Francisco for the Richey home.

Los Angeles brought more photographic frustrations (a proposed exhibition in Japantown never materialized) and more memories roused. A week after her arrival, she carried out a symbolic act of transformation, with Tina Modotti, photographer, conducting last rites for bohemia's Madame de Richey. Her gesture bespoke the ebb and flow of tides within her, one "possibility of being" (as she liked to say) ceding place to another, a vestigial self sloughed as a stronger, truer Tina emerged.

> I have been all morning looking over old things of mine here in trunks— Destroyed much— It is painful at times but: "Blessed be nothing." From now on all my possessions are to be just in relation to photography—the rest—even things I love, concrete things—I shall lead through a metamorphosis—from the concrete turn them into abstract things—as far as I am concerned—and thus I can go on owning them in my heart forever.

Back in Mexico City, Tina and Edward watched the annual May Day demonstration from Pablo O'Higgins's roof, where Tina put into practice her new ideas about picture making. Hand-holding the Graflex, she shot down onto a streaming throng of campesinos, their tilting sombreros and varied shirts creating a pulsing overall pattern. Figures jostle and surge as if the four sides of the photograph will not long contain them. In *Workers Parade,* Modotti has put multitudinous humanity under a microscope to discover a powerful solidarity of class. Pivotal in the photographer's career, the image conjoined her formal and social concerns, pointing the way to a forceful vision utterly her own.

Recognizing its eloquence, Frances Toor featured *Workers Parade* in a late summer issue of *Mexican Folkways,* the bilingual magazine she had launched to spotlight the "creative spirit" of indigenous Mexico. Drawing upon a stellar roster of contributors—the likes of Jean Charlot, Carleton Beals, Monna Alfau, Diego Rivera, Pablo O'Higgins, José Clemente Orozco, and Tina Modotti—*Mexican Folkways* served up essays, photographs, drawings, poetry, and lyrics of popular ballads and argued that the quintessence of Mexicanness resided in the nation's indigenous cultures. In seven years of publication, *Mexican Folkways* would express (ironically, under the editorship of a foreigner) one vision of what it meant to be Mexican.

From the inaugural issue, advertisements for "PHOTOGRAPHS EDWARD WESTON–TINA MODOTTI—Av. Veracruz 42—Tel. Ericsson, Condesa 38" appeared regularly in *Mexican Folkways.* The publicity was no doubt good business, but also an expression of Tina's friendship for Frances. Sociable and blunt, given to bouts of pedantry but relishing a good off-color joke, Frances Toor had come to Mexico a Berkeley-trained anthropologist on a summer teaching stint. Quickly falling in love with the country and its people, she disencumbered herself of a dentist husband and settled in. A squat figure in khakis and boots, Frances enjoyed nothing more than hoisting herself into the saddle to scour the Mexican hinterland for the vernacular art objects she and her circle adored. Back in the city, she would hunker down at her Underwood, full lips pursed, thick glasses perched upon her round nose, to pound out texts on the art, food, music, and dress of the Mexican Indian.

Frances's friendship was all the more precious to Tina given the inevitability of Edward's parting. Although the thought of being alone was laced with financial as well as emotional anxieties, Tina never accepted offers, which must have been made, to set herself up as some richling's wife or mistress. By May, her separation from Edward looked imminent—one lucrative portrait commission remained for him to complete—until an assignment from Anita Brenner stayed his departure. Contract in hand for what became her best-seller, *Idols Behind Altars,* Anita hired Edward to make two hundred reproductions (seventy were eventually used) of objects and architecture at sites around Mexico. Illustrations for a "spiritual inventory of what Mexican life was and is," the photographs comprised images of carved polychrome Madonnas, colonial-era ex-votos, painted calabashes, Catholic altars, Jaliscan pottery, *petate*-lined huts, saddlery, carved chairs, and reproductions of paintings by Francisco Goitia, Diego Rivera, Jean Charlot, and José Clemente Orozco.

Straightaway, Edward requested help from the delighted Tina, and, on the morning of June 3, accompanied by Brett and trailing suitcases, cameras, tripods, and the teenager's butterfly nets, they left Mexico City to begin the job. Skirting craggy-peaked volcanoes, they bussed southward on one of the few roads that torrential rains had not churned into mud.

"Have you read about the terrible floods in Mexico?" Tina inquired in a letter to the Richeys.

> All over the country, including in the capital, it has rained heavily this year and in some parts it was so bad that whole towns have been washed out— For our traveling it is bad also because there are little towns without railroad and the only way to get to them would be in automobiles but the roads are so bad that it makes it impossible. We have gone at times on horse back but we have so many cameras and suitcases which makes horse back riding difficult— It is necessary to engage an extra horse and man to carry cameras and it makes it very expensive. But no matter which way we go it is pleasant and interesting.... How Robo would enjoy traveling around Mexico. I think so often of him.

Even more worrisome than travel conditions was the six-month-old Cristero revolt, which had erupted when the Calles administration abruptly enforced anticlerical clauses in the 1917 constitution. The church, in effect, went on strike, with priests black-marketing Masses and cathedrals disgorging rioting zealots. Soldiers raped nuns and sacked chapels while campesinos shouted *"¡Viva Cristo Rey!"* as they hacked to death "atheistic" schoolteachers. Eighty thousand Mexicans would die in the brutal conflict. It was hardly the ideal moment for foreigners to roam the countryside taking pictures in churches. Edward and Brett doffed their hats at every shrine, while Tina kissed "the greasy hands of lecherous priests" and demonstrated such "tact and sympathy for the Indians" that the threesome escaped with nothing more than tongue-lashings and threats.

Anita's assignment called for two months of travel beginning in Puebla, a devout city tightly packed with overwrought cathedrals and austere convents. The photographers set up tripods one day at José Luis Bello's palatial home, a cabinet of curiosities where busts of Napoléon shared tabletops with Guerreran devil masks. Another morning found them in the nearby villages of San Francisco Acatepec and Tonantzintla, whose churches dazzled with a brightly hued profusion of scampering putti, fat-cheeked martyrs, birds, flowers, and vegetables, imagery nominally Catholic but hardly familiar to the Vatican. That was Anita's point precisely: Mexican culture was syncretic, with an Indian idol lurking behind every Catholic altar, a mother goddess inside every Madonna.

From Puebla, the trio dropped south into the semitropical, pistachio-colored city of Oaxaca where, under watchful Zapotec and Trique eyes, they photographed black Coyotepec pottery and the Virgin de la Soledad in her hefty gold crown. Finishing in town, they sweltered by country bus and horseback to the intricately mosaicked ruins at Mitla, a grand roofless Dominican monastery at Cuilapan, and the market towns dotting endless valleys ringed by stormy blue mountains.

Their Herculean task occupied nearly all of the couple's waking hours. As shadows lengthened, they would close their cameras, pausing for *mole oaxaqueño* or enchiladas washed down with beer before returning to the pleasant downtown Hotel Francia. Throwing blankets over the curtain rods, setting out trays and filling Edward's rubber raincoat with hypo, they would improvise a darkroom, developing films that they washed in the fountain of the open-air patio, fragrant with night-blooming jasmine and canopied with stars.

Tina and Edward generally kept up a good-natured relationship during the *Idols Behind Altars* expedition, though one letter from Edward to

Johan, postmarked Oaxaca, spewed out a vituperous attack on intelligent, independent women. Nonetheless, the photographers' personal work reveals two utterly different mind-sets and two Mexicos. Edward's is exquisitely textured, largely unpeopled, and aestheticizing, while Tina's shows a place of vibrant, active, closely knit Indian communities. Turning her back on photographic traditions that viewed Indians as specimens to be cataloged or as accessories to a bucolic landscape, she took a keen interest in how indigenous Mexico dressed and worked, what it created, and how it lived.

Her approach was informed by *indigenismo*, which one intellectual defined as a "willingness to [see the Indian as]...a rock upon which the future civilization and culture of Mexico has to be built." The idea that indigenous peoples were the quintessential Mexicans had gained currency among many artists and intellectuals, and Tina's warmly sympathetic approach bore a strong resemblance to that of Diego and other Mexican painters who were her contemporaries. Inevitably, her imagery and theirs intersected. In both Modotti photographs and Rivera murals, one sees *cargadores* bent double under their loads, men wearing traditional palm-fiber raincoats, and the intricate patterns of rural markets.

Back in Mexico City in July, Tina and Edward closeted themselves for ten days of printing before departing to the rustic western state of Michoacán. They found the first stop, Pátzcuaro, to be a charming lakeside jumble of red-roofed houses, cobbled byways, and beached canoes. "[W]e are quite *crazy* about Pátzcuaro!" Edward reported to Anita. The village was fertile photographic ground, as well. Prowling the market, Tina made images which reveal the intensity of her encounter with rural, indigenous Mexico. She depicted Purépechan women wearing finely patterned rebozos, homespun pleated skirts, and wide sashes. In the glint between two storms, she caught sombreroed Indian fishermen mending nets stretched up to dry. Charmed to be serenaded by roving music makers, she made their portrait, which she captioned, "Young musicians of a village band—mostly all Indians—barefooted but oh how they can play!"

Following the gaze of hundreds of astonished dark eyes, the trio found folklore of another kind. The monocled René d'Harnoncourt, his six-and-a-half-foot frame bedecked in plaid knickers and spats, had come to town on a buying trip for Fred Davis's Mexico City shop. Years later, d'Harnoncourt would direct New York's Museum of Modern Art, but, in the mid-1920s, the impoverished Viennese-born count had just landed in Mexico, where he survived on catchpenny jobs. The gringos spent their evenings together, René chatting in fractured English and booming out renditions of Austrian folk songs and the "Marseillaise" as his companions developed films.

Days later, in the shudder and sway of the descent to Uruapan, "Tina gave a horrified 'O!'—then she was speechless...." She had glimpsed a headline announcing the funeral of their old friend Manuel Hernández Galván. A politician and general (both hazardous professions in 1920s Mexico), Manuel had been gunned down by a rival as he fraternized in a Mexico City tavern. The death of the virile charmer with whom she had probably known a brief intimacy stung Tina with its cruel capriciousness. Hernández Galván had been in the midst of a reelection campaign, and he now stared at them everywhere from a chlorine green poster, savagely soaked and flayed by unrelenting rain.

By the time the threesome reached Guanajuato, Manuel's hometown, where they had planned to dine with him, Edward was in the foulest of moods. "Rain fell every day of our stay in Guanajuato," he growled to his *Daybook*. "I recall mines, mummies and a dismal, reeking landscape.... My love for Mexico turned to something near to hate." Tina photographed a typically steep staircased street and ramshackle houses clinging to the sides of a rock-strewn arroyo, but Edward had no stomach for photography. In what resembled an antique birdcage, the couple descended the shaft of a silver mine, alighting two thousand feet under the earth, to find a little shrine adorned with crystals. Edward's *Daybook* quoted their guide: "'The miners sing hymns as they descend to work...and one slipped off the other day. He made a nasty mess.'" Mexico, Tina knew, was the saddest as well as the most joyful place on earth.

Edward tied up the project's loose ends in Mexico City that fall, and, on November 6, Anita scrawled in her diary, "Weston *fini!*" Meanwhile, Tina continued to photograph in her looser, less rarefied style. Taking her subjects from the life stream of Mexico, she cast an especially sympathetic and respectful eye upon working-class women. Some kneel at metate stones to clap-clap tortillas, while others, wreathed in children, hunch over washboards and tubs. A braid-wearing girl of humble origins sits writing in one image that conjures up Mexico's quasi-evangelical campaign to eliminate illiteracy, as well as the provocative notion of education for working-class females.

Probably in a wistful mood, since her desire for a child never dimmed, Tina made a series of photographs of Luz Jiménez, the Salas' cook, and her baby daughter, Conchita. A dignified woman of broad, flat face, long braids, and smooth, chunky body, Luz was a favorite model among painters. Their images often emphasize her sculptural qualities, while Tina's evoke the tender bond between mother and child as well as the materiality of sun-warmed skin, silky baby hair, and cottony fabric.

A photograph of Conchita suckling at Luz's breast was among Tina's contributions to the big "Exhibition of Modern Mexican Art," where it drew raves from critics and casual viewers alike. Edward also participated in the show, but his mind was elsewhere. During his last weeks in Mexico, he attempted to seduce Mary Louis Doherty, a pretty, good-natured Iowan who taught English to Indian children, but Mary rebuffed him on grounds of his relationship with Tina. "More kisses and embraces in the dark-room," read Edward's account of the rejection. "'But this must end, Edward. We have all believed in the legend of Edward and Tina, you are leaving now, and I want to still believe. It was a beautiful picture.' 'But I insist, M. darling, that I have no one else, not by the farthest stretch of imagination!' M. would not surrender her fabulous picture."

The strain between Tina and Edward must have eased when Tina found a picture postcard of a bullfight addressed in Edward's hand to "Srta. Tina Modotti, 7 Calle Dolorosa, Mexico, D.F." No street in Mexico City bears the name Dolorosa, signifying "painful" or, colloquially, "an account to be settled." Perhaps Tina was simply staying for a few days at Carleton Beals's rooming house on Dolores Street and Edward misaddressed the card, for his Spanish seemed incapable of subtle poetic allusion. His message, however, was heartrending. "Dearest Tina," he had written, "The leaving of Mexico will be most remembered for the leaving of you. Thank you for your love[,] Edward."

But intransigence had become a habit between them. The next Saturday, they were sitting stiffly side by side in a cab speeding down the Paseo de la Reforma toward the train station when Edward darted a glance in Tina's direction. Seeing her velvety eyes welling with tears, he sought her lips for a lingering final kiss. The day after she saw his train pull out, Tina sat packing in the eerily silent, half-naked, half-cluttered house. She slid a volume from among those remaining on the bookshelf, leafed through its pages, and paused before setting pen to paper. Nietzsche's expression of "man's comprehensiveness and multiplicity, his wholeness in manifoldness" swam between the lines before her eyes:

> ...I want to write you at length Edward—but not now—I cannot see now—. You know that poem of Ezra Pound on page 172— You are *that* to me Edward— No matter what others mean to me *you* are *that*—only you were embittered and had lost faith in me—but I never did because I respect the manyfold possibilities of being found in all of us and because I accept the tragic conflict between life which continually changes and form which fixes it immutable....

The anthology *Modern American and British Poetry* lay open to Ezra Pound's *Canto LXXXI:*

> *What thou lovest well remains,*
> > *the rest is dross*
> *What thou lov'st well shall not be reft from thee*
> *What thou lov'st well is thy true heritage*
> *Whose world, or mine or theirs*
> > *or is it of none?*

Tina flipped the book shut and thrust it into a box.

Mexico City (1927–1928)

B Y JANUARY 1927, Tina was settled in a redbrick apartment house angling off Abraham González Street at its intersection with Atenas. Sagging and tilting under the weight of its years, the Zamora Building was not much to behold, but it was conveniently located, fifteen minutes from the city's center, in a pleasant neighborhood of family-run greengroceries, car-repair shops, and middle-class flats. Most important to Tina, the building was also home and office to Frances Toor, her closest friend and confidante.

Deposited on the fifth floor by a creaky elevator, visitors entered Tina's apartment, to fall under the charm of an unpretentious, light-soaked living room. Its focus was a table, circled by attractive black-and-gold hard-backed chairs. Over a meal or a stack of papers, one could glance up to arched French windows, their balcony encumbered with potted plants silhouetted against a vast patchwork of rooftops. Arrayed around the freshly painted white room were a chest of tiny drawers, a bookcase, a couch (propped with bricks to adjust for the building's slope), and Tina's cumbersome steamer trunk. Gifts from friends gradually found their places: a delicate inlaid box, her portrait drawn by Diego, Vocio's quilt, and photographer Manuel Alvarez Bravo's small black-and-white print of a lichen-covered rock.

The apartment also included a pocket-sized kitchen, guest room, bath, and Tina's room, crowded with a bed, typewriter table, and dresser, where stood Edward's portrait of her mother. On the *azotea*, she converted a windowless servant's chamber into a darkroom stocked with trays, printing frames, lamps, scissors, tongs, measuring cups, brown glass jugs for chemicals, and rolls of paper in gunmetal tubes. "Her studio was always in simple good order," recalled writer Emily Edwards, "and this easy efficiency was in whatever she was doing."

Both financial necessity and emotional refuge, hard work left the photographer few idle moments in the months that followed. By stepping into the shoes of the ailing José María Lupercio as documentarian of Diego Rivera's murals, she brought in a heftier income than with portraiture alone. In March, she dashed off a breathless note to Edward: "Lately I have been oh so busy with copies—Sunday worked again at the Segretaria—more fragments of new frescos. Diego is so enthusiastic about my copies that he would like me to even repeat the ones Lupercio has done already—too big a job however, I said no—shall send you some copies by and by—."

Painting from the ground up, Diego had arrived at the third floor of the Ministry of Public Education, where he was mythicizing the revolution in a series of richly anecdotal panels teeming with figures. Overhung by low porticos and swept by bands of light and shade, the frescoes rimmed doorways and elevators, flanked a long staircase, and extended down a murky corridor. At times, Tina maneuvered her tripod in close. Other times, she pulled back to make images revealing how painting and architecture were wed. Plagued by curious rubberneckers—Diego on his scaffolding had become a popular Mexico City tourist attraction—she dodged crowds by working on Sundays or, if all else failed, diving under the black focusing cloth.

In April, Tina printed several hundred-image sets of mural photos, mailing one to Edward and dropping off others for sale at Aztec Land and the Sonora News Company. She also turned her camera toward frescoes by Máximo Pacheco and José Clemente Orozco. A twenty-two-year-old Indian painter, once Diego's assistant, Máximo was immersed in his first mural, commissioned for a remote suburban school. Tina recorded it as something of a labor of love, refusing to accept a centavo from the artist and never seeing much cash from print sales. The Orozcos, on the other hand, were ordered and paid for by Anita Brenner (who later seethed over Tina's "black betrayal" when the photographer offered the set to another writer, who published it in *Studio* magazine). A dark-complexioned man, myopic and withdrawn, Orozco sneered at his archrival Rivera and refused to glorify the Mexican Indian on grounds that racial thinking was divisive. His famous caricatures were pure acid, and the murals Tina photographed revealed a dynamic, tormented vision of religion, mythology, and revolution.

Stamped "Tina Modotti-Fotografia," Tina's reproductions found all kinds of uses. From California, insurance executive Albert Bender paid fifty cents apiece for fifty, which he donated to the San Francisco Museum of Art. Meanwhile, Tina's neighbor B. Traven, a peripatetic adventurer and writer (best known for his novel *The Treasure of the Sierra Madre*), called for a steady stream of the prints, which he envisaged as stills in a documentary film about the Mexican Revolution. Journalist Ernestine Evans came to town to cull illustrations for her monograph on Diego Rivera, while Alma Reed, a cultural promoter taking Orozco's career in hand, played with the idea of exhibiting prints in the offices of New York's top architects, who might award commissions to the painter. Rivera packed a set of Tina's reproductions when he traveled to Moscow, so that he could show his work to Alfred H. Barr, soon to take the helm of New York's Museum of Modern Art. By definition, frescoes cannot travel, and aficionados unable to journey to Mexico City experienced the mural phenomenon through Tina Modotti's virtuoso documentation.

Laid low by influenza, Tina nonetheless dragged herself to the annual May Day demonstration, which she viewed from a balcony of the National Palace (a privilege she perhaps owed to Diego), photographing wave after wave of marchers inundating the immense plaza below. In the weeks that followed, as unseasonably torrid weather gripped Mexico City, she charged back into the darkroom, where an "avalanche of work" engulfed her. Reassuring Edward that her health was *"very good now,"* she admitted she had

> undertaken too much lately and I never have a minute to myself—
> it would keep me sufficiently occupied just to print the frescos of
> Diego—I sell quite a lot of copies—but beside that I have
> promised the Cuetos copies of their things—then more new frescos of Orozco for Anita—then some portraits—Lola Cueto's—the

german's—and again I had to do Frances—it was after all simpler
to do her over than to have her get after me all the time—.

Generous, congenial souls, Tina and Frances beat a well-worn path
back and forth across the Zamora Building's fifth-floor hallway. Frances
cared for Tina during her convalescence, and Tina, ever thoughtful, showered her friend with attentions, from one of Vocio's handmade handkerchiefs to an ever-sympathetic ear. Frances's days were usually monopolized
by *Folkways,* for which Tina made dozens of photographs, some published
as art and others illustrating articles on bread making in Janitzio, Judas
piñatas, or Mexican masks. She also faithfully advertised her mural prints
in the publication (using lists whose sequencing, she confessed to a client,
was "rather mixed up...since the numbering was done at different times
much confusion was aroused"). With an editorial nod to her burgeoning
artistic reputation, Frances designated Tina a contributing editor. Self-
conscious about her meager education, Tina assumed the honorific with
quiet satisfaction.

Rising at seven for morning coffee, followed by a workday during
which she more or less successfully fended off intrusions, Tina was back in
her living room around five, reviving herself with a cup of tea or glass of
red wine and a smoke. A knock on the front door might bring artistic col-
laborators such as poet Germán List Arzubide (who thanked Tina in print
for her gracious assistance with his fledgling magazine *Horizonte*) or painter
Gabriel Fernández Ledesma, editor of the highly respected art journal
Forma. Years later, Fernández Ledesma told of one quiet afternoon conversation suspended when an organ-grinder's mellifluous air distinguished
itself from the low drone of the city. Tina rushed to fling open a window,
and, as the whimsical tune swelled louder, he sensed a wave of relaxation
and well-being breaking over her.

Late afternoons also brought Frances, Anita, Carleton, Mary Doherty,
Xavier Guerrero, bearing gossip, the latest issue of *New Masses,* or an out-
of-town visitor. Tina sometimes pulled out a stack of recent Westons as
convivial chatter in English and Spanish bounced around the room. "One
eats spicy meals and drinks excellent beer and everyone lingers to tell stories," reported a gringo visitor who socialized in Tina's circles. As evening

settled in, Tina might depart for an Anti-Imperialist League rally, dine with a friend on inexpensive rice and eggs at a Chinese restaurant, or make an appearance at a party. "*¡Ay, Tinita!*" someone would sing out as the door opened and she began rounds of greetings and *abrazos*. Sporadically, she resurrected her own *tertulias* on Friday evenings, sometimes slipping into the bedroom, exhausted, at ten o'clock, leaving guests to their revelries.

A snapshot by writer Abe Plenn registers the Tina her friends knew. Braced against a wall, hands thrust deep into her pockets, she throws the photographer a look mingling amusement, patience, curiosity, and weariness. At thirty, Tina's face has filled out and matured, but the most striking changes to her appearance are self-imposed. She sports her favorite darkroom garb, baggy coveralls cinched with a rough leather belt, and a no-nonsense coif with nary a wandering strand. The old soignée Tina still materialized occasionally. Introduced to the photographer at a reception in late 1926, writer and educator Adelina Zendejas mistook her for "a woman of the high aristocracy because she was of…an extreme elegance…."

Tina's self-assured mien belies her own sketchy emotional self-portrait from this period. "I am always so nervous and lack…serenity of mind," she confessed to Edward. Reaching into a deep reservoir of strength, she refashioned a purposeful life, and it was perhaps to that effort she referred when she later cryptically mentioned the "work she had to undertake to form her personality." Yet anxiety took its toll on her spontaneity and high spirits. Militant Juan de la Cabada, later a distinguished writer, came away from their first encounter with the impression of an animated but not entirely happy woman. "She was vital, not joyful but vital," he remembered, adding, in the dazzled manner of so many, "She came across as an angel, came across as light." "At that time in Mexico City there were people more beautiful than Tina Modotti," said another, "but her beauty was different. It was an inner beauty that gave her a magnificent presence."

Many were unaware of Tina's gnawing sorrow over the loss of Edward. The pair's incompatibility notwithstanding, she thus tallied her emotions in the first year without him: "I suffered much…even knowing that our separation was definite." She made assiduous efforts to stay in touch, exchanging letters, photographs, books, and sentimentalities. "To keep in contact with you means so much to me Edward—" she wrote that spring. And, two years later: "Oh Edward, for a few moments to be near you..." "Tina dear," he responded to one outpouring of appreciation, "if I have been an important factor in your life, you have certainly been in mine. What you have given me in beauty and fineness is a permanent part of me, and goes with me no matter where life leads."

Edward would have delighted in the anecdote with which Tina regaled a handful of friends one evening. At Chapingo, she reported, some of the "Dieguitos" had plunked down trowels and buckets, refusing to pick them up again for fear of being possessed. Diego had dozed off, rolled from his scaffolding (pushed by demonic forces, in some opinions), and was knocked unconscious for several minutes. His entourage feared the artist dead, and several alleged to have encountered his ghost. Tina spun her tale apparently unaware of its denouement. According to Diego's biographer, Bertram Wolfe:

> In the middle of the day he was brought back from Chapingo, carried by three men, when Lupe was at her dinner. She was infuriated by his prolonged absences—he had not been home the night before at all—and attributed them to his new Italian model. When the men told her that Diego had fallen from the scaffold she answered, "Throw him on the couch in the corner. I'll tend to him when I have finished my dinner." It was not until one of the men fetched a doctor, who declared that Diego's skull was cracked, that she really paid any attention. The matter became a scandal throughout the city....

Laying claim to the titles of favorite model and wife of Mexico's renowned painter, the high-strung Lupe was doubly roused to fury by the season's juiciest tidbit—that Diego and Tina were in the throes of an impassioned affair. Tied down by pregnancy and a young daughter, Lupe lacked even a decent audience for savaging her rival. To Tina, she spit out a venomous, accusatory letter, which the photographer must have countered with her (and Diego's) version of the situation. "Tina is [Diego's] little megaphone, I scarcely doubt," snipped Anita.

Lupe's allegations and persistent innuendo are the only clues that the affair transpired. All the same, work threw Tina and Diego together constantly, their mutual fondness was obvious, and both had eyebrow-raising reputations. Moreover, Diego stood in the thick of the politics of the radical Left, speaking commandingly, if sometimes fancifully, of issues very much on Tina's mind.

To Diego, nothing would have been more natural than physically consummating his visual love affair with a splendid nude model. Next to painting, he most adored beautiful women, and, curiously, they usually counted the artist's elephantine size and odd froglike countenance among his notoriously seductive charms. And Tina, at an emotional loss over Edward's departure, may have turned for solace to the other artistic "genius" in her life, who, like Edward, had paid her the supreme compliment of "immortal portraits," destined for a place in art history.

Neither Tina nor Diego fell in love with the other, and, if they indulged in trysts, these were episodes in a long, vital friendship. Nothing could mollify Lupe, however, and the alleged affair tipped the already-rocky Rivera marriage. In September, Diego steamed off to the Soviet Union for the Bolshevik revolution's tenth-anniversary festivities, returning in spring to find Lupe living with another man.

Meanwhile, Xavier Guerrero was appearing ever more frequently at Abraham González Street. A Tarahumaran Indian from the vast northern state of Coahuila, Xavier was a handsome fellow with liquid black eyes, copper-hued skin, satiny mane, and small body packed into overalls. At fourteen, he had landed a job adorning a businessman's villa with songbirds and flowers, but his youth was most keenly marked by the revolution's bloody chaos and bright hope. When the fighting sputtered out, Xavier moved to the capital, where he assisted various muralists, earning a reputation as a technician versed in half-forgotten indigenous methods, and fell in love with novelist Katherine Anne Porter, who refused his offer of marriage. He joined the Party and soon occupied half a dozen positions as *responsable* of this and secretary of that. Xavier still took on mural projects and made woodcuts for *El Machete,* but his art making was scattershot. If he occasionally dozed off in long-winded Central Committee meetings—Diego loved to twit "the sleeping monkey," according to their comrades—it was of no importance, for Xavier's radical credentials were unassailable.

Since their meeting in Los Angeles five years earlier, Tina and Xavier had frequented the same circles. Yet the references to the Mexican that pop up from time to time in Edward's journal and Tina's letters cast only a dim light on the relationship, whose shape is indistinguishable. Had Tina and Xavier enjoyed a casual simpatico connection? A staunch friendship? An off-and-on love affair? Did Tina's passion for politics breathe new emotion into her dealings with Xavier? In any case, her affection quickened and intensified until she loved Xavier (she later told him) "as I never before was able to love" and that emotion was "the greatest pride of my life."

Xavier Guerrero seems an unlikely candidate for such fervor, but while many deemed him slow-witted and stone-faced, Tina must have perceived a decent man with a deliciously dry sense of humor and what Jean Charlot called "a nature pitched finer than most." Preoccupied with the miserable lot of the Mexican poor—dirt farmers, stunted waifs, withered Indian *abuelitas*—Xavier "helped her to understand Mexico in all of its contradictions," submitted Rafael Carrillo. "Now the country with its physical beauty was not simply a source of pleasure. She began to see close up the hard, sacrificing existence of our people." Moreover, Xavier looked beyond this dark, brutish life to the promise of a glorious Red dawn. Like Edward, he was a man obsessed.

It was no doubt Carleton Beals who introduced Xavier and Tina to the leftist novelist John Dos Passos, in Mexico to scratch around for new material. Tina was eager to show her prints and talk photography with the cosmopolitan New Yorker (Dos Passos was unimpressed with Stieglitz's cloud series, she gossiped to Edward, "too vague…and with such absurd titles"). She snapped a picture of Dos Passos, in a dark suit and gone-tourist serape, mixing with a group of peons as he did on the evangelizing expedition described in his memoirs:

> I did get in several days of walking with a young fellow of mostly Indian blood named Xavier Guerrero.
> Xavier was a painter of real talent, but he was renouncing his art out of dedication to the Communist Party. We walked around from village to village in the chilly mountains back of Toluca. We ate off the Indians and slept on straw mats wrapped in insufficient serapes. Cold and fleas made sleep uneasy. There was a bare sculptural magnificence about everything: the mountains, the prickly pears,

the maguey, the broad darkly molded faces. I sat looking and sketching while Xavier, who ought to have been doing the drawing, spread the gospel of Lenin and Marx among the villagers.

They talked a great deal about *los enemigos.* Xavier kept explaining that los enemigos were the capitalist oppressors, but it occasionally came out that when these people talked of los enemigos they meant the Indians on the other slope of the mountains.

We don't know if Tina accompanied Xavier on treks among the Indians, but he gave her pictures of the Tarahumaran people, speaking gravely of "the roots of the class war" and "classless culture of the future." And she gratefully acknowledged, "You were the one who opened my eyes, you were the one who helped me when I could feel the pillar of my old beliefs shaking beneath my feet." Tina had seen so much in Mexico, but she took a further look, with more depth of field, as a photographer might conceive of it, and without warning, everything had changed. How *could* she have been so shortsighted?

As if to prove the point, she collected some of Ella Wolfe's friends, in town from New York, for a morning excursion to the sprawling shantytown called Colonia de la Bolsa. With Edward, she had tossed around the idea of such a visit, but it had never materialized. Now, traipsing through la Bolsa, her eyes "big, bright, sad...shining but at the same time...melancholic," she absorbed the brute realities of its welter of ragpickers, silent women with nothing more than thin rebozos and prayers for protection, half-naked bundles of children, their faces bleak and apathetic. The group's purpose was not slumming, however, but, rather, a tour of educator Miguel Oropeza's exemplary school for destitute boys, which was plunked in the middle of appalling squalor. Students were trained in useful vocations—carpentry, baking, sewing, farming—and governed by syndicates they ran themselves. As the visitors departed, profoundly moved, tears washed Tina's dust-caked cheeks.

Her next letter to Edward blurted out her admiration for Oropeza's accomplishments, suggesting that the visit fed the activist flame blazing within her. Distressed over the wretchedness of Mexico's dispossessed, Tina saw no course other than intensifying her efforts on their behalf. She tasted again the trauma and pain of her childhood and was able to trans-

mute that recollection into compassion and resoluteness. Lacking the skeptical, probing personality of a Carleton Beals as well as Diego's knack for
insouciantly mixing art and activism, Tina drew no boundaries around her
political engagement. It was not in her to dabble in militancy. At once effi-
cient and starry-eyed, she undertook whatever the cause required, whether
hawking newsletters, translating articles, or typing manifestoes.

Rather than allow what Anita was calling "mystic radicalism" to inter-
fere with her photography, Tina abandoned themes of flowers and architecture to focus on the soulful and heroic qualities of the Mexican masses.
She fixed her lens upon the sun-raked, dust-whipped, harshly beautiful lives
of laborers and campesinos. Many Modotti photographs reveal a complicity between the photographer and her subjects, viewed not only as individuals but also as representatives of a time and a people. Tina's bent for
symbolization, her search for meaning, is everywhere evident in these
images, but as an animating spirit rather than heavy-handed sloganeering.
And, despite her preoccupation with social and political content, the photographs rarely lose their crisp elegance of form and subtle handling of tone.

Mexican workers conjoined with their tools and burdens became a
favorite theme. Tina shot a silent, tattered bakery boy, a wide bread basket
appended to his head, and a day laborer so encumbered by his load that he
appears to be nothing more than legs for a bundle of boards. Along her
sidewalks hobble a dark, crooked woman, somehow eking out a living from
the mound of sticks on her back, and a striped-shirted plant seller who bal-
ances his wares like an extravagant topknot.

In *Hands Resting on Tool,* Tina focuses on a pair of rough-knuckled,
dusty hands poised on the well-worn handle of a shovel. Every shape and
shadow balanced and battened into place, the image is both abstract and
brimming with the materiality of light clinging to metal and sun toasting
the skin. Another photograph depicts toilworn hands and feet, the latter
seemingly inseparable from a pair of shabby sandals. White cotton trousers
suggest that their wearer is an Indian. Shadows and a glimpse of a second
man seated next to the first evoke a gathering, which is presumably taking
place during an interlude of repose in a day of labor. One can imagine the
shouted proclamations and debate of a political meeting. For once, the
Mexican Indian's hands and feet are idle, but, more subversively, his eyes,
ears, and mind are not.

Sometimes Tina took a directorial approach with her subjects, as in *Worker Reading "El Machete,"* an advertisement of sorts for the Party daily. Positioning a young laborer in a band of sunshine, she deploys a series of shapes to nudge viewers' eyes toward the newspaper's masthead and headline, which she brings right to the surface of the picture. *Worker Reading "El Machete"* is one of several Modotti photographs that find synergy in combinations of image and text. If today it seems a beautifully composed study of man with newspaper, the picture must have electrified Tina's contemporaries with the nervy immediacy of its promise, or threat, of a literate proletariat partaking of the Communist press.

In one series, the photographer depicted the unearthly beauty of industrial storage tanks and construction sites, their webs of stone, steel, and timber ensnaring solitary workers. Four such photographs were published in *Forma,* along with an article lauding Tina for "paying deserved attention to new forms of activity as a possible source of new forms of beauty...." The images were intended to complement the staccato poetry of Germán List Arzubide for a book the pair had been planning. Deposited with Tina when Germán went to Europe, the manuscript was a casualty of the vicissitudes of her life, and *The Song of Mankind* was never published.

Meanwhile, Tina carried on with her magazine photography assignments, one of which turned macabre. Gabriel Fernández Ledesma had hired her to shoot the design for a carved door at La Merced open-air art school. The former convent's patio enclosed a menagerie of animal models: raccoons, a coyote, an armadillo, a fawn, and Panchita, the mascot spider monkey Tina liked to cuddle. Over the weekend, the coyote had somehow broken loose and slaughtered the others, whose corpses were being collected as Tina arrived on Monday morning. "They pulled Panchita out from under a pile of rocks," remembered Fernández Ledesma, "and everyone was horrified because Panchita showed us her own intestines...with such a painful look...and I have vivid recollections of Tina Modotti's face at that moment, so filled with anguish, so different from her usual calm, dreamy expression."

More sweeping dramas gripped Tina's attention that summer. In strategically important Nicaragua, where a civil war was raging, United States Marines had disembarked to tip the scales toward conservatives, thus checking the spread of the Mexican revolution. A spiritualist peasant named Augusto "César" Sandino repulsed U.S.-brokered peace accords, however, and vanished with his ragged guerrilla band into the misty Segovia Mountains. From that outpost, he broadcast his patriotism and pride in the Indian blood coursing through his veins. In the name of anti-imperialism, national liberation, and deliverance of the oppressed, Sandino's little army then slashed down the mountainsides in a fierce attack on the vastly superior U.S. forces occupying the town of Ocotal. Progressives around the world rallied to the cause of the humble Nicaraguan.

Mexican Communists vied for Sandino's allegiance with the Hands Off Nicaragua Committee, where Tina again showed herself to be an effective organizer and fund-raiser. When the Central American rebels presented the committee with a U.S. flag snatched from under marines' noses, she was there with her Graflex to record the moment. Later, List Arzubide smuggled the same Stars and Stripes past New York immigration officials to an international anti-imperialist conference in Frankfurt, Germany. Striding into the assembly hall, he flashed the flag—now emblazoned with the words NICARAGUA LIBRE—as hundreds rose to their feet and broke into a thunderous "Internationale."

Tina's political imagination was fired not only by Sandino but also by the shoemaker Nicola Sacco and fishmonger Bartolomeo Vanzetti, behind bars since their 1921 convictions for a vicious robbery and double murder in South Braintree, Massachusetts. Italian-born anarchists, the two were widely considered victims of an egregious miscarriage of justice fueled by xenophobia and antianarchism. When the Mexican Left set up a united front on the prisoners' behalf, Tina eagerly took turns at the mimeograph machine and in the crush of protesters at rally after rally, and when the Italians were executed on August 22, 1927, she was no doubt convinced that the democratic system had forever besmirched itself. Writing to Edward a few days before Sacco and Vanzetti went to the electric chair, Jean Charlot observed dryly, "Tina goes hard on social work."

Tina's letters to Edward were tender, collegial, and solicitous. Though her ideas about photography had diverged from his quest for "pure form" and "quintessence," her admiration for his art was unwavering. When she undid a package from him of monumental, luminescent, and razor-sharp close-ups of seashells, she was dumbfounded. "My God Edward your last photographs surely 'took my breath away!' I feel speechless in front of them— What purity of vision they convey— When I first opened the package I couldn't look at them very long they stirred up all my innermost feelings so that I felt a physical pain from it...nothing before in art has affected me like these photographs...."

She showed the prints to Rivera, Orozco, and René d'Harnoncourt, carefully noting their comments and writing to Edward at length about her own reactions to the work. The incident made her realize how much she hungered for cozy photography chats as in the old days. Though acquainted with a dozen photographers, she felt deep artistic kinship with none until she met Manuel Alvarez Bravo. She picked up the ringing phone one day, to hear a timid male voice: Might it be possible to meet the artist whose work he so admired in *Forma* and *Mexican Folkways*?

Manuel was a scrawny twenty-five-year-old government typist and novice photographer who found in Tina a cohort and mentor. He would call her after work, and she would let him know whether or not it was a good day to come over. If so, she would bring out her latest photographs and Edward's, and the pair would talk until interrupted by a stream of other visitors. Manuel often arrived bearing a monograph on this painter or that photographer and, sometimes, eerily beautiful, unsentimental prints of rocks, skulls, and handmade toys, early works in his seven-decade career as Mexico's preeminent photographer.

Like a specter from the past, another visitor trotted into Tina's apartment that summer and stayed a month. Willowy and frail-looking, her eyes dark smudges in her pallid face, Vocio had gamely braved high seas and Mexican railways to see dear Tina. Rather distinguished-looking in silk dresses and cloche hats, she startled acquaintances with her fussy, folksy manner. "They were so very different," observed Emily Edwards, who stopped by one day. "The slim, conventional older woman seemed the younger of the two—an ageless maturity was Tina's."

Tina shepherded her guest to San Angel, Coyoacán, Puebla, Cuernavaca, and the storybook "floating gardens" of Xochimilco. The well-touristed village's pink-walled church, canals dotted with swaying water lilies, and luminous mingling of water and sky had long enchanted Tina. Once she might have filled her viewfinder with architectural studies, but now, as if Xavier led her by the hand, she turned from de rigueur snapshots of Vocio in the flower-bedecked flatboats to photographs of the village's

Indian toilers. Together, Tina and Vocio later captioned the prints: "Market scene—Xochimilco"; "Indians getting fertilizer from the bottom of the canal at Xochimilco"; "Indians carrying loads of corn husks for the making of 'tamales.'"

One weekend was wrapped around a photography session at Robo's burial place in the American Cemetery. "It is such a beautiful place there, so quiet and well kept," Vocio reported to her daughter, Marionne. "The lawn's green and cut and the walkway swept as clean as a floor. There is a bench at the foot of his grave in the path, and we sat there a long time and talked, waiting for the sun to shine on his grave as it was cloudy and the sun has to get above the trees too."

That evening, Tina developed the negatives, intending to make contact prints the following afternoon. Instead, she found herself on Sunday scurrying between a parade of visitors in the living room and her darkroom stacked with negatives. Vocio again took up her pen: "She is busy all the time making pictures for somebody.... An American lady friend of Tina has come in for a little visit.... There has been someone here all the afternoon and evening, and Tina can't get anything done. She wanted to print some of those pictures we took of Roubaix's grave yesterday. There has been four different persons here this afternoon and evening. One came while we were eating dinner...."

After the door closed on the last visitor and twilight crept into the corners of the room, how much did Tina explain to Vocio, one wonders, of the frenzied talk of protest rallies and political agendas? Pablo O'Higgins said of Tina that she "never [pretended] to be anything she wasn't." It is true that she never made herself out to be richer, better educated, or more gifted than she was, but, for a friend or a cause, she would willingly twist the truth, and with the radical reordering of her articles of faith came a less spontaneous and more circumspect personality. Though she was able to accommodate disparate worlds and sets of friends, explaining these, one to the other, became burdensome. Tina parceled out different parts of herself to different people, making few attempts to reconcile her various communities. She never revealed to Vocio that Edward ("Mr. Weston" or "Weston" in their conversations) had been anything but teacher and colleague, and her letters to Edward are generally mute on the subject of politics.

Yet she did inform him that she had proudly joined the Communist party. Her comrades were about six hundred in number, many foreigners, an impoverished, scrappy, self-important, and starry-eyed lot. Like most of them, barely conversant with Marxist theory, Tina was less intent on familiarizing herself with Marx and Lenin than on observing Communist codes of conduct, written and unwritten. Being a model Communist, she believed, meant letting her old preoccupation with personal and sexual self-expression fall by the wayside. She took for granted that the Party's needs transcended her own and ungrudgingly subordinated individual freedom to working-class solidarity.

For all their own sleeping around, Communist men liked their Communist women respectable. Perhaps believing that Tina's conduct too closely matched bourgeois stereotypes of free-loving Bolsheviks, some comrades took a dim view of her nude modeling and reputation for indiscriminate affairs. She discussed the matter with Alexandra Kollontai, Moscow's brilliant and gracious successor to Pestkovsky. An influential Left oppositionist, Ambassador Kollontai had challenged the Soviet leadership on theoretical matters, including decommodifying love and integrating women's liberation into Communist ideology (thereby getting herself assigned to remote outposts such as Mexico City), but her conversations with Tina were more down-to-earth. The envoy advised her, Tina said later, that

> in middle-class circles of Mexico City and among foreign residents I did not have a good reputation because I had posed nude for Weston and because of that famous mural by Diego Rivera at Chapingo…. [Kollontai] had always been an honest revolutionary, a good Communist, had loyally served her country; as for her personal life, she considered it a private matter. That conversation pleased me because her ideas coincided with mine; notwithstanding, I had had moments of depression and uncertainty because some friends and comrades, women or men, had expressed serious and unjust criticisms of me.

In spite of her words, Tina simply relinquished a decade-long career as an artist's model, never again striking a pose, nude or clothed, for painter or photographer. To Anita, she mentioned another intended change in her lifestyle: "to simplify life, in particular with men," meaning that she put a stop to blithe, simultaneous intimacies and purely physical relationships. She became a one-man woman, and that man was Xavier Guerrero, who moved in with her. Behind him trailed half the Mexican Communist party, whose Central Committee met in her living room.

Moscow, meanwhile, had turned its attention to Mexico's Communist-front groups, and its ranking Comintern member on the spot was Vittorio Vidali, who stepped from the train and into Tina's life in the autumn of 1927. Tina was charmed by the infectious laughter of the twenty-seven-year-old Italian oozing street smarts and easygoing swagger. Both jocular and peremptory, Vittorio had handsome darting eyes, a large forehead, dark hair, and mobile mouth, from which, in a pleasant, raspy voice, he delivered a stream of opinions, anecdotes, and advice.

Their connection brokered by Party secretary Rafael Carrillo, Tina appeared at the newcomer's hotel room one day, efficiently arranged a move to cheaper lodgings, and invited him home. He recalled:

> We spoke of many things: of the situation in the United States;
> ...of the small Italian colony in Mexico City, composed, for the
> most part, of disreputable elements. "With much effort," Tina told
> me, "I was able to form an antifascist organization to carry out a few
> actions against fascism. But it is not enough, and what is lacking is
> not only the solidarity of those Italians, most of whom are fascists,
> but also the support of the important Mexican organizations. They
> don't really care what's happening in Italy because they are preoc-
> cupied with the problems of their own country. The Party and the
> Anti-Imperialist League are helping us, but it's not enough. Surely,
> your presence will help to create something more serious and
> effective."

To Tina's delight, Vittorio was not only a compatriot but practically a neighbor, having grown up in a suburb of Trieste, forty-five miles from Udine. From a brood of eleven, born to a couple of unskilled workers, he had lived the kind of dreary, gnawing poverty in which a few drops of vinegar in water often had to substitute for a glass of wine. At seventeen, he was a strong-arm socialist; at twenty-one, a founding member of Trieste's Communist party. When shoot-ups with local fascists got out of hand, he high-tailed it over the Alps and knocked around the world awhile, eventually surfacing as a Chicago-based agitator for the Italian section of the U.S. Party. The years that followed were measured out in one- and two-night stands in New England mill towns, Pennsylvania coal-mining settlements, and anywhere else rife with frustrated, grimy-faced Italian laborers. Arrested in 1926 for having entered the country illegally, Vittorio got himself to the Soviet Union, from which he emerged a crack Comintern agent trained by state security forces. Using the pseudonyms Enea Sormenti and Carlos (or Jorge) Contreras, he rolled up his sleeves and began waging professional revolution in Mexico.

As Tina and Vittorio chatted, one matter or another brought to Tina's door Ursulo Galván of the National Peasants' League, *El Machete* editor Rosendo Gómez Lorenzo, painter and labor organizer David Alfaro Siqueiros, and the strapping campesino José Guadalupe Rodríguez. José arrived with bottles of Durango red wine, and, switching from Italian to Spanish, militant to hostess, Tina whipped together dinner (chances are, her standby, spaghetti with butter and cheese).

Walking Vittorio to his hotel later that evening, Rosendo painted a picture of the role the Abraham González Street apartment played in the life of the Mexican Communist party. "As you see, we also have our 'salon,' Tina's home. That's where the ruling circles of the Party, Party youth and the Anti-Imperialist League meet. It's the reference point for peasants' and workers' delegations coming from around the country. Her address is the only one delegates of foreign organizations carry in their pockets when they come to Mexico...."

Humbled by Vittorio's revolutionary prowess, Tina was quick to defer to her overbearing compatriot. One day, she brought out a favorite quotation from Nietzsche: "What is done out of love always occurs beyond good and evil," by which she apparently meant beyond hackneyed notions of the right way to live. Misinterpreting or simply reacting to the mention of the "petit bourgeois" Nietzsche, Vittorio pounced upon the dictum and, grabbing Tina by the shoulders, shouted, "Well, this is too much!... To me it seems that when a person says this, he believes in heaven and hell and it's a *bit* arrogant!" Falling silent, she never again allowed a reference to Nietzsche to cross her lips in the presence of Vittorio, who pronounced her "a very reserved woman, always" and remained ignorant of certain aspects of her life until decades later.

Had Tina been a man, her talents and connections would have promptly won her a seat on the Party's Central Committee, but among Communists, as elsewhere, reigned the presumption of male superiority and privilege. She herself would have refused the label "feminist" for its bourgeois associations, arguing that middle-class women merely confronted men of their own class, while proletarian women struggled shoulder-to-shoulder with proletarian men. Tina handled most of the unsung day-to-day chores for Red Aid and, using the name Tina MacRichey, rented P.O. Box 2317, used to collect mail for various Communist-front organizations. Her free-of-charge "family portraits" of Party committees and meetings were taken for granted. In Mexican art circles, she was known as an independent spirit, but, in the political arena, she never aspired to leadership and happily played the role of dutiful Party helpmeet.

Tina's remarkable year of 1927 also saw the first of a series of still lifes using a repertoire of objects evoking Mexicanness, Communism, and revolution. One image juxtaposes a sombrero, hammer, and machete; another, a bullet-laden bandolier, guitar, and ear of corn; a third, simply a hammer and sickle. No mere agitprop, these are graceful, uncommonly ordered photographs in which a soft, crisp light plays over objects, and no space remains inert. Echoing Mexican popular artists' delight in the materials they employ, Tina gives us corn kernels rippling hard to the touch, sickles casting a dull sheen, and cartridge belts reeking of old leather. Both elegant still lifes and virtual tinderboxes to her contemporaries, the images forge an immediate and eloquent connection to the complex circumstances of 1920s Mexican radicalism.

In some circles, the series was roundly criticized as the "debasement and diminution of [Modotti's] art," while others discerned the originality of her seamless synthesis of ideology and form. *Mexican Sombrero with Hammer and Sickle* appeared on the cover of *New Masses,* a widely read, topical monthly of the radical Left. The prestigious publication prompted a proud, chiding note from Tina's brother Ben: "...you little liar, you once told me that one cannot express social concerns through the art of photography. You are the one who has proved yourself wrong." Tina also prevailed with *Bandolier, Corn, Guitar,* which would be among her submissions to a big Mexico City exhibition the following summer. "Miss Modotti triumphed with her clearly Mexican art," opined *El Universal Ilustrado*; "her portrayal of a cartridge belt, of a guitar and of an ear of corn represents, according to the artist, 'the revolutionary songs of Mexico.'" The show revealed that Modotti and Alvarez Bravo (who contributed spare, unpicturesque images of a feather duster, paper birds, and a ceramic frog) worked a wide aesthetic chasm apart from other photographers. "Gee, I wish you had seen it," Tina told Edward of the accumulation of misty, bucolic landscapes and sentimentalized portraits of paupers; "it surely was a mess!"

In late 1927, Tina photographed in the Veracruz hill town of Jalapa, where she accompanied Xavier to a peasant organizing conference. She made the popular *A Proud Little Agrarista*, an emblematic close-up, from a low, heroicizing angle, of a youthful campesino who wears his sombrero like a plaited halo. So arrestingly does light glance off the textures of cloth, straw, and skin in this portrait that one is reminded of Susan Sontag's observation: A photograph is not only an image but also "a trace, something directly stenciled off the real, like a footprint or a death mask." In Jalapa, Tina also portrayed open-air meetings of campesinos and a peasant family pleasantly swamped by its harvest of corn.

The images put a face on the Party's attempts to reinforce its ties to radical rural groups, thus stepping up pressure on the Calles administration for agrarian and social reform. Economic development through foreign investment had become the Callista byword, and deals made over cocktails in politicians' Cuernavaca villas were taking priority over land redistribution. The government's drift to the Right gathered speed after the arrival of U.S. ambassador Dwight Morrow, who skillfully eased the two nations past a long deadlock on subsoil rights, and U.S. oil companies got back to business in Mexico. All the while, glib revolutionary rhetoric continued to pour out of the National Palace, and, from abroad, Mexico still appeared a bright beacon of social justice.

The outing to Jalapa was one of Tina's last with Xavier, for Moscow abruptly summoned the Mexican to a three-year course at the International Lenin School, a training institute for up-and-coming Communist cadres. Xavier's categorical mind-set led him simply to put his affairs in order and depart for the Soviet Union. Apparently not invited to accompany him (they spoke of a visit), Tina escorted her companion to the train station, returning with such a serene expression that Vittorio shook his head over the woman's lack of affect. Stoicism and self-control were precisely what Tina believed the Party required of her. If her distress was intense, Moscow's representative would be the last to know.

Resigned to await Xavier's return, she sent him weekly packages of clippings from the Mexican press. Among them, no doubt, was "Against the Fascist Terror," *El Machete*'s report about the Anti-Fascist League's biggest rally yet, organized by Tina in protest of the assassination of imprisoned Perugian worker Gastone Sozzi. From the podium, she delivered a clear-voiced indictment of the Italian government while, in the audience, Mussolini's informer took mental notes for the Ministry of Foreign Relations, with a copy to the Ministry of the Interior. He singled out

> two Italians whose names until today were unknown to the colony here.... Both say they represent the international Antifascist League about which I have spoken several times in my reports, and both used very violent language against the regime. One is an Enea Sormenti [Vittorio Vidali], who claimed to be an Italian refugee and who holds the presidency. The other is a certain Tina Modotti, who described present-day Italy as "transformed into an immense prison and a vast cemetery."

Endorsed by the Communist party, the meeting took place in its fine new headquarters on the upper floors of a squat red *tezontle* building at the corner of Isabel la Católica and Mesones streets. Offices opened onto the open-air courtyard of the building blessed, from its rooftop, by a chiseled colonial-era saint, whom Tina carefully cropped from her official photograph.

One late spring evening, lights blazed from the windows of *El Machete*'s workroom as Tina leaned over the desk of editor Rosendo Gómez Lorenzo. The pair translated an article from the Italian press, Tina rendering each sentence into rough Spanish as Rosendo mentally corrected her grammar and typed. They were interrupted when a strikingly handsome twenty-five-year-old man strode into the room.

"Ah, sorry, sorry, you are working," came the resonant Cuban-accented voice.

"Yes, but it's okay," replied Rosendo. "Comrade Modotti, Comrade Mella."

Tina looked up, and her glance briefly locked onto the young man's lively coffee-colored eyes. Julio Antonio Mella was lean of face, with full lips, a tousle of curly black hair, and a broad-chested, well-muscled body. Peering at Tina and Julio Antonio through his spectacles, Rosendo perceived Cupid's arrows flying in both directions. The encounter so flustered her, Tina later confided to a woman friend, that she was momentarily incapable of speaking or thinking rationally. Yet she had a glancing acquaintance with the figure in the gray workman's shirt, and the two had even been introduced at a Sacco and Vanzetti demonstration.

Every militant in Latin America knew the exiled Cuban revolutionary by reputation. Mella's contagious vitality, mesmerizing oratory, uncompromising attitudes, and physical prowess had given rise to a mythic persona. He was David to Cuban dictator Gerardo Machado's Goliath, "the Adonis of the left," "young, beautiful and insolent like a Homeric hero."

With Tina, Julio Antonio displayed an uncharacteristically bumbling, boyish quality. "Please, continue working," he said, seeming to conclude the exchange, then disappeared into the warren of offices. Twice he returned with questions, but when Rosendo invited him to accompany them to a Chinese restaurant down the street, he declined on grounds of too much work. No sooner were the two seated at the Café Canton, however, than Julio Antonio appeared, asking for the keys to Rosendo's office but settling in for coffee and talk.

Born Nicanor MacPartland, Mella was the love child of Cecilia MacPartland, an Irishwoman, and her well-to-do mulatto lover, Havana tailor and businessman Nicanor Mella. The boy's grandfather was Gen. Ramón Mella, a glorious independence hero of the Dominican Republic. When he was seven, Nicanor's mother abruptly quit Cuba, leaving her sons to their father's strict Catholic upbringing. Shamed by his illegitimacy and confused by a legacy of mixed nationalities, mixed races, and mixed messages, Nicanor coped by throwing himself into obsessive activity. He excelled in swimming and rowing and, enrolling as a law student at the University of Havana, quickly emerged as the undisputed leader of the sclerotic institution's reform movement. Rattling the university's gates was only the beginning, however, for Mella believed that the school's corruption mirrored that of Cuban society. Vowing to rid the island of injustice and U.S. imperialism, he cofounded Havana's tiny Communist circle, soon folded into the fledgling Cuban Communist party.

Two incidents propelled Julio Antonio Mella's fame far beyond the island. When a Soviet freighter dropped anchor in Havana harbor and Cuban authorities forbade shore leave to its seamen, Julio Antonio swam through shark-infested waters (as the legend goes) to extend fraternal greetings and savor four well-publicized hours in the floating workers' paradise. A few months later, an explosion rocked a Havana theater, and Mella's archenemy, Cuban dictator Gerardo Machado—a fleshy ladies' man and great admirer of Mussolini—saw his chance to silence the young agitator. Mella was thrown in jail, whereupon he promptly declared a hunger strike, languishing for nearly three weeks until the newspapers were filled with medical bulletins and blurry pictures of the bearded militant sinking toward death. So thunderous was the public outcry that Machado was obliged to unlock his prison doors. Fearing an anonymous bullet in a dark alley, Julio Antonio hopped a banana boat out of Cuba.

He blew into Mexico like a tropical storm, entangling himself in national and international affairs, yet his obsession and his battle cry—the name of the magazine he edited and had smuggled into Havana—was *Cuba Libre*. Every spare moment was devoted to planning his homeland's liberation from the tyrant Machado.

Rosendo's perception about the spark between Modotti and Mella had been accurate. From the time they met, the two were inseparable and deeply in love. Yet Tina systematically repulsed Julio Antonio's romantic overtures. He was married, to a Cuban woman named Oliva Zaldívar Freyre, who marched at his side in demonstrations but yearned for a private as well as a public life, and this he was unwilling to give her. When she got pregnant, she left Mexico to give birth, in Cuba, to a daughter, whom Julio Antonio never saw, and there was talk of divorce. Tina's trepidation about the romance was not linked to Oliva, however, but to Xavier. In the time of her free and easy liaisons, the prospect of having two lovers would have left her unperturbed, but as a Party member, she believed sexual adventuring (with two members of the Central Committee, no less) to be a disruptive breach of duty.

Their mutual devotion to the cause notwithstanding, the two men were utterly different. Julio Antonio exuded vehemence and energy; Xavier seldom lost his sweet-tempered reserve. Julio Antonio freely strayed from the paths of Party orthodoxy; Xavier was ever dutiful. Julio Antonio burned with desire for her; Xavier penned husbandly letters packed with curt, stolid advice. He scolded Tina for lending her apartment for a friend's drunken party and responded unsympathetically to her lament that she had no money to buy clothes: "I'm sorry about your clothes, you call it tragic or nearly tragic: you exaggerate, and I am certain it is your Italian-ness combined with a little bit of Mexican-ness. I will send you something from here, but…don't expect anything like [you had] in Los Angeles.…" Tina's nightmares must have catapulted her seven years into the past, the features of Xavier in Moscow blending with those of Robo in Mexico City, and Julio Antonio in Mexico City mutating into Edward in Los Angeles.

Ceding finally to "a clear and inevitable reality," Tina acknowledged that she was no longer in love with Xavier, but she refused to make any commitment to Julio Antonio until she had resolved matters with the Mexican. Half a dozen options—traveling to Moscow for a face-to-face discussion, holding everything in abeyance until Xavier's return, even committing suicide—swam through her mind, and still she vacillated. Baffled by such distress, Julio Antonio tortured himself with the thought that she was not over her infatuation with Xavier. Tina scrupulously telephoned Vittorio, just back from Moscow, to inform him of the situation and apparently heard no objections to a liaison with Julio Antonio.

Close upon the heels of that conversation came Julio Antonio's departure for Veracruz, the jumping-off spot for his audacious expeditionary force, whose landing in Cuba was to trigger a large-scale uprising on the island. From his hotel in the Gulf Coast city, Julio Antonio reminded Tina that, the bid to change Cuban history notwithstanding, his future lay in her hands.

"My dear Tinísima…" he began, using the tender cascade of syllables that was his (and, coincidentally, Assunta Modotti's) pet name for her:

> Just a few lines after the telegram.… It may be that you think the telegram imprudent, well, you are in the habit of being frightened of all that there is between us. As if we are committing a great crime by loving each other. However, nothing is more right, natural

and necessary for our lives. You can imagine that your face never left me during the entire journey. I can still see you grieving, body and soul, giving me a final farewell as if you wanted to come to me. Your words also are caressing my ears.... Well, Tina, sorry to run on, but I am in agony. I think I am going to lose my mind. I have had too many painful thoughts these last few days, and today the wounds are still open from this separation. The most painful of my life. If you have calmed down, write. Put a little peace in my mind. Each time I think about my situation, it seems that I am at the entrance to a cemetery. I love you, seriously, tempestuously. As something definite. You say that you love me just as much. If we work this out, I have the conviction that our life will be something productive and grand. But you repeat to me the same thing as before, that you are not ready for solutions. As for me, Tina, I have taken my life into my own hands and have brought it to your balcony, the accomplice of our love. Sometimes I think I am a child and that you have pity for me. If not, explain what kind of love this is which brings me to desperation. Tell me if I have any hope. If you don't want to be in Mexico, we will go together to Cuba or Argentina. Tina, it is not in me to beg but, in the name of that which we love, give me something certain, something which is more than smoke....

As Tina read Julio Antonio's entreaty, the fog of uncertainty dissipated, and she sat down to draft a pained, solicitous, and self-reproachful message to Xavier:

There is no doubt that this will be the most difficult, most painful, and most terrible letter I have ever written in my whole life. I've waited a long time before writing it, mainly because I wanted to be very sure of the things I am going to tell you....

X., sometimes when I think of the pain I am about to cause you, I feel more like a monster than a human being, and I'm sure you will think this is true. At other times I see myself as the poor victim of a terrible fate, with a hidden force that acts on me, despite myself, the way it acts on life. But I would be the first to reject these elements: "fate," or "hidden force," etc. Well, then, what remains? What is it that I am? Why do I act in this way? I sincerely believe that I have intrinsically good feelings, and that I've always tried to do good for others before I've thought of myself, not to be cruel for its own sake. That's the proof that when I have to be the way I'm being with you now, I suffer (perhaps more than you) because of the consequences.

But I should tell you what it is I have to tell you: I love another man. I love him and he loves me, and this love has made it possible for something to happen which I thought could never happen: to stop loving you....

Mailed on September 14, Tina's letter arrived in Moscow some twenty-three days later. Guerrero's cold and terse wire flung back: "RECEIVED YOUR MESSAGE. GOOD-BYE."

Chapter 9

Mexico City (1928–1929)

A N ABRUPT CHANGE in the Cuban exiles' plans to liberate
their country from dictatorship quickly brought Tina and Julio
Antonio together. As their flotilla was preparing to launch itself across the
Gulf of Mexico, word reached Veracruz that Machado's spies were wise to
the project, and Mella postponed the raid indefinitely. He doubled back to
Mexico City, where he heard from Tina of her letter to Xavier. Emptying
out his dingy rented room near Lecumberri Prison, Julio Antonio joyfully
hauled a few meager belongings to Abraham González Street.

Toasting their life together with a glass of wine, Tina and Julio Antonio embarked upon a period of unbridled passion and sheer bliss. They
brimmed with tender gestures for each other. "We were very happy, Julio
Antonio and I," she once said. "Like all dreamers, Julio Antonio had illusions, about soon traveling to Cuba, which he thought the best place to live.
He was going to teach [me] how to swim. We were really just like two
sweethearts." When she found the apartment empty because Julio Antonio
had a meeting, dinner would be waiting, the table set, a piece of candy or a
blossom laid next to a note: "Tonight we can't eat together..."; "I leave
thinking of you...." Life was luminous and full of promise.

Seven years younger than Tina, Julio Antonio lovingly dubbed her
"little mother," as she cosseted and fussed over him. At the same time, the
relationship was charged with eroticism. He adored "that back with that

black hair, loose as a flag," and scandalized gossip avowed that she had photographed his erect penis.

Not one snapshot survives (if any were ever made) of the lovers together, though a handful of Tina's photographs evoke their day-to-day life. Her camera captured Julio Antonio dozing in the grass, pounding at his typewriter, and mixing in a street demonstration. In an emblematic profile, he is viewed from below, jaw strong, eyes scanning distant horizons, and features resolute, as if they belong on the head of a coin. Embodying aspirations to social justice and national self-determination, the image was to be widely printed in newspapers and magazines after Mella's death. Familiar to two generations of Latin Americans, it was superseded as an icon only in the 1960s, by Cuban photographer Alberto Korda's omnipresent photograph of revolutionary Che Guevara.

A magnet for all kinds of people, Julio Antonio brought a new collection of friends and acquaintances into Tina's life. The student crowd, of various political stripes, congregated in the afternoons at Alfonso's, a Chinese restaurant on Argentina Street where all ran long tabs. Over heaping plates of chow mein and tall glasses of *horchata,* around tables piled with newspapers, jackets, and books, they debated politics and political theory to the verge of fistfights. The bubbly, bespectacled dental student Rogelio Teurbe Tolón held forth in the thick of the commotion, as did Alejandro Gómez Arias, a brilliant intellectual about to be elected president of the National Student Confederation, and Baltasar Dromundo, sad-eyed, impassioned, and articulate. Sometimes Tina would float in, smiling but rarely laughing, seductive yet not coquettish, attending to each person, though rarely taking the floor in their free-for-alls. Julio Antonio's cronies found her an extraordinary woman.

Though Julio Antonio pocketed a generous eighty-dollar monthly allowance from his father and Tina was by now earning a reasonably good living, their money flew into various collection baskets and the hands of needy comrades, and the pair seemed rarely able to scrounge up a peso between them. With his pal Juan de la Cabada, Julio Antonio lunched on the cheapest fare he could concoct, banana sandwiches washed down with plenty of milk. Nonetheless, among Cuban émigrés, Abraham González Street was known for its hospitality. Sprawled around the living room and feverishly holding forth on strategies for insurrection, guests would dive into mounds of spaghetti and quaff red wine serenely distributed by Tina before closeting herself in the darkroom.

Among Julio Antonio's companions, Tina struck up a particular friendship with a prankish, wisecracking twenty-one-year-old painter named Frida Kahlo. Her pelvis shattered in a horrendous bus accident, Frida was shackled in corsets and often racked with pain. But to see her palling around with the law student Germán de Campo, one would not have guessed it. They made an irrepressible pair, "Germancito," a plump, witty, cane-twirling dandy, and Frida, petite and strangely attractive with a dark, penetrating gaze and eyebrows that joined.

Frida quickly fell under Tina's sway, joining the Party and shedding her schoolgirl blouses and baubles for the workman's shirts and A-line skirts that Tina deemed proper for a Communist. For a time, Frida's only adornment was an enameled hammer-and-sickle pin, a gift from Tina. Even more momentous than her conversion to communism, however, was the young woman's encounter with Diego Rivera at one of the lively *tertulias* Tina still threw from time to time. When the muralist ambled in, packing a pistol, and silenced the phonograph by plugging it full of bullets, her interest was piqued. She began to frequent the Ministry of Public Education, watching him paint and startling other visitors by calling him *"mi cuatacho,"* meaning "my big pal." Diego was invited to call at the Kahlo family home in Coyoacán, and, as he tells it, his knock on the door was answered by a whistled version of the "Internationale" from a nearby tree before the overall-clad Frida climbed down. Before long, Tina and Julio Antonio were running into the pair at campesinos' demonstrations and protest meetings, and Frida became active in the Communist Youth Association.

September found Tina rarely at the Ministry of Public Education, for she had received a flood of orders from José Clemente Orozco, now settled in New York. In characteristically convoluted fashion, the artist wrote his close friend Jean Charlot to describe photographs that Tina should take of his Mexico City murals. "Easy to sketch from memory in his letters, Orozco's photographic directives posed substantial problems when weighed *in situ*," Charlot recalled. "Tina's paraphernalia was old-fashioned even for that day, and it took much ingenuity to fit her bulky box camera and tripod along the staircases and under the low arches of the Colonial building. For days we worked throughout the daylight hours, stopping only

for a beer and sandwich brought by Tina's friend Julio Antonio Mella."
Giving Orozco's murals her undivided attention, Tina decided that his art,
less particularistic than Rivera's, was superior: "...I feel the genius," she told
Edward. "His things overflow with an inner potentiality.... You can begin
where he leaves off and that is very satisfying...."

Ironically, the quality Tina admired in Orozco's paintings was lacking
in her own preachy *Contrasts of the Regime* series. Appearing over several
months on the pages of *El Machete,* which normally served up uninspiring
head-and-shoulders shots of Soviet bigwigs, the photographs were poorly
reproduced, and many fall short of the vigorous composition characteristic
of her best work. Nonetheless, they broke ground as virtually the first critical photojournalism to appear in the Mexican press during the postrevo-
lutionary period. Undoubtedly, Tina's efforts were informed by her
familiarity with the German worker-photography movement, which
empowered the masses to photograph the world around them with a proletarian eye. She dubbed the series her "propaganda pictures."

Labeled, with bitter irony, *The Protection of Children,* one depicts a sad-
eyed young water carrier, cowled in a tattered rebozo, amid a confusion of
buckets, jugs, planks, and crates. "Millions of children like this are seen in
Mexico," reads the caption. "They work hard at jobs inappropriate to their
ages, twelve or fifteen hours a day, almost always for food. And what food!
Nonetheless, the Constitution...." Another image picks out two abject figures crumpled on the pavement in front of what looks to be a bar: "The
high council on health makes countless rules covering one and all, but this
sight can be seen everywhere." Still others are paired photographs that contrast the lots of Mexico's rich and poor. Flanked by wholesome, starchy-
collared children, a nanny pushes a baby buggy in a leafy setting as five
waifs huddle together in the squalid Colonia de la Bolsa. "Even in Children
Does Capitalism Show Its Brutal Contrasts," the reader is told. With such
captions binding the photographs to an antigovernment message, *El Machete*
effectively locked out other possible interpretations. Mostly uncredited
(either in rejection of "bourgeois individualism" or because Tina felt
uneasy about signing her name to a project of such blatancy), the pictures
bear witness to her desire to remove photography from the middle-class
living room and search into the ways it could be used to effect social
change.

Tina persevered with direct action, as well. As president of the Anti-Fascist League of Mexico, she convoked the public to an October rally marking the sixth anniversary of Mussolini's march on Rome. A shoulder-to-shoulder crowd packing a union hall heard her proclaim fascism a danger for all people, denounce the Vatican's coziness with Mussolini, and urge Mexico to break diplomatic relations with Italy. She then relinquished the podium to Diego and Julio Antonio, who eloquently analyzed the origins of fascism, a last desperate hurrah of the capitalist system.

As 1928 drew to a close, Tina accepted Vocio's offer of a holiday trip to Los Angeles, then thought better of it. Instead, at end-of-the-year gatherings in Mexico City, she and Julio Antonio were a radiant presence, two tailors' children whose plain, somber garments offset their own glow. In December, they attended "Cuban Night," organized by an exiles' association in a hall leased with the proviso that the event eschew political propagandizing. Halfway through the evening, a cohort of intruders inexplicably tacked up a tissue-paper Cuban flag, which Julio Antonio removed in order to comply with the terms of the rental agreement. His gesture was greeted with belligerent catcalls that swiftly degenerated into a fist-swinging melee. From Havana, in the weeks that followed, erupted a volley of accusations from publications friendly to the Machado regime that Julio Antonio Mella had desecrated the flag.

The first days of 1929 found him firing off telegrams and letters defending his actions in the Cuban-flag incident. On Thursday evening, January 10, he huddled with Tina at International Red Aid's Isabel la Católica Street offices. "Carbó, *La Semana*, Havana, Cuba," he scrawled on a slip of paper. "Ask you completely refute slanderous campaign initiated our enemies. Never profaned flag. Details mail. Affectionately, Mella."

Putting a signature to the draft, the pair drew up chairs with Red Aid stalwarts Vittorio Vidali, Rogelio Teurbe Tolón, and Peruvian journalist Jacobo Hurwitz Zender for another interminable, smoke-hazed committee meeting, this one to plan a shelter for families of persecuted militants. When they adjourned shortly before nine, Tina and Julio Antonio lingered briefly with the others before striking out for *El Machete*'s offices, two blocks north, where they dashed upstairs to wheedle from editor Rosendo Gómez Lorenzo an advance copy of Friday's paper.

As the pair left the building, cold stung their cheeks, and they stepped briskly on the two-block walk to La India, a dismal, low-ceilinged neighborhood bar where Julio Antonio was keeping a 9:00 P.M. appointment. Earlier that day, a Cuban named José Magriñat—known to Mella's entourage as a gambler, two-bit delinquent, and informer—had phoned to dangle the offer of useful tips about Machado's machinations. Though comrades had tried to warn him off the meeting, Julio Antonio maintained that it was valuable to mine the enemy for information, and he agreed to talk with his compatriot that evening.

Shivering as the raw night air penetrated her thin coat but untroubled about the rendezvous, Tina accompanied Julio Antonio to the corner of Bolívar and República de El Salvador streets, where La India's saloon-style doors, shaped like champagne glasses, swallowed her companion into its raucous, sour-smelling darkness. A corpulent, heavy-jawed fellow, Magriñat sat tossing back glasses of beer as Mella approached. Tina, meanwhile, set off for the cable office on San Juan de Letrán Street in a bustling garment district rapidly emptying out for the night. Her steps hollow in the cavernous building, she put through Julio Antonio's night letter to *La Semana*, then stood awaiting his arrival.

The clock in the lobby was ticking off 9:25 when Mella's brown-overcoated, broad-hatted figure bounded in. As they left for home, picking their way along San Juan de Letrán's uneven pavement, Julio Antonio repeated Magriñat's message: Two Cuban gunmen—one tall, blond, and mustached, the other short and dark—had come to town carrying orders to kill him.

Tina was inwardly terrified and outwardly calm. Her body stiffened and her stomach began a slow churn as other recent warnings flooded into her head. From New York's community of Cuban exiles had come word that, in the aftermath of the fumbled invasion, Cuban strongman Gerardo Machado had judged the moment right to pick off Mella, and Diego Rivera, just back from the Caribbean nation, had admonished his comrade not to leave the house at night.

Believing it her duty, as a Party member and as Mella's *compañera*, Tina allowed herself no quivering remark or look of fright. Pablo O'Higgins once said of her that she "exercised great vigilance over herself, always acted with much gracefulness, with a valiant attitude.... [She never seemed] defeated or whiny; on the contrary, she straightened her head, walked quickly, always did it as if she dominated the situation, even if inside she was afraid." Julio Antonio, young and cocky, dismissed Magriñat's message as twaddle.

The apartment was twenty minutes away by foot. With Tina scurrying to keep pace with Julio Antonio's long stride, they entered Independencia Street, narrow and sinister as a tunnel, and poorly lit save for the shuddering beams of passing automobiles. A left turn put them on a wide, littered stretch of Balderas, where eerie shadows of mannequins shifted in the vitrines. They considered waiting for their usual trolley, then rejected the idea as too dangerous. Five short blocks down Morelos Avenue, the pair rounded a final corner onto Abraham González, and the edge of their building came into view. Tina leaned into her conversation with Julio Antonio. A sulfur yellow streetlight glared above. Her right hand dug into his overcoat sleeve; her left was thrust deep within her own coat pocket.

As they passed the stone wall of a coal-distribution yard, two sharp cracks burst from behind. Tina tasted hot, bitter gunpowder as she felt Julio Antonio's arm slipping from hers. One bullet had shattered his left elbow; another penetrated the spinal column, searing his lung, liver, vena cava, and stomach.

Shouting and flapping his arms, his Texan-style hat spiraling off, Julio Antonio bolted obliquely across the street, in the direction of home. In front of the variety store at number 19, some 150 feet from where the shots had exploded, he staggered, and the pavement reeled up into his face. Tina lunged behind on suddenly unsteady legs. At that moment, she said, "I didn't even think of the danger to myself. Seeing Julio Antonio run, I ran behind him, only trying to help him. Nothing else mattered. I didn't even turn around to see who was shooting." Finally overtaking Julio Antonio as his back crumpled down the building's facade, she knelt to cradle his head in her lap, brushing his forehead with her lips, smoothing his dark curls, and frantically imploring the shuttered windows beginning to pop open, "A car, people, a car!"

Realizing that Magriñat had set him up, Julio Antonio bellowed, "Magriñat has to do with this!"; "Pepe Magriñat knows all!"; "Know, everyone, that the Cuban government has had me assassinated!"; and "I am dying for the revolution!" Lowering his voice, he said, "Tina, I'm dying." She answered, "No, you aren't going to die. You're too young.... I don't want you to die, Julio Antonio." A bright red stain inexorably worked its way through his shirt, sweater, and coat and onto the sidewalk.

A teenaged boy loped up to gawk, and the harried neighborhood cop arrived at the scene. He let fly a question or two, answered only by pleas for a car, before running to phone in his report of a shooting. Across the street, a factory worker, stepping out for a brief errand, took in the situation with startled almond-shaped eyes. Among the curious converging from all sides were Tina's neighbors, the fifteen-year-old Campobello sisters, sent to fetch Frances Toor, who came running up as Red Cross paramedics bundled Julio Antonio into an ambulance that wailed off toward San Jerónimo Hospital.

As he was being undressed and prepared for surgery, Julio Antonio urged the doctors to operate immediately. District police commissioner Fernando Carrillo Rodríguez, misinformed that the Cuban ambassador had been shot, rushed in to take the victim's declaration. Julio Antonio's mellifluous voice was thinning, yet he managed to emit a statement. "I was accompanied by Tina Modotti..." he quavered, thrusting responsibility for the shooting directly upon Machado. By the time Carrillo Rodríguez read the words back to him, Julio Antonio, his hand too enfeebled to sign, his voice unable to speak, could only nod.

The commissioner then tracked down Tina, trembling, desolate, and hopeful. Nearby sat the blood-soaked pile of Julio Antonio's clothing, topped by his little red appointment book with matching pencil and the folded copy of *El Machete*. "Your name?" The words "Rose Smith Saltarini" dropped from her lips. She was an English teacher, a widow from San Francisco, California, and she lived at 21 Lucerna Street, she said.

Admitted into the harshly lit operating theater as Julio Antonio went under chloroform for two hours of surgery, Tina quivered and was braced by Frances. Diego Rivera and then Carleton Beals talked their way in. Tina undertook desperate mental negotiations with fate: "If the price is that I never see him again or that I see him in the arms of another woman, it does not matter. The important thing is that he live...." Dr. Díaz Infante completed surgery, pronouncing it a technical success yet shaking his head over the wounded man's chances for survival. A confusion of artificial respiration and injections ensued, but "life was slipping from [Julio Antonio] with cruel certainty for half an hour of agonizing suspense." At 1:40, doctors drew a sheet over Julio Antonio's head, and Tina collapsed, convulsed with grief, into Frances's arms.

Julio Antonio's death crashed upon her like a thunderbolt. Just hours before, he had been at her side, vital and adoring, her sweetheart, her comrade, her companion, her child, her "tropical jungle, blue sky and color of the earth." He inhabited all that she saw, felt, and did, and, already, she must have dimly perceived that his loss would drain her life of meaning and hue. All that remained to her were his words: "I am dying for the revolution!"

Tina had little time for reflection, however, as police hustled her past reporters vying for interviews and into the van, which then sped to the Sixth Precinct station on Victoria Street. When agents probed her declaration, she promptly conceded that she had been untruthful. She rescinded everything and began again, explaining her desire to keep her name out of the papers and thus safeguard her reputation with well-to-do clients whose portraits were her bread and butter. In truth, she had perhaps simply panicked and surrendered to the old impulse to concoct a story.

Dawn was muscling into the sky as Tina left the station for the Juárez Hospital morgue, where Julio Antonio had been autopsied and laid out, cold and mutilated, upon a concrete slab. Meanwhile, news of the shooting had spread like wildfire across the city, and the throng which had huddled in San Jerónimo Hospital's courtyard to hear Carleton Beals's shocking words—"Mella is dead"—now stirred about the morgue. One group of comrades haggled for release of the corpse while others clustered silently in the formaldehyde-reeking drabness. Diego made sketches (used years later for a mural at Manhattan's New Workers' School), and a plaster death mask was molded. Someone helpfully sprinted over to Abraham González Street to pick up Tina's Graflex, with which she made tender photographs of her companion. Death had given him a childlike quality and sweet smile. The camera set aside and comrades allowing her some privacy, she saw their precious final moments alone slip away.

By early morning, Tina was home, slumping bleary-eyed and desolate. When a pounding came at the door, she opened, to find a reporter eager for a scoop. He beheld a woman with red-rimmed eyes and mussed hair, shabbily dressed in an old gray sweater, black skirt, and mended stockings, caked here and there with blood. At first steadfastly refusing to respond to the newsman's questions, Tina abruptly released a torrent of words, all the while rubbing her forehead with her fingertips, as if "trying to get rid of an image," or fixing her eyes upon some distant object. As he scribbled away, eyes lifting from time to time to roam the bohemian "love nest," the phone jangled with news that comrades had carted Julio Antonio's corpse through the streets to lie in honor at Party headquarters. Cajoled into a photograph before the reporter departed, Tina ran a comb through her hair, then stared into the camera, her skin ashen, her eyes heavy-lidded and devoid of light.

Believing that mourning clothes carried the wrong symbolic import, she donned a navy blue suit and cerulean blouse with white polka dots. "For me, Julio Antonio is not dead" was her message to the world. "He will endure and live forever in the affection of his friends and in his great work." In the days that followed, some read signs of indifference in her choice of clothing and her intermittently successful attempts to will her face into an expression of serenity.

Tina arrived at Party offices, to find Julio Antonio's coffin in the second-floor conference room, outfitted with red-and-black draperies, red lightbulbs, and banks of carnations. An endless line of grief-stricken mourners had already begun its shuffle through the unheated and lugubrious chamber, and a newsboy handed out, right and left, a special edition of *El Machete* tacked together overnight. Tina joined the stiff-backed honor guard flanking the coffin as photographers jockeyed to frame shots of her with the hammer and sickle of Mella's shroud. Flashbulbs popping at her out of the penumbra, the still-sleepless Tina must have struggled not to sway or collapse.

But Tina's difficulties with the press had just begun. Astonishingly, in their coverage of Mella's death and the search for his assassins, the city's leading dailies would attempt to convince readers that, bored with her lover, Tina had paid for him to be gunned down by a rival for her affections. "A woman of steel dressed in flesh," she was not a victim of the crime, they theorized, but, rather, its instigator.

Speaking with one voice, Cuban exiles contended that Mella's slaying had been ordered by Machado (so vicious that he regularly fed his opponents to sharks in the Bay of Havana, they explained) and that the Cuban-flag incident had been an attempt by agents provocateurs to discredit Mella in the eyes of his compatriots and thus blunt outrage over his assassination. The Cubans' words were duly recorded and buried on page eight, while lurid innuendo about the life and loves of Tina Modotti rolled into the headlines on a high tide of ink.

In propounding the crime-of-passion theory, the right-wing press served as mouthpiece for Mexico City's general inspector of police, ex–private eye Valente Quintana, who was ingratiating himself with his superiors by besmirching Tina Modotti and, through her, the Mexican Communist party. According to Carleton Beals, Quintana (who had visited Cuba, where Machado pinned a medal or two on his chest) colluded in the assassination by protecting "the owner of red light houses on Cuatemotzén Street," where the killers had fled.

As a foreigner and a woman, Tina Modotti was useful to those eager to tar Bolshevists with the brush of depravity. Morally dismembered and strewn across the pages of the city's leading newspapers, she was left to be devoured by xenophobes, misogynists, and reactionaries. "The interesting Italian was wearing a black skirt and gray sweater molded onto her agile body," proclaimed *El Universal.* She was a Mata Hari who "lights her match in the half-light of passionate chambers," interjected *Excelsior.* "Drama goes with her, has been born with her and will die with her." In a day when women who smoked in public were branded whores, reporters made a point of mentioning her habit. Newsmen invented imaginary lovers for her and took seriously a crank who claimed to have watched her disrobe in Chapultepec Park. Somebody threw in the dime-novel theory that, being Italian, she was a fascist spy employed to lure Mella to his death.

If Tina had no inkling of the ordeal she was entering into, it was partly because her dealings with the mainstream press had always been pleasant. In her presence, reporters had half-forgotten their assignments, and editors had happily given a green light to features about her pictures and exhibitions. The aftermath of Mella's killing caught her unaware of how different the stakes had become.

Moreover, Tina was an "incorrigible innocent," as Vittorio Vidali once wrote, "not only...incapable of hating, but also she did not even understand the hatred of others." Trusting the press and the police to conduct a thorough investigation of the crime, she had faith that "the truth would come shining through." In the presence of scandalmongering reporters and power-hungry functionaries, she was almost unfailingly polite and unruffled.

Her first hint of what lay ahead came as she answered a Friday-afternoon legal summons. As she ran up the courthouse steps, a bystander thrust into her hand *El Universal Gráfico,* whose headline shrieked, THE PASSION MOTIVE. "It's a lie," she snapped back. "This is not a crime of passion." *El Universal,* meanwhile, offered its afternoon readers the full text of Mella's autopsy report, detailing the contents of his stomach as if laying out a feast to be plucked by vultures.

In the courtroom, Tina was made to repeat her story to stern-faced Judge Alfredo Pino Cámara, dubbed "the celebrity judge" for the high-profile cases over which he presided, and a bevy of his assistants. Afterward, flanked by Party leaders, she made her way to Valente Quintana's offices, where the hard-eyed, glabrous-cheeked little investigator pumped her with questions until nearly 9:00 P.M. When she dragged her way home, she discovered that the police had sealed off her apartment.

After a night of troubled sleep at the home of friends, Tina returned, haggard and grim-faced, to Abraham González Street. She stepped out of the elevator on the fifth floor, to find herself face-to-face with Police Chief Casimiro Talamantes, a big-boned man whose steel gray hair poked straight up from his head. Talamantes announced that she was under house arrest, amounting to twenty-four-hour police surveillance, before trundling her back downstairs and through a curious crowd to the assassination site. There, she was made to endure a reenactment of Julio Antonio's death. Photographers clicking away, inspectors bombarded her with questions of where, when, who, and how, and she responded graciously, unwilling to reveal publicly the rawness of her pain. Duty required that she sideline her own emotional needs in order to bring to light the vile deeds of Machado's henchmen.

Hustled back home, Tina watched, lips pursed and hands in pockets, as inspectors swarmed through her home, fingering objects, rummaging through desk drawers, and seizing pictures, letters, notes, and diaries. Photographs of Karl Marx and the hammer and sickle, prominently hung on the living room wall, must have fueled agents' zealousness to dismantle the place. Their hopes of finding sensitive political documents were apparently dashed by Tina's precautions, but they impounded nearly every memento of her short time with Julio Antonio. She could only have felt the intrusion as symbolic rape. When she departed for a 2:00 P.M. interrogation in the office of the procurer of justice, policemen were still ravishing her home.

In death as in life, Julio Antonio Mella galvanized the Left. On Friday, an angry crowd had massed around the high-walled Cuban embassy, hurling stones and chanting, *"¡Viva Mella!";* "Death to Machado!"; and "Death to the corrupt press!" At nightfall, protesters stormed out of Party offices to lead a round of volatile demonstrations that ended in shrieks when police turned fire hoses on the crowd in front of the National Theater.

The next morning's sun beamed on Mella's funeral procession, a long, sluggish stream wending its way through the capital for nearly six hours. Bobbing along at its head was the fallen hero's casket, shouldered by comrades and surrounded by trucks bearing panels of red and white flowers arranged into a hammer, sickle, and star. Brightly colored banderoles identified the Mexican Student Federation, the Anti-Imperialist League of the Americas, the Mexican Communist Youth Association, the International Center of Working Women, and on and on, in a roll call of the nation's militant and student organizations.

From the Communist party building on Mesones, the throng streamed to the National Palace, the School of Law, and the assassination site before converging onto the Paseo de la Reforma, Mexico City's Champs-Elysées. At each stop, speakers clambered atop automobiles to shout themselves hoarse with accusations against Machado and his thugs; at each departure, the "Internationale" swelled, filling the boulevards and echoing off the walls of bourgeois mansions. Detained until late afternoon by the procurer of justice, Tina missed most of the outpouring of grief and anger, arriving to claim her place near the head of the cortege only as it approached Chapultepec Park, whose Pantheon Dolores cemetery held Mella's gravesite.

As she marched the last mile to Julio Antonio's burial, Tina's posture communicated dignity and resoluteness taxed to their limits. She wore a felt toque pulled so low that one could barely see her eyes, shadowy pools constantly on the verge of spilling over. She could only have dreaded the coming moment, when she would give up Julio Antonio to the earth and to history.

With the crowd teeming in the watery light beneath the cemetery's giant eucalyptuses, Diego Rivera hammered out the final words—"Enough tears, comrades! Let's sing the 'Internationale!'"—before Julio Antonio's coffin was lowered into a symbolic third-class ditch. Tina's last minutes near him offered little opportunity for catharsis and comfort, however. With the inspirational melody ringing in her ears, she had to wrench herself away to keep a 5:30 appointment with Chief Inspector Quintana. Out of view of the multitude, she slowed her pace, dolefully and distractedly making her way back to the police station.

Three witnesses to the crime, all giving an account different from Tina's, had also been summoned to Quintana's offices. Ludwig Herberich, the German owner of the Sanitary Bakery at 22 Abraham González Street, had been idling in the doorway of his establishment when the fatal shots rang out. José Flores, an apprentice butcher, and student Anacleto Rodríguez had been chatting in the vestibule of their building next door. Cooling her heels with the men in Quintana's waiting room, Tina repeatedly raised her newspaper, as if to read, then lowered it again to study the faces—two dark-skinned and startlingly young, one pale and complacent—as if by careful scrutiny she might uncover the truth of the curious story they were telling.

Quintana sent for Tina first. The building unheated on a Saturday evening, she wore gloves, and one of the detectives huddled in a woolen coat. Motioning her to a straight-backed chair under a map that sliced the city into precincts, Quintana commenced his grilling as reporters gathered round: "How were you walking with Mella? Arm in arm? And on which side?"

She leapt from the chair, seizing the startled detective's arm to demonstrate. "Yes, we were arm in arm. I was on the side of the wall, and he on the outside. I was holding his left arm, like this."

"How do you explain, then, that Mella took a bullet in the left elbow, the same one that you were covering with your arm, and another wound on the left side, without your being hurt?"

Nonplussed, Tina paused. "I can't explain it.... I don't remember exactly how I was holding Mella's arm; probably I was grasping it lower or higher, like this.... I don't remember, but, yes, I was on that side, so I felt the flashes of gunpowder on the right side of my face."

Having scored a point for the morning papers, Quintana called for the two youths, who affirmed that they had seen three people, two men and a woman, striding down the west side of Abraham González Street, not the east, as Tina insisted. Though Tina's apartment was situated on the west, the trio had inexplicably crossed to the opposite sidewalk, when one man dropped back to plug bullets into the other. Ludwig Herberich's testimony was more precise. He had watched three people—Mella, Modotti, and a short man in a dark overcoat—enter Abraham González Street from the direction of the Paseo de la Reforma, to the west, then traverse the street. The short man halted, positioned himself behind Mella, and fired, before fleeing on foot.

"Oh, this is enough to drive me crazy!" Tina surrendered to her frayed nerves. "Where did you make that up?"

"No, señora," responded the baker. "I saw the three come from the Paseo de la Reforma side."

"That is not possible. I came with Mella from the Morelos Avenue side, in the direction of Bucareli Street. We didn't cross the street until after Mella was wounded, and I helped him get to the place where he fell, but nobody, not one person, was walking with us. Surely, you are the victim of an optical illusion, and probably the assassin came near us and, from a distance, appeared to be in line with Mella and me. I've said that the assassin came very close to us, and it's possible that you didn't see things right."

"No, señora, I see very well. It is not true that you came from the Bucareli side. You came from the Paseo de la Reforma side."

The session disintegrated into a verbal free-for-all, during which Tina posed several pointed questions, causing the young men to waver in their recollections. Herberich, however, refused to budge, and Quintana hurled accusations that Modotti was lying. Even as she blurted out her frustration, Tina remained courteous and apparently artless: "*¡Caramba!* I can't say anything more than the truth. You should believe me. I swear it upon the soul of my mother...." Privately, she was convinced that the witnesses had been bribed.

As the interrogation dragged on, Quintana reached for a letter confiscated that morning from Tina's apartment, the first of the documents police would play out like a good poker hand. Written by Xavier Guerrero, the note was signed "X" and postmarked Moscow. Distressed when Quintana read Xavier's words aloud, Tina accused the detective of impertinence and refused to reveal the writer's identity as reporters present at the interrogation chortled over the revelation of a "mysterious Mr. X."

Banned to a chilly hallway as José Magriñat took his turn, Tina wrapped herself in a serape and tried to rest. Meanwhile, the Cuban denied that his meeting with Mella had been a pretext to pinpoint the revolutionary's whereabouts. On the contrary, it was Mella, not he, who had sought the appointment, to request a contribution of eighteen pesos to cover costs for his magazine, *Cuba Libre.*

Quintana then put the hulking, insolent Magriñat face-to-face with Modotti, who came undone under the stare of the man she believed to be Julio Antonio's killer. She "shook noticeably, fidgeting with her hands and feet; she wanted to smoke but could barely light the cigarette. Magriñat stared her down, as though trying to dominate her, and her appearance seemed to indicate he succeeded." Relishing the situation, the Cuban taunted Tina about her claim not to have seen the face of Mella's assassin.

Remarking upon Tina's fatigue, Quintana halted the session around midnight. Though she tartly informed the detective that she would never tire of shedding light on the crime of Abraham González Street, Tina was relieved to gather up her belongings and prepare to depart. At that moment, however, a mental telepathist and would-be criminal psychologist from the United States, one Professor Maximilian A. Langsner, popped up in Quintana's offices. Police had sometimes used Langsner in baffling cases, though the charlatan's latest claim to fame was driving blindfolded through rush-hour traffic to publicize a Chrysler dealership. The investigation degenerated into grotesquerie as Tina was sent into an immediate one-hour session of hypnosis with Langsner. Afterward, he prattled to newsmen that Julio Antonio Mella's murder was indeed a crime of passion and that Tina's true love could be found in Moscow.

On Sunday morning, plainclothesmen were camping in her living room as Tina sought to sleep. Hawkers sold *Excelsior* to cries of "Tina Modotti refuses to name assassin of Julio Mella!" and "Tina's version of crime absurd!" as pressmen readied photographs lifted from Tina's darkroom for Monday's edition. To the snapshot of Julio Antonio asleep, they attached the imaginative caption "Photographic study made by Tina Modotti during Julio Antonio Mella's lifetime in order to give them both an idea of how he would look after death."

Meanwhile, telegrams rained upon Mexican president Emilio Portes Gil, out of town to recover from the flu. Leftist groups urged energetic action against the true culprits and the severing of diplomatic relations with Cuba. From the president's private secretary, Adolfo Roldán, in Mexico City, came word that a broad spectrum of public opinion was enraged over Mella's slaying and convinced that the government had reasons to cover up the killers' identities. "TINA MODOTTI COMPANION MELLA HAS BEEN IMPRISONED," Roldán's telegram to his boss continued, "AND IS TREATED WITH HARSHNESS THAT INSPIRES COMPASSION FOR HER DEJECTED STATE AS RESULT NERVOUS SHOCK." Apparently, Gen. (and future Mexican president) Lázaro Cárdenas, Mexico City mayor José Manuel Puig Casauranc, and others had Roldán's ear over the relentless assault on Modotti. On Monday morning, Puig Casauranc strode into police headquarters to exact a briefing and demand impartiality in the case.

Communists also had no intention of letting Mella's assassins escape as Modotti twisted in the wind. Pulling Diego Rivera down from his scaffolding, Party leaders put him in charge of an independent inquiry into the case. Diego was everywhere during the Mella affair: holding Tina's hand, interviewing witnesses, investigating leads, chiding police for wasting time on the passion theory, and orchestrating the Party's own reenactment of the crime. Shoulder-to-shoulder with comrades near the stone wall on Abraham González Street, he rolled his bulging orbs and said, rebukingly, "What kind of country is this that investigates crime using hypnotism? If the police can't do better than that, maybe the proletariat should take its place."

Wearing the same black coat that had taken her through Robo's funeral, Tina also spoke at the session, riveting her eyes upon reporters. "I have not said that my true love is in Moscow," she objected. "I also implore that [the press] no longer speak of my 'lovers,' but rather my 'companions.' It is not that I deny the first term; it's that the second is more appropriate."

Tina's feistiness may have been aroused by a Sunday-evening visit from her female comrades. Last light had already slipped from the sky, and the tall windows were drawn tightly shut, shielding Tina from nothing, however, since Quintana's agents lounged inside the apartment, and her belongings—what remained of them—were topsy-turvy. Surrounding Tina in the sparsely furnished living room, the women spoke in quiet, urgent tones of what should be done, seething, no doubt, because a man would never be dragged through the mud for his liaisons.

On Monday morning, professing that she no longer wished to conceal her love life, Tina granted an interview to sketch her relationships with Robo, Xavier, and Julio Antonio (though not Edward, whose nude photographs of her she knew to be in police possession). Graciela Amador, Concha Michel, Luz Ardizana, and others, meanwhile, drafted a statement of solidarity to the scandalmongering *Excelsior*.

> ...*Excelsior* is a cowardly liar for attempting to stamp the humanly impeccable personality of Tina Modotti with an appearance of amorality, which only exists in the atrophied mind of the editorialist and his underlings.
>
> We who for years have shared Tina's life of work and struggle; we who have known so well her much bitterness and her few joys; we who truly admire the moral force of this exceptional woman; we who also admire her as an artist and, finally, who judge ourselves highly honored to count her in the first rank of our militants, we can do no less than to declare it loudly so that everyone knows who Tina Modotti is.

As the week began, police pulled more confiscated "evidence" from their sleeves. Pairing Tina's photograph of a .45-caliber pistol with a .45 cartridge retrieved on Abraham González Street, they concluded that she possessed a picture of the murder weapon. The .45, she explained, had once belonged to Xavier Guerrero, who gave it to her to sell in partial repayment of a debt. Its purchaser, Swiss economist Fritz Bach, confirmed Tina's account, and, in any case, Mella was killed with a .38. Police then aha'd over an envelope covered with a drawing of the neighborhood, believed to be a blueprint for the crime until it emerged that the handwriting was Mella's and the map intended for a newly hired maid.

By Tuesday, a sea change was occurring in the Mella affair. Tina began showing up in court with a lawyer, the aging leonine liberal José María Lozano, and police purported to have discovered that Nicanor Mac-Partland was not Julio Antonio Mella's rival for Tina's affections, but, rather, the same person. Most significant, with a nod from President Portes Gil, Puig Casauranc announced that Valente Quintana had been dismissed from the case on grounds of bias, and agents began to move in on Cuban suspects.

Though police were acknowledging that the passion theory had withered, Judge Alfredo Pino Cámara was not yet prepared to relinquish it. The aim of Tuesday's session, he enjoined—small black mustache bobbing up and down on his fleshy face—was to "discover in [Tina], her true modality, her feminine psychology." Under the banner THE SENTIMENTAL PROBLEM OF TINA MODOTTI, *El Universal* advised its readers that "Tina Modotti, romantic and emotional, is prone to grand passion."

Still dogged by plainclothesmen, Tina girded herself for the ordeal in a smart black felt hat with silver cherry ornaments and the pale sweater and black skirt she had worn on the night of Julio Antonio's death. Facing a circle of functionaries and reporters around Pino Cámara's conference table, she chain-smoked her way through the interrogation by Telesforo Ocampo, Jr., an ambitious young lawyer with matinee-idol looks. As Ocampo made a show of laying siege to the "deep secrets of her past," she maintained her composure, gluing her eyes to the plumes of smoke ascending from her cigarettes.

> "Did you not have a relationship with another person [at the time Mella was courting you]?"
>
> "I had no spiritual bond with any other person when I became close to and fell in love with Mella; earlier I had cut off a previous attachment."
>
> "Do you know Xavier Guerrero?"
>
> "Yes, I met him in Los Angeles, California, where he was commissioned by the Secretary of Industry, in 1923, to exhibit popular art."
>
> "What political ideas did he have?"
>
> "He was and is a Communist, affiliated with the Communist Party of Mexico."

"Whom do you believe had stronger ideas about Communism, Mella or Guerrero?"

"Both."

"Are you sure?"

"Absolutely."

"Do you not consider it an outrage to a person or a lover to carry on a romantic correspondence with another? In other words, having intimate relations with one, would it not be an outrage if one wrote of love to another?"

"I consider it so."

"Did you love Guerrero very much?"

"In his time, yes."

"Do you, having relations with Mella, think it good to receive gifts from another person?"

"Oh! Yes, from friends."

"No, I'm talking about people who have amorous intentions. Is it honest, licit or moral to receive these gifts?"

"If I knew that they were doing it with amorous or self-interested intentions, I would not accept it, but there are many ways of giving a gift."

"Can you affirm to us if Guerrero professed great love for you?"

"Yes, I can affirm it, but the love he had for me was less than the greatest love of his life, that which he felt for the revolution, being ready to sacrifice himself for it."

"Do you believe that when a person feels great love for another, he sacrifices her for an idea?"

"If the person is worthy, yes. Revolutionaries' love is not something isolated from their activities, but rather is related to their political ideals...."

"Did you ever tell Mella of your relationship with Guerrero?"

"Yes, from the first moment, then I felt a great struggle inside myself."

"What was Guerrero's intimate conduct with you? Was he tender or did he have some difficulty with you?"

"Yes, he was very tender, and we had absolutely no difficulty."

"You were never threatened by him?"

"Never..."

"Did you know Mella's secret political work?"

"His secret work, no."

"Then explain this: 'I do not want the others to know what you know.'"

"It is from the trip Mella took with the intention of entering Cuba to foment a revolution, but he did not want his Communist friends to know it."

"He wanted to foment a revolution in Cuba?"

"Of course, those were always his intentions...."

As if Ocampo's probes of her romantic and political life were not sufficiently stinging, Pino Cámara ordered Tina to read from two most intimate pieces of correspondence, Julio Antonio's love letter written in Veracruz and her own message of adieu to Xavier Guerrero. The press reprinted both in full, thus inviting not only Tina's well-heeled photography clients but also all of Mexico to rummage around in her personal life. Her distress must have been boundless.

Though the passion theory was clearly flimflam, Tina remained suspect for the discrepancy between her testimony and those of the three witnesses. Events broke in her favor when an electrician named Antonio Ojeda Basto donned a suit and tie to present himself at the main police station and offer a vivid account of the events of January 10. On his way home that evening, Ojeda Basto had made his habitual stop at the Sanitary Bakery to pick up a loaf of bread for breakfast. He found the establishment's front door locked, though light seeped from its edges. Reaching his building, he climbed the stairs to his apartment, only to discover a burned-out lightbulb, which sent him back outside for a candle from the variety store across the street. As he set foot on the sidewalk, two shots exploded to his right. His eye caught one man ambling toward Morelos Avenue as another spurted in the opposite direction, a woman scrambling hard behind. At first mistaking the running man for the aggressor, Ojeda Basto sank back into his doorway as the fellow plunged to the pavement directly across the street. The woman went down after him, scooping him into her arms and wailing pitifully for a car to get him to a hospital. When the electrician approached the couple, his first inquiry to the woman was about the attacker. Receiving no answer, he rushed home to phone for an ambulance, then returned, recognizing the wounded man as Julio Antonio Mella, whom he knew through the General Confederation of Workers.

"What happened, Comrade Mella?"

"They have had me killed on orders of the Cuban embassy. Machado has ordered me killed."

As a crowd collected, two well-dressed men braked their automobile and sidled up to Mella. Taking advantage of the hubbub, one lifted the wounded man's shirt and sweater, then signaled the other, "He's done for."

His testimony called into question, Ludwig Herberich allowed that the three people coming from the Paseo de la Reforma might have been a different group, since he had not really been paying close attention. Herberich's statements and motives remain obscure. A partial explanation came on Wednesday evening, however, as Judge Pino Cámara presided over another reenactment, this one at the exact time of the murder. The police officer playing the baker's role perceived that the dazzle of the streetlight under which the assault had occurred caused a foreshortening effect, and thus perhaps the mysterious third figure described by witnesses stood at some distance from Mella and Modotti.

On January 17, as her name was officially cleared, Tina's eyes briefly regained their old sparkle. José Magriñat was arrested, only to be released a few days later for insufficient evidence. The case floundered and went nowhere until 1932, when it was reopened under pressure from Mella's widow. Large sums of money were traced from Havana via New York to Mexico City, but the public never learned whose pockets had been lined. Though reimplicated, José Magriñat walked free until 1933, when Machado was overthrown and Communists reportedly plugged a bullet into his henchman.

During the affair's last headline-grabbing days, *Excelsior* took advantage of the stash of items seized in Modotti's apartment to dip Mella as well as Modotti in vitriol. Underneath an unflattering photograph of Julio Antonio's wife and another of the Cuban entwined with an old girlfriend, the newspaper began serializing embarrassing excerpts from his adolescent diary, never informing readers that its expressions of immature enthusiasm and confused libido were those of a sixteen-year-old. Mella came across as "amorous, egotist...inexperienced, and burning for power and glory...."

Excelsior also purported to possess scandalous nude photographs of Tina and Julio Antonio. These images alone, sniped an editorial, were grounds to "deprive Mella of posthumous honors and to relegate his concubine to the category of feminine species who sells or leases love." Buttonholed by Rivera and by Tina's old friend the caricaturist Miguel Covarrubias, *Excelsior's* editor in chief pulled the supposedly damning pictures out of a desk drawer. Mella's was an identification photo required for membership in a Havana rowing club, and Modotti's was a nude by Edward Weston. The image, the artists archly informed the editor, resulted from Tina's work as a professional model for the celebrated North American photographer, and the nude was a longtime theme in Western art.

Tina initiated a lawsuit against *Excelsior* for its characterization of her as a harlot, though she had lost faith in legalities. Ten days after the murder, she stood in her small photo laboratory, exchanging observations with a *La Prensa* reporter who had taken a fairly evenhanded approach to the case. Without makeup, her hair summarily pinned back, she wore a long Japanese kimono whose colors, thought the newsman, brought out the ivory tones in her complexion. She wore oversized slippers, which she halfheartedly attempted to conceal. Chatting with the reporter, Tina turned her attention to the tray of fixing bath into which she was gently submerging a print. "This photograph was taken two days before the tragedy," she explained.

A group portrait made at a committee meeting, the image depicted Julio Antonio Mella surrounded by comrades, among them David Alfaro Siqueiros, Sandalio Junco, Vittorio Vidali, and Rogelio Teurbe Tolón. Viewed through the trembly liquid, the boyishly handsome Julio Antonio gazed straight ahead, forever young, vibrant, combative, and fraternal. Tina's heart must have been broken at the thought of photography's magical yet wretchedly inadequate ability to steal from death.

Tina herself sometimes appeared transformed in photographs taken in the aftermath of Julio Antonio's murder. In one, she stands arms folded across her chest, head slightly tilted, eyes staring and expressionless, and mouth gathered up into what resembles a smirk. Although she would never utter the words, her posture announced devastation so deep that a dispirited defense of her body was all she could muster. A terror had installed itself within her, the terror of having surrendered her heart and soul to someone who took them with him to a violent end.

More than a decade later, at the time of Tina's death, she still carried in her purse a small picture of Julio Antonio Mella.

Chapter 10

Mexico City (1929–1930)

THE MARTYRED JULIO ANTONIO MELLA swiftly became "a symbol around which everyone...in Mexico revolve[d]," and Tina a requisite presence at meetings and observances. In a letter to Edward, she acknowledged "so much suffering" and bemoaned a heart "full of pain and bleeding...." She yearned to "give vent to all [her] pent up emotions," yet cut herself short. "...I cannot afford the luxury of even my sorrows today—I well know this is no time for tears; the most is expected from us and we must not slacken—nor stop halfway—rest is impossible—neither our consciences nor the memory of the dead victims would allow us that." She ruthlessly choked back her grief and refused to indulge in moping around in ashes and dust.

Sometimes pointedly donning the outfit she wore on the tragic night and pulling a beret low over her forehead, Tina steeled herself to step briskly from her apartment, across the very pavement once splattered with Julio Antonio's blood. A photograph of one Communist assembly catches her, with her left hand propped on her hip and her right clamping a cigarette, as she waits her turn to speak. Sad, dusky, and matter-of-fact, her eyes stray around the meeting hall, solid with attentive cadres. A portrait of Mella affixed to the wall dwarfs the panel of Party chiefs flanking her. Tina was on hand in January when an army of peasants packed the city's largest theater to pay its respects to the fallen leader, and in February, she took the spotlight before throngs of militants and sympathizers at a six-hour memorial meeting. A Russian chorus performed "Immortal Victims," the crowd thrilled to Eisenstein's epic *Ten Days That Shook the World,* and Tina exhorted the hero's admirers to fight, not weep. "In Mella," she assured a hushed auditorium, "they killed not only the enemy of the dictatorship in Cuba, but the enemy of all dictatorships....I affirm that the assassin of Mella is the President of Cuba, Gerardo Machado."

Or so she believed, and probably correctly. However, ultimate responsibility for Julio Antonio Mella's slaying has never been established, and one plausible theory holds that he was liquidated by the Comintern, in a plot perhaps rigged with Machado or Mexican authorities. If so, the linchpin of the affair would have been Stalin's man in Mexico, Tina's close friend and later lover, Vittorio Vidali, whose charm belied an ambitious and ruthless operative. It is hard to say if accusations against the Party, which began circulating not long after Mella's death, ever reached Tina's ears. If so, she no doubt dismissed them and held firm to her belief in Machado's culpability. But one shudders for her to imagine a scenario in which she unwittingly lived with the man behind the murder of the love of her life.

Tina was aware, however, that while Communists put a gloss of Red hero on Julio Antonio Mella, he was actually a maverick. In 1927, Soviet chief Joseph Stalin had ousted archrival Leon Trotsky from Soviet Party ranks, and a great schism was opened between Stalinists, on one hand, and, on the other, a loose collection of opposition Communists, Left socialists, and Trotskyites. Julio Antonio's friendliness with Spanish Left oppositionist Andrés Nin during the Cuban's 1927 visit to Moscow was taken as one of several signs of his deviance, but, in any case, Julio Antonio was temperamentally incapable of the blind obedience required of Stalinists.

Moreover, he rejected the Soviet leader's strategy of building socialism in only one country, the U.S.S.R., and when the Comintern dictated confrontation rather than collaboration with progressive bourgeois forces, Mella spurned the Party line. He believed in closing ranks against the Yankees, and he meant to use a Left political alliance to deliver Cuba from the dictator Machado. His plan to invade the island, thereby touching off an insurrection, was destined to win no favor with Party stalwarts. Rather than go by the book and seek permission from the Mexican Central Committee, Mella and his cohorts had plotted their invasion surreptitiously, though he took Tina into his confidence. Shortly before the little flotilla was to weigh anchor, he had cautioned her: "You KNOW NOTHING, understand? when it comes to them [the Party leadership]."

Apologists for various political viewpoints can select from a myriad of confusing and contradictory stories about Julio Antonio Mella's relationships with Communist colleagues during the last months of his life. One tale recounts that Moscow's representatives excoriated the Cuban at a Latin American conference but the Mexican Central Committee repudiated all charges against him. Others have it that Mella was expelled from Communist leadership, and perhaps from the Party altogether, and may or may not have been reinstated. According to one source, Vidali went to Havana, where he got hold of a resolution from Cuban Communists that Mella should submit to Party discipline. Confronted with the document, Julio Antonio hurled invective at his comrades and fired off an insulting letter of resignation but later reconsidered and apologized for the sake of unity.

Mella was a charismatic, internationally recognized figure, and his heterodoxy posed a delicate dilemma for Vittorio Vidali. That the pair vied for Party leadership, and that Vittorio was possibly in love with Tina, put a second edge on their polemic. The two revolutionists were like earth and air, picaro and paladin: one a favorite son of the Comintern, and the other Cuba's would-be liberator. The Spanish Left oppositionist Julián Gorkin maintained that Vittorio barked at Julio Antonio, some twenty-four hours before the slaying and in front of a dozen witnesses, "Always remember, comrade, there are only two ways out of the International, expulsion or death!" Victor Alba, a historian and anti-Stalinist Marxist from Spain, submitted that "Mella...[was assassinated] by a double agent on the contemporaneous orders of Cuban dictator Gerardo Machado and of the 'advisors' of the Comintern [Argentinean Vittorio] Codovilla and Vittorio Vidali."

There is reason to be skeptical that Moscow would dictate Mella's elimination in 1929, several years before the onset of the Soviet terror. Yet documents recently unearthed in Moscow archives suggest that the tyrant was ordering political executions well before the mid-1930s. Why would Moscow's finger point to distant Latin America? A former secret agent for Fidel Castro, Juan Vivès, reports that after Stalin chose Havana as his headquarters for clandestine operations in the Western Hemisphere, he demanded that the disruptive Mella be silenced, using Machado as the fall guy. By Vivès's account, a Cuban Communist employed by Vidali slipped five thousand pesos to Machado's Mexican agents in payment for the murder.

If Julio Antonio's assassination is shrouded in confusion, so is the matter of Tina's political affiliation. One opinion is that, won over to her companion's point of view, she had dropped her Communist orthodoxy. "Frankly, her true affiliation is...anti-fascism with a tinge of socialism," reported *La Prensa* at the time of Julio Antonio's death. "Strictly speaking, she is not a Communist." *Excelsior* chimed in that the couple pursued ends similar to those of Communists but used other means, and Carleton Beals attested that "she was pictured as an agent of the Communists, though she was no Communist at the time, for Mella had been at odds with the Communist line and, I believe, had just broken with the party, though this is now concealed, and he is considered a martyr." Yet not a word about internecine quarrels escaped Tina's lips, and upon Julio Antonio's death, she flew back into the Party fold. Hers was a high-minded, bighearted communism that, magnanimously or naïvely, sidestepped tactical debates and dismissed factional struggles. Now, another dimension was added to Tina's militancy, for she moved into the powerful, all-explaining Party as into a great emotional sanctuary.

"[W]hat of her now?" Tina's friend Anita Brenner had inquired of her diary in the days following the tragedy. "The logical thing would next be [an affair with the painter, Dr.] Atl, then psychoanalysis, then spiritualism, then the Church penance and absolution...the attitude would be logical not for her sins but because of her temperament." But the irreverent Anita misunderstood that Tina's extraordinary psychological suppleness had failed her at last. Incurably brokenhearted and reeling from her public savaging, Tina nonetheless tenaciously and perversely suppressed the urge to attend to her own emotional needs. Her responses to the deaths that framed her Mexican experience were utterly dissimilar. After Robo's loss, she had surrendered herself to a tide of grief, eventually discovering fresh creativity and happiness, but upon "the tragedy of my soul" that was the death of Julio Antonio, she rigorously interiorized her pain. Left unattended, the wounds festered, and her suffering was long and deep.

In a study of the "protean personality," psychiatrist Robert Jay Lifton argues the coexistence in certain individuals of two seemingly opposing life forces, proteanism and fundamentalism. Those who lead improvised and eclectic lives, he observes, are apt to respond to emotionally devastating and chaotic situations by self-surrender to a religious or political ideological system. "However the self may seem to be falling apart, 'fundamentalism provides explanations that put everything back together again,'" he writes. "The self becomes increasingly totalized, ensconced in an all-embracing ideological structure."

To say that Tina surrendered herself to the Stalinized Party is not to say that her deepening commitment to Communist militancy was mere visceral reaction. She had behind her, after all, half a decade of well-considered, hard-fought political battles. But the Party took on the additional role of emotional prop, and estrangement from its ranks would have left her feeling useless and wasted. She became increasingly self-disciplined, chary, and rigid. It was a measure of her steady transformation that, while she had long juggled disparate circles of friendship, socializing with non-Communists now seemed expendable.

Monna Alfau stopped off at Abraham González Street one day, and the two women were their usual gracious selves. "I saw dear Tina last week," Monna wrote Edward; "she is a brave girl and very much to be admired. She has gone through a lot of sad things but she is a strong female, a faithful friend. We do not see her as often as we would like to, but we know that she is busy all the time. She never comes to see us or goes to see anybody; but everybody loves her just the same and understand[s]." But it was virtually the last time the pair came face-to-face, and six months later, Monna vented her indignation that "Tina has sacrificed everything to this damn Communist Party."

At times Tina could hardly remember the gleeful days of her early friendship with Monna, when Mexico had burst upon her with the joy of an exploding piñata. "I am living in a different world Edward," she admitted, "strange how this very city and country can seem so utterly different to me than it seemed years ago! At times I wonder if I have really changed so much myself...."

Another generation attracted by Mexico's romantic radicalism now bandied about Tina's name as a curiosity for tourists in the know. The poet Kenneth Rexroth, then twenty-three, gawked at her in a crowded café "where [artists] all hung out along with heavily armed politicians, bull-fighters, criminals, prostitutes, and burlesque girls. The most spectacular person of all was a photographer, artist, model, high-class courtesan, and Mata Hari for the Comintern, Tina Modotti. She was the heroine of a lurid political assassination and was what I guess is called an international beauty. I had outgrown my fondness for the Kollontai type and she terrified me."

Another newcomer that spring was pretty, nineteen-year-old painter Ione Robinson, who pulled in from Los Angeles for a stint as Diego's assistant. Ione was amazed

> when I saw Tina, that she could be a *femme fatale,* or an accomplice in a sensational crime. I had expected so much that I was disappointed, for she wore heavy blue overalls and her face was without makeup of any kind, accentuating a sallow, brownish skin. Her hair grows too low on her forehead, and it was parted in the middle and pulled into a bun on the back of her neck, but her eyes were really striking, and so was the manner in which she held her mouth half open when she was not speaking.

Upon Ione's arrival, Diego had conducted the young woman to Tina's flat, where she was to stay for several days. As they talked, Ione's eye went straight to Julio Antonio's portrait, framed in black and adorned with a freshly cut miniature rose, and to his death mask looming chillingly over her bed. Occupying the living room, its once-pristine walls penciled with quotations from Marx and Lenin, was Tina's other houseguest, her twenty-five-year-old brother Ben. A zealous militant who was as humble as his sister before Party intellectuals, Ben had arrived for a seven-month stay and hired on in a Mexican cement factory. Her visitors notwithstanding, Tina found time to give unstintingly to the cause, managing Mexican Red Aid and allowing Communist meetings to overrun the apartment.

Meanwhile, requests for Modotti photographs poured in from all sides, and only by keeping a tight hand on her schedule could she more or less meet the demand. With uncommon self-discipline, she regularly burrowed into the darkroom.

By 1929, her work was becoming a fixture in the burgeoning international picture press. In Germany, it appeared on the pages of the lively *AIZ* (Workers' Illustrated Newspaper), a weekly by and for the proletariat, and

in France readers viewed Modottis in the experimental journals *BIFUR,*
Monde, L'Art vivant, and *transition* (alongside Man Ray's cameraless rayo-
graphs, James Joyce's *Work in Progress*—later titled *Finnegans Wake*—and
other avant-garde art). She was also the darling of the New York monthly
New Masses, which ran four Modotti covers within a year. In June 1929, it
was *Mexican Miner's Wife Picketing Before a Mine in Jalisco,* a photograph
probably posed on Tina's roof, despite its title. The photographer's model
was Communist militant Benita Galeana, seen walking with resolute and
unhurried gait toward a distant aspiration. Benita shoulders a wind-
whipped banner whose wedge converges with her figure to make a bold,
intriguing shape. The photograph was to appear over various titles, unsurprisingly, since it summarizes and idealizes protest for social justice.

Other calls for pictures arrived from the Brussels-based *Variétés,* the
British *Journal Almanac,* and a photography salon in Portland, Oregon, but
they were answered tardily, if at all. Some months earlier, when New York's
Creative Art wanted images for a Mexican theme issue, Tina had apparently
improvised with prints she had on hand. Editor Lee Simonson complained
to Carleton Beals, who was coordinating things on the Mexican end: "The
pictures Tina Modotti sent won't do.... I must have her famous one of the
Mexican hat scene in the market place and other fine ones of that series
showing the Mexican environment." But he never got the hat scene and had
to string out the Mexican theme in two issues. Sixteen reproductions of
Rivera murals, all Modottis, and three Orozcos, probably her work as well,
appeared in January, and February brought five more reproductions, seven
examples of her creative work, and an essay by Carleton Beals who wrote
most evocatively of her early still lifes such as the two lilies, which, he said,
"she has depicted with a delicacy and innocence reminiscent of the angel
trumpets of Fra Angelico, but depicted in some gray dawn of which Fra
Angelico never dreamed." Her subjects and approach had changed, he went
on to say, and "the inner spirit of modern life reveals itself in her newly
developed love of signs, or script, the flow of printed word, which imparts
to some of her pictures an animated sort of stillness, a taut tenseness."

Meanwhile, portraiture and reproductions continued as Tina's major
source of income. Among Mexico City artists, it was a must to have one's
work photographed by Modotti. She was overwhelmed by orders from the
Contemporáneos, a set of painters who quested after "Mexicanness" in for-

mal values, and from Frances Toor, who commissioned dozens of shots of masks for a *Mexican Folkways* essay by Miguel Covarrubias. Meanwhile, portrait sitters trooped in and out of the apartment, among them the Soviet news agency TASS's correspondent Joseph Freeman, politician Ramón de Negri, art patron Antonieta Rivas Mercado, and swank Boston socialite Alice Leone Moats, married to a chewing-gum magnate. "Tina has been photographing her," Ione Robinson wrote home; "she has not been able to get a good shot yet and is annoyed with Mrs. Moats, but grim in her determination to take something good, so Mrs. Moats comes to Tina's nearly every day with boxes of beautiful clothes from Chanel and Vionnet to be photographed in." Though Tina uniformed herself in coveralls or white shirt, dark skirt, and sensible shoes, some part of her still adored fashion, and Ione noticed that Tina eyed her own frocks "like a nun who has renounced all worldly possessions."

Mrs. Moats found an opportunity to take Ione aside and mention confidentially that radical, red star–wearing elements of the sort found around Tina were potentially damaging to a girl's reputation. Shrugging off the advice, the painter took in

> a small party Tina gave to celebrate [Siqueiros's return from a Comintern conference], and when I came in he was sitting in the middle of the room like a prophet, talking with an energy that had everyone spellbound. He…is a green-eyed Mexican, very handsome with white skin and black, curly hair. Several other members of the old Syndicate were at Tina's. [Artist] Fermín Revueltas… was sitting in a corner very 'lit up' and dressed like an Indian. [Painter] Carlos Mérida, who speaks French and English, talked to me about Paris and his life with Modigliani…. Then there was Dr. Atl, a funny little man with a beard who paints very badly…. Pablo O'Higgins was there too; he used to be Diego's assistant and comes from California, though you would never know it except for the color of his hair. Pablo lives on a roof, and is an ardent Communist. Of course, everyone who comes to Tina's is a Communist….

Among Communists, as others, conversations turned to presidential elections that year. Having institutionalized the revolution by creating the National Revolutionary party (the precursor of today's PRI), synonymous with both the Mexican state and his own machine, ex-President Plutarco Elías Calles was running the country from his Cuernavaca mansion through a string of puppet presidents. Callistas chose the compliant Pascual Ortiz Rubio as their candidate for president, while former minister of public education José Vasconcelos threw his hat into the ring for a moral crusade against corruption and subservience to the Yankees. Meanwhile, Communists made common cause with Red trade unionists and a peasants' group to propose one Pedro V. Triana.

On Sunday, April 7, in Tizayuca, a dusty dairy-farming village and bastion of communism in the state of Hidalgo, both Triana's campaign and Red Aid's new publication for workers and peasants were launched with great fanfare. Astutely timed to coincide with the tenth anniversary of the murder of campesino hero Emiliano Zapata, the event drew a large and enthusiastic crowd. Sunshine poured like warm honey over brown-skinned peasants streaming into town as banners gently fluttered, a brass band blared, and notables nosed through the thronged central plaza on horseback. It was the sort of comradely event Tina adored, replete with rounds of revolutionary songs. Rousing choruses of "Vive Lenin! Down with the King!" topped her favorite, "Red Banner." Yet she quickly fell to work documenting the occasion, scrambling to high places for plunging crowd shots and tilting her camera upward for a photograph of Diego delivering finger-wagging oratory about the failure of the bourgeois revolution.

In truth, the photographs' suggestion of a benign village fair is misleading, for Mexico had become a seething volcano, liable to erupt at any moment. The Comintern's hotheaded new policies dictated tactics of belligerence and class confrontation. Communist parties worldwide were ordered to cut all ties to the powers that be and set up rival people's governments. In Mexico, the traditional, right-wing election-year insurrection was under way, and the Party's strategy was to recruit workers and peasants into armed militias that loyally charged into combat side by side with the Mexican army. The uprising quelled, however, the masses were to outflank authorities and retain power in liberated territories, where long-promised land would be distributed and the people would govern through soviets.

In a panel at the Ministry of Public Education, Diego painted a scenario for the brewing insurrection. Here Tina again wears the assassination outfit, though her pullover is no longer gray but, rather, bright Bolshevik red. She and Frida Kahlo, clad in a workingman's shirt and star pin, distribute rifles and bullet-laden bandoleers to the insurgent masses as Siqueiros, Vidali, and Mella, his eyes locked with Tina's, look on. The setting is a factory overflowing with workers, one of whom incites comrades to rally round peasants already off to battle outside. Hammer-and-sickle insignias are brandished, along with a banner appropriating Zapata's slogan, "Land and Liberty."

As the government bolstered a reputation for tolerance by allowing the artist to script revolution on its ministry walls, police went on the offensive against the Communist menace, suppressing a number of publications and threatening foreign radicals, such as Tina, with the "33," a reference to the constitutional clause authorizing summary deportations without trial. On May Day, with Tina taking photographs for *El Machete* and *Labor Defender,* a demonstration turned bloody when participants encircling the U.S. embassy were beaten by riot squads. Guerrilla skirmishes followed, peasants were forcibly disarmed, and soldiers responded to a Communist Youth appeal not to fire upon the masses by dragging the militants off to prison. Police swarmed through Party headquarters, smashing printing presses and padlocking the building. Only days after he had sat talking in Tina's living room, the congenial campesino leader José Guadalupe Rodríguez was ambushed and summarily dispatched by a firing squad.

Tina lived the crisis hour by hour, and it was probably not until after Ben's departure for New York in August—the last she would see of her family for a decade—that she conceded she could no longer bear the stress. She fled Mexico City, crawling by rickety trains to the remote Mexican isthmus southeast of Oaxaca. There, on a dry and rocky lowland bitten by hot-chili-pepper winds, the towns of Tehuantepec and Juchitán sprawl around crumbling market plazas. A torpid guest house, surrounded by blazes of bougainvillea and clumps of high, shimmery coconut palms, offered Tina a room, where, shuttered into a murky stillness, she could spend long hours alone with her ragged sorrows.

The region is fabled for its women, known as Tehuanas. Dressed in flamboyant crimson-and-vermilion-embroidered *huipiles* and sweeping ruffled skirts, their jet black hair braided with a rainbow of ribbons and their ample bosoms ablaze with jewelry fashioned from gold coins, self-confident and bawdy women glide through the dusty streets like majestic sailing ships. Tina marveled as they hawked live iguanas and oversized tortillas, lolled in brightly hued hammocks, and danced together at afternoon *velas* that shut down the town. The women running its markets, with the men bending low in the fields, marked the culture as a matriarchy in the popular imagination. Mexico City's intellectuals admired the Tehuanas' regal bearing and pride in their Zapotec heritage, and painters had begun to use their images as icons suggesting an unbowed, authentic, anticolonialist Mexico. Their dress later became the rage in some artistic circles and painter Frida Kahlo's trademark.

During her interlude on the isthmus, Tina made dozens of images, most off the mark of her usual meticulously composed and richly connotative work. In the streets, she was obliged to photograph quickly, but not aggressively, and the women sometimes flashed smiles, while they were known to throw stones at men. Here cluttered with detritus, there blurred by passing life, Tina's pictures depict gossiping vendors, a welter of children bathing in the river, and two generations of women crowned with lovely painted gourds. Later, she made contact prints, mailed to family and friends with scrawled captions. To Edward, she apologized: "I am sending you a few of the snapshots done in T[ehuantepec], forgive me but I am just sending you from the ones I happen to have duplicates on hand, of course I have many more done while there, but alas, mostly are in the same condition as the ones I am sending you, either messy or moved...." She was in the habit of begging pardon, however, for photographs that did not square with his aesthetic, and it is possible that her pictures hinge on an impulse to try straightforward description of street life. If unsuccessful as artworks, the results were more faithful to the Tehuanas' everyday experience than were idealized Indian beauties that spoke to Mexico City's desire for intellectual metaphor. Carleton Beals affirmed that Tina now sought "a perfect snapshot. The moving quality of life rather than still studies absorbs her."

Yet she also made emblematic portraits, such as the carefully arranged *Woman of Tehuantepec,* dignified by traditional apparel, a distant, clear-eyed gaze, and her position above the camera's lens. *Mother and Child* belongs to Tina's occasional series on maternity. Wearing a nondescript dress and viewed in profile, from chin to the arc of her pregnant belly, Tina's subject is an Everywoman anchoring, with one solid arm, a hefty naked child. As if to continue her meditation on womanhood and fortitude, Tina attached

her Graflex to a tripod and backed up to a mud-and-wattle wall, using a
long cable release to click off a self-portrait. By donning the Tehuana's distinctive garments, Tina symbolically assumes her reputed strength, and in
picturing herself in "quintessentially Mexican" dress, the photographer
declares a deep and abiding identification with the country that she now
knew she would have to leave. The image is a spiritual passport, and a tal-
isman of her love for the Mexican people.

As she poses, Tina's haze of sorrow has dissipated, and her face is
open and unstrained. This was virtually the last picture of the vibrant,
luminous Tina. In rare future photographs, her vulnerability would be
shielded with an averted or watchful look. A snapshot made in Mexico City
a few months hence shows an unsmiling woman with arms folded impatiently across her chest, as if she were her own bodyguard or, in Vittorio
Vidali's expression, "a kind of castle with her drawbridges always up, inac-
cessible."

The breathing spell on the isthmus had offered Tina the rare luxury
of keeping creative photography in the center of her attention. With political work and picture-taking chores for the Party absorbing much of her
time, she believed that the quality of her artistic work was in decline. In
July, she had mailed to Edward a package of prints for a group show at the
Berkeley Art Museum. Distressed by the low standard of pieces about to
fall under the master's eye, she gingerly touched upon the idea of renouncing creative photography altogether:

> Only twenty and now that they are all wrapped and ready to
> send I wish I could omit about half of them. I am sure that if it
> wasn't for the trouble of undoing the package I no doubt would dis-
> card at least ten. Really Edward it takes a lot of nerve on my part to
> send to this exhibit, and *especially* to send to you the poor efforts of
> these last two years of work. But I have written you enough already
> so that you will be prepared for the worst..... You know Edward I
> still retain the good standard of photographic perfection, the trou-
> ble is that I have lacked the necessary leisure and peace to work sat-
> isfactorily.... At times I feel that it would be more honest on my
> part to give up all pretences and not do any more photography, out-
> side of the purely commercial and portraiture work. Yet it is a sac-

rifice and it hurts me to even think of that, so I go on but the results never satisfy me.

As Tina fretted over the aesthetics of pictures sent to Edward, she was equally preoccupied with issues of content, taking as a consequence of her political beliefs that she must no longer dwell upon lyrical or abstract imagery. Manuel Alvarez Bravo remembers her enthusiasm as they leafed through German photographer Albert Renger-Patzsch's *The World Is Beautiful,* a book of images so trenchant that one is caught up short, as if never before having truly perceived forests, flowers, or factories. "She liked that book," Alvarez Bravo recalls, "but one day I bought a monograph on a French painter, I don't remember which one, a young painter, good, I liked him quite a lot, and I showed it to her and then I clearly saw how sad she was to distance herself from [art for art's sake]." Tina believed that such images were not truly apolitical, but, rather, served the individualistic interests of the bourgeoisie. The masses, on the other hand, had no use for flowers or landscapes, but they needed pictures helpful in their struggle to displace capitalism and organize social revolution. Tina's words to Edward had barely touched upon her dilemma. Was it possible, she wondered, to make photographs which were neither simpleminded agitprop nor exercises in bourgeois formalism? Could she serve the interests of her class without betraying her own aesthetic principles?

Diego was struggling with similar issues, but, when Tina returned to Mexico City that fall, news of Diego was along other lines. The painter had recently married nineteen-year-old Frida Kahlo, Tina informed Edward, and the newlyweds threw a raucous reception that left guests telling confused and contradictory stories. One partygoer recalled that the event took place on Tina's *azotea,* festooned with drying lingerie, which "made a good atmosphere for a wedding." Tina's letter to Edward did not linger on the nuptials, however, for she had a more consequential announcement: "But the most startling news about D[iego] is an other one, which will be spread through all the corners of the world tomorrow.... Diego is out of the party."

With a Stalinist shakedown under way, Mexican Communists were divided by bitter and confused factional disputes. A rash of charges was slung at Diego, among them his coziness with the government, which now awarded him the only two major mural commissions, thus collapsing the once-heterogeneous mural movement into a single painter and style. At a fractious Central Committee meeting, he voted, tongue in cheek, for his own expulsion: "I, Diego Rivera, general secretary of the Mexican Communist party, accuse the painter Diego Rivera of collaborating with the petit-bourgeois government of Mexico and of having accepted a commission to paint the stairway of the National Palace of Mexico. This contradicts the politics of the Comintern and therefore the painter Diego Rivera should be expelled from the Communist party by the general secretary of the Communist party, Diego Rivera."

In the communication with Edward, Tina coldly spelled out her response to Diego's purge: "He will be considered, and he is, a traitor. I need not add that I shall look upon him as one too, and from now on all my contact with him will be limited to our photographic transactions. Therefore I will appreciate if you approach him directly concerning his work."

Tina's attitude is surprising not only because Diego had dropped everything to defend her from infamy but also because he had staunchly allied himself with Julio Antonio in many a Party row. In years to come, even at the height of her Stalinism, Tina would put personal loyalty ahead of political orthodoxy, but now, in a siege mentality that saw enemies descending upon the Party from all sides, she uncharacteristically tossed away a six-year friendship. To do otherwise would have placed her in an uncomfortable situation with comrades, but also Diego's antics must have galled her, and she found it unconscionable to be in the good graces of a government that made little effort to bring Julio Antonio's killers to justice.

Approached with the financially tempting offer of a job as official photographer of the National Museum, Tina, unlike Diego, had refused on principle to work for the regime. Yet, with rumblings about deportations growing stronger and plainclothesmen staking out her home, she knew that departure was inevitable and tried to cobble together some savings. She consigned photographs to Fred Leighton, an ex-reporter who was opening a Mexican handcraft shop in Greenwich Village, and she agreed to a (presumably paid) endorsement in Agfa's professional newsletter. The photo supply house's August bulletin carried this handwritten statement: "I believe that Agfa Bromide paper has everything required for portraits of the highest distinction and quality, from excellent tonal range to subtle grays! Tina Modotti." By winter, she had squirreled away two hundred dollars.

Meanwhile, boxes of her books went to Edward for safekeeping, and she chatted to a German reporter of plans to live in Berlin or Munich. In a note to Anita Brenner, in New York, Tina voiced the need to "test myself anew, reaffirm myself...a spiritual need," yet Mexico held her with "I almost dare say snake like attraction...." The uncertainty was frazzling, though she wisely tried to carry on with photography as if nothing were ever going to change.

It was probably around this time that Tina positioned her camera in front of the National Pawnshop, a government agency in Mexico. Before her crept a motley line of men and women, young and old, Indians and mestizos, anyone desperate enough to exchange a ratty treasure or two for quick cash. In Tina's photograph, exuding disillusion with Mexico's regime, the establishment's barred windows, closed door, and unwelcoming facade inspire thoughts of official imperviousness to the masses' plight. "People waiting in front of the national pawn shop to go and pawn their poor belongings," Tina scribbled on the back. Her note to Anita had touched upon the Marxist stance she takes in the photograph. "I look upon people now not in terms of race [or] types but in terms of classes," she explained. "I look upon social changes and phenomena not in terms of human nature or of spiritual factors but in terms of economics."

Tina also occupied herself with photographic studies of artist Louis Bunin's puppet workshop at a suburban training institution for Indian teachers. A Russian-born Chicagoan, Bunin had come to Mexico as Diego Rivera's assistant, but he was moonlighting as an instructor in marionette making, scenery changing, and jiggling wire-webbed crosspieces to give life to the little personages. The idea was that puppet theater could be usefully employed at up-country schools to present parables on such subjects as disease prevention and the evils of alcoholism. Bunin also produced spectacles both lighthearted and serious, causing a big stir in some circles with Eugene O'Neill's *The Hairy Ape*, a caustic allegory about the psychological disintegration of a snarling ship's stoker in the face of an antagonistic bourgeois world.

Given her fascination with stagecraft, figurines, and hands (a recurring photographic subject), Tina found Bunin's workshop to be a wellspring of imagery. She distilled its visual clutter into brooding, starkly elliptical visions that were tragicomic metaphors for manipulation, subjugation, and the human condition. The photographs resonate with the high political dramas being played out in Mexico City, and Tina could only have taken wry pleasure in seeing herself in the indignant, dogtrotting figures before her lens. Coincidentally, the subject of this final Mexican series nearly matches that of her slight, charming early work, the papier-mâché cowboy playfully labeled *My Latest Lover!* That these images are poles apart in content, mood, and sophistication speaks to both her personal and photographic trajectories.

A desire to propose a modernist model for up-and-coming photographers was doubtless among the impulses behind Tina's decision to arrange for a retrospective of her work. "I am thinking strongly to give an exhibit here in the near future," she informed Edward in a newsy letter. "I feel that if I leave the country, I almost owe it to the country to show, not so much what I have done here, but especially *what can be done,* without recurring to colonial churches and charros and chinas poblanas, and the similar trash most fotographers have indulged in," a reference to costumed "types," the trite standard fare of many photographers.

Tina Modotti's only major exhibition in her lifetime opened on December 3, 1929, in the vestibule of the National Library and under the patronage of the newly autonomous National University. Spanning her career from the early flower studies to a dramatically angled shot of a worker hoisting an enormous beam (*New Masses'* September cover illustration), the show displayed matted prints salon-style, with Julio Antonio Mella's portrait hung above the others like a crown jewel. In her red-inked manifesto penned for the occasion, Tina rejects the title "artist," claiming to be "a photographer, nothing more." Declaring her indifference to debates over whether or not photography is art, she champions images that put to advantage the medium's intrinsic qualities and contends that photographs are "the most direct means for fixing, for registering the present epoch," and thus grasping its truths. By imbuing the photographic document with sensitivity and an understanding of how it can be useful in the historical advancement of the proletariat, she concludes, one can make of the photograph "something worthy of a place in social production, to which we all should contribute."

Consistent with her credo, Tina had repudiated "perfect platinum prints for wealthy collectors," which rendered photography a font of consumable objects for the bourgeoisie. Instead, she was making more humble gelatin silver prints and seeking the widest possible audience, arranging for an extension of exhibition hours to accommodate the schedules of the working masses. Never before had Mexican peasants and laborers seen their lives illuminated and heroized in photographs. A typographers' group baptized a printing press in her honor, and a contingent of overall-clad textile workers from Puebla buttonholed her with news that, much to their boss's annoyance, they were calling one mechanical loom "La Tina." But her triumph was at best bittersweet.

One baffling incident speaks to the tangled political web in which she was ensnarled. Among the photographs on exhibit was a close-up of Julio Antonio Mella's typewriter, an image her companion had admired as "the typewriter you have socialized with your art." His comment alluded to the fragments of text on a piece of paper rolled into the machine. We see the words "inspiration...artistic...in a synthesis...exists between the..." Their author, as Tina surely knew, was none other than the demonized Leon Trotsky. Not only did she exhibit the photograph bearing Trotsky's phrases but Tina also printed the full citation, without attribution, at the top of her photographic credo. Shocking to comrades and particularly curious in light of her hidebound judgment of Diego, it was an act that could swiftly derail a Party career in the paranoid atmosphere of 1929. The only plausible explanation seems to be Tina's guilelessness, coupled with a veneration of anything associated with Julio Antonio. With his death, the photograph had taken on the meaning of a spiritual portrait of the revolutionist, who had aspired to literary as well as political authorship and regarded the typewriter as his most potent weapon. "Many have fallen. Many more will fall," Julio Antonio had written presciently. "But not a single idea, not a single principle has been killed."

The exhibition closed with a reception, where Tina was thrilled by David Alfaro Siqueiros's speech, equal parts art history lecture and political harangue. The Mexican student leader Baltasar Dromundo, a sentimentalist and brilliant speaker who had been close to Mella, also addressed the assembled crowd. His then bride remembered that Baltasar was smitten with Tina,

> sending her flowers, serenading her, writing poetry to her.... She used to phone him at the house and he would [immediately] leave. It didn't matter to him at all that I was jealous...and she was absolutely oblivious.... I was a young little thing of eighteen and she didn't even take me into account.... [She] spoke in such an exalted manner...of her amorous interest [in him], an intellectual and amorous interest, but without wishing to make any commitment. She spoke of her freedom and of how she could never belong to anyone.

In responding to Baltasar's gestures of courtship, Tina must have realized the diminution of her emotional capacity. With these phrases, she dedicated to him a Weston portrait in which she wears an air of distress:

> Baltasar—no words could express better than the look on this face the sadness and pain I feel at not being able to give life to all the marvelous possibilities I envision and whose rudiments already exist, awaiting only the "sacred fire" which should emanate from me, but which, when I seek it, I find extinguished. If you will allow me to use the word defeat in this case, I will tell you that I feel defeated for having nothing more to offer and for "having no more energy for affection." I have to admit this, I, who have always given so much of myself, have given all of myself with that exaltation which transforms the gift into the greatest voluptuousness for the giver....

Tina was, Baltasar lamented, "like my native land—sad, painful and splendid."

Meanwhile, police continued to tighten the screws on Communists, raiding a joint meeting of the Central Committee and Communist Youth and hauling thirty comrades off to jail. Like all Comintern parties, Mexican Communists constituted a dual organization: an open political group, on one hand, and, on the other, a covert operation with ties to Soviet intelligence. Government repression brought the Party's clandestine structure into its own, and, acting with some impunity owing to her high profile and connections, Tina turned her hand to undercover work. She proved herself valiant in one perilous situation after another, and Vittorio remembered that she was both acutely aware of the potential cost of her actions—"calumnies, hates, difficulties with work, jail, expulsion from the country"—and absolutely unflinching.

Sometimes paired with Pablo O'Higgins, Tina dispensed supplies and shunted messages among imprisoned comrades. Pablo, too, saw Tina dancing gracefully on the razor's edge, especially when called upon to pass him a letter in plain day near Alameda Park, a district swarming with police. He had memories of "a difficult and stupid situation, [but] she pulled it off magnificently...." Tina also made regular calls upon the jailed comrade Julio Rosovski, who had safeguarded the names and telephone numbers of hundreds of Communist operatives by memorizing them before destroying all written trace. Julio had not counted on his own arrest, however. On each of her visits, Tina toted a double-capped liter of milk, and, from one time to the next, her comrade furtively scribbled lists on tiny slips of paper inserted between the tops, which Tina carried away on the empty bottles.

Hoping to leave the country on her own terms, Tina looked to Nicaraguan rebel leader Augusto Sandino, in Mexico on a desperate quest for support and swiftly headed for an acrimonious break with the Communists. A small, dark, nervous man with a head as smooth and oval as an egg, Sandino wore fatigues, a dull red kerchief, and tall boots, conveying the impression that he had just stepped out of battle. When he attended an Anti-Imperialist League gathering at Tina's apartment one evening, she drew the *guerrillero* aside and volunteered to join his partisans, holed up under deplorable conditions in the Segovia Mountains. It was the first but not the last time that Tina was to poise herself for martyrdom, not for the glory, but, rather, it seemed, out of a romanticized yearning to die serving the people and thus tread the same tragic path as Julio Antonio. Sandino was undoubtedly disarmed by her request, and his melancholy, careworn eyes brightened. "And what does Tina wish to do in the Segovias?" But even as she put words to her desire to document the Sandinista struggle, he shook his head, for he judged his followers' conditions unbearable for a European woman.

On February 5, 1930, when a Catholic fanatic shot and wounded
newly inaugurated president Pascual Ortiz Rubio, the government had its
pretext to administer a coup de grâce to Communists (and Vasconcelos
supporters). Tina's friends Juan de la Cabada and Rosendo Gómez Lorenzo
were carted off to a penal colony, Siqueiros was thrown behind bars, the
notorious general Eulogio Ortiz threatened Luz Ardizana with rape by a
bullfighter, and Vidali disappeared into the back alleys of Mexico City.
Two days later, agents rapped at Tina's door and hustled her off to a district jail, where, for nearly a week, she shivered in a dank cell. Her only visitor was an old friend, Mary Louis Doherty, called in by one of Tina's
photography clients, Mexico City mayor Puig Casauranc. Mary brought
"medicine or anything that Tina wanted" and then went home and "cried
and cried and cried.... There was Tina in the prison in a cell and yelling to
me out the window, you know, crying wanting to get out."

But when Tina's cell door clanked open, it was not to release her but,
rather, to trundle her across town. Without the remotest idea of what was
happening, she was terrified. Her destination proved to be Lecumberri
Prison, the forbidding stone-walled "Black Palace" normally used for sen-
tenced prisoners. As a heavy door slammed shut and the lock rattled behind
her, Tina found herself buried in an isolation cell with a "little barred skylight, too high to look out from" as her only light source, and she was overcome with panic. Even more distressing than the physical hardship was the
thought that not one soul knew her whereabouts. She later scavenged a few
sheets of paper to write Beatrice Siskind, a friend of her brother Ben in
New York:

> ...I am strictly incommunicado. I asked if I could have callers and
> meals from outside but to no avail. Now I will not enter into details
> about the physical discomfitures—they are pretty bad as you can
> suppose, a regular cell of iron and stone, an iron cot without mat-
> tress, an ill smelling toilet right in the cell, no electric light, and the
> food, well, the usual food of prisons, I guess. But all this is nothing
> compared to my mental anguish in not knowing anything from the
> comrades. I especially worry about the foreign ones, whose names
> I won't mention, but perhaps you know which I mean.... I am sure
> the comrades nor anybody else know I am here.... It still all seems

like a bad dream to me and at times I feel my mind going around but I control myself by sheer will-power, whose capacity, in me, I had never before realized.

Tina tried to smuggle out the communication, along with a plea to Mary Doherty that she contact a lawyer and a government official, but both letters were intercepted. All the while, Tina was reciting, as her mantra, Nietzsche's words: "What doesn't kill me, strengthens me." Comrades eventually discovered what had happened to her, and she had at least one visitor when Luz Ardizana talked her way in with an argument that the prisoner might need "female things."

After thirteen days, Tina was yanked from her cell and, in another thunderbolt, accorded only forty-eight hours to leave the country. In the reigning climate of hysteria, it was a simple matter for the "vile yellow press" to dispense with Tina Modotti in the public mind. Mexicans "swallowed with their morning coffee" (Tina's words) that she was "the chief of a secret society of bomb throwers" who planned to assassinate the president but was beaten to the task. In a bitter frame of mind, she imagined breakfast-table conversations: "...who would have thought it eh? Such a gentle looking girl and who made such nice photographs of flowers and babies...."

To help with the move, Tina mobilized friends who were not languishing in prison or who had not disappeared underground. Mary generously put in long hours packing, selling, and giving away seven years' accumulation of belongings. She offered the kitchen stove to one of Tina's guards, and he "was delighted and very kind." The two women dashed to Sanborn's House of Blue Tiles restaurant so Tina could bid farewell to her old friend Fred Davis, and Mary's chum Eugene Pressly dropped by to lend a hand. In a letter to Edward, Mary sketched the scene: "Tina's leaving the house on Abraham González.... This curious collection of secret police and other culprits and weeping servants and [Frances's maid] Leonora in a pulque stupor (unable to keep up under the strain—she is so sentimental) and Tina dressed in character—blue shirt and tam o'shanter—Eugene and I officiating in an amazed sort of way."

To Mary, as no doubt to Tina, the experience had a hallucinatory quality: "Tina was putting herself through this ordeal for the sake of saving Humanity.... I suppose the 'movement' needs its martyrs and Tina makes a very effective one but it does seem to me too dreadful to have this sort of underworld drama being acted out seriously so close to home. I still can't believe that all these happenings of the last year or more have anything to do with our Tina."

Manuel Alvarez Bravo and his then wife, photographer Lola Alvarez Bravo, stopped by, and Lola was appalled to find Tina's apartment, ordinarily "very simple, very orderly, very functional," in disarray, with "packages, boxes and bundles everywhere." The couple purchased her eight-by-ten-inch view camera and asked if they could retrieve some prints from the trash. Tina was "so different from how we knew her," Lola observed, "so hurt, with such a deep pain, so pale and exhausted: well, the harm they had done her was such that even the guards themselves felt bad at times, and once when I was with her they went out on the balcony to give her a bit of space and peace. They stayed on the balcony smoking and killing time until we finished chatting with her, said goodbye and left."

On an impulse, Lola and Manuel collected their young son and hied themselves to the train station at the hour of Tina's departure. Depressed and resentful that a lack of time had forced her to leave dozens of loose ends, Tina arrived, trailing Mary and a bevy of policemen. Lola recollected that Tina, tears pooling in her eyes, took the boy's head in her hands and planted a kiss in his hair. "I'm leaving," she murmured, "and I hope I come back to see you and to see Mexico in other circumstances better than these." Manuel's lasting memory was of sitting in the train with Tina, a bundle of nerves in the minutes before departure. It was "a very powerful moment, very moving. I was with her up in the compartment, she on the window side and I beside her, and then they blew the whistles, they blew the whistles, the conductor came around, I got off, and that's when I said *adiós*." Until the train clattered out of the station and picked up speed, Tina was too stunned to cry.

On February 25, a dingy, rodent-infested Dutch freighter sloshed out of Veracruz harbor. Embarking on a five-week zigzag journey toward its home port of Rotterdam, the SS *Edam* counted among its third-class passengers a trio of deported Communists: an Austrian waiter, a young shoemaker named Isaak Rosenblum, and the notorious Tina Modotti. The vessel's swing from its berth, lights glancing off the water and the harbor receding, hardly penetrated Tina's consciousness, for she was wrapped in "a kind of a haze and a veil of irreality."

She was traveling on an Italian passport valid only for return to Italy, which, if she did end up there, would mean certain imprisonment and possibly death for a Communist. But her U.S. document had expired in January 1927, and she had no other option for departing Mexico. She also carried a French transit visa permitting nonstop travel from Boulogne, where she was to debark, to the Italian border. The freighter's port calls depended upon fluctuating cargo schedules, however, and, even as Tina sailed, messages were flying among the legal departments of Red Aid's European sections to arrange for her petition for political asylum, in France or elsewhere.

Hugging the Mexican coast, the *Edam* put in first at Tampico, where Tina and Isaak were permitted to stretch their legs onshore. As they filed back on board, the two found their paths blocked by a seemingly befuddled man unwilling to budge. Tina snapped nervously, "But who is this idiot in front of me? Who is this man who won't move?" Pivoting to fix her in the eyes, he growled, "What's it to you, lady?" Tina's jaw dropped, for she realized she was looking at none other than Vittorio Vidali, masterfully disguised and clutching the passport of Peruvian Communist Jacobo Hurwitz Zender.

Having evaded a police dragnet, Vidali was en route to Moscow. It is difficult to ascribe motives to his hop aboard the *Edam*. He later claimed that he acted on Party orders to save Tina from Mussolini's clutches, but it is unclear how he could have done so. Perhaps he answered a yen to have her to himself for five weeks, and, without doubt, this man, who once brashly traveled halfway around the world using a collaged Russian love letter as passport, was amused by his own bold stroke.

Free to prowl the ship at sea, Tina was kept under close surveillance in port. At New Orleans, she was locked up onshore for eight days, alone in a vast white-walled room whose barred windows recalled a jail and whose unmade beds gave her "the strange feeling that corpses have laid on them." Writing to Edward, she flashed a wicked sense of irony: "The worst of this forced idleness is, not to know what to do with one's time—I read—I write—I smoke—I look out of the window into a very proper and immaculate american lawn with a high pole in the center of it from which top the Stars and Stripes wave with the wind—a sight which should—were I not such a hopeless rebel—remind me constantly of the empire of 'law and order' and other inspiring thoughts of that kind—." Afterward, she set about writing a letter (to the editor of the Peruvian magazine *Amauta*) denouncing Mexican capitulation to Yankee imperialism.

From time to time, the drum and clap of thunderstorms drowned out distant echoes of Mardi Gras, which was in full swing. Vittorio, meanwhile, went carousing, and Tina heard an account of the festivities when he convinced port authorities he was a distinguished Latin American journalist and thus wrangled forty-five minutes with the detainee. Under a matron's watchful eye, the pair conversed in double entendres, which must have included mention of the visiting German warship *Emden,* whose crew had paraded through New Orleans and whose officers were supplying the social whirl with much-admired Teutonic dash. The *Times-Picayune* lumped the story of the "internationally famous [Communist] Tina Medotti...held in the immigration station" with that of a "Communist agitator" taken to court on charges of smuggling inflammatory German-language Bolshevik tracts into the *Emden.* Vittorio must have relished the article, or perhaps he had insider knowledge of the comrade's subversive activities, because, forever after, he confused the names of the two ships and always testily insisted to interviewers that he and Tina had sailed to Europe on the *Emden.*

The vessel next docked in Havana, where Tina was hustled through tropical heat to the gloomy Tiscornia military quarantine center. No trace remains of the thoughts that came into Tina's mind in Julio Antonio's hometown. One wonders if she was conscious of how her lover's death had finished off Mexico's freewheeling and optimistic 1920s, and how something vivid and bounteous in herself had slipped away with the era. Her spirit shaded into weary but determined vigilance. After three days, she was put back on board, and, foam bursting from its sides, the *Edam* at last moaned and creaked toward the Atlantic. The Cuban coastline trembled briefly on the horizon, then dropped from sight.

Part IV

Тов. МОДОТТИ

Berlin and Moscow (1930–1932)

AS DAWN BROKE watery and weak on April 2, 1930, Tina's train was snaking through low hill country. Gazing heavy-lidded at damp, mole-colored field stubble and half-combed tangles of brush, she mentally replayed the scene of twenty-four hours earlier.

Bypassing Boulogne, the *Edam* had docked in Rotterdam, with Tina sequestered in her cabin. When Vittorio stuck his head into the door, he found her gray with fear and intent upon embracing him because, she said, "Who knows…anything can happen, including that we never see each other again." For long minutes, she waited as the palaver to decide her future took place in the port's customhouse. The first to have his say was Mussolini's stout, goatee-wagging envoy, who demanded that Dutch immigration officials hand over the "dangerous Communist, a terrorist, wanted by Italian authorities," a woman so potentially unruly that she would require a crack police escort to Il Duce's ship, which was anchored nearby. Red Aid attorneys scoffed, pulling out a duly authorized clearance for her to remain in Dutch territory for one day, along with documents vouchsafing a six-month residency in Germany. With her heart no doubt pumping madly, Tina was at last escorted from the ship into the office where the Italian was still working up a lather. To her immense relief, she and Isaak were, minutes later, whisked off by Red Aid comrades, who fed and feted them before depositing Tina on the train that now carried her bravely to the future. By

nightfall, she would clatter into Berlin's drafty, high-vaulted Hauptbahn-
hof, crawling with dark bundled figures and emblazoned with advertisements for cigarettes and beer.

In short order, Tina joined up with Vittorio and Isaak. Although the
sun flirted with Berlin, cold stung their cheeks as the threesome strolled the
banks of the Spree River, a glossy silver ribbon winding through the city.
"Tina is elegant, and her face has healthy colors," Vittorio wrote, reliving
their walk. "She is a beautiful woman, graceful and slim, and, her composure notwithstanding, she expresses a robust love of life. She is still young
and seems even younger with the high part that divides her head, the tailor
gray suit which becomes her, the scarf around her neck." Over cups of
steaming coffee at one of the venerable mirrored cafés lining Unter den
Linden, they spoke with comradely affection of Tina's situation.

Her primary consideration was to settle where she would be "most
useful to the movement," but she also had to earn a living. France and Spain
were options, and although Vittorio was prodding her to go to Moscow, she
refused, perhaps believing that Western Europe was better suited for a professional photographer. In Berlin, Tina could put to advantage her smattering of the language, a handful of German acquaintances made in Mexico,
and the city's vast Communist network of organizations, clubs, publications, mail service, and two daily newspapers.

But her optimism was strained, and her mood darkened as the time for
Vittorio's departure drew near. "Tina is silent," he recalled; "she answers in
monosyllables. It is understood that she is tormented by doubts and uncertainties. Nor is the weather very propitious for us; when we go out, the sky
is leaden. Tina sees herself pale with fatigue and incertitude. For the first
time, I see in her look, always sweet and serene, a sign of disturbance,
almost desperation."

"Dear, lovely Tina!" Edward had lamented in his *Daybook*. "You seem
so much more remote in Germany—so the paper stated [your] destination—for now I cannot picture your surroundings." In 1930, the third-
largest metropolis in the world, Berlin was fast, cosmopolitan, seamy, and
staggering in its contrasts. Close by grand hotels and operas stood soot-
streaked tenements hung with limp rags, and fur-coated matrons brushed
up against pasty-faced scavengers pawing through refuse bins. The streets
smelled of benzene, stale beer, grilling sausages, French perfume, and

Tina Modotti, Untitled, c. 1926–1929; gelatin silver print.

OPPOSITE, TOP: *Tina Modotti, Untitled, c. 1926–1927; gelatin silver print.* OPPOSITE, BOTTOM: *Tina Modotti,* "Indians getting fertilizer from the bottom of the canal at Xochimilco," *1927; gelatin silver print.* ABOVE: *Tina Modotti,* "A stall in the Alameda selling Indian wares," *c. 1926–1929; gelatin silver print.*

TOP, LEFT: *Tina as she liked to dress for darkroom work.* TOP, RIGHT: *Tina at a Mexico City demonstration.* BOTTOM, RIGHT: *Edward Weston,* Xavier Guerrero, *c. 1923.*

A portrait of Vocio by Tina.

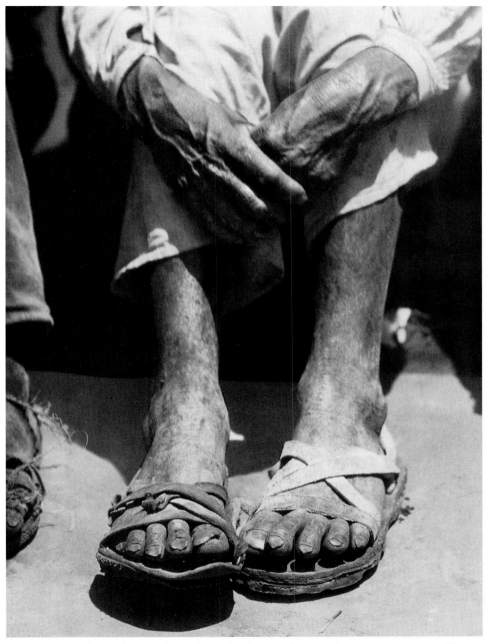

OPPOSITE, TOP: *Tina Modotti,* Hands Resting on Tool, *1927; platinum print.* OPPOSITE, BOTTOM: *Tina Modotti,* "People waiting in front of the National Pawn Shop to go and pawn their poor belongings," *c. 1927–1929; gelatin silver print.* ABOVE: *Tina Modotti,* Untitled, *c. 1927; gelatin silver print.*

Tina Modotti, Child in Sombrero, *c. 1927; gelatin silver print.*

N
E
W
MASSES

A Photograph by Tina Modotti

Soldier of Christ | **The Right to Death!**

Did God Make Bedbugs? | **Awake, Negro Poets!**

The Greatest Living Criminal

15 CENTS   **OCTOBER, 1928**

Tina Modotti, Mexican Sombrero with Hammer and Sickle; *cover of the October 1928 issue of* New Masses.

Tina Modotti—1928

ABOVE: *Tina Modotti,* Julio Antonio Mella, *1928; gelatin silver print.* OPPOSITE, TOP: *Tina Modotti,* Mella's Typewriter *or* La Técnica, *1928; gelatin silver print.* OPPOSITE, BOTTOM: *Inspector Valente Quintana* (seated at desk) *and his colleagues interrogate Tina.*

TOP: *With a police officer at a reenactment of Julio Antonio's assassination.* BOTTOM, LEFT: *Police searching Tina's apartment.* BOTTOM, RIGHT: *Tina awaits her turn to speak at a memorial for Julio Antonio Mella.*

TOP: *Tina's photograph of* Distributing Arms, *a fresco panel by Diego Rivera at the Ministry of Public Education, c. 1928–1929*. From left, *David Alfaro Siqueiros, José Guadalupe Rodríguez, Frida Kahlo, Julio Antonio Mella, Tina Modotti, and Vittorio Vidali*. BOTTOM, LEFT: *Tina Modotti,* Woman with Flag, *1928; palladium print by Richard Benson*. BOTTOM, RIGHT: *Tina (left) at the Tizayuca rally in April 1929*.

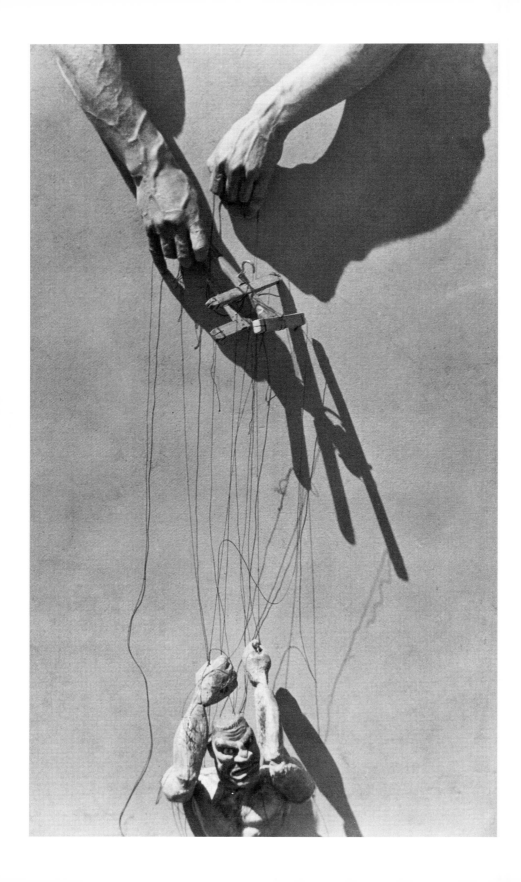

OPPOSITE: *Tina Modotti,*
Hands of a Puppeteer,
1929; gelatin silver print.
ABOVE: *Tina's snapshot of
Vittorio Vidali taken aboard the
S.S.* Edam. BELOW: *Eugen
Heilig's photograph of Tina
promoting* AIZ, *Germany,
1930.*

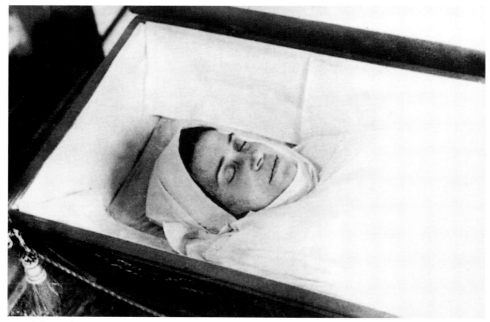

TOP: *Tina and Vittorio in their room at Moscow's Soyuznaya Hotel.* MIDDLE: *"María" with Spanish Communists Isidoro Acevedo and Esteban Vega.* BOTTOM: *Tina in her coffin.*

garbage. Rattling around wide-eyed and disoriented, Tina noticed bustling open-air soup kitchens, movie palaces ablaze and lively with boisterous crowds, strutting, sharp-tongued prostitutes, apothecaries' iron shutters ritually cranking up and down, and the budding green thickets of the Tiergarten. From this turbulent, snarling scene, her eyes picked out "the strain [which] shows on the people; they never laugh, they walk the streets very gravely, always in a hurry and seem to be constantly conscious of the heavy burden which weighs on their shoulders."

She had arrived in the waning days of the Weimar Republic. Already tottering under the burdens of its World War I reparations debt and disastrous rates of inflation, the nation had plunged into catastrophic economic depression following the Wall Street crash of 1929. A quarter of its population was jobless, and the parliamentary process had degenerated into a frenzy of dealing and scheming. Adolf Hitler's tirades were finding friendly ears, and, for the first time, Tina saw flesh-and-blood fascists in the form of Nazi Brownshirts striding along Berlin's boulevards.

The country's ideological battles also enflamed the German art world. The Bauhaus school's Communist director, Hannes Meyer (whom Tina would later befriend), was on the verge of resignation forced by municipal authorities, who feared that the stunts of "Red Bauhaus brigade" students would cost them votes. Painter George Grosz savagely caricatured Weimar society, and printmaker Käthe Kollwitz was making haunting lithographs and drawings of the heroic poor. Tina admired both artists, whom she hoped to meet but apparently never did. Already, the Nazi presence was weakening Berlin's rich creative community, and, before long, the city would begin hemorrhaging artists, writers, and intellectuals.

For the time being, Tina's mind was fixed on nothing more than four walls and a darkroom. For several days, she stayed with the Wittes, an academic couple she had met in Mexico City. "[H]ow can I praise sufficiently that exquisite and heavenly creature called Lady Witte!" Tina blurted out in a letter to Edward. But, probably fearing that troubles would rain down on her hosts should Mussolini's operatives discover her whereabouts, Tina reluctantly declined the good woman's offer of a charming "Tina's room" to call her Berlin home. Instead, she lit on a shabby rooming house and began scouring the city for a darkroom to borrow or rent. When that proved impossible, she was obliged again to pound the pavement in search of lodgings, this time with the rare luxury of running water so she could work at home. Eventually, she found two rooms in the Pension Schulz, a Communist safe house on Tauentzienstrasse, just off the busy cabaret- and café-lined Kurfürstendamm. Obligingly, the landlady never entered her name in the guest register, required by law to be submitted to police.

Installing a darkroom was irksome, not only for the trouble involved but also because purchases of an enlarger and chemicals consumed too much of her $420 nest egg and encumbered her with belongings when staying a step ahead of Mussolini might mean a hasty departure. Though she scrimped on everything in Berlin, Tina found her days were a losing race between the cost of establishing herself as a photographer and the need to spare her cash reserve.

Setting up the lab turned out to be only one in a litany of bewildering complications recited to Edward:

> Have I told you of my surprise on arriving here to discover that throughout all Europe different sizes are used altogether for films, papers, cameras, etc. That was my first trouble. I [am] kept awake at nights wondering what to do: either I should have sold my graflex or order films from the U.S. I decided to do the last of these two things since nobody would have interest in my graflex on account of its format. Naturally I could not afford to buy another camera unless I could first sell this one. Then came the problem of all my negatives 8 by 10. I brought absolutely nothing from Mexico outside the graflex. I needed a printing frame 8 by 10 and have had to have it made to order. Paper that size I have had to order in larger quantities than I wished to, otherwise the factory here would not cut it special. You would be surprised perhaps to know that most photographers here still use glass plates. Then there is the trouble of different standards of measurement: you know, not grains, but grammes. A hell of a mixed up affair. And on top of it all, the difficulty of the language! I tell you I have almost gone crazy.

Another perplexing issue was how to earn a living from her camera. Tina held up the options one by one, and not only Germany's economic depression but also its photographic culture seemed to conspire against her. She told Edward that the quality and quantity of portraits offered by even the most humble photo shops deterred her from opening a studio, but the problem was also the incompatibility of business publicity and semiclandestine living. When offered a position as a journalist, she declined on grounds that "I still think it is a man's work in spite that here many women do it; perhaps they can, I am not aggressive enough."

Tina's rejection of reportage came as the profession was being revolutionized by the commercialization of small-format Leica and Ermanox cameras. Using modified movie-camera film, these devices made possible a rush of thirty-six shots before changing film (whereas Tina was in the habit of loading her camera for each new exposure). Moreover, their lightness and compactness allowed photographers to stalk a subject and capture action at its peak. The model of the new photojournalist was Erich Salomon, who wormed his way into courtrooms and diplomatic conferences, where he brazenly clicked off indiscreet candids, leaving people sometimes none the wiser until their faces stared out from the newsstands. Yet such an approach was wholly against the grain of Tina's preferred practice: meticulously composing her photograph on the camera's ground glass and processing each negative and print in the manner of a skilled artisan.

Bombarded with advice to lay aside the cumbersome, conspicuous Graflex, Tina played with a borrowed 35-mm camera, but she was frustrated because she could not envision the print in its finished size. "Besides a smaller camera would only be useful if I intended to work on the streets," she reasoned to Edward, "and I am not so sure that I will. I know the material found on the streets is rich and wonderful, but my experience is that the way I am accustomed to work, slowly planning my composition etc. is not suited for such work. By the time I have the composition or expression right the picture is gone. I guess I want to do the impossible and therefore I do nothing."

Yet Tina did experiment with street photography. She adopted the astute tactic of loitering around tourist landmarks, poised to swoop in photographically on the life they attracted. The zoo offered a broad-beamed bourgeois couple for her lens, and, at the Neptunbrunnen Fountain, she framed a bronze nude and two passing nuns. The images have a distanced, ironic quality, as if their subjects (utterly unlike those she would have chosen in Mexico) barely stirred her interest enough to make her want to possess them visually. Her photography was manifestly not thriving on fresh impressions. She told Edward it was "crap," and Berlin's "nasty, cold, grey miserable" weather added to her ugly mood as well as her photographic frustration. Open up her lens and slow her shutter speed though she might, negative after negative proved underexposed, and she seemed unable to compensate for "this damned light after Mexico!" Depression and self-doubt welled up, but she resolutely tamped them down: "I have enough self confidence and realize I must not undervalue my capacities."

As for Mexico, she thought it wisest to lock out of her mind even simple thoughts of the sun agreeably stinging her shoulders. Berlin held no rich troves of associations and memories. Rarely was she touched with affection, and she found herself dying by inches. "Well, there is nothing to do but go ahead," she wrote Edward; "I recall often that wonderful line from Nietzsche you told me once: What does not kill me strengthens me. But I assure you this present period is very near killing me." After nights spent tossing and turning, she would rise to a dull, rain-spitting sky and check hungrily for mail, so vital that she kept a logbook of correspondence. Though all happiness eluded her, she refused to unburden herself to acquaintances, believing that she "must solve my own problems and not bother friends too much."

Yet she found "kindness...like a ray of sunshine" in friendships with the Wittes and Eugen Heilig, a Communist who directed the worker-photographer agency Unionfoto, which Tina had joined in hopes of commissions. Pleasant, slender, and dark-eyed, Eugen made no bones about his opinions of the Nazis and social injustice, yet he brimmed with a puckish humor that did her heart good. A devoted father, he liked to bicycle with five-year-old Walter to a frog pond where the pair traded stories over tins of sardines. The boy also tagged along on a visit to Tina's room, where a shimmering crystal chandelier impressed itself upon his young memory. When he grew bored and restless, she dug out a brightly painted Mexican fish. Her friendship with Eugen was important enough to her that she offered him a portrait of Julio Antonio Mella, with her companion's name penciled on the back.

Eugen was a photographer who worked for the magazines *AIZ* and *Der*

Arbeiter Fotograf, both the brainchild of Communist public relations wizard Willi Münzenberg. The two magazines published Tina's images, Mexican and German, although, in the collective spirit, her work was not always credited. Many of the publications' photographs were by workers, employed or jobless, and, while often technically amateurish, they pierced German working-class realities—demonstrations, hunger, strikes, unemployment lines—as an outsider's images could not. "Even the type of propaganda pictures I began to do in Mexico is already being done here," Tina explained to Edward; "there is an association of 'workers-photographers' (here everybody uses a camera) and the workers themselves make those pictures and have indeed better opportunities than I could ever have, since it is their own life and problems they photograph." Another door slowly closed in her face.

Nonetheless, on Sundays, she joined in *AIZ*'s agitation tours, trucking to villages where she and her comrades documented living conditions and proselytized the rural masses. Eugen's camera caught Tina as she talked over *AIZ* with two stooped peasants, and, again, as she peered through the Graflex's viewfinder at the crowd milling on a lakeside beach. Her clothing leaps to the eye: She is enveloped in a long skirt, sweater, scarf, and felt cloche, while most of the locals wander around in swimming trunks. Sunny or no, Berlin left her cold and lonely.

We know little of Tina's political activities during the six months she remained in Berlin. Probably she plunged into translating and typing for Red Aid and the Anti-Imperialist League, where she received her mail (though the family wrote her directly, using the name T. Richey). She struck up a friendship with the league's codirector, Virendranath Chattopadhyaya, known as Chatto. From a distinguished Bengali family, Chatto was the patriarch of European-based Indian nationalists, a legendary host and energetic consensus-builder who had turned to communism for allies in the anticolonialist struggle.

Tina's militancy extended beyond the walls of Red Aid and the Anti-Imperialist League. The honeymooning Anita Brenner visited that summer and got "the willies" from the way her friend cleaved to the Party, and Baltasar Dromundo recollected a letter in which Tina explained that her Red Aid work now entailed a more direct struggle against fascism. How that translated into missions, we can only guess, but it was almost certainly on behalf of Red Aid that Tina traveled to Switzerland (where she picked up false identification papers) and on to Spain.

The vagaries of the mission put her at Seville's Ibero-American Exposition, a much-heralded Hispanic trade fair that boasted manicured grounds, gewgaw national pavilions, demonstrations of flamenco dancing, and other trappings of such events. Mexico's presence took the form of a vaguely Aztec building where light filtered through stained-glass windows onto displays of salsa, pharmaceutical products, vanilla, cigars, and contemporary art, organized by her old friend Gabriel Fernández Ledesma. Culled from the 1928 exhibition in which Tina had participated, the photographs exhibited were signed by Manuel Alvarez Bravo, Roberto Turnbull, Hugo Brehme, and a dozen other figures from her past. Here we must allow Tina a few hours awash in nostalgia, especially when phantoms came dancing down an even longer corridor of time. They wore the faces of a young Italian immigrant roaming San Francisco's Panama-Pacific International Exposition and the actress Robo draped in black lace and called his "Spanish girl." Tina purchased a deluxe red-covered set of forty views of the exposition and dispatched it to the Richeys. "To dear Vocio and Marionne!" she wrote on the title card. "Pictures of a country much dreamed about by our dear Robo—Affectionately yours, Tina."

Back in Berlin, Tina added photographs taken in Germany and Switzerland to her Mexican portfolio for a modest exhibition at the Joachimstalerstrasse studio of photographer Lotte Jacobi. It was Tina's gift for companionship with people of all ages that had led her to Lotte. Through mutual acquaintances, Tina had befriended thirteen-year-old John Frank Jacobi, and he took her home to meet his mother. A fourth-generation photographer and remarkable portraitist, Lotte was an unpretentious and firm-minded woman with an intense gaze and prematurely gray-streaked hair. Parading before her lens that year were, among many others, actor Emil Jannings, artist Käthe Kollwitz, painter Max Pechstein, actress Lotte Lenya, conductor Wilhelm Furtwängler, and the entire Communist slate in September's parliamentary elections. Finding Tina a "delicious" person and a talented artist, Lotte loaned her cameras, organized the show, and included her work in the offerings of the Jacobi Studio's small agency, which supplied pictures to newspapers and magazines.

Among those who saw Tina's exhibition was the peripatetic Czech

Egon Erwin Kisch, the most famous Communist reporter in Europe. A burly bon vivant with a big, infectious sense of humor, Kisch later wrote that "every person who saw these photographs never forgot [Tina Modotti's] name," but it was the Mexican, not the European, images that enthralled him. With Mussolini's agents monitoring photography listings for Mexican exhibitions or other signs of the "dangerous Communist Medotti," press coverage was virtually nil. The association with Lotte seemed auspicious, but, by the time of the exhibition, Tina found herself hopelessly out of tune with Berlin, and even her relationship with photography was rocky. "I have felt like giving up photography altogether," she had confided to Edward, "but what else can I do?" Most distressingly, her money was fast disappearing.

As she mulled over her future, thoughts of family drifted into Tina's mind. Around the time of her arrival in Berlin, Assunta and Mercedes had returned permanently to Italy, settling in Trieste, not far from Tina's sister Gioconda and nephew Tullio. The move is surprising, given the Modottis' antifascist opinions, but both women had been at loose ends in California, and Assunta must have been eager to know her grandson. They were ignorant, however, of financial hardships in the offing and were doubtless unaware that Gioconda, hard-pressed to raise her child on seamstress's wages, was supplementing her income with occasional prostitution. For Tina, the change meant the possibility of a family reunion, say in Switzerland, but this was proving unfeasible, with Italian authorities probably balking at the Modottis' request for travel papers.

In September, Vittorio returned to Berlin, to find Tina thin, nearly penniless, and sagging in spirit. Her thoughts of Italy had persisted, but now they coalesced into the idea of doing undercover work in her homeland. Several times, in years to come, Tina was to make official application to the Party for this assignment. She would ask almost timidly, as if hers were an unseemly request for a lavish gift, and, always, her petitions would be denied out of fear that her long absence would give rise to an awkward action or slip of the tongue that would unmask her as a Communist agent.

In his response, Vittorio was less nuanced than the Party chiefs. "Are you crazy? They'd put you in jail immediately." But he granted that he had submitted the same request.

He asked if she were homesick for Mexico.

"No. I left behind a world that now seems full of ghosts."

"Do you have other plans?"

"I have no plans. In any other country, I would find the same conditions from the point of view of work."

He coaxed her to go to Moscow, and she promised she would if nothing caught fire within the month.

In early October, Tina gave up on Berlin, again pared her possessions, and boarded a train bound for Leningrad. On the eleventh, the Comintern's Italian section notified the German section that Tina Modotti had arrived in Moscow to work for International Red Aid.

In 1930, Moscow beckoned to Communists from all over the world. According to psychologist Winifred Gallagher's study of how surroundings shape perceptions and behavior, when pilgrims' expectations are high, such meccas "have the capacity to promote physical and psychological change." Three years earlier, Vittorio's first voyage to Moscow had disciplined his mind and touched his heart, and he came away rhapsodizing about "a large, almost Oriental village which calms the nerves with its patriarchal peacefulness."

Tina discovered a city that was anything but bucolic. Its tattered web of half-paved streets was cluttered with ramshackle construction sites and swarming with crowds of Muscovites, who seemed peasants next to fashionable Berliners. Families doubled up in cramped apartments, and everybody's days were consumed by long chases after food and supplies. In those lean years, shop windows stood empty except for shelfworn cardboard cutouts of vegetables and eggs. The city's rattletrap trams were a spectacle, for not only were they spilling with passengers but also their sides bore crude and bizarre plywood bunnies, reminders that raising rabbits for meat was a patriotic act. Yet one's heart uplifted at the sight of ruddy-cheeked Pioneer Youth and "millions of children, workers' children who before had had nothing and could hope for nothing, were eating, singing, dancing, holding hands in the new nursery schools, freed from squalor and disease and neglect." At midnight, Moscow's carillons chimed out a solemn "Internationale," followed by a wild, joyous pealing of bells, as if to say, *Here* humanity has been reborn! *Here* the great experiment in solidarity and courage is under way!

On its Red Square end, Tverskaya was the grandest of Moscow's boulevards, but the asphalt petered out only a few blocks beyond. Midway stood the Soyuznaya, a shabby old residence hotel for foreign Communists where Vittorio had been living. Tina was assigned a small room with double curtains and hissing radiators, which she plastered with wet towels to combat the dryness. Children squalled in the close quarters, and tenants ceaselessly shuffled to and from communal bathrooms under the eyes of all-seeing, all-knowing floor monitors. Officially, cooking was forbidden, but, in the evening, the corridors were pervaded with odors of smoked fish, kasha, *chai,* fried eggs, and cabbage leaves swimming in broth. Tina arranged a few sprigs of dried flowers in a beer stein, hung her portrait of Mella on the wall, and called the Soyuznaya home.

Two meetings monopolized her thoughts as she settled in to life in Moscow. At the first, she arranged to clear the air with Xavier Guerrero, still a student at the International Lenin School and living practically across the street at the Hotel Lux. An hour after striking out for the appointment, Tina slumped in Vittorio's room, recapitulating how painful it had been. Xavier had played the stone idol. "He didn't want to speak. He just listened to me, silent and solemn as always. Finally, he only said that he did not intend to discuss my letter or my explanation. Now there was nothing more to be said between us and, for him, I do not exist."

Tina's distress over Xavier's rebuff was swiftly eclipsed by her awe before Elena Dmitrievna Stasova, who directed MOPR, the Russian branch of International Red Aid, and, de facto, the entire organization. From an aristocratic and politically radical family, the Communist grande dame had served as Lenin's secretary and confidante. He had been partial to her undercover name, "Comrade Absolute," but, to the Russian people, Stasova was simply the "old Bolshevik." Peering at Tina through round, black spectacles, she looked the kindly though indomitable dowager. Her salt-and-pepper hair was carefully pinned back, while a grandmotherly brooch and Party medals glinted side by side on her bosom. She directed that Tina be paid a resettlement stipend and admitted to the ranks of MOPR's readers of the foreign press.

While still a newcomer, Tina discovered that the Soyuznaya housed many refugee families from South America and Italy, who knew scarcely a soul in Moscow and spoke not a word of Russian. All of her generous impulses were aroused by their plight, and from interviews made decades later, a picture of Tina knocking at their doors comes into focus. "Do you need anything today?" she would inquire in Spanish or Italian. "What can I do? Are the children all right?" Argentinean émigrés Luis Checchini and his wife were struggling to care for two infants as they learned the ropes of the Soviet system. Through MOPR or on her own, Luis recalled, Tina grappled with the interminable lines, black market, and rationing coupons, not to mention Moscow's freezing, snow-scudding streets. Her tactic was to join any queue she came across, not knowing if it would lead to kippers or alarm clocks. She often returned to the Soyuznaya unfazed and bearing the miraculous liter of milk. "...Tina was literally our salvation, and, if I say 'our,' it is because I am referring to all the Latin American émigrés."

Whereas once Tina had given of herself emotionally and physically "with...the greatest voluptuousness," the generosity which now came to the forefront had her humbly distributing material comfort and good cheer. A feeling of belonging, always important to her, was even more so after the terrible loneliness of Berlin, and she reveled in the kinship of the international working class. "Tina felt as if she were in a big family; she was satisfied," Vittorio observed. Boundless selflessness helped to dispel her solitude and anesthetize the emotional pain that never subsided. Blessedly little time was left over to think about herself.

At 9:30 each morning, Tina would pin on badge number 25 as she clocked in at MOPR, a humming bureaucracy occupying a four-story building of czarist vintage on Ogarev Street. She worked at a table in the bright natural light of the readers' pool downstairs, where she was lucky enough to fall heir to an ancient, eccentric Adler typewriter. Most but not all of her colleagues were Russians—Bertha, Shevelova, Laurence, Utkes, and Marusha, by name—and she joined their fold as a protégée of Vittorio Vidali, who ranked a private office down the hall. Among the administrators upstairs, Tina befriended MOPR's accountant, Marie, a seasoned German comrade married to an official of the secret police.

On November 23, Tina signed a memo, officially accepting from Comrade Jorge Contreras (Vittorio Vidali) a sheaf of Latin American, Italian, Spanish, and Portuguese files as well as a short-term plan of work. She buried herself in reading, translating, and analyzing the foreign press and quickly turned her hand to writing, as well. For the December issue of MOPR's magazine, she produced an essay on Latin America and then buckled down to monthly submissions signed "Tina Modotti," "María," or "Julio Antonio." Her competence and efficiency were rewarded with a promotion from reporter to chief reporter. The pace quickened as she was assigned visits to Red Aid's founding director, the elderly German militant Clara Zetkin, and liaison work with intellectuals such as writer Maxim Gorky and Lenin's widow, Nadezhda Krupskaya. She shepherded foreign delegations around Moscow and delivered talks in factories. Red Aid eased the suffering of refugees, rescued orphans, and fought fascism, racism, colonialism, and anti-Semitism, and Tina was put to shame by the thought that she had straggled into full-time militancy so late and so ignorant.

Officially, her day ended at 4:00, but cell meetings, Russian lessons, and mandatory training in Marxism-Leninism had to be squeezed into the hours remaining. MOPR's politically sophisticated atmosphere made Tina self-conscious about her lack of knowledge of Communist culture, and she supplemented her classes with diligent reading in the Marxist corpus, plunging headlong into *Das Kapital,* although never finding time to finish it. As hungry as ever for meaning and symbol, she tried to "put into her head a completely different vision of the world from the historical, political and social point of view." She was not voluble about her newfound understandings, however, but rather increasingly self-contained and withdrawn. Friends found her "always the same, always silent."

With Vittorio, too, Tina was undisclosive, even after the two began living together in 1931. She had pulled into Moscow, to find him a married man and father-to-be. As he told the story, the matrimony ensued from the briefest of affairs, though he lived for a time with the child's mother. In those days, Soviet marriage and divorce were casual matters requiring half an hour's paperwork in the appropriate office. By the time Vittorio severed the relationship in the fall of 1931, most of his acquaintances assumed he was married to Tina. The two never spoke of matrimony, however, and Vittorio's sexual peccadilloes no doubt continued apace.

Four years younger than Tina, he was physically changed since their Mexican days. His body had thickened, the once coal black hair had thinned and faded, and a fleshy moistness had settled about his mouth. A rabble of appetites, Vittorio wolfed his food, downed a few glasses too many, and was quick to swing a fist. He possessed a rough-edged, bullying charm that some found irresistible and others repugnant. Implacably ambitious and deeply committed to communism, Vittorio skillfully negotiated Moscow's labyrinthine political intrigues, though he was known to let gut reactions cloud his judgment. In Tina's eyes, he was a font of knowledge and an affectionate, optimistic companion. She soothed his unruly moods and called him by the delightful Italian baby talk name of "Toio."

For some eleven years, Tina and Vittorio formed a couple, although they would be apart as often as together. Tina wrote of her new intimacy to Frances Toor, who told their friend Joseph Freeman, "I heard from Tina some few months ago and she wrote me that Life is again good to her in matters of love, because there is a new man in her life whom she loves and who loves her." Finished with fiery, soul-stirring affairs, Tina found a comforting domesticity as Vittorio's companion. Keeping both feet on the ground, they formed the sort of conjugal bond that proceeds from a long friendship and daily collaboration at the office. They shared impoverished Italian childhoods, three years of friendship in Mexico, a wide circle of friends, and the arduous existence of Comintern cadres. She kept house for him, and, in the evening, they attended Comintern functions and "festivities organized by comrades' families, [where] she never refused to dance or to have a glass of wine or beer or a little glass of vodka or cognac." They rarely quarreled, but, when they did, Vittorio knew just how to bruise her emotionally, with the hurled epithet "high class whore." Tina's history of free and happy sex had become a shameful secret, and she would uncharacteristically burst into tears.

As Tina's love for Edward had once fused with enthusiasm for photography, the relationship with Vittorio pivoted around their militancy, and, for a time, she proudly called him "my husband who is politically better educated than I." After her death, Vittorio was to set himself up as Tina's interpreter, and virtually the only accounts of some periods of her life after this point are those in his voluminous memoirs. Written in the 1970s and early 1980s, these should be read skeptically, for they are politically revisionist, recasting Vidali's unalloyed Stalinism as idealism and reasonableness. Vittorio polished up his problematic relationship with Tina so that he would shine brighter in its reflected light. He would later make a point of writing and visiting her siblings, and they remained in his sway.

Many who knew the couple never got over their puzzlement that

Tina would choose Vittorio as her *compagno di vita*. Surprise that such a finely sensitive woman did not recoil at Vittorio's coarse personality ushered in speculation that the relationship held "for political reasons. She knew a lot of things.... Otherwise nobody could stay with a guy like that, sharing his bed." From the vantage point of some seven decades, the heart of the question becomes: How could Tina, drawn to communism by its promise of social justice, involve herself with a man who was capable of countless thuggish and morally reprehensible actions? Over the years and from many sources, Vittorio was charged with sinister deeds, including indiscriminate executions of prisoners during the Spanish Civil War and participation in a string of political assassinations. Since 1927, he had been in the service of the Soviet secret police (the GPU and NKVD, predecessors of the KGB), a connection he consistently denied.

Tina was most likely familiar with many of Vittorio's deeds and approved of them in the abstract. More than ever in the thrall of Marxist idealism, she knew what one commentator called Communists' "inner radiance: some intensity of illumination that tore at the soul...a kind of exaltation...that can be understood only, perhaps, by those who have loved deeply...." Tina "was a woman very passionate about the idea," mused one comrade; "it was reflected in her gaze, in her voice," and almost anything done in the name of the idea, the victory of the proletariat, seemed justifiable. Whether robbing banks or dispensing with enemies of the people, "revolutionary necessity" had long been part and parcel of Bolshevik culture, or, in Lenin's words, "Everything that is done in the proletarian cause is honest." Tina would have nodded assent at the words of one Party member, who justified Stalinist-era excesses with the image of breaking to harness an extraordinary animal: "This is a mighty beast we have got hold of, this idea of socialism. It has brought to the surface elemental pain and need. It has got hold of *us* now but if we hang on and ride the beast we will have hold of it, and then a new day will dawn."

Tina's all-consuming passion altered not only her relationship with Vittorio but also that with Edward. Having come so often into mental view during her photographic travails in Berlin, he now swiftly receded to the past. Three months after moving to Moscow, Tina had sent her last message to Edward:

I have been living in a regular whirlpool ever since I came here in October, so much so that I cannot even remember whether I have written to you or not since my arrival....

I have never had less time for myself than right now; this has its advantages but also drawbacks, the main one being the utter lack of time to devote to you, for instance, if only through a few badly scribbled words! There would be so much to write about life here, but no hay tiempo [there is no time]—I am living a completely new life, so much so that I almost feel like a different person, but very interesting.

We don't know if Edward responded, but he labeled the communication "Tina's last letter to me." He would report a decade later to their once mutual friend Miriam Lerner that "Tina has cut off all her old friends. I have not heard from her in years. She is right considering her place and position. She would not be the same Tina to us, we would not be the same to her. Better to have memories."

Edward would have recognized Tina, however, in her solicitude for Angelo Masutti, the sixteen-year-old son of newly arrived Friulian Communist émigrés. A lean, curly-haired, and eager young man, Angelo hired on as Vittorio Vidali's assistant at MOPR. The adolescent secretly disliked his boss, whether in a jovial mood or sputtering with rage, and still remembers his distaste when the older man draped an arm around his shoulder and queried, "Well, Angelo, what do you think of Moscow now that you're here?" For Tina, Angelo sometimes translated and typed (two-finger style), and he once contributed an essay about bureaucracy to the wall journal, a glorified bulletin board common in Soviet organizations, for which she was responsible.

Angelo's appointment book for 1932 reveals Tina's attentiveness to her compatriot during his first days in the Soviet Union:

21 February: Dinner with Tina at Lux restaurant.
22 February: Dinner with Tina.
25 February: Had lunch at MOPR restaurant with Contreras and Tina.
26 February: Lunch at Lux with her.

25 March: Typed for Tina.

3 April: Typed in Spanish for Tina.

5 April: Typed for Tina.

On June 13, 1932, Tina arranged permission for Angelo to visit the Soyuznaya, where, at a table in the room she shared with Vittorio, she showed him her Leica, the first small-format camera he had ever set eyes upon. Apparently, she had at last sold the beloved Graflex and purchased a Leica with help from one of the many foreigners traveling in and out of Moscow. Hers was a 1932 model, unavailable in the Soviet Union, equipped with a 50-mm Elmar lens and the first built-in light meter.

The camera was loaded with Agfa film, and Tina expertly adjusted its aperture and speed before placing it in Angelo's hands.

"Take my picture."

This was Angelo's first attempt at photography, and he fumbled with the focusing ring before clicking off a snapshot of her, sitting against the light, and a second, half-turned toward the window. Vittorio then squeezed in next to Tina, and Angelo exposed a third negative. Seeing the boy's excitement and aware that he dreamed of being a cinematographer, Tina gestured toward the camera. "Keep it," she offered, and he did, for more than three years. Two weeks after loaning him the Leica, she invited him back to the Soyuznaya to see her portfolio, which astonished the adolescent and set him on the path to a career in professional photography.

Angelo's tenure at MOPR was short. Admitted to the fall session of the state film school, he requested and received a memorandum of release, signed by Vittorio and endorsed in Tina's now-cramped hand: "He will be seventeen years old in October. I agree he shall go to the school and leave our apparatus. Of course we lose a good worker but he also needs to study a profession." Written in English, her statement was dated August 16, 1932, her thirty-sixth birthday.

Tina had graduated from Red Aid's collective workroom to an office, either occupied solo or shared with Vittorio, but so rarely was she on hand that Angelo sometimes wondered if she actually worked there. "She was not often in Moscow," he remembered. "She went on missions. She came and went." The clandestine solidarity missions on which Tina was embarked stirred her blood and satisfied her deeply by the directness with which they allowed her to minister to the masses. In March, she had ferried funds to Polish workers imprisoned during a general strike, and she later slipped in and out of Romania, Hungary, and other countries where the movement was illegal. By temperament and strength of purpose, Tina was manifestly gifted for covert work, and, even physically, Vittorio judged her "truly the ideal type: a beautiful presence, elegant, and with her simple, sweet face and a good passport, she crossed all borders." Though well aware that arrest could bring torture, years behind bars, or death, she never lacked the courage of her convictions.

One of Tina's closest calls would come later, when she received a directive for a mission to Spain. By this time, she was an old hand at false credentials, clandestine mail drops, note keeping in cipher, and detecting police decoys. While Red Aid colleagues were fed the story that Tina Modotti had fallen ill, she was striking out for Madrid, Barcelona, Reus, and, again, Madrid. There she was arrested one morning as she sallied forth from a hotel in search of breakfast and cheaper lodgings. Under interrogation, she remained stoic and silent, and, while police hunted up a matron for a body search, she very professionally profited from the wait to slip from a pocket her Red Aid credential and scrap of notes with the intention of "making them disappear," perhaps by swallowing them. But she had only time enough to slap the papers between the pages of a newspaper. The matron quickly discovered them, and the documents sufficed to get her escorted to the border on the next train, probably saved from worse by her refusal to panic.

Her work in Moscow was more mundane. She compiled statistics, items, and citations, which she added to the steady stream of exhortative essays flowing from her typewriter. Intended mainly for the magazines and pamphlets with which MOPR deluged the masses, some were translated into various languages and sold like pocket books for a few cents.

Tina's seven-thousand-word opus—entitled *5,000,000 Widows, 10,000,000 Orphans: Women! Do You Want That Again?*—links antifascism with pacifism, a Comintern position with tremendous appeal to Europeans still suffering the effects of World War I's horrors. Here Tina flails away at capitalists who would cynically manufacture another war in order to convert worldwide economic depression into personal wealth. Turning directly to women, she takes to task "fascistic-military women's organizations" (in the United States, the women's auxiliary of the Ku Klux Klan, the Daughters of the American Revolution, the Amazon League, and the Girl Scouts) and chastises bourgeois do-gooders who believe war can be averted by petitions to the League of Nations. The treatise concludes with examples of "women bravely doing their revolutionary duty" and a citation of Lenin that muddies the clarity of her call to throw down arms, distinguishing between "imperialist war" and revolutionary insurrection. *"What will proletarian women do in an imperialist war?"* asks "the great father of the working masses, the immortal leader of all exploited, oppressed peoples and races.... *Will they merely curse the war and all that goes with it; will they simply call for disarmament? Never!... Proletarians must master the art of war, not to kill their brothers, the workers of other countries, but to triumph over the bourgeoisie and thus put an end to exploitation, poverty, and war...."*

Equally dutiful and doctrinaire was her analysis of the situation of Mexican peasants toiling on foreign-owned coffee plantations. Ironically, she rebuked capitalists for inhumane treatment of campesinos as (unknown to her) an appalling famine organized by Stalin was cutting down millions of Soviet peasants. Occasionally, Tina's account of hacienda life lapses into vivid detail: Three times a day, we learn, Indian workers down white lightning distilled from sugarcane, which stupefies them into submissive slaves, while priests terrorize them with apparitions of eternal damnation. But Tina's text is mostly a vast gray field of words, nothing at all like the powerful photographs she once made of the same subject.

For a time, Tina was responsible for the children's page of MOPR's Russian-language magazine, and here she devised a humorless fictitious correspondence between Tina Alberti, an Italian girl living in Milan, and Cesare, her compatriot, whose family has emigrated to New York. Called "Black Shirt and Red Scarf" (references to fascist garb and to the kerchief worn by Communist Pioneer Youth), the story heaps equal scorn upon fascists and capitalists. "Dear Cesare," it begins:

> I am writing to you. I am Tina Alberti. Do you remember me?...
> We have a bad life. You will ask, why? For almost a year, my father has had no job. His factory was closed, and all the workers

thrown out. Mama is dead. She was beaten to death during a May Day demonstration, and Giuseppe, my older brother, has been in prison for three months....

In our school all the children are put in departments and groups. We have sailors, foot soldiers, gunners, and sanitary workers. The commanders are officers and instructors. They are very hard and punish us for everything, even the slightest fault. In the summers, they send us to camps where we live like soldiers.... Our captain says this is necessary because we all belong to the State and must at any moment defend him against his enemies—the Communists and their friends....

From New York's Little Italy comes the reply:

Hello, dear Tina...

We have been living here for two years. We live in the Italian part of town, not far from the East Side. I do not go to school because my father and sister are unemployed, and all of us must make a living. If only you knew how difficult life is here. Until last month, Papa sometimes had work, and we could pay the rent, but now he earns nothing. The owners threw us out, and we are living in a small lean-to that we built from scrap materials. The rain comes in, but it is better than living in the street.

As the story continues, Cesare is snared into the army by offers of free food. But he refuses to learn to kill Communists and escapes to don the red scarf and fight fascism.

That the once-vibrant pen of Tina Modotti turned sectarian and flat speaks to the completeness of her intellectual surrender and to a perception of a world crisis so acute that playfulness and metaphor were inexpedient even in writing for children.

Organizing educational exhibits had become another of Tina's specialties. In "Photography as a Weapon for Agitprop for Use by International Red Aid" (reprinted in Germany's *AIZ*), she shares practical tips about employing images as tools for explaining "white terror," exchanging information, and propagandizing. But she also addresses the medium more conceptually in a passage that conceives of photographs as evidence, surprisingly denying their ambiguity and suggesting that each picture holds an absolute and unmalleable meaning:

> Nothing is more persuasive and expressive than what we can see with our own eyes. However graphically we describe an attack upon a workers' demonstration by armed police, or the body of a worker trampled underfoot by mounted police, or that of a negro lynched by a brutal and bloodthirsty executioner, no drawn, verbal or written image will ever be as telling as a photographic reproduction. The photographer is the most objective of graphic artists. He takes only what is offered to his lens at the split second of the release. A photographic image can be understood in any country, by all nationalities...irrespective of language, title and explanations.

In contrast, *AIZ* never published a photograph without a caption to affix its meaning (Tina's *Hands Resting on Tool*, for example, had appeared as *We Are Building a New World*), and the Marxist writer Walter Benjamin was arguing that photographs seductively transfigure misery into beauty and that only text could "rescue [a picture] from the ravages of modishness and confer upon it a revolutionary use value."

Tina's second anniversary at MOPR coincided with the organization's first international conference, which brought to Moscow delegates from fifty-two countries. Simultaneously, preparations were proceeding apace for the fifteenth-anniversary celebration of the Russian revolution. Armies of hammering, sawing, and shouting construction workers invaded the streets, while electrical wires and makeshift bleachers sprung up everywhere. So brightly illuminated that midnight resembled high noon, Red Square was transformed into a spectacle of billowing banners proclaiming "Workers of the world, unite!" Presiding over everything was a thirty-foot-tall Lenin with outstretched arms. Well traveled though she was, Tina was impressed by such theatrical grandeur.

To foreign comrades descending from trains, the Red Army Band offered a vigorous "Internationale." MOPR staffers cheered and waved, factory delegations stepped forward with comradely hugs, and Pioneer

Youth handed out conference pins, along with cigarettes, fifty per delegate per day, a gift from the Soviet people. Comrades swarmed through Red Aid offices, making inquiries, stumbling upon old friends, convening ad hoc meetings, and departing by factory-provided limousine for guided tours past the fairy-tale domes of St. Basil's and the surging Moskva River. At the Hermitage Theater, the conference was launched in a mise-en-scène of red flags, green foliage, and another oversized Lenin as Red Aid's senate of venerable elders—Kun of Hungary, Katayama of Japan, Pieck of Germany, Marty of France, and Stasova of the Soviet Union—offered greetings in two dozen languages, followed by long rounds of speechifying.

Besides her work as an interpreter, Tina played hostess to two honored guests. One was the elderly "Mother Mooney," who had traveled to the Soviet Union to campaign for the release of her son, Tom Mooney, still imprisoned in California for allegedly masterminding the 1916 San Francisco bombing that Tina well remembered. The other was Ada Wright, the mother of two of nine African-American youths who had been accused of rape in Alabama's notorious Scottsboro case. Tina tirelessly trekked around the city to plenums where delegates rolled up their sleeves to review progress on a country-by-country basis and map strategies for capitalist, socialist, colonialized, and semicolonialized sectors. Her most visible contribution to the event, however, was the exhibit "The Work of International Red Aid," installed at the Palace of Nobility, behind a facade swathed in banners and decorated with a rotating globe. "Inside this vast building," noted one French participant, "our comrades from the Soviet section installed a remarkable exhibition about MOPR: photographs, charts, pamphlets, handouts, and posters, in all languages and from all countries, are carefully classified and arranged so that, at a glance, one can judge the formidable power of our Red Aid around the world."

After two weeks, delegates scattered to tour factories and collective farms around the Soviet Union, with Tina shepherding a Latin American group to the distant Caucasus Mountains. Later, by order of Stasova, she was honored with a medal and a three-hundred-ruble bonus for her work at the conference, the apotheosis of her career as a Communist cadre.

Chapter 12

Moscow and Paris (1932–1935)

LOANING THE LEICA to Angelo Masutti effectively closed Tina Modotti's photographic career. In his 1974 memoirs, the Chilean poet and Communist Pablo Neruda invented for her a grandiose gesture of renunciation: "This Italian revolutionary, an extraordinary artist with a camera, went to the Soviet Union...to take photographs of its people and monuments. But she was caught up in the uncontainable rhythm of socialism in full progress and flung her camera into the Moscow River, vowing to consecrate her life to the most menial work of the Communist Party." Lotte Jacobi, visiting Moscow in 1932, found Tina's situation more problematic. "She seemed less well than in Berlin, thin and...I don't know, but she didn't seem well. I asked her how she was, and she told me that she was terribly busy. I said to her, 'Are you still taking photographs?' And she said no, that there was no time for that when so much had to be done, at Red Aid, well, lots of things. She seemed to consider photography a luxury and to believe that one had first to help people and later perhaps take photographs."

Tina had arrived in the Soviet Union intending to photograph at the big November 7 celebration, and plans were afoot to show the work in New York. Perhaps she did take pictures, but the exhibition never occurred, and, if she harbored hopes that, as in Mexico, her images would incarnate the nation's glorious heyday, these quickly withered before Soviet realities.

From the beginning, the Bolshevik regime had looked favorably upon photography for its "scientific objectivity" and supposed ease of comprehension by the masses. In the 1920s, the Soviet worker-photographer movement had thrust cameras into the hands of the proletariat, instructed to chronicle the nation's victorious leap forward. Meanwhile, art photographers engaged in radical, restless experimentation with photomontage, multiple exposures, and offbeat angles, seeking a yield of metaphors for the dynamism and promise of Soviet society. By 1930, however, freewheeling attitudes had been sharply reined in, and the state-sanctioned Union of Russian Proletarian Photographers was monitoring work for its adherence to the Party line. Pictures by formalists, sentimentalists, and nonconformists met with stern cries of "bourgeois escapism!" In one version of a frequently told story, avant-garde photographer Alexander Rodchenko's portrait of a Pioneer Youth drew rebukes for the girl's air of fatigue. In another, the picture was considered to be on a "dangerous, erroneous, bourgeois-formalistic" Left path because of its subject's upward gaze: The proper Soviet look was straight ahead. Overtly experimental work was decried for kowtowing to foreign influence, and, with a 1932 decree, Stalin made social realism the official art style of the Soviet Union.

Enormously proud of her photographic achievement, Tina could not help but recoil from the thought of prescriptive photographs. She "was unhappy because there was no [artistic] stimulation there, nothing," remembered Mexican singer Concha Michel, who went to Moscow in the early 1930s. "They did not appreciate her photographic art. They only wanted to use her to make some politician's portrait or something...."

Yet well-intentioned friends urged Tina to continue with the camera. From New York, writer Ernestine Evans contacted Comrade Doletsky of the Soviet news agency TASS: "I have asked Tina Modotti who is one of our best known American photographers to come and show you some of her Mexican photographs. I am certain that both you and Press Cliché will be interested in her work. I think she ought to be using her camera during her stay in Russia." Perhaps that meeting set in motion the offer of a position as official Soviet Communist party photographer, which Tina refused.

Around Tina's unwillingness to compromise her photographic principles accreted other reasons to put the camera aside. Some were simple and specific: Moscow's dingy light, irksome rules about photographic permits and authorizations, and the unavailability of three-and-a-quarter-by-four-and-a-quarter-inch sheet film, which rendered the Graflex useless.

More important, her relationship with photography had been undermined by doubts that gnawed at her long before she set foot in the Soviet Union. Could pictures effect change in the world? If not, was photography simply egotistical self-indulgence? Unable to give her creative work the fullness of time it demanded, why should she continue to push out unsatisfying second-rate pictures? And, with unparalleled iniquity menacing the working class and the world dividing into camps of good and evil, was it not incumbent upon her to lay aside that puny weapon, the camera, in favor of the most direct and forceful action she could muster? Tina's quest for transcendence remained intact, but it was redirected toward the ultimate victory of the proletariat. Perhaps it was no longer necessary to photograph the hammer and sickle when the Soviet flag was invested with mystical power.

Despite her conviction that giving up photography was morally right, the decision was painful, for it was tantamount to amputating the best of herself. But her distress was probably tempered by the thought that it was only provisional.

Tina's dilemma was not uncommon among idealistic artists and writers of the crisis-torn 1930s. Thousands soon would rush to defend with their lives the cause of Spanish freedom, whose first foreign victim was British painter Felicia Browne. In Cuba, the writer Rubén Martínez Villena (who knew Tina in Moscow) surrendered his pen for the people, avowing, "I will never write poetry as I have done up to now.... I no longer feel my personal tragedy. I am now of them and of my party." German playwright Bertolt Brecht summarized the feelings of many artists: "What kind of times are they, when /A talk about trees is almost a crime/ Because it implies silence about so many horrors?"

Tina discussed the issue with Vittorio, but he had little use for art and could muster no more than support for whatever she decided. She raised it again with Pablo O'Higgins, who had arrived in the Soviet Union in 1931 on a one-year scholarship to the Moscow Art Academy. She told Pablo that "this, and no other, was her place and that she had to take very direct and immediate action as a revolutionary." Having decided that "all art was mere childishness in the face of the great oncoming wave of world change," he approved. Yet he continued to paint, and with enough passion to get thoroughly steamed up over the academy's requirement that students copy plaster casts and to complain bitterly until accorded special dispensation.

One wonders if Tina measured her artistic loss against that incurred by the brilliant film theorist and director Sergei Eisenstein, whom she and Pablo looked up one day and found wallowing in despair. Sergei had just returned from a year in Mexico, where he shot *Que Viva Mexico!*, a filmic symphony that showed every sign of being a cinematographic landmark in the making. As the project dragged on, wildly behind schedule and over budget, Eisenstein's chief financial backer, writer Upton Sinclair, had called a halt. An ugly quarrel ensued, and, his assurances notwithstanding, Sinclair never forwarded the footage to Moscow after it was processed in Hollywood. Tina and Pablo paid their visit around the time Sergei learned that his material had been turned over to the producer of Tarzan movies to splice together into something profitable. Sergei "was going to commit suicide and who knows what," recalled Pablo, "because he had been there for a year, and what was he going to do? Naturally, we tried to help him as much as we could.... Well, to comfort him and say 'No, you're not going to do that.'"

More memories of Mexico sprang from Tina's 1932 "autobiography," the long questionnaire put before all Comintern cadres. She carefully enumerated her services to the Mexican Party, but the association with Julio Antonio Mella went unreported, as did her acting career, replaced with a seven-year stint in a milliner's shop. As a member of the Soviet Communist party, Tina next had to undergo the *chistka*, or "cleansing," which spared none the discomfort of sitting before a local plenum to confess all sins, political and personal, and submit to questions shot by everyone from Party boss to charwoman. As laconic as she was allowed to be, Tina cleared the hurdle (while fully one-third of her comrades were ejected as suspected class enemies). Not long thereafter, she took a position on MOPR's Executive Committee, near the pinnacle of the worldwide organization.

In the early spring of 1933, Tina and Vittorio won a month's reprieve from Moscow's rigors and vacationed at the pleasant little Crimean resort of Foros. They sunned themselves in a botanical garden fronting on the sea, tended to Vittorio's lumbago and Tina's fatigue, and hobnobbed with Lev Kamenev, a prominent Soviet oppositionist. Expelled from the Party with

Trotsky, Kamenev had been banished to Siberia, from where he was now wending his way to Moscow to make further confessions of error. Turning a deaf ear to Vittorio's political gambits, the worldly old russet-bearded comrade charmed Tina with discourses on photography and painting, fueled by sips of good Georgian wine. Socializing with political deviants boded ill for Tina's future in the Soviet Union, but, Vidali tells us, she still "had almost no interest in the multiple internal Party questions of the day.... She didn't want to know anything about them, and I never heard her express any judgment about personality issues in the USSR or other countries." Few had any idea of how high the stakes had become: Three years hence, Kamenev would be tried as an enemy of the revolution and shot.

Tina's indifference to political maneuvering left her prey to sectarian squabbles among various apparatuses. Back in Moscow, she and Vittorio were summoned to a secret meeting with the powerful Red Army intelligence chief, Jan Karlovich Berzin, who bid them join Richard Sorge's master spying operation in Japanese-occupied China. Working in Shanghai under the cover of a pro-Nazi German reporter, Sorge was feeding the Red Army valuable intelligence about Germany and Japan. Military espionage was a far cry from international solidarity work, and the alacrity with which the couple accepted Berzin's offer bolsters suppositions that Tina was by now willing to undertake any task the Party requested. Her only misgivings about the assignment apparently involved neither safety nor ethics, but, rather, picture taking, for the proposal called upon her to become Sorge's photographer. Presumably, her job would center on copying lifted documents, but the idea of signing up for all-purpose photography made her squirm.

As far as one can tell from Vidali's later account of the episode, Berzin was making a stealthy grab for two of MOPR's top staffers. Yet, rationalizing that it was all for the same cause, Tina and Vittorio did not believe they owed Stasova the loyalty of informing her. She got wind of the deal nonetheless, and, refusing to yield an inch to the Red Army, she sat the couple in front of her desk for a frosty announcement in her most Olympian manner: "...your little trip to Shanghai has been canceled." Vittorio thought, "How the devil does this woman know everything?" But Tina must have felt some measure of relief. Having formally extricated the pair from the military mission, Stasova reassigned them to International

Red Aid's regional office in Paris. Traveling with a Soviet passport in the name of Tina Kontreras, as well as false Costa Rican papers, Tina was to hopscotch through Warsaw, Prague, and Geneva, then rendezvous with Vittorio in France.

In the winter of 1933, the political storm long brewing in Europe had broken violently over Germany. Named chancellor of the Reich, Hitler began his reign by terrorizing the Communists. The Party's Berlin headquarters was raided, its meetings suppressed, and its publications banned as part of a strategy to incite a Bolshevik uprising, which Nazis would then manipulate into triumph at the ballot box. Failing to trigger the expected revolt, Hitler availed himself of other methods. On February 27, 1933, Germany's parliament building, the Reichstag, burst into flames, an act of arson almost certainly engineered by its own Nazi president, Hermann Goering, who raced to the crime scene, ranting, "This is the beginning of the Communist revolution! We must not wait a minute. We will show no mercy. Every Communist official must be shot, where he is found. Every Communist deputy must this very night be strung up."

Five leading Communists were charged with arson, while thousands of others suffered beatings, imprisonment, torture, and murder. Cunningly throwing the German people into a panic over a supposed Communist conspiracy, Hitler wiped out individual liberties and coaxed the Reichstag into ceding constitutional powers to the chancellor. Great waves of refugees fled the country, many for Paris, already teeming with asylum seekers from oppressive regimes in Hungary, Poland, Romania, Turkey, Italy, and Morocco. Hard hit by the Great Depression, France saw wages collapse and unemployment lines swell, and the discontented vented their spleen at aliens encamped in their midst. Immigration quotas were enacted, applications for work papers were systematically denied, demonstrations turned violent, and xenophobia wreaked havoc on working-class solidarity. It was rich terrain for International Red Aid.

Based in Paris, the organization's European office, as Tina and Vittorio quickly discovered, was a grand name for little more than Stasova's directive, a few scrawled phone numbers, and a mail drop. With a phalanx of seasoned comrades, the pair was to use methods both legal and illegal for shunting funds and instructions among Europe's national sections, spiriting Communists out of Germany, participating in campaigns on behalf of the

Nazis' victims, organizing fund-raising and membership drives, and running Moscow's errands on the Continent. Vittorio played the role of pugnacious, risk-courting chief of operations to Tina's assiduous and modest deputy.

From Moscow's insularity, they had stepped into "a den of espionage and counterespionage, of informers and provocateurs, of agents paid only to infiltrate our organizations and our apparatuses." Any indiscretion could be fatal. Cafés swarmed with loutish Blackshirts spoiling for a good brawl, but, more insidiously, Italian agents and would-be snitches vied for Mussolini's bonuses, while the French counterespionage service combed the city for Soviet agents. Tina and Vittorio undertook a conspiratorial life of fleeting encounters, careful detours, juggled credentials, and minutely orchestrated plans sometimes jettisoned at the last moment.

Never relaxing into a pattern likely to catch the eye of a meddling concierge or neighbor, the couple moved incessantly. They squeezed into the dreary suburban bungalow of their Romanian colleague Franz, found a bed in the studio of a Dutch painter friend, checked into an unobtrusive hotel in a working-class district, or persuaded the typesetter Sirletti to put them up for a few nights. Most of their hosts could offer only cramped spaces lacking plumbing and adequate heat, but from time to time, the pair enjoyed the luxury of Germaine and Marcel Willard's charming, comfortable flat on the rue des Beaux-Arts, a picture-postcard street lined with art galleries and lively cafés.

The utility company worker François Le Bihan and his wife, Germaine, also regularly put a roof over their heads. On the top floor of a tranquil brick building in the square du Véxin, wedged into the tangled streets of the unfashionable nineteenth arrondissement, the Le Bihans' apartment was well suited to Tina and Vittorio's purposes. Here they slept and worked in the same room, sequestering themselves to map strategies and hammer out texts. They were but two of a parade of foreign revolutionists through this Communist safe house. While some visitors spoke freely of their homelands, Tina and Vittorio remained mute on the subject. Although they spoke flawed French—Vittorio's had an odd, childish lilt—their hosts knew neither their nationalities nor their true names. Vittorio was called Raymond (though his residence permit listed Julio Enrique, a history professor from Guadalajara, Spain), while Tina became Lina.

Tina was friendly with Germaine (who was Catholic, not Communist like François, but deemed trustworthy nonetheless), and the two women occasionally chatted after dinner as fourteen-year-old Cécile half-listened. The adolescent's overarching impression was of a woman discreet "from every point of view.... I wouldn't say she was secretive, but very discreet." Years later, upon learning that Tina had been a great photographer, Cécile was "dumbfounded because I never would have guessed it.... I don't know if I lacked imagination, but I didn't expect her to be anyone out of the ordinary."

A slight, weary brunette, her hair scraped into a bun and face devoid of makeup, Tina was unfailingly outfitted in a pullover, plain skirt, low-heeled shoes, and navy blue beret, all inexpensive, simple, and clean. Outdoors, she added a long navy blue coat and a scarf. She was a quiet, circumspect creature whose every movement was modulated and whose silky dark eyes sometimes flashed a look of anguish. To the adolescent Cécile, Tina was not particularly beautiful but, rather, looked "like my mother, like a mother." The observation would have satisfied Tina, who now found that good looks potentially sapped her effectiveness as a militant.

Yet Cécile spent little time puzzling out Tina and Vittorio, since she found nothing particularly intriguing about the couple. For a time, they tried to coax her into practicing English with them, but, much to her parents' chagrin, she was tongue-tied. It was not until four or five years later, when Cécile had matured and the pair began dropping by on their way to and from Spain, that the trio grew closer. Vittorio wanted to spirit the young woman off to the war, where her fiancé was fighting in the International Brigades, but Tina firmly put her foot down. "She was the moderating element, that was clear.... They were completely opposite in character."

The dissimilarity was one reason for their effectiveness. Often working from the local French Red Aid's avenue Mathurin-Moreau offices, on the site of present-day Communist party headquarters, the pair launched into their tasks. Vittorio labored over a policy analysis of political asylum issues, while Tina had her hands full publishing the trilingual monthly *MOPR* and participating in international campaigns for the German Communists Thaelmann and Dimitrov, the Brazilian Prestes, the Hungarian Rákosi, the Romanian Pauker, the Italian Gramsci, and the Americans Tom Mooney and the Scottsboro defendants. She trudged all over Paris collecting signatures from intellectuals, who would have included writers Henri Barbusse, André Gide, Louis Aragon, Anna Seghers, André Malraux, Romain Rolland, and Egon Erwin Kisch. For the pamphlet *Droit d'asile* (*Right of Asylum*), she reflected upon the plight of Europe's political refugees. Tina's text alludes to her former Mexico City neighbor B. Traven, whose 1926 German-language novel, *The Death Ship*, had just been published in English:

> The pursuit of man across the world is poetically described by Traven in *The Death Ship*, the suffering of a man without passport pursued around our planet, but this suffering has today become the cruel lot of thousands of unhappy people. Because the bourgeois press, for understandable reasons, speaks only rarely of expulsions and extraditions of emigrants, it is difficult to offer precise statistics about this matter. One thing remains certain: expulsions are increasing from year to year and month to month.

The solitary sufferer "without passport," or rather with too many passports, was, of course, also Tina herself. She now appeared a remote, lonely, yet vital figure preoccupied with the "victims of bourgeois class justice." Tina's prose sounds formulaic, and her proposed solutions are reductive, yet the breathless slogans seem outpourings of her soul: *"Vive la solidarité internationale! Vive le Secours Rouge International! Vive l'Union Soviétique!"* ("Yes to international solidarity! Yes to International Red Aid! Yes to the Soviet Union!")

Nothing is known of Tina's leisure time in Paris, where every street put before her more diversions than Moscow could dream of. Talkies had just made their European debut, photographers André Kertész and Robert Capa were publishing picture essays in the illustrated press, and museums beckoned on every side. Yet it was an unhappy time in France, with the economy in shambles and cynical, corrupt politicians riding merry-go-round governments for all they were worth. The Party line held this situation to be all to the good, since capitalism inevitably disintegrates into fascism, useful in sweeping away lingering vestiges of bourgeois democracy, thus clearing the path for proletarian revolution. On February 6, 1934, the Communist prognosis seemed correct as a violent fascist demonstration (bearing hallmarks of an attempted putsch) unseated the latest French prime minister. Party doctrine notwithstanding, Communists succumbed to an acute case of jangled nerves, and the French Left quickly put together a massive counterdemonstration. At the same moment, in Vienna, fighting erupted between a self-styled people's army called the Schutzbund (League of Protection) and the forces of Austria's Christian Socialist chancellor, Engelbert Dollfuss. Tina put her hands on fifteen thousand francs just raised in the "Lenin, Liebknecht and Luxemburg campaign," and, with Vittorio, she slipped swiftly into Vienna.

Under pressure from the spectacular electoral gains of Austrian Nazis, Dollfuss had attempted to outflank the far Right by adopting its agenda. With a nod from Mussolini, the Austrian had dissolved parliament, banned all political parties save his own, and generally dismantled constitutional government. In response, outraged members of the Schutzbund barricaded themselves in Vienna's vast tenement projects, intending to topple the authoritarian regime.

Accounts of the uprising are contradictory. Contemporary historian Gordon Brook-Shepherd underscores the restraint of Dollfuss's response, which alternated between radioed appeals for surrender and spatters of howitzer fire that left 140 insurgents dead and 400 wounded. In contrast, Red Aid documents describe apartment houses ripped apart by howitzer balls and clattering rounds of machine-gun fire. The crack of rifles mingled with frenzied screaming and bursts of shattering glass as government forces tortured and summarily strung up their prisoners. In the Communist version, rebels hobbled from pockmarked, blood-smeared buildings, leaving eighteen hundred comrades dead and one thousand wounded.

With other Red Aid delegates, Tina threaded her way through the housing projects, interviewing inhabitants and taking notes. She met scores of heartbroken women who asked how they could put food into the mouths of children and elderly parents. Their men were dead, they told Tina, or jammed into prison camps where they had to survive on watery, potatoless slop. At Kaisersteinbruck, inmates were succumbing to typhoid fever, and Woellersdorf was hit with an epidemic of dysentery. Tina shored up destitute families with cash payments, deployed teams of Red Aid doctors and lawyers, and made plans for orphans to be transported abroad. Sporadically, shouts and falls of footsteps announced that police were bearing down upon the tenement house where they were working, and the Red Aid delegation would scatter to the four winds.

As always, Tina's heart was laid open by working-class suffering. She conjugated communism with compassion and was ultimately happiest in ministering directly to the people. Among the scores of survivors interviewed that week was Frau Muenichreiter, the pretty brunette widow of a shoemaker hanged in the insurrection. Though it is impossible to say if this particular woman passed before Tina (or if Tina wrote the account that follows), such encounters filled her days and such tragedies were her tragedy.

> Three children hover around [Frau Muenichreiter], two boys and a little girl. The boys, attentive and thoughtful, as are proletarian children who have known from infancy the suffering and anxieties of their class, answer with an astonishingly acute political instinct.
>
> Muenichreiter's wife is a proletarian woman, gentle and modest, with an open face and simple gestures. Her speech is also modest and simple. She speaks seriously and without tears of this most terrible thing which has befallen herself and her children. But, from time to time, one notices that the corners of her mouth are quivering. It is the only sign of the depth of her sorrow....
>
> Muenichreiter's wife, who at first stayed home to care for her three children, carried hot soup to her husband on the line of combat. He had only swallowed a few spoonfuls when white guards attacked them. As Muenichreiter pushed away the barely touched bowl, rifles were already spitting fire.
>
> Muenichreiter's group fought to the last bullet before trying to disengage itself. It was then that Muenichreiter was wounded in the shoulder and arm. His best friend, wounded in the head, fell beside him, and Muenichreiter thought it wrong to leave the dying man. And it was to this last act of proletarian solidarity, this last attempt at first aid, that he owed his arrest.

Like most Schutzbund members, the Muenichreiters were Social Democrats, not Communists, but Red Aid asked few questions of victims of capitalist repression and extended helping hands to Communists, socialists, trade unionists, liberals, and those without affiliation. Yet, the Party line decreed it "impossible to struggle against fascism without struggling against social democracy" and held progressive agencies to be anathema. Using the alias George Contreras, Vittorio authored a pamphlet vilifying the Matteotti Fund, an Italian Socialist group that had teamed up with the Quakers to care for Vienna's victims. By conventional Stalinist epithets, the Matteotti Fund represented "social fascism," "nefarious sabotage," and a "Trojan horse within the workers' movement." As for the Schutzbund rebels who were not imprisoned, hundreds made a dash for the Soviet Union, where, greeted with much fanfare, they entered into hero lore as exploited workers who had risen up against their capitalist oppressors. Three years later, all would be carted off to perish in gulags.

Back in Paris, Vittorio sauntered one May day into the place Saint-Germain-des-Prés, after a convivial lunch with politico Jacques Duclos and lawyer Marcel Willard. A gentleman accosted him, and, within minutes, Vittorio found himself whisked off to jail by the Deuxième Bureau, the French counterespionage unit, which planned to press charges of spying for the Soviet Union. On Willard's advice, Vittorio confessed to lesser counts of violating interdictions on political activity by foreigners and was swiftly deported to Belgium. Meanwhile, Tina had sweated out Vittorio's failure to appear at their makeshift office. Aghast at the possibilities of his arrest and an imminent police raid, she finally closed the shutters, ripped compromising dossiers from their shelves, and shoved them with burning matches into a trash can. Black smoke billowed, but Tina persisted, grim and purposeful, until overcome by smoke inhalation. Fortunately, a German colleague happened by, and, taking in the situation at a glance, he flung open the windows and revived his limp comrade.

Upon discovering what had befallen Vittorio, Tina and a clutch of coworkers hastened to Brussels to take counsel with him. Sifting through the repercussions of this turn of events, the group determined that the European office should be split in two, with one set of comrades functioning openly and legally while the other went underground. Tina was chosen to head the "shadow Red Aid" while Vittorio, stripped of his cover and useless in France, received word to report back to Moscow.

As the couple awaited the docking of a Russian freighter in Antwerp, they went sight-seeing in Gent, Liège, Charleroi, and Namur. The high-light of the spontaneous vacation was Bruges, where Tina was enthralled by the Rubenses and the Brueghels, and the twosome spent an evening con-suming mussels and French fries at a sidewalk bistro. When the band struck up, Vittorio took her for a spin on the dance floor, where he was all smooth-ness and she as awkward as ever. Tina confided to her companion that the "stay in Paris had given her a global vision of her tasks; she felt more secure and liked the work because she was convinced of its usefulness." Showing "uncommon vivacity" and "deep conviction," she opened up about dangers she had confronted and her realization that she was "capable of controlling her doubts and fears."

The six months that follow are shrouded in mystery. Circumstances suggest that Tina often worked at the Willards' apartment, where her dossiers were shielded by a law forbidding searches and seizures in attor-neys' homes. A lonely, tenacious figure, Tina dipped deeply into her reser-voirs of sangfroid and courage. Covert work was, as a seasoned colleague maintained, "worse than [wartime] trenches," and thus it was habitually assigned to "the most self-denying, the most sacrificing, the one who accepts the possibility of not surviving."

We catch up with Tina in August when, as "Renée," she organized a three-day World Congress of Women Against War and Fascism, held at the Left Bank meeting hall La Mutualité. Stasova herself attended the confer-ence, lecturing to fifteen hundred delegates on "the liberated Soviet woman" and casting an approving eye on the exhibition Tina had installed on the mezzanine. Photographs, drawings, and charts drove home the con-ference's theme that capitalism equals warmongering. In collaboration with Australian-born writer Ella Winter, Tina prepared a thirty-page handbook bearing the typically zealous title *Women under Fascist Terror! Women on the Front of Solidarity and Combat!* The publication offered an inventory of pub-lic-aid programs quashed by capitalists in favor of the arms race and a country-by-country roster of "white terror" cases for use by Red Aid and its sister organizations.

Even as she typed it, the term *sister organizations* must have startled Tina. Alarmed at the confidence with which the Nazis threw their weight around Central Europe, the Comintern was in the midst of a historic pol-icy shift. Shelving its posture of hostility toward progressive Left parties,

Moscow had ordered bourgeois democracy preserved long enough to defeat fascism. Ink was not yet dry on the unity pact by which French Communists, Socialists, and Radical Socialists created the Popular Front, and, already, groups such as the Matteotti Fund were no longer bullied and reviled. The idea of working-class unity seized the popular imagination, and, amid a sea of ardent faces and proudly raised bent-arm salutes, Tina sang a gloriously resolute "Internationale."

October 1934 saw political and personal events unfolding in rapid succession. In Spain, a well-armed united Left uprising swept the northern mining region of Asturias, winning prompt support from the Comintern. Red Aid launched an appeal "for urgent and powerful solidarity," and, grabbing her Guatemalan passport, Tina leapt aboard a southbound train. Detained at the border, she doubled back to Paris, where she found a directive to return to Moscow.

As Tina was reestablishing herself in the Soviet Union, Vittorio saw her as a person different from the one to whom he had bid farewell five months earlier. The empathetic helper had lost ground to the sectarian operative, and she was "more reserved, less talkative, more rigid in her judgment about the relationships between Party and comrades." Vittorio's observations bespeak Tina's further drift toward psychological capitulation to Stalinist doctrine as ultimate truth. She had stopped growing and evolving as an individual. Her creative life had atrophied, her sense of humor flagged, and she had few points of reference outside the Party. As decrees rolled off its machinery, she mentally slotted them into the implacable march toward proletarian revolution. In Vittorio's judgment, 1934 was "the year in which Tina most developed as a revolutionary." He added, rather ominously, "When she spoke, she knew. When she knew, she spoke."

He further reports this statement from Tina: "I convinced myself that the slogan 'the Party is always right' is just and necessary." Ever quick to assent to the Party line, she now went further, suggesting that imagination be stifled and personal convictions ignored in the name of discipline. Such an attitude was to inform the coming years of false confessions and groveling surrender of many oppositionists. "A true Bolshevik has submerged his personality in the collectivity, 'the Party,' to such an extent that he can make the necessary effort to break away from his own opinions and convictions, and can honestly agree with the Party—that is the test of a true

Bolshevik." So spoke Comrade Pyatakov, a former deviant who recanted in 1928 and remained the most loyal of Stalinists until his execution in 1937. But Lenin's widow, Nadezhda Krupskaya, who kept her distance from Stalin, characterized the idea "the Party is always right" as "psychologically unacceptable."

Within weeks of Tina's arrival, the infamous murder of Leningrad Party chief Sergei Kirov was to trigger the Moscow trials, which would be followed by years of monstrous carnage and terror. Paranoia quickly insinuated itself into nearly every relationship, and the nation crawled with informers and inquisitors. Acquaintances began to vanish by night, and in December came mass deportations to Siberia and the Arctic.

As a low-hanging cloud of fear descended upon Moscow, Vittorio presented to Red Aid's Executive Committee his long-anticipated report on political asylum. According to his account of events, he upbraided the Soviet Union, as well as other nations, for their bureaucratic attitudes toward refugees and endorsed a more humanitarian approach. Stony silence, followed by a barrage of criticism, met his remarks, and Comrade Shevelova was "almost screaming when she said that my observations were an inadmissible insult to the Soviet people." In the meeting's aftermath, friends turned cool, Stasova stopped calling, and Vittorio was placed under surveillance while a commission investigated his "case." Despite her adamancy about discipline, Tina, a pillar of quiet strength, steadfastly stuck with him during these "difficult moments, of anguish and humiliation."

The critical juncture came at a Red Aid cell meeting, one of thousands held around the country to consider the Central Committee's secret missive "Lessons of the Events Connected with the Evil Murder of Comrade Kirov." Tense and waxen, Stasova stood stiffly at one end of a room where the half-light heightened a feeling of portentousness. As the assembly's "reporter," Shevelova summarized Kirov's biography, read and analyzed the Central Committee's letter, and, eyes glued to Vittorio, discussed Comrade Stalin's bid to root out double-dealers. Vittorio's memoirs recount that he leapt into the breach, condemning those who discredited the Soviet Union through insensitive officialism and cleverly shuffling Stalin's arguments into his own. The strain palpably eased as Stasova wrapped up the meeting. Vittorio's affair saw its denouement when she shipped him off to Spain with funds raised for Asturian rebel families, a mission probably calculated to save his life, and Tina was once more alone.

One foreign resident remembered:

> The [Kirov] tragedy came in a season of the country's greatest triumph—this winter of 1934–35 was the first one that the majority of the people had spent in comfort. The necessities were stored up, and now there were the materials and energies for luxuries— the small things that one can get along without, but one would *rather* have them: new grocery stores with new kinds of food were the most evident victory over necessity, carrying all those not entirely necessary articles called *delicatessen*. Japanese silks appeared in Mostorg, in payment of Japan's debt for the Far Eastern Railway. There were more than one kind of shoes and one kind of hat. Heavy and war industries had caught up on the rubber problem, and there were plenty of overshoes and galoshes. The closed shops and the special *valuta* (foreign currency) stores for foreigners were abolished, and those goods made available to all.

Moscow was gouging out its first subway line "which was going to show how a socialist country could learn from and surpass capitalist engineering and decor," and the city's residents, Tina included, cheerfully turned out on Red Sundays to carry rocks and finish off surface work. When the Metro opened that spring, nobody could stay out of it or stop marveling at its comfort and design.

That Tina helped build the subway is one of the few pieces of information we possess about her life in 1935. We also know that she pulled out of the Soyuznaya, making do with room 23 at 152 Rozhdestvensky Boulevard, farther from the city's center, and that she resumed the routine at MOPR. French journalist Simone Téry journeyed that year to Moscow, where she alighted at Red Aid to interview Stasova. "[B]ehind the vigorous figure of 'the old Bolshevik,'" Téry later recalled, "...was [Tina] diminutive, sweet, discreet and smiling." The implication is that Tina was content, yet it was a trying time for her. Life as a MOPR bureaucrat was a comedown after the dangerous and useful activity she had known in France. She pushed through her typewriter a chapter on Latin America for the pamphlet *Fifteen Years of White Terror,* but she later told Vittorio she had accomplished little else. On top of that, her reputation had been tarnished in some circles, along with his, and she felt what she termed "a special watchfulness," meaning the need for caution and probably a surveillant's eye upon her.

Though Tina had few confidants, she enjoyed a wide circle of friends and acquaintances, among them several Italian families who were longtime Moscow residents. She discreetly socialized with MOPR colleagues and with members of the city's Political Emigrants' Club. She also knew many players in the Soviet Union's burgeoning film world, and she moved to the fringes of a coterie of cinematographers, film school students, and directors.

Its central figure was Sergei Eisenstein, who was teaching a famous course in directing at the film academy. Years later, Vittorio dredged up dim recollections that, in his absence, Sergei had been instrumental in organizing a brief exhibition of Tina's photographs at Moscow University. Tina also knew German director Max Kahana, with whom she had collaborated on a documentary about Red Aid produced by Mezhrabpom, MOPR's film unit. Renowned for high-quality feature, documentary, and propaganda work, Mezhrabpom was a haven for foreigners seeking entrée to the world of Soviet cinema. Thus, when twenty-three-year-old American Jay Leyda, later a distinguished film historian and writer, rolled into Moscow in the fall of 1933, he naturally gravitated toward Mezhrabpom, which sponsored his application for admission to the academy.

Leyda had arrived in the Soviet Union with baggage bulging. As a favor to New York gallery owner Alma Reed, he was returning to Tina a big stack of her photographs, probably the Orozco mural reproductions used in Reed's just-completed monograph on the Mexican artist. Leyda passed the images before Eisenstein's admiring eyes but was unable to give them to Tina until her return from Paris nearly a year later. Jay had also brought to Moscow his ten-minute film *A Bronx Morning,* an abstracted light-and-shadow vision of the borough and an exploration of the idea that a gesture could have "more than one use, more than one meaning." By screening it for Sergei, he won admission to the director's course.

When Tina and Jay met at last, he found her "almost as monumental as a political worker as indeed she was monumental as an artist." As it turned out, Alma Reed was not their only mutual acquaintance. Raised in

Dayton, Ohio, Jay had briefly studied photography with Jane Reece, of all people, and he was probably familiar with Reece's gauzy pictures of the exotic Madame de Richey, now good for a hearty laugh.

Details are sketchy, but it seems that Tina was deeply involved in at least one film project. Later, word reached her former acting cronies in San Francisco, who spoke of Tina when they gathered to prepare a WPA-sponsored history of local Italian-American theater. "Her work in the Russian cinema," they reported, "most importantly, her film on the Baku region, was widely acclaimed." It is conceivable that a Modotti movie molders in a Russian storeroom, or, more likely, that she took part in a project such as Igor Savchenko's short propaganda piece *People Without Hands*. Jay Leyda's history of the Soviet cinema reports that Savchenko, a director active in the mid-1930s, came to the capital from the Baku Theater of Young Workers.

Meanwhile, a consensus was building at MOPR that, with Vittorio out of favor in certain influential circles, Tina would be safer from arrest outside the Soviet Union. A description of a proposed Paris job for her circulated that fall, but by the time Vittorio pulled into Moscow on a November furlough, arrangements were under way for Tina to join him when he returned to Spain. On Saturday, December 21, Vittorio struck out for Madrid via Paris as Tina hastened to put her affairs in order, and Jay Leyda mailed a postcard to his classmate, Tina's former colleague Angelo Masutti. "Angelo," he had written, "Please be at Tina Modotti's room at 8 o'clock on the night of December 23rd. [Novelist and scriptwriter Pyotr] Pavlenko will read his scenario. Jay Leyda." Though Tina kept Jay's entourage in the dark about her imminent departure, the low-key gathering of colleagues stood in for a farewell party.

Not only was she too cautious to discuss her departure, but she also no longer revealed the events of her life by mail. Out of prudence and fatigue, she had allowed her once-flourishing correspondence to shrivel. That autumn, her sister Mercedes had replied to a letter from Vocio, petulant over lack of news from Tina:

> Tina is in the same place and the address is the same, if you care
> I will give you the one we have, maybe you have a different one,
> Hans Mosiman, Burglistrasse 35, Winterthur, Swiss. You must put
> Tina's letter in another envelope but don't write anything on it, it

will be forwarded to her. She says she is very busy, hasn't had a vacation this year so far. Ben and J. [Yolanda] complain because they haven't heard from her for over a year. She writes Mother about once a month, she says she is well but very tired and that must be the reason because Tina always was a good correspondent.

Without waiting for Mercedes's response, Vocio had dispatched to Tina's former address a letter that eventually reached Moscow. Tina replied on Christmas Eve, with her departure imminent, though she breathed not a word of it. From opaque, featureless phrases, she squeezed a tone of affection:

> I was so glad to receive your letter of Nov. 10th. You are perfectly right in complaining of my long rude silence, I have no excuse other than the lack of time and yet I know that that is no excuse at all. I do hope you will forgive me and not hold it against me, because I assure you that though I have not written for so long still I do think so very often of you both and of our pleasant life together.
>
> I am working very hard but I am very happy with my life and my health is also good although I cannot manage to put up any flesh no matter how much I eat.
>
> I know you would like me to tell you something more in detail about my life and about life in general here but there is so much to tell that I just have not the heart to start; besides I believe that you have a chance to read considerably on things here. So many books have been written on the life here and besides there are several publications devoting considerable space to this country....
>
> I heard that my little sister has gone East but I also have not heard from her for a long time, though in her case also I am the one to blame because I never answered her letters, so you see dear Vocio and Marionne you are not the only ones whom I have not written to.
>
> I hear from mother about once a month but now with the trouble going on there I have been for over 6 weeks without news and I am beginning to worry; things are just awful there and it surely is

the duty of us all to try and stop that crime, you know what I mean
I am sure.

As if to distract the two women's attention from the impersonality of
her letter, Tina popped into the envelope a postcard of St. Basil's Cathedral
on which she had typed: "This church is a beautiful work of art. Now with
the reconstruction of the city, the church will be moved farther away from
the red square in order to make the square larger. It is being preserved as
one of the most precious works of art of that far back period." Although she
encouraged the Richeys to keep up the correspondence, using the address
of an Italian friend in Moscow ("don't put my name on the envelope, not
necessary"), the letter was doubtless her last communication with Robo's
family.

A day or two later, Tina procured twenty-five rubles for travel
expenses and departed the Soviet Union forever. Though a directive to take
all of her possessions signaled she should not plan on returning, she
entrusted her friends, the Regent family, with the Leica, recently retrieved
from Angelo, and a bundle of photographs. Like flotsam deposited on a distant shore, these would remain in Moscow until long after her death.

Tina traveled west convinced "that the Soviet Party accepted the
decision of the Communist International to send me to Spain again and
with [Vittorio] because it wants to get rid of two bothersome people."
Although the Stalinist era's worst nightmares were still to come, she had
had a taste of fear by night. Yet Tina's faith in communism was bright and
intact, and she harbored no remorse about the choices she had made.

To be sure, she was unaware of how ruthlessly and cynically the
Soviet tyrant was manipulating the idealism of millions. But, as a believer
in historical materialism, Tina summarily rejected the idea that Stalin or
anyone else could transform the party of the proletariat into the machinery
of dictatorship. The immense authority of the Russian revolution easily
eclipsed any disconcerting episodes in Moscow.

Moreover, the Party seemed the world's brightest hope against the
tyranny of Hitler and Mussolini. Tina's antifascism was not only intellectual but also deeply personal, and she laid to the fascists' charge everything
from her unhappy Italian exile to Julio Antonio's murder by Machado, "the
tropical Mussolini." So rabidly did she demonize fascists that, after speak-

ing with a retinue of Blackshirts in Spain, she was to express disbelief in their fascism on grounds that they were peasants and workers and seemed genuine human beings. "[I am an antifascist] because I am an enemy of tyrannies," she had once explained, but the Party's powerful mystique blinded her to its reign of terror.

Tina saw lingering doubts as nothing more than gaps in her political education. Ultimately, her communism was a matter of faith. The idea of life outside the Party was unthinkable, and, as another true believer put it, "If I were convinced that the Soviet Union did not justify my faith, the world would become a hopeless, dreadful place for me." Communists of Tina's generation were passionate creatures, observed one scion of the movement, and

> the law of passion is such that it is *all*; and when a thing becomes all, people do terrible things to themselves and to one another.
>
> Thus, among the Communists, men and women who gained the courage to plunge after freedom were in the end not free. Men and women who had great intelligence were in the end in no position to use that intelligence. Men and women who were eminently reasonable and clung to the beauty and decency of reason were in the end a caricature of reason....
>
> And surrounding the whole of things was the longing; *responsible* for the whole of things was the longing, the longing aroused by the vision of loveliness that was Marxism and could not be let go of even when the vision became a trap, a prison, a shriveling of the soul rather than the exultant charging of the soul it had been in its beginnings.

Tina's enthrallment with the Communist world notwithstanding, she was happy to be in Paris, where she and Vittorio strolled along the banks of the Seine. During the past year and a half, the couple had been together no more than three months, and their letters had wisely skirted all topics save cheerful greetings and predictions of successful missions. During the interlude in France, it quickly emerged that the relationship had frayed, a change Vittorio attributed to the discrepancy between his forthrightness and sensuous love of life and Tina's tight-lipped political compulsiveness:

...the veil present between us during the previous encounter continued or rather was becoming thicker. Distance and a mutually difficult life had contributed to making us an "all political" couple, common in the Communist Party....

In facing this experience, which was painful for me, I swore that I would never turn "all political." I wanted to be myself, in flesh and blood, with my personality, my good qualities and my defects, always capable of saying what I thought and considered just.... I would not renounce these principles, not even for the love I felt for Tina. She knew it.

A somewhat different interpretation is that Tina wished to retreat from the emotional intimacy of the early days in Moscow and thus recast the relationship as "all political." The couple still had sexual relations, yet—while Vittorio's memoirs made a point of how Tina "liked making love...generous love, full of fantasy, complete"—theirs was not the sensuous rapport he would have us imagine. More to the point was her comment repeated by a Spanish friend: "I was madly in love with a Cuban, I was married to him, and they killed him—I think he was the love of my life and I don't think I'll ever love again the way I loved my husband...."

Always closemouthed around Vittorio, Tina became even more so. After he struck out first for Spain, she paid a call on the Le Bihan family, to whom she spilled news apparently withheld from him: She had learned that she suffered from a heart condition.

Part V

María

Spain (1936–1939)

INETEEN THIRTY-SIX got under way with a victory. In February's legislative elections, Communists, Socialists, and anarchists—united as the Spanish Popular Front—built their campaign around amnesty for workers jailed in the brutal repression of the Asturian revolt. Unexpectedly, the Left triumphed, and jubilation swept the masses as prisons disgorged inmates and the Popular Front stepped into power.

Despite endless celebratory parades and choruses of the "Internationale," the government had little time to rest upon its laurels. Only five years old, the second Spanish republic had spawned bitter enemies, and now these came to the fore. Monarchists plotted the restoration, paramilitary groups stockpiled weapons, and fascists set about destabilizing the regime with a spate of kidnappings and assassinations. Ensconced on vast estates, the reactionary landed aristocracy dug in its heels against attempts at agrarian reform.

It is likely that Tina and Vittorio were in Spain as Moscow's top envoys to Red Aid, which could now function openly. Even before the elections, the pair had devoted what time they could spare from the amnesty campaign to restructuring the understaffed and disorganized operation. Tina crisscrossed the country that spring, knitting together a volunteer corps and revamping publications, including the newspaper *Ayuda,* for which she zealously penned articles about "white terror" cases.

In Madrid, the couple stayed at the home of Matilde Landa and Paco Ganivet, well-to-do converts to communism. In their early forties, they were a fashionable and attractive pair, the parents of a beautiful five-year-old daughter. Pale and willowy, Matilde had delicate features, coal black eyes, and dark hair, which she, like Tina, parted in the middle and wound into a bun. Not only did the two resemble each other physically, Matilde also shared Tina's serene manner and strong will. They became fast friends.

On May Day, the women marched together in a vast workers' parade that choked the city and horrified moneyed, conservative *madrileños*. The crowd carried portraits of Socialist prime minister Largo Caballero, Stalin, and Lenin, and orators promised proletarian revolution. With the Popular Front victory, Spanish Communists had been roused from years of listlessness, and the Comintern was bolstering its contingent of foreign "advisers."

Spring turned to summer, and the air was thick with rumors of an impending military coup. On July 17, as wealthy Spaniards holidayed by the sea and the tense nation sweltered under oppressive heat, right-wing generals gave the nod for garrisons to rise against the constitutionally elected progressive government, and Spain burst into flames. The rebellion found Tina working in the southern city of Córdoba, from which she escaped, though insurgents established a foothold in the region. She rushed back to Madrid, where every other wall was suddenly covered with hammer and sickle graffiti, and citizens offered greetings of *"¡Saludos antifascistas!"* A crowd seeking weapons mounted a furious attack on the Montaña army barracks, where insurgents were trapped, and churches were set ablaze by mobs who assumed the Catholic establishment's complicity in the right-wing rebellion. Populist parties and labor unions began forming surging, ill-disciplined militias, many of whose members believed that time was ripe for overthrowing centuries of tradition and launching the revolution.

Tina saw the Spanish Civil War as part of the fascists' international conspiracy against the working class and thus an opportunity to fight for her homeland as well as for Spain. Mussolini supplied men and matériel to the rebels, while Italian antifascists were flocking to the Loyalist cause with cries of *"Oggi in Spagna, domani in Italia!"* Tina confided to young Agueda Serna Morales (who inspired Hemingway's Maria in *For Whom the Bell Tolls*) that the battle against fascism "was not, for her, a theoretical question but, rather, the consequence of all that she herself had suffered because of fascism; that in her country, Italy, she could not struggle and, for that reason, Spain was her last remaining bulwark. I will never forget what she told me on that occasion: 'If we lose here, we lose everywhere.'" Spain was the crucible of antifascism, and Tina's final chance for personal happiness. If the republic triumphed, she believed, "it will completely change my life and the lives of others around the world who are persecuted by fascism as I am." The acuteness of her desire made Tina as dedicated, disciplined, and indefatigable as anyone in Spain.

Following Communist convention, she took a nom de guerre. Tina's shape-shifting identity and career as a revolutionist (companion to Nicanor MacPartland, better known as Julio Antonio Mella, and Vittorio Vidali, self-christened Carlos Contreras and Enea Sormenti) had already brought a series of names and aliases. In Spain, she sometimes called herself Carmen Ruíz Sánchez or Vera Martini, but most knew her simply as María.

An Italian, Spanish, and Mexican name, common in any Catholic nation, María evokes "the servant, the mendicant, the one who comes from the country," the humble, silent woman in black. Tina's use of the appellation, in profoundly religious Spain, where Mariolatry flourishes, also begs association with the Virgin. Like Mary, Tina became a paragon of devotion, gentleness, asceticism, and grief. She sought the most abject and dangerous tasks. Her face was inscribed with a sorrowful realization of humanity's suffering, and "she spoke slowly and sadly, as she herself was enveloped in sadness."

Though Tina could have restricted herself to Red Aid's administrative duties, she chose to work where conditions were most primitive and war's savagery most appalling. Perhaps she was newly fatalistic because she intended to disregard the heart trouble that was responsible for her swollen ankles and extreme fatigue. Remembering Nietzsche, she adopted the motto "Live dangerously." Vittorio recalled, "Tina was always in the front lines of danger," or in the throes of unsung toil. A comrade who helped with the periodicals project remembered that she never pulled rank, but, on the contrary, volunteered for inglorious tasks. "If something had to be done, Tina did it: clean the offices, sweep, do everything that needed doing because it was impossible to hire employees or anything, and all the work was done by volunteers. Tina always chose to do what others wouldn't do."

After armed conflict erupted, she could be found mopping feverish brows, helping the elderly to shelter, emptying bedpans, or holding the hands of those not expected to survive the night. "I met María," one Spanish mother informed her soldier son. "I lack words to describe her to you. I can only tell you that she is admirable."

One of Tina's first wartime endeavors was to administer, with Matilde Landa, the vast and ultramodern Hospital Obrero, the Workers' Hospital. With most of the army medical corps mutinous and the Spanish Red Cross in disarray, Red Aid had stepped in to run medical and sanitary installations. Lacking not only personnel but also such essentials as antibiotics, beds, painkillers, and stretchers, hospitals barely functioned. Neither Tina nor Matilde knew the first thing about institutional management, but they improvised and collaborated with the medical officer in charge, Dr. Juan Planelles, a portly, energetic, and droopy-eyed Catalan who "dreamed of a Spain patterned after Russia." Juan and Matilde also shared the powerful position of political commissar, charged with indoctrinating staff and guarding against treasonous activities.

Until the arrival of Mary Bingham de Urquidi, the English-born wife of a Mexican embassy official, the Hospital Obrero was bereft of professional nurses. Touring the facility on her first day, Mary approached the entrance to its huge white ceramic–walled, red tile–floored kitchen. A battery of gas stoves lined one wall and refrigeration units another, while alcoves were filled with row after row of pantry shelves. Before a chopping block stood a big-bellied French cook, stripped to the waist and brandishing a butcher knife. Mary's guide, Lola,

> called to a woman inside, who was…wearing a long nun's gown. She introduced her as Marie. Marie was French and was in charge of the kitchen and the cooks. She said that she had never had anything to do with kitchens. Her English had a funny accent, a mixture of French and American due, she said, to having lived in Brooklyn, N.Y.
>
> "Marie," I asked, "Why did you come to work in a hospital?"
>
> "I am a Communist," she answered, "and you?"
>
> "I am not a Communist, nor ever could be. I am a nurse. My mission here is not political, only humanitarian."

"Too bad you are not a Communist. However, there are all kinds of people and politics in this hospital. We will appreciate your work anyway. I am at your disposition in this kitchen. Let's have a cup of coffee."

Mary never found out that Sister Marie was the erstwhile Mexican photographer Tina Modotti, who had taken to wearing the nuns' habits discarded by nurses when they fled. A disguise could be useful in gleaning information, and the hospital was a nest of intrigue. The recent sudden deaths of some one hundred patients had been a mystery until it was discovered that Tina's predecessor, Sister Amalia, a secret fascist sympathizer, was poisoning the food. Refusing to the end to reveal from whom she took orders, Sister Amalia was led into the garden and finished off by an amateur firing squad as Tina assumed the kitchen duties.

Fueled by a roasted barley brew that passed as coffee, Tina ran herself ragged, scrubbing on her hands and knees, scouring pots and pans, and trotting back and forth across the hard tiled floors. Her eyes turned red-rimmed, and her legs swelled so severely that doctors ordered her hospitalized for several days to rest.

Tina and Matilde shared the hospital's travails with a twenty-six-year-old Cuban-bred Spanish woman named María Luisa Lafita. A short, vivacious brunette with enormous blue eyes, María Luisa and her husband, refugees from the Caribbean island's repressive regime, had knocked on Red Aid's door one day asking to see the officials in charge. Vittorio and Tina inspected their credentials and, when these proved in order, welcomed the pair not with a formal handshake but, rather, with the warm hugs and kisses of working-class kinship. It was a gesture María Luisa would remember with emotion all her life.

When hepatitis brought Dolores Ibarruri, called "La Pasionaria," to the Hospital Obrero, she was entrusted to Tina and María Luisa. Dressed all in black like the devout Catholic she once was, La Pasionaria toured the republic, inspiring citizens and soldiers with soaring, dramatic oratory that made her the most famous Communist in Spain. "Women of Madrid!" she pleaded. "Do not hinder your husbands from going to war. It is better to be the widow of a hero than the wife of a miserable coward!" She rallied armies with the cry *"¡No pasarán!"* ("They shall not pass!").

Threats rained daily upon the Communist matriarch, and Planelles barked out orders that no one save Tina and María Luisa was to enter her room. By then, both had trained in the use of pistols, rifles, and grenades. Though staff members were forbidden to attack enemy soldiers, the two knew they must do anything necessary, even go under fire, to protect a patient, especially one as precious as La Pasionaria. For five days and nights, Tina alternated with María Luisa as her bodyguard and nurse.

Spain's early harvest of atrocities brought to the Hospital Obrero a convoy of wounded militiamen. Six years later, Tina told French journalist Simone Téry that she would "never forget" their arrival. "She said nothing more," recalled Téry, "but I saw how her face still changed when she evoked this first vision of war." Many of the victims were adolescents, in excruciating pain from fractures, bayonet stabs, and shrapnel wounds. Amputations had to be performed without proper instruments, and surgery continued around the clock. From that time on, beds were filled with broken-bodied soldiers, for only eleven hospitals were functioning in all of Madrid as insurgent general Francisco Franco drove his troops up from the south, ever closer to the capital.

Not long afterward, a distress call sounded from a children's tuberculosis sanatorium in the mountains north of Madrid. Not all religious orders had sided with the fascists, and the nuns who operated this facility were aiding the loyalist cause by concealing a handful of soldiers. Although nearly surrounded by troops, the sisters had caught sight of Republican flags and were unconcerned until shells began riddling the building's walls. When they shepherded their charges onto the patio to show attackers that they housed only children, fascist planes swooped down, spurting machine-gun fire and dumdum bullets that took out hunks of flesh as big as a man's fist.

With their colleague María Valero, Tina and María Luisa rushed by ambulance to collect the wounded and take them back to Madrid. In the appalling bloodbath, many children had lost arms and legs, and others were dying of internal bleeding. As aircraft continued to strafe the sanatorium, the trio heroically carried the small victims to waiting vehicles. "We saved many children," María Luisa recalled, "and then when we brought the children to the hospital…the wounded militiamen, even some who had serious wounds, right away asked if it were possible to donate skin, and the same wounded men who had gone to defend liberty in the trenches were trying to save the lives of these children...it was a very beautiful gesture."

For the first six months of the war, Tina sallied back and forth between the working-class district of Cuatro Caminos, home to the Hospital Obrero and Red Aid's regional office, and the agency's national headquarters in a fashionable downtown district unlikely to be a target of fascist bombs. She worked two full-time jobs simultaneously. Vittorio enumerated her responsibilities outside the hospital: "organizing the sanitary service of the army...organizing orphanages, organizing family visits to soldiers to inspire them, to organize all this not just in Madrid, but around Spain." Under her guidance, Red Aid set up a first-aid post for each militia unit, opened stretcher factories in Madrid and Valencia, trained paramedics and nurses, and converted a subway train confiscated by workers into a traveling hospital. By year's end, the national medical corps had been reassembled, and Red Aid could wind up most of its sanitary and medical work. But children and the elderly still had to be evacuated from danger zones, orphans cared for, and women urged to knit gloves, socks, and mufflers for soldiers at the front. The organization published newsletters and posters, distributed donations from abroad, trained aid workers, and handled mail for foreign volunteers. When the government decreed that no civilian could own more than one blanket, Red Aid collected the others and trucked them to the front.

Tina ploughed through all obstacles, leaving a trail of memos, telegrams, and letters, carefully dated and marked "received" or "noted" and signed "María." She spoke in a low voice and avoided the spotlight, but colleagues had no misgivings about her abilities. "She was modest and reserved. Nonetheless, she had a very strong personality. She impressed me very much," recalled Manuel Fernández Colino, a Cuban volunteer. "When she spoke, it was not as if someone were reciting the Bible or dictating some theoretical lesson. She spoke simply with great self-assurance. She immediately inspired your confidence." To Flor Cernuda, an earnest adolescent who came to Madrid straight from her village in La Mancha, Tina "would pass by without saying a word yet something remained where she had passed.... She was so gentle and tranquil and, at the same time, so incredibly active. Today she was organizing, out of nothing, a transfusion center.

Tomorrow, she would be finding a location for a day care center or orphanage. And, the following day, taking care of those left behind by dead soldiers or arranging for blankets and warm clothing to be sent to the front. She never rested."

Tina was most talkative and relaxed in the company of Matilde and María Luisa, to whom she recounted her past. During long-winded Red Aid meetings, she sketched other participants, and when she showed the drawings to María Luisa, the two would burst into peals of laughter. Staying for several weeks in a borrowed house, Tina somehow put her hands on sugar and chocolate and found time to bake. María Luisa remembered that she "shared because this is Tina's character, to share…she knew how to make *churros* [fritters], and also made chocolate candy…and she gave them to others. She always tried to make friends with those things, with great affection and respect.…"

Such frivolous moments were rare, however. More often, Tina sternly drove herself through the day. Though equally obsessed with winning the war, Vittorio was in his element in Spain, which was to see the apogee of his career. Military commander Enrique Castro Delgado found him "brusque, heavy-drinking, womanizing, and terribly ambitious." A burly figure in a leather aviation jacket and dangling binoculars, Vittorio was a moving spirit of the Popular Army's Fifth Regiment (so named because four regiments were normally stationed in Madrid). In the first hours of the insurrection, Communists had gathered on the patio of a former convent to put together the crack fighting force, which Herbert Matthews of the *New York Times* called "one of the great revolutionary military units of all time." Recruits took an oath to go always forward and never retreat, and those who disobeyed orders could expect to be shot. At a time when nearly every trade union was pulling together a group of ten or twelve fighters who gave themselves a peppy name, such as the "Red Bullets," and took off in search of a front, the Fifth Regiment trained its men to salute, care for their weapons, and believe in the slogan "Discipline is not servility, it is—Victory!" As political commissar (a rank equal to military commander), Vittorio was the unit's ramrod, and he proved quick-witted, courageous, and imaginative. He once chartered a marching band to teach recruits how to keep step, and he bombarded enemy lines with rockets stuffed with brightly colored flyers inviting Franco's legions to desert.

In the early days of the war, when both were working in Madrid, Tina and Vittorio saw each other often. They never took an apartment of their own, staying instead at friends' homes, Red Aid offices, or hotels. For a few weeks that autumn, the pair used a house on Príncipe Vergara Street, adjoining the Red Aid dormitory where Flor Cernuda lived. Its walls were thin, and from time to time, the young woman overheard a fracas next door. "María was capable of raising her voice. I lived wall to wall with her and Carlos [Vittorio], and sometimes the two had discussions, and then you realized that here were two extremely strong personalities," she recollected. "No, I don't know what they were talking about, it isn't important to me. It happened only rarely, but…one could see that María was capable of wearing the pants in the family, as Spaniards say."

On one occasion, Flor witnessed an uncharacteristic outburst from Tina:

> And once I saw her agitated and furious…. At Red Aid headquarters we shared a bathroom, and once María forgot her comb there. A few minutes later when she went back to get it, it had disappeared. Someone had taken it…. You can't imagine the state she was in. She got angry as if it were a great tragedy. She ran through the halls shouting curses, but, unfortunately, in Italian. I couldn't understand what she was saying…. It really impressed me to see María, always so tranquil and serene, in such a state of nerves.

By early November, a gusty, rain-laden wind was sweeping the streets as the rebels advanced toward the gates of Madrid. To prepare for the final thrust of battle, Hitler's Junkers and Mussolini's Fiats showered incendiaries and bombs on the population. Their screams of *"¡Aviación!"* drowned out by air-raid sirens, *madrileños* would drop everything to make frantic dashes into the subway. Trucks packed with soldiers and sandbags rumbled down the streets, and mortars were heard belching west of the city. The tension grew unbearable, and, when panic seized Madrid, the republic's president and his cabinet, as well as a large contingent of Soviet advisers, slipped away by night. A *New York Herald-Tribune* reporter cabled home: "Madrid is…a doomed city…which will haul down its republican flag whenever…Franco so decides."

Tina pushed herself to the limit to evacuate the helpless and transfer Red Aid's national headquarters to the coastal city of Valencia as Communists undertook methodical preparations for the capital's defense. Fifth Regiment headquarters throbbed with activity as Vittorio churned out inspirational messages and bellowed into loudspeakers at rallies, "We give the guarantee that Madrid is unconquerable…Madrid will not be taken by the enemy come what may."

With Franco poised to attack at dawn on November 8, Vittorio spent the night before "in a prison briefly interrogating prisoners brought before him, and, when he decided, as he almost always did, that they were Fifth Columnists, he would shoot them in the back of their heads with his revolver. Ernest Hemingway [in Spain as a journalist] told [*New York Times* reporter Herbert Matthews] that he heard Vidali fired so often that the skin between the thumb and index finger of his right hand was badly burned." A letter from Hemingway to filmmaker Joris Ivens situated the episode at a garbage dump and identified the victims as well-to-do, upper-class (and thus possibly fascist) young men arrested haphazardly in Madrid's streets.

For such morally reprehensible acts, many considered Vidali a barbarian, even in the context of war. At the same time, the confident energy with which he engaged the Fifth Regiment in the dramatic and highly symbolic struggle for Spain's capital gave rise to the legend of Comandante Carlos. After ten days of bloody combat, which sometimes saw raw foreign volunteers and civilians grappling hand to hand with Franco's troops, the rebels retreated, and Loyalists scored a resounding victory in the Battle of Madrid.

In the midst of the city's chaotic evacuation, Tina had set aside twenty minutes to write her monthly letter to Assunta, to whom she was regularly forwarding a portion of her paycheck:

> I have been far from Paris for a few weeks now, and this is probably why I have not received your letters. Just imagine, Mama, that barely two weeks ago I received your letter of July 9!… Around the end of September, I sent you the money, and I hope, dear Mama, that you received it…. I'm very well and, as always, thinking often of my dear Mamacita, and I hope with all my heart that her health is good and continues to be, even though winter is now upon us….

But Tina's words may have never reached the Modotti home, for her letter was opened by Trieste police, who forwarded copies to the Italian Ministry of the Interior and state security police. The same batch of confiscated mail enclosed a note from Ben Modotti to Mercedes as well as François Le Bihan's reply, by necessity uninformative, to an anxious inquiry from Mercedes concerning Tina's whereabouts. "There is always a mix-up in our letters and most of them get lost, I mean those to Tina," Mercedes complained. "I don't think all of them get lost. I'm more inclined to believe they get censured."

In December, when a communication from Mercedes finally fell into Tina's hands, it brought news that, two months earlier, their mother had died of bronchitis, complicated by a broken leg. Not long after receiving the devastating letter, Tina appeared without warning at Fifth Regiment headquarters. Steering Vittorio into a corner, she placed her hands upon his shoulders and, weeping softly, announced, "My mother died." To Mercedes, Tina replied with a natural dignity so like Assunta's:

Dear sister,

Only a week ago did I receive the letter in which you tell me of the death of our dear mother. Your previous letters, in which you speak of her fall, her successive illnesses, etc., I never received. Nonetheless, I am deeply and eternally grateful to you for the very sensitive way in which you gave me the news, which has helped me to bear this terrible blow. Even so, I could not find it within myself to answer you immediately. My only desire these days has been to be near my sisters and brothers because their presence, yours especially, would have helped me to bear the terrible pain; would have filled a bit of this terrible emptiness which our blessed mother has left behind her.

As I write you, I have to make an enormous effort not to be overwhelmed by my tears; I must be strong. I know that, under other circumstances, I would have been able to see my mother again during these past ten years. This thought arouses in me a profound anger over the very circumstances which have prevented it. And the thought which tortures me perhaps most is this one: that the separation which prevented our dear mother from seeing again her faraway children made her last years of life so sad. And this: that she so suffered during her life and had the right to spend her final years surrounded by all of her children.

Imagine my situation, Mercedes: for three months I suspected nothing and continued writing to our dear mama (I don't know if the letters ever arrived). And our mother had already abandoned us forever....

Tell my sisters and brothers that for me the memory of our mother is like a bond that keeps us united in thought despite the distance separating us.

Following Assunta's death, Tina fell into a prolonged depression, and Vittorio insisted that she see a doctor, who prescribed bed rest.

The loss of her mother after a decade of separation translated into another reason to detest the fascism that had kept them apart. In late December, Tina traveled to Paris for an international conference on German amnesty, where she delivered a "short, vigorous speech":

> Until the time of their liberation by the Popular Front, we fought for [those taken prisoner after the Asturian revolt], not only for humanitarian reasons, but also because they are the best sons of the Spanish people: José Manzo, González Peña and all those who are today in the front lines of the struggle for free Spain. In the midst of the torments of the atrocious war that it is our lot to live, our thoughts go out to [imprisoned German Communist party chief Ernst] Thaelmann and all our German brothers whom Hitler wants to kill after having deprived them of liberty. Long live the struggle for Thaelmann and for all antifascist prisoners in Germany!

Back in Valencia, Tina was behind her desk for only a few days when insurgents launched a fierce surprise offensive, threatening the vital Madrid-Valencia highway, and she had to scramble to coordinate civilians' departure from the Jarama River valley. At the beginning of 1937, the Fifth Regiment had been reconfigured into the International Brigades, a Communist-organized foreign volunteer corps, and Vittorio now served as chief of propaganda for the entire people's army. He roamed the Jarama front in a truck with a loudspeaker mounted on the back and harangued the enemy, mostly Mussolini's forces, about not firing on their Italian brothers.

Meanwhile, a situation was developing so disastrously in southern Spain that both Tina and Vittorio were summoned to Valencia for hasty consultations. After fascists overtook the seaport of Málaga, on a narrow plain between mountains and the Mediterranean, they subjected Republican soldiers to savage reprisals and ordered tens of thousands of civilians to vacate the city. The departure via the one remaining route, a coastal highway to Almería, five days by foot to the east, swiftly turned into "the most terrible evacuation of a city in modern times."

It was decided that Tina and Matilde Landa would join in a humanitarian relief effort with Canadian doctor Norman Bethune and his blood-transfusion unit, installed in a one-and-a-half-ton Renault truck. An outspoken and eccentric man, Bethune had appeared at Red Aid offices three months earlier to propose that he organize a system of supplying blood at the front. After some hasty fund-raising abroad, the Canadian established blood banks for Madrid and front hospitals. By equipping the truck with a refrigerator, sterilizing unit, and vacuum bottles, he devised, for the first time in the history of war, the means "to carry blood-banks, not to base-hospitals or even dressing stations, but direct to those bleeding on the field...[offering medical care] under falling shells and by the flare of explosives."

As Tina and her colleagues reached the Málaga-Almería highway, fascist planes were strafe bombing and tanks pursuing the column of fleeing refugees. Trapped between sheer stone cliffs and the sea, a shuffling, bleeding, terrified mass of humanity crawled toward Almería. For one aid worker the scene evoked an "Old Testament exodus spread out before us: the illusion heightened by the donkeys and the grey-white single-piece cloak folded like a hood round the heads of many of the women and children; others in black, with long thick shawls draped over head and shoulders: all swarthy, dark-skinned: all with differentiations of dress and color almost obliterated by the dirt and dust which enveloped them."

Bethune's group administered first aid and trucked the most defenseless from the spots where they collapsed into Almería. Baked by the sun all day, Tina shivered as soon as it dipped into the sea, but no one dared to build fires, which might draw more bombing. She toiled side by side with Matilde, who won her deepened respect as "an extraordinary woman with an incredible capacity for work." Norman Bethune gave words to their experience:

> Our car was besieged by a mob of frantic mothers and fathers who with tired outstretched arms held up to us their children, their eyes and faces swollen and congested by four days of sun and dust....
>
> Children with bloodstained rags wrapped around their arms and legs, children without shoes, their feet swollen to twice their size crying helplessly from pain, hunger and fatigue...a solid stream of men, women, children, mules, donkeys, goats, crying out the names of their separated relatives lost in the mob. How could we choose between taking a child dying of dysentery or a mother silently watching us with great sunken eyes carrying against her open breast her child born on the road two days ago.... Here was a woman of sixty unable to stagger another step, her gigantic swollen legs with their open varicose ulcers bleeding into her cut linen sandals. Many old people simply gave up the struggle, lay down by the side of the road and waited for death....

When the inferno had subsided and Almería was clogged with sleeping refugees, German and Italian aviation pounced upon the town, dropping ten enormous bombs, which killed dozens more. Still dazed by all that had happened, Tina described to Vittorio the sum of the region's miseries. "Truly an atrocious experience," she concluded, "even worse than Madrid. War is hateful, but this massacre of women, children and old people is the most horrible act. I hate war and never want to see another." She realized she had been tempered by events of the past months: "I never would have believed that I would be so strong and not lose my head in a situation where the wind of collective insanity is blowing."

As Tina believed that no effort was too great for the cause, so, too, she thought none too small. She arranged herself with particular care and chose simple, dark but rather elegant clothing. U.S. social worker Constance Kyle visited Tina in her Valencia office and found her "lovely, very well-groomed, in a good-looking tweed suit, the light from the window behind her desk shining on her dark hair." Tina turned forty that year, and, in María Luisa's opinion, she was "very well kept up and very beautiful.... Black hair, that Italian hair, which is like Mexican hair, pure Mexican, that shiny blue-black hair, that's how Tina's was, absolutely, and a very good complexion, never changing...." But old friends such as Mexican writer Juan de la Cabada, who traveled to Valencia in 1937, saw only how much she had changed: "She was not the same woman because years do not pass without leaving a trace. One is marked by suffering [which doesn't show itself in some people]...but with certain very passionate temperaments such as hers, no? Very intense as she was, well, it doesn't go away.... She was the picture of sadness, she was stamped with great sadness."

De la Cabada was attending the Congress for the Defense of Culture Against Fascism, an international gathering of pro-Loyalist intellectuals, at which Tina represented Red Aid. Vittorio recounted that, during the conference, photographers Robert Capa, David Seymour (known as Chim), and Gerda Taro (who would be crushed to death by a tank three weeks later) urged Tina to pick up a camera once more. "No," she reportedly replied, "two tasks cannot be done at the same time." Also present at the meeting were writers André Malraux, Rafael Alberti, Pablo Neruda, María Teresa León, Ilya Ehrenburg, Ernest Hemingway, and Octavio Paz, who told this story about Tina:

> With my wife [writer] Elena Garro...we frequented in Valencia a café which was a rendezvous of anti-Franquists of all political directions...one day a man came up to our table calling himself an agent of the services of investigation. He asked only my wife to accompany him to the offices of the International Red Aid, saying that one of her Mexican friends wished to speak with her. Thus Elena met with Tina Modotti, who seemed at the moment to have a personal office. "We know that you and your husband are frequenting company that could turn out to be very dangerous," she said. Elena did not understand, and la Modotti explained to her that the café was a rendezvous of Trotskyite and anarchist elements, of traitors to the revolution and enemies of the people, and another series of phrases along these lines. She concluded by warn-

ing her that if she continued to be seen with similar people, the consequences could be very serious for us. From that day, there began for me all those doubts that later distanced me definitively from the Mexican Communist party.

Besides Communists and Social Democrats, Republican forces counted anarchists, Trotskyites, syndicalists, and members of an anti-Stalinist Marxist party known by its Spanish acronym, POUM. Believing the war and the revolution to be synonymous, many opposition leftists were as intent upon fostering a classless society as on knocking out the fascists. Communists disagreed, judging the moment inauspicious for proletarian revolution, and, with the Soviet Union its only powerful foreign ally, the government was exceedingly attentive to Moscow's wishes. Soviet "advisers" swarmed over the country, and the NKVD [Soviet secret police] operated with impunity in extending Stalin's purges to Spain. "In Catalonia, the elimination of Trotskyites and of anarcho-syndicalists has already begun: it will be conducted with the same energy as in the USSR," bragged the Soviet newspaper *Pravda* in December 1936.

Five months later, a war within the war erupted in Catalonia's capital, Barcelona, a stronghold of the Left opposition. Communist-backed police launched an assault on the anarcho-syndicalist-controlled Telephone Exchange, thereby touching off fierce street battles between anarchists and POUMists, on one hand, and their erstwhile comrades-in-arms, Communists and Catalan authorities, on the other. Vilified by Communists as fascist and Trotskyite, though it was neither, the POUM was declared illegal, and its leader, Andrés Nin, kidnapped, tortured, and murdered by Soviet agents while Spanish Communists looked the other way. This was none other than the Andrés Nin who had briefly befriended Julio Antonio Mella a decade earlier.

Nin was widely known in Spain and abroad, and his disappearance elicited an international clamor, but, to this day, mysteries remain about his fate. Vittorio Vidali has been implicated in numerous accounts of the affair, among them that of then Communist minister of education Jesús Hernández, who tarred the Italian as "one of the main executors of the NKVD in Spain." Documents recently unearthed in Barcelona lend credence to Vittorio's claim that he was not present during Nin's sequestration and interrogation, though he was almost certainly aware of what was transpiring. As it turns out, the POUMist was held for a time at the home of Constancia de la Mora and Hidalgo de Cisneros, highly placed Spanish Communists and close friends of Tina and Vittorio. Did the idea of the ruthless Communist assassination of a man Julio Antonio admired ever give Tina pause? If so, she kept the thought to herself.

Tina's role as a prominent Communist and senior Red Aid official dictated that she, too, participate in counterespionage activities. Writer and diplomat Fernando Gamboa, who had known Tina in Mexico, attended the intellectuals' congress, where he "heard very bad things about Tina, the only such things I've heard in my life, from people who said that she was very tyrannical when she was at Red Aid in Valencia...she had been hardened by years of war, by the horrors of war, of which she saw the very worst."

Tina was also involved in intelligence work at Albacete, headquarters for the International Brigades. A Comintern idea, the Brigades drew to Spain some forty thousand volunteers of many political stripes, eager to defend the republic and combat fascism. The Communist party riddled the operation with secret police, and *New York Times* reporter Herbert Matthews identified Vittorio as their chief, presiding over "*checkas* [Soviet-style interrogation squads] at Albacete, the International Brigade Center, and several other places." Some of those judged and executed were fascists, spies, traitors, and deserters; others were leftists who refused to pay obeisance to Stalin.

In his encyclopedic history of the International Brigades, Spanish scholar Andreu Castells cites Vittorio as head of the anti-Trotskyism section and Tina as assistant chief of counterespionage, reporting to Pauline Marty, the wife of notorious International Brigades commander André Marty. Not only does Tina's pattern of collaboration with Vittorio lend weight to the allegation, but also recent research by Brazilian historian Dainis Karepovs offers a case in point. Karepovs has brought to light evidence that Tina was instrumental in the Communist assassination of International Brigades volunteer Alberto Bomilcar Besouchet.

During Tina's January stay in Paris, a French Party official had entrusted her with a message, which she relayed to the Spanish Party's Central Committee:

Dear Comrades:

    The message cited below was sent by the Communist Party of
Brazil to our comrades in Paris who have asked me to transmit it
to you so that you may take the necessary measures:
    "Lieutenant Alberto Bezouchet is currently in Spain. After he
left Brazil it was discovered that Bezouchet had passed over to
Trotskyism. He left a proof which is a true provocation against
the revolution of national liberation, and thus it is urgent that all
comrades be notified so that they not permit him to use the name
of the Brazilian Communist Party."
    This message was delivered to me in Paris on January 20, the
date of my return [to Spain]. I am taking the liberty of sending a
copy of this message to the Political Commissar of the
International Brigades [the Italian Giuseppe di Vittorio].

    With Communist *saludos,*
    María
    (of International Red Aid—calle Montornes, 1)

    The man in question, twenty-five-year-old Brazilian career soldier
Alberto Bomilcar Besouchet, was the youngest of four brothers, all Communists. The Party had expelled the three elder Besouchets, however, for
their critical attitudes, and the trio embraced Trotskyism. Alberto, meanwhile, took part in a failed Communist uprising against Brazilian dictator
Getúlio Vargas and wavered between Stalinism and Trotskyism. The first in
Brazil to enlist in the International Brigades, Alberto penned an open letter
of farewell to comrades before departing his homeland. A brash gesture, his
missive extolled the Spanish Popular Front for "breaking, one by one, the
rotten teeth of the international bourgeoisie." Though the message's content
toed the Stalinist line, its language did not. Increasingly paranoid, Communists held certain expressions such as "international bourgeoisie" to be Trotskyite code, and thus they refused to print Alberto's letter. It finally appeared
in a Trotskyite newspaper, which noted that the "political position of comrade Alberto is still vacillating," and the young man sailed for Europe, having pocketed a letter of recommendation from a Brazilian Left oppositionist
to POUM leader Andrés Nin.

After reaching Spain in February 1937, Alberto fought bravely on various fronts. By the time he was wounded in Guadalajara, he had attained the rank of colonel and was serving on the staff of a prominent Spanish general. During May's Barcelona street battles between Communists and their Left allies, Alberto vanished. Within the Communist bureaucracy, there was later confusion over his whereabouts. A certain A. M. Elliott was to sign a memo dated January 15, 1939, which listed "BESOUCHET (Brazilian). Had relationship with Trotskyites. Died during the events of May [1937]."

But Elliott was misinformed about the time of Besouchet's death. In September 1937, Brazilian Stalinist Honório de Freitas Guimarães, alias Castro, sent a letter to "Jack," who may have been Vittorio Vidali. As Dainis Karepovs suggests, Besouchet was, in all likelihood, interned in a Communist prison, and Castro's message probably responded to a request for written accusations against him. The charges centered on Alberto's suspect relationships with his brothers as well as with an "adventuress" named Elsie Houston, a Brazilian singer recently divorced from Trotskyite surrealist poet Benjamin Péret. Houston was also the sister-in-law of a Trotskyite from São Paulo. Freitas Guimarães mentioned a price for Alberto's release: "I suggest that measures be taken to control his activities and, if nothing more serious is found, that our Spanish comrades make him understand that he must cut all relations with people who are entirely on the other side of the barricade. It would be very good if he could be brought to make written declarations against Trotskyism and his brothers' position, which we could publish in our press."

But Alberto may have been unwilling to go along with the scheme, for the Besouchet family was later informed that he "had been shot during the International Brigades' final retreat from Barcelona (in October 1938), together with anarchists and Trotskyite prisoners," and his friend Apolônio de Carvalho, another Brazilian volunteer, confirmed that Alberto was "assassinated in cowardly fashion" at the end of 1938.

One memo that ended up in Comintern archives reads like a tombstone's inscription:

BESOUCHET, Alberto, origin BRAZIL
lieutenant

according to information from Brazilian C.P., communicated by
comrade Maria of I.R.A.,
calle Montornes 1,
24 January 1937,
Trotskyite

Tina most likely never set eyes upon Alberto Bomilcar Besouchet,
and she may have been unaware of his valor and commitment to antifascism. She did understand, however, that, by acting as informant to the
Spanish Party (and taking it upon herself to notify the International
Brigades' political commissar, charged with ferreting out ideological
deviants), she was condemning Besouchet to prison and possibly death.
Locked into the Communist apparatus, Tina did not take exception to the
Party's purge of its enemies in Spain. Blinded by tyrannical self-discipline,
desperation to win the war, and a belief in the value of correct ideology, the
woman who braved hails of gunfire to save children's lives sacrificed
Alberto Besouchet (and no doubt others) for what she believed to be the
good of the cause. Questions about Tina's moral stance during the Spanish
Civil War have previously centered on Vittorio's barbarous acts and how
she responded to them. Unlike her companion, Tina never physically
harmed anyone, but it is now clear that she shared his responsibility for
Communist atrocities.

"All are young like Julio Antonio Mella," Tina once sadly reflected to
Vittorio of foreign combatants of her acquaintance who were dying in
Spain. "If he were alive, he too would come to fight for the defense of the
Spanish republic." Yet, with tragic irony, Tina helped send to his death
another brave, idealistic Latin American, the same age as Julio Antonio at
the time of his murder. Did she ever conceive of how Mella's assassination
had set her on the path toward participation in an act as despotic as that
which had cut him down?

In all likelihood, Tina's involvement in the Besouchet affair was not
an isolated incident. Was she disturbed, at the time or in later years, by the
thought of her role in Stalinist imprisonments and eliminations? The
answer is murky, though one is tempted to turn to a bitter comment she
reportedly made to Spanish general Valentín González, who had quarreled
with Vittorio: "You should have shot him. You would have done a good

thing. He is an assassin. He has dragged me into a monstrous crime. I hate him with all my being. Yet, despite that, I must follow him until death. Until death."

Meanwhile, the war was going from bad to worse as rebels wrenched northern Spain from Republican control, and the Loyalist offensive at Brunete quickly bogged down. Tina continued to devote "all my minutes, all my hours" to the cause, which occasionally meant pleasant visits with writer Antonio Machado, whom Red Aid had evacuated from Madrid to the village of Rocafort, outside Valencia. A modest, contemplative widower in his sixties, Machado was a lonely man who could barely manage the tasks of everyday living. Yet he is, in the opinion of many scholars, Spain's greatest poet since the seventeenth century. He called Tina "the angel of my house," whose atmosphere he evokes in "Meditation," penned in Rocafort:

> *Night has come to the garden—*
> *the sound of running water!—*
> *and everything smells of jasmine,*
> *the nightingale of scents.*
> > *The war—how asleep it seems*
> *from this to the other sea....*

But in April 1938, the enemy reached the Mediterranean, cutting the republic in two and putting the Valencian sector in enough danger that Machado had to be moved to Barcelona, along with Red Aid headquarters. Official pronouncements notwithstanding, Loyalists' pessimism deepened, and nerves were badly frayed as sirens shrieked, beacons crazily roamed the sky, and fascist bombs hurtled nightly into the Catalonian capital.

Perhaps feeling guilty to be alive when so many were perishing, Tina continued fearless in the face of physical danger. Vittorio recalled a hair-raising boat trip, the first of several she would make between Barcelona and Valencia:

> The organization of the aid [to refugees from fascist-occupied zones] had to come from Barcelona and Valencia, now separated by enemy territory.
>
> It was then that it was decided to send María and the others to Valencia, crossing in motorboats a sea dominated by enemy coast

guard and aviation. Some of these boats had been machine gunned and sunk. It seemed to me that "María" was too tired and did not feel very well. Thus I tried to intervene to prevent this trip, but she firmly disagreed: "I feel fine," she said, "and I want to go." They embarked on a dark night with a heavy sea. I found out later that there were problems with the motor and they had run the risk of attack in enemy territory.

In the last weeks of the war, Tina would make an equally grueling plane trip from Albacete to Barcelona. A malfunctioning radio caused the first flight to be aborted, and, on the second, enemy Fiats ruthlessly pursued the aircraft. It finally landed under fire in a swampy field as soon as Barcelona's dim necklace of lights came into view. Throughout the ordeal, Tina was serene, and when the airmen praised her courage, she responded with a little smile of satisfaction.

Over the summer and fall of 1938, Tina rarely saw Vittorio, who was preoccupied with an offensive on the Ebro. In November, they came together at a national Red Aid conference, held in Madrid to remind the world that Spain's capital remained in Loyalist hands. On the last evening, as Vittorio was hosting a dinner for foreign observers, the enemy unleashed a fierce aerial attack, which was to cost fifteen hundred lives. One mortar projectile shot through the window of Red Aid's dining room and landed on the guests' table. Five people died immediately, and many were gravely wounded. Tina, who was not attending the event, dashed to the site as soon as she heard the news. Ambulances were converging from all sides as she threaded her way through the wreckage and crowds to the victims. She briefly attended to Vittorio, whose right arm and thumb had been badly sliced up by falling glass, then turned to the more seriously wounded, such as Melchiore Vanni, alias Bonnet, the Italian director of Paris's International Coordinating Committee for Aid to Spain. In the confusion, Vittorio was trundled off, and Tina would spend the night combing Madrid's hospitals for her companion. He recalled that, the next morning, "when I awakened from the anesthesia, I found her with me, her head leaning on the bed, she was sleeping."

For Tina's work in such tragedies and her everyday efforts, a delegate from Albacete had proposed at a Red Aid solidarity conference the previous summer that Comrade María be honored as the organization's top activist, and his motion met with deafening applause. Now French Red Aid published a pamphlet paying homage to four colleagues in Spain, among them "María Ruiz":

> of her we can say that she is the very image of humanist sentiment and internationalism. She has struggled against reactionary forces on the fronts of many countries. Her sick heart is always sensitive to the sufferings of others. But her feminine tenderness and her dedication to work, for which all around her love her, do not diminish the firmness of her character, which, together with her intelligence, give her a deserved place in the ranks of the directors of this great solidarity organization.

Their words notwithstanding, Tina's French comrades were aware that Red Aid was in decline. In an important speech, Comintern chief Georgi Dimitrov reprimanded MOPR for its bloated bureaucracy, and already Stasova had departed in disgrace. Accused of Trotskyism, she made a personal plea before Stalin and was spared arrest. There was talk of overhauling Red Aid, but its suppression was linked to the Stalinist agenda, and most national chapters folded in 1939.

If the demise of a cause to which she had devoted thirteen years was painful to Tina, even more so was the departure of the International Brigades, negotiated as part of the Munich accords. Sick with the knowledge of impending defeat, she watched from the official reviewing stand as troops made a final parade in Barcelona. Days later, she described the event to Vittorio, weeping as she lamented, "It's not fair that it should end this way. We've been fighting for almost three years. I saw combatants from all the battles, mutilated and wounded, marching in their sashes, with bouquets of flowers, but there was no joy, only sadness in their faces and tears in everyone's eyes; likewise the people saluting them and covering them with flowers were touched. I felt anguish in my heart, and I thought about how this was the end." Vittorio ventured that the war might still be won. "You always were optimistic," she countered.

It was not long before insurgent forces began swallowing up Catalonia from the south. In the weeks that followed, nearly half a million people fled before the fascist onslaught, and pandemonium erupted. Cars, trucks, donkeys, and carts jammed every road between Barcelona and the French border, and towns along the way were clogged with desperate, half-starved, rain- and snow-drenched refugees. Many carried nothing but children and, knotted into old handkerchiefs, handfuls of dirt from their villages. All the while, the enemy was mercilessly bombing the sad cortege.

Using any conveyances available, Tina ferried old and infirm Party officials into France. After Barcelona fell, she found herself in Red Aid's Figueras office one day when a bomb leveled the building, but she miraculously escaped death. Not long afterward, as insurgent armies were closing in, an official errand took Tina's old friend Fernando Gamboa, on the staff of the Mexican legation, to a village not far from Figueras. The embassy's Hispano-Suiza limousine rolled into a nearly deserted plaza, remembered Gamboa, and

> there, to my surprise, sitting alone at one of those outdoor coffee shops, was Tina. I asked, "What are you doing here?" "Just waiting," she replied. We embraced affectionately. She was waiting for the army which was on its way to that small town, and she knew that Carlos was coming with it. I told her that she was in great danger and that she could not go along with the army—I even added as a joke, you are not in Mexico, you can't be a *soldadera* [camp follower]. I tried to persuade her to come with me...in a half hour we could be in Guyana, which was where the embassy was set up.... I see her now—a different Tina—a tired woman.... Well, she refused my offer firmly.... I left, it was more or less at about six in the evening, the sun was shining but gave no warmth. The whole scene, the entire situation reinforced by the winter sun, the peasants escaping from the mountains, the army retreating and the image of Tina, sitting alone, with that waiting, searching, contemplative look....

Tina had already bid farewell to Matilde, who secured permission from the Party to remain in Spain and fight on. Matilde would be arrested, tortured, and condemned to death, a sentence later commuted to life in prison. Several years hence, on the day she was to be dragged into a church and forcibly baptized, she fell, jumped, or was pushed several stories to her death. Afterward her husband, Paco, returned to Spain from exile in London and killed himself by leaping from a building.

On February 9, 1939, Tina departed for France, just ahead of Franco's armies, with nothing but the clothes on her back. Grizzled and badly in need of a bath, Vittorio came out later, and when the pair joined up at the Spanish consulate in Perpignan, Tina's first words to her companion were from a poem by Antonio Machado:

> *And when the day for the final voyage is here*
> *and the ship that does not return heads down the stream,*
> *I'll be aboard, you'll find me traveling light*
> *and nearly naked like children of the sea.*

Penniless, they made their way to Paris.

For a month, the couple stayed in the lovely rue des Beaux-Arts apartment of their old friends Marcel and Germaine Willard, whose sixteen-year-old son, Claude, gave up his bedroom to them. Claude later remembered that Vittorio was "chatty and amiable," while Tina seemed "an ardent woman." The pair disappeared each morning and returned in the evening to join the family for supper. After they retired on the first night, Tina covered the lamp with a newspaper, silently undressed, and climbed into bed.

"You're anxious," Vittorio remarked.

"Yes, and still stunned. In these last ten days, everything has changed so quickly that I still don't really understand what happened or what will follow."

As they discussed the situation, it was evident that Vittorio considered Spain a major strategic loss, while Tina felt the defeat as an aching void, a personal tragedy, and a source of bitterness and confusion.

"What will we do, Toio? I seem to be caught up in a cataclysm, and I can't get my bearings. It's the first time this has happened to me. From the time I left Barcelona, people walking to the border or about to cross, and even afterwards, kept asking me 'Is it straight ahead?' and I didn't know how to respond."

The next morning, Vittorio awoke early, to find his companion still sleeping. He saw that her face was lined with sadness and guessed she had spent part of the night crying. For the first time, he noticed her crop of gray hair.

Days later, the affable British Communist Tom Bell arrived from Moscow, and, after vigorous handshakes, the trio settled in at the Willards' to thrash out Tina and Vittorio's future. From Dimitrov and Stasova, still respected in Comintern circles, came a message that the couple could either rest in the Soviet Union or travel to the United States to organize aid to Spanish refugees. Although both Tina and Vittorio were persona non grata in the United States, their mentors strongly advised the second option, since six months in a Russian sanatorium would likely turn into fifteen years in Siberia. Tina yearned to do undercover work in Italy, but her request had again been denied. They chose the U.S. option but held Mexico as another possibility.

After the Willards' concierge had to fend off police inquiries concerning Vittorio, the pair moved to the Hotel St-Pierre, on a narrow street across from the School of Medicine. Pleasant if threadbare, the St-Pierre was filled with Mexicans on their way home from Spain, among them Fernando Gamboa, painter David Alfaro Siqueiros, and diplomat Renato Leduc, living with British painter Leonora Carrington.

On March 15, Mexican ambassador Narciso Bassols, a fellow Communist, gave Tina a visa as a Spanish refugee, and the U.S. embassy later issued her a transit visa. Vittorio departed first for New York, while Tina moved to the Parisian suburb of Melun-sur-Seine to care for several ailing comrades, including Melchiore Vanni, who did not yet know that he was dying. It was not until April 1 that she finally sailed from Cherbourg aboard the *Queen Mary*.

She traveled third-class as the widowed Spanish professor Dr. Carmen Ruíz Sánchez. The sea was heavy, and her passage to New York proved slow. Shortly before her departure, Melchiore Vanni died, and a few weeks earlier, Antonio Machado had succumbed to pneumonia and the punishing trek across the Pyrenees. "And when the day for the final voyage is here," echoed his words, "and the ship that does not return heads down the stream/I'll be aboard, you'll find me traveling light/and nearly naked like children of the sea."

Mexico City (1939–1942)

O N APRIL 6, 1939, twenty-six years after the adolescent Tina Modotti had sailed into New York, the *Queen Mary* carried the woman calling herself Dr. Carmen Ruíz Sánchez toward the Statue of Liberty and the silhouetted skyline of Manhattan. After the ship docked, however, she did not join other passengers pressing their way down the gangplank; rather, she followed port officials' instructions to remain aboard. Onshore, thirty-seven-year-old Yolanda Magrini impatiently awaited a reunion with her sister, whom she had last seen in 1926. A tiny, opinionated woman who read voraciously, Yolanda shared Tina's love of flowers and her knack for thrifty chic. Two years earlier, she had wed Italian-American radical and washing machine salesman Peter Magrini, but the marriage quickly fell apart. Peter fought in Spain with the Abraham Lincoln Brigade, while Yolanda's application to serve as a volunteer ambulance driver had been denied. Instead, she opened a modest photo studio on Staten Island and made herself useful to the Communist party.

Tina's transit visa notwithstanding, she was never permitted to exit immigration facilities, and Yolanda, baffled and frustrated at her sister's failure to appear, tried unsuccessfully to force her way onto the ocean liner. Unprepared for the vast numbers of Europeans fleeing repression and war, U.S. authorities had placed increasingly stringent controls on Spanish haven-seekers. All of the ship's Republican passengers were detained.

Meanwhile, the port's Communist network ferried messages between Tina and Vittorio, who had been in New York for nearly a month but was lying low to elude the FBI. After a week, Tina embarked on the SS *Sibony*, bound for Mexico, which had announced its willingness to accept up to fifty thousand Spaniards.

Six days later, as her ship closed in on Veracruz harbor, Tina panicked and experienced severe heart palpitations at the thought that the border police might recognize her. Because of her previous deportation, she was entering Mexico illegally, and, if detected, her future looked bleak. Every other country in which she had ever resided was virtually closed to her, and Europe teetered on the brink of war. Even more terrifying than the prospect of becoming an international outcast, however, was that of stirring a hornet's nest of scandal in the Mexican press.

But Tina cleared customs without incident and joined up with a Party emissary, who accompanied her to San Angel, a leafy town of cobblestone streets and colonial villas, south of Mexico City. Vittorio had flown down from New York and was staying with retired Spanish-born diplomat Martín Díaz de Cossío, a member of the Committee to Aid Spanish Refugees. Díaz de Cossío lived with his stunningly beautiful velvet-eyed wife, twenty-six-year-old Isabel Carbajal, and their two sons.

One Saturday not long afterward, writer and professor Adelina Zendejas, a casual friend of Tina's in the 1920s and now Isabel's confidante, lunched with the Díaz de Cossíos at their San Angel home. She was briefly introduced to a houseguest named Carmen, an austere-looking woman with fright etched into her face and a voice that Adelina found oddly familiar. That afternoon, Adelina, Isabel, and Martín went to the movies. As Martín was buying their tickets, Isabel asked her companion, "Doesn't María remind you of anyone?"

"What is she called, María or Carmen?"

"Well, both."

"She isn't really Spanish, is she?"

"No, she's not."

"No, but her voice reminds me of someone."

"Come on, think, Adelina."

"Well, let's see, Isabel. He's Carlos Contreras, right?"

"Yes."

"Then she was the wife of Julio Antonio Mella."

"Yes, it's Tina Modotti."

The episode makes plain not only how dramatically Tina's appearance had changed but also how loath she was to unmask herself, even to a politically compatible friend. She attempted to live incognito and became petrified with fear when she was recognized. Stopping on the sidewalk one day for a car exiting a parking lot, she heard a knock and looked up, to see Felipe Teixidor rolling down his window to greet her. Tina's hand flew to cover her face. "That's all," remembered Felipe's wife, Monna Alfau, "and we never saw her again, but another person, to whom the same thing happened, insisted and said to her, 'Look Tina, you know who I am, and I know who you are. Why are you hiding?' 'Good God, don't say anything. I'm afraid they'll deport me again,' replied the poor thing."

Tina dreaded vilification and expulsion not only for herself but also for Vittorio. Her companion was among the high-level Stalinist functionaries slipped into Mexico by its pro-Soviet envoy to France, Narciso Bassols, under the guise of granting asylum to Spanish Republicans. Among them were disciplined NKVD mobile brigades, trained in liquidations on foreign soil, who rolled into Mexico City with the intention of settling a sum of old scores. Objections to Red terrorists sounded in some quarters, and the newspaper *La Nación* decried the return of the treacherous Sormenti (Vidali). In his later account of Communist skullduggery, journalist Ralph de Toledano singled out "veterans of the Fifth, or NKVD, Brigade, the blood-saturated and terror-drenched *Quinta brigada* which conducted the purges in Spain and prepared now [in Mexico] for new purges of old enemies and wavering friends."

Cafés along Mexico City's fashionable Avenida 5 de Mayo filled with weavers of intricate webs of intrigue. Spanish Falangists busied themselves with organizing a pan-American fascist league, Nazi businessmen and spies attended to the Führer's interests, and Soviet agents masqueraded as diplomats. The Communists were keeping a row of enemies in their sights, particularly Leon Trotsky, who had been living in Mexico since 1937. Hounded around the world for a decade, Trotsky had found sanctuary when Tina's former friends Anita Brenner and Diego Rivera interceded on his behalf with Mexican president Lázaro Cárdenas. Though Trotsky's political philosophy won few adherents, the heretic's presence humiliated

Stalinists, whose comrades abroad cast slurs upon their manhood. For two years, Trotsky and his wife, Natalya, had been guests at Frida Kahlo's family home in Coyoacán. But in the aftermath of Trotsky's affair with Frida and Diego's break with the Fourth International, the Russians moved across town to a quasi-fortress girded by twelve-foot-high walls, laced with trip wires, and guarded around the clock.

A number of Soviet agents carried orders to liquidate Trotsky. One was Leonid Eitingon, an expert in "wet affairs" who disposed of generous funding from the Kremlin. Eitingon was seconded by the ignoble fat man Vittorio Codovilla and by Vittorio Vidali, whose right hand was Pedro Martínez Cartón. A Spanish printer and soldier said to be callous, dogmatic, and ruthless, Martínez Cartón reportedly couriered from Moscow a list of Stalinist prey. Officially, Vittorio took up journalism, writing a column for *El Popular,* the organ of a powerful alliance of industrial unions known by its Spanish acronym, CTM, and run by the shrewd Vicente Lombardo Toledano.

May Day dawned to a pure azure sky. Fists raised, Tina and Vittorio marched alongside Spanish exiles and CTM bosses in the traditional parade to the Zócalo. Afterward, the couple repaired to a garden party at the suburban home of a Spanish economics professor. Suddenly, Tina was swept into an enormous bear hug by her old friend, political economist Alfons Goldschmidt, whom she had not seen since Berlin days. Still the soul of good-natured kindness, Alfons had been widowed and had fled Berlin for New York City, where he married fellow German Communist Leni Kroul. When Alfons was invited to teach and consult with the Cárdenas administration on the nationalization of the oil industry, the newlyweds had made Mexico their home. A handsome, bookish, throaty-voiced woman, Leni had endured Hitler's prisons and a tragic love affair before fleeing Nazi Germany. She and Tina became close friends.

A few days later, Tina and Vittorio had to leave the Díaz de Cossío household. Unable to afford a place of their own, they accepted Adelina Zendejas's invitation to stay at her Morelos Avenue apartment in central Mexico City. Like an old lover encountered unexpectedly after a decade, the capital was familiar and respectably dull. Half again as big as in the 1920s, it boasted gringo-style luncheonettes, movie palaces whose marquees trumpeted Cantinflas comedies, and serape-hung curio shops squeezed between stony, blackened ex-convents and churches. Billboards for Montezuma beer and Palmolive soap topped the blocky office buildings lining nearby Juárez Avenue, where fleets of taxicabs cleared paths with their horns. The odor of exhaust fumes mingled with those of grilling onions and meat from vendors' stands, and Indians wandered around peddling everything from *huaraches* to parakeets to novelty toys. The street bustle was still overwhelming, except on Sundays, when everyone flocked to Chapultepec Park or the bullfights, leaving the neighborhood empty and sad.

During the months that Tina and Vittorio found a home with Adelina, their hostess would frequently return from work and find the table set or a small bouquet of marigolds arranged in a vase. "[W]hat [Spanish poet Antonio] Machado said about being an angel who floated about, whose hands took care of things, that was Tina," Adelina observed. "She was an angel.... I've never felt the presence of someone that way. She never spoke of what was not her business. She knew how to listen, but, as she was listening, she considered what was being said, and, at the end, she gave her opinion almost always very firmly. She was extraordinarily sensitive."

In contrast, Adelina found Vittorio "a caveman." "Ay, he shouted, he insulted people, he talked like a machine gun, he was very violent, also rude," she said. "She was very delicate. I never heard her use obscene language, and Vidali used every sort of offensive expression, Mexican, Spanish and Italian. All together, he said them. Besides, he ate, well, he didn't eat, that's not the word, he pounced upon his food.... Also devilishly in love with women...and he was attractive to them...because he was very joyous and always wisecracking." Leni Kroul also got to know Vittorio, and she shared Adelina's repulsion. "He was the scariest guy I ever met," she recalled. "How powerful he was! I think he spoke about that. He had to shoot somebody, you know. How could this wonderful, soft, beautiful woman be married...." She paused. "There was a nobility about her, a calm, beautiful woman, and then this brutal, boom-boom guy."

It leapt to many eyes that Vittorio was in fine fettle, while Tina seemed mortally tired. Unable to shake off the demons of her past, she assumed an aura of silent suffering and dignity. "I would observe Tina, even at pleasant moments...when there were joyful things, and I always saw something sad in her," remembered Adelina. "One day I said to her, 'Tina, come here. What is it that you're missing?'"

She replied, "It's that I saw so much horror during the Spanish war."

Adelina lived only two blocks from the spot where Mella had been shot. Another time, she said to Tina, "I think that Julio Antonio's shadow has not left you."

"It's because coming to live in your house has made me relive many things," she explained.

That summer, equipped with a false U.S. passport, Tina departed Mexico City on a double mission. She traveled first to New York, where she was at last reunited with her siblings Yolanda and Ben. There she consulted with aid workers on Spanish refugee issues, in which she was deeply involved, and called upon high Party functionaries to talk over the plan that she and Vittorio return to the United States.

She was staying in the plush 340 East Fifty-seventh Street town house of Martha Dodd Stern and her husband, Alfred, Communist sympathizers who would later flee the country under indictment on charges of spying for the Soviet Union. A thirty-one-year-old honey blond southern belle whose long past included affairs with writer Carl Sandburg, sculptor Isamu Noguchi, and Nazi Gestapo chief Rudolf Diels, Martha was the daughter of William Dodd, an ex-ambassador to Hitler's Germany. She had accompanied her parents to Berlin, where she flirted with fascism before embracing communism. The about-face was chronicled in her gossipy best-seller, *Through Embassy Eyes,* which had hit bookstores shortly before Tina's arrival. Pillars of Communist high society, Martha and Alfred lavishly entertained the likes of Party chief Earl Browder, writer Lillian Hellman, and actor Paul Robeson.

One of Tina's closest friends, Constancia de la Mora, was also a houseguest of the Sterns. The rebellious scion of prominent, aristocratic Spanish stock, Constancia had joined the Party in the early days of the war. She had directed the Republicans' press censorship office in Valencia and now resided in Mexico City with her husband, ex–air force chief Hidalgo de Cisneros. Constancia was a tall, handsome, heavyset woman with a sweet, low voice. She had come to New York to put finishing touches on *In Place of Splendor,* her autobiography and intimist account of the Spanish Civil War, which would make her the toast of East Coast radicals. Although Constancia's manuscript had already passed through many helping hands, it required further revisions, a task she entrusted to Tina and a former

Spanish Red Aid worker, the Cuban Manuel Fernández Colino, who was living in New York. In speaking to Constancia, Manuel was astonished to learn that the María he had known in Spain was none other than Tina Modotti, the companion of Julio Antonio Mella. To Tina, Manuel spoke volubly and affectionately of Julio Antonio, once his classmate in Havana, but, while she responded to his comments about the Cuban's politics, she was still incapable of casual conversation about their love affair.

Carrying U.S. travel documents, Tina set sail from New York to Europe, exhausting herself with a transatlantic mission to deliver funds to a contact in Switzerland. The money was a payoff for the release and transport of important Communists from the French camps where nearly half a million Spanish refugees remained interned. Along the way, Tina jotted a note to Mercedes, whose reply, addressed in care of François Le Bihan's Paris address, was intercepted by Italian police. Now savvy enough to garble her messages, Mercedes misdated the letter, which told of awaiting Tina's news "from Roberto's country [Mexico], and this last one instead reveals to me your return. Then that means that things didn't go as you hoped and you had to make a sudden return.... Of you, dear one, I know so little, and I would give anything to find out a few details, and I must content myself just with knowing that you are safe and sound (the most important thing, I know). Well, patience, maybe someday...." But Mercedes and Tina were never again to set eyes upon each other, and Mercedes's dreams of returning to the United States faded away. She lived out her days in Trieste, not far from their sister Gioconda, with whom she quarreled bitterly.

Back in New York, Tina got reacquainted with her brother Ben, living with friends on Sixty-eighth Street, and her sister Yolanda. At the trio's last long visit, in San Francisco thirteen years earlier, all had brimmed with zestful energy, but the intervening years had dealt rather harshly with the six Modotti siblings. From Los Angeles came news of their younger brother, Beppo, who had married a woman named Laura Landi. To escape surveillance by the L.A. Police Department's notorious Red Squad—still in dogged pursuit of the three Communist Modottis—Beppo had been calling himself Joseph Landi. His marriage was turning sour, however, and he was on his way to becoming an alcoholic.

Before leaving the city, Tina took counsel with former colleagues at International Labor Defense, the local section of Red Aid, about the possibility of resurrecting the organization with headquarters in New York. Though Party chiefs had nixed plans for Vittorio's move to the United States, Tina also discreetly inquired about residency papers for herself. It wouldn't be surprising to learn that she briefly dreamed of a position with a revitalized Red Aid (which her administrative skills, international experience, and mastery of six languages easily qualified her to direct). Neither the agency nor Tina's permit showed any hopes of materializing, however, and when she took leave of Ben, she said, *"Addio!"*

"Why did you say 'farewell,'" he challenged, "and not 'see you later'?"

"Impossible," she replied "I am already dead. I can't live in Mexico."

Perhaps Tina was referring to Mexico City's altitude, dangerously high for someone suffering from heart disease, to her anxiety over calumnies in the press, or to the cruel ghosts of her past. In Mexico, she was haunted by former lives, painful to remember and impossible to forget. Many of those aware of her identity saw her as a shocking shadow of what she had once been. One woman, to whom she was introduced by a mutual friend as Tina Modotti, thought her a pathetic figure, "already very much the little old lady...badly dressed," and impossible to reconcile with Edward Weston's vital and seductive model.

Settling in Mexico City also kept Tina unhappily distant from Yolanda and Ben. She regarded the closely knit Communist community as surrogate kin, however, and she liked to call the Party "our big family." Some have speculated that, disgusted with Stalinist brutality, Tina wanted to renounce Communism, but this is unlikely. One does not easily turn away from a cause to which one has sacrificed health, happiness, love, family, and beauty. She retained a strong sentimental attachment to the Party and kept faith in its messianic promise. "Out of fear of nothingness, [the Communist] obstinately follows a dead illusion," once mused ex-Comintern official Jesús Hernández; "he prefers faith, however feeble it may be, to the absence of faith. The person who can, from one day to the next, declare himself an atheist has never believed in God." When it came time to renew her Party credentials, however, Tina declined, out of concern for her status as an asylum-seeker.

And she no longer acquiesced to every decision made in the Kremlin. On August 24, 1939—the day of Tina's return to Mexico City from New York—news flashed around the world of Stalin's signature of a nonaggression pact with Adolf Hitler. Like many Communists, Tina was shocked and horrified at her leader's cynical betrayal. With antifascism at the heart of her political belief system and Nazi death-dealing in Spain fresh in her mind, she refused to accept Hitler as any sort of ally. "But how can we align ourselves with Hitler?" she exploded to Vittorio. "Sooner or later, he will confront the Soviet Union. Germany is an anti-Communist country. I don't agree." Vittorio's realpolitik argument hailed Stalin's clever play for time, but Tina was unswayed. "OK, that's all OK, but I... with Hitler, never!"

The cold light of political reality also shone upon the supposedly apolitical Continental Congress to Aid Spanish Refugees, convened in Mexico City in January 1940. From the Comintern came orders that Communist delegates were to sabotage the conference and lash out at the French government, which had reacted to the Stalin-Hitler accord by banning the Communist party. In retaliation, France was to be excoriated for ill treatment of Spaniards in exile. The Party's tit for tat had the effect of withholding assistance from refugees in dire need. Working as an interpreter at the congress (a position that, some believed, amounted to being a listening post for information useful to Party superiors), Tina must have faced conflicting impulses of Communist duty, on one hand, and, on the other, dismay over a policy that flew in the face of her deep-felt commitment.

Ultimately, however, such frustrations probably reinforced Tina's loyalty to the Party. Social scientists studying religious sects that predict a second coming observe greater devoutness and tightened emotional bonds among the faithful when the Messiah fails to materialize as expected. Believers experience the episode as a trial of faith, although there is a limit to such blind devotion. Presumably, Tina never learned—and thus was not put to the test—that Vittorio was acting as an intermediary between Mexican Communists and a Nazi spy named Max Weber, as part of an Axis plot to overthrow the Mexican government and convert the country into a base of operations against the Allies.

There were other mysteries in Tina's relationship with Vittorio, which even close friends found difficult to plumb. Theirs was a complex, symbiotic connection which mingled affection, disgruntlement, and mutual dedication to the cause. One is tempted to believe that Tina tried to extricate herself from the partnership but that her Communist superiors pressured her to remain. Vittorio's connection to a selfless Spanish Civil

War heroine, known for "a tact, a delicacy, a beautiful human comprehension," was advantageous to an operative, and Tina would have quickly hewed to Party wishes.

If she chafed at the relationship, few were aware of it. The two led somewhat separate lives, carried on like married folk when they were together, and rarely squabbled. Friends remember that once, traveling outside Mexico City, Tina opened a letter from Vittorio which read, "It is a desert here without you," and she glowed with delight. But he was an inveterate pleaser, and, although the pair would live together until the day Tina died, their romance was long finished. Vittorio had seduced Isabel Carbajal, and, with Tina's knowledge, they were carrying on a liaison. Unlike Martín Díaz de Cossío, who was shattered by his wife's infidelity, Tina seemed indifferent to the affair, and the two women remained friends, though the deliciously fresh Isabel occasionally referred to Tina behind her back as "the old lady."

Resigned to her lot, Tina endeavored to shape a life. In an attempt to rekindle their friendship, she visited Frances Toor, now a renowned authority on Mexican popular art, whose guidebooks had become tourist bibles. But Frances reviled Tina for her Stalinism, and the two women exchanged rancorous words. After she calmed down, Tina complained to Vittorio of Frances and her ilk: "They're not the same now. They hate Russia and the Communists. They've made a lot of money and they have a lot of money. They're not friends now, and it's better to lose them than to see them."

Another pressing order of business was to make a living, but Tina was ineligible to accept work until her legal status was resolved. On January 27, 1940, she wrote to Minister of the Interior Ignacio García Téllez (who, in 1929, as rector of the National University, had lent his patronage to her exhibition):

> Your private secretary informed me that I had not been deported by presidential decree but rather by administrative act, and, if I understood correctly, this facilitates the solution of my case. But I have already been in Mexico for a few months, in the abnormal situation of which you are aware, without an official document to legalize my stay and allow me to move around freely and look for a job.... I know very well that, in fact, you are offering me

your country's hospitality; your generous gesture is, for me, invaluable and cause for profound gratitude....

As Tina's case advanced, ex-Mexican ambassador to Spain Adalberto Tejeda used his good offices on her behalf, and Adelina put in a word with García Téllez, with whom she had contacts. When Tina was summoned to the ministry for an interview, Adelina loaned her a smart hat and gloves "because I didn't want them to see her down on her luck." She came home "radiant," Adelina recalled, "because, at last, they had given her legal status in Mexico." Subsequently, Tina received a "beautiful letter" from outgoing President Cárdenas, who annulled her 1930 expulsion, although she still had to renew regularly her status as a political refugee. It was "as if she had been reborn," Adelina thought, "but right away I saw the sadness come back." Still fearful that her presence in Mexico could become a lightning rod for scandal, Tina often used the identity of María.

She began grinding out a living as a translator, tackling political articles, a book about imperialism, and texts by Stalinist union boss Vicente Lombardo Toledano. Her poverty notwithstanding, she also threw herself into volunteer work, most enthusiastically anything on behalf of Spanish émigrés and their children, and the nascent Giuseppe Garibaldi International Association. Nominally a broad antifascist coalition, the group was tightly controlled by the Communist party. For its newsletter and tracts, Tina slogged through editorial chores, translations, and errands, and she often kept a mimeograph machine clunking away far into the night.

Yet she never lacked time to minister to needy friends. When Alfons Goldschmidt died in January 1940, leaving a terribly stricken young widow, Tina simply appeared on the doorstep of Leni's Paseo de la Reforma apartment and stayed for several days to console her. "I called Tina the revolutionary Madonna," Leni later said in a low, emotion-laden voice. "She came to me, too, when I was in tremendous pain, and she was wonderful. There was a softness and a warmth. I was devastated, and then Tina came to me.... I will never forget it. There was so much dignity and compassion...." To bring balm to Leni's sorrow, Tina told her about "the assassination of her lover and how she was devastated and how she had no peace after that...."

Increasingly, Tina had to pay for bursts of activity with days when she dropped in her tracks. Her skin took on a creamy yellow cast, and painful, bloated ankles and feet sometimes caused her to plop down as soon as she walked into the house and trade her shoes for slippers. She consulted Dr. Enrique Rebolledo Cobos, who probably confirmed earlier diagnoses of congestive heart failure and prescribed more rest. When *El Machete* editor Rosendo Gómez Lorenzo stopped by for a visit, he was aghast at how tired and aged Tina looked. "She still bore traces of her former beauty," he noticed, "but very tired." Writer Fernando Gamboa agreed that she seemed "very bad, you know, very bad. She was horribly worn out, much more so than when I saw her in Spain...very faded, faded, with a bad color.... It was very accentuated. It was obvious that she was wretched."

Around the time of Alfons Goldschmidt's death, Tina and Vittorio took up residence in a shabby studio apartment on Pedro Barranda Street, in a working-class district near the Monument to the Revolution. A faint echo of the invincible, shape-shifting Tina sounded in her rapt attention to domestic matters. She joyfully undertook the project of decorating her first home in over a decade. "You traipsed through this slum building," remembered Leni, "and then Tina's apartment! It was two different worlds. It was all painted in white, and she had used the cheapest native furniture.... There was a serenity in the place. And I remember the light. She didn't have any lamps, you know." To filter the glare of naked bulbs, Tina covered them with Japanese paper suspended with string from the ceiling. Guests sat upon a sort of futon, called "a Turkish bed," purchased at the Lagunilla Market. One friend recalled that it was "harder than the devil," but arranged with "a very pretty little bedspread that María surely made, had sewed herself, and with a few small pillows...." Tina scrubbed, dusted, did the laundry, and ladled out to Vittorio heaping plates of pasta and polenta. He bragged of her housekeeping, yet, ironically, now that Tina was taking an interest in home life, she found herself cheated of the intimate companionship she had often known in the past.

Yet the pair kept up an active social life, which revolved around dinners, parties, and occasional Sunday outings. They socialized with Constancia de la Mora and Hidalgo de Cisneros, whose Veracruz Avenue apartment was the favorite gathering place of Spanish émigrés; ex-general Patricio Azcárate and his wife, former Red Aid administrator Cruz Díaz, whom Tina adored; and Pedro Martínez Cartón, married to a German-born Communist who used the alias Carmen Salot. The Italians Mario and Anna Maria Montagnana were members of their social set, as were the Swiss couple Hannes and Lena Meyer. Tina was also close to Leocadia Prestes, the courageous matriarch of the Brazilian Prestes family, who was living in Mexico City with her four-year-old granddaughter, Anita. Leocadia thought Tina "an adorable person...of great human sensitivity, an extraordinary woman," an opinion shared by one of Tina's most frequent callers, Pablo O'Higgins. As devoted as ever, Pablo was now a leading player in a socially engaged artists' group, the Popular Graphics Workshop.

In April 1940, Tina's former friend Bertram Wolfe, the leader of the New York–based anti-Stalinist Lovestonite party, made reference to Vittorio and Tina's clandestine work in a letter to a like-minded friend in Mexico City. "[A]s to the dry cleaning establishment," he wrote, "Sormenti [Vidali] and Tina are known to us." Vittorio was at the time no doubt deeply involved in details of the plots against Trotsky. The first, an armed assault on the old revolutionist's Coyoacán villa, was launched during the night of May 24. Led by hotspur painter David Alfaro Siqueiros, a squad of Communists and artists disguised as policemen, reportedly including Vittorio Vidali wielding a Thompson machine gun, kidnapped a guard and stormed the house. They pumped over two hundred bullets into the bedrooms but missed their target, who dived under the bed with his wife. Vittorio was interrogated about the attack and released for lack of evidence. Trotsky would die three months later when Ramón Mercader, a Catalan-born agent whom Vittorio had known in Spain, brutally drove an ice pick into the Russian's head. Whatever Vittorio's role in operating the Stalinist apparatus of terror, Moscow was pleased. He was later to win promotion to the staff of Soviet ambassador Constantine Oumansky, NKVD chief for the Americas, who ordered him to plan a secret international military brigade, which would be deployed in the event of war between the Soviet Union and the United States.

During the weeks leading up to Trotsky's assassination, Tina was absorbed in a wholly different project. It is probably a measure of Vittorio's inattention to her activities that he erroneously said she had picked up the camera again to make photographs for Constancia de la Mora's planned (but never published) second book, *Mexico Is Ours*. Using words and pictures, the book was to tell the story of how reformist president Lázaro Cárdenas had breathed new life into Mexico's revolutionary agenda. Laura and John Condax, two young Philadelphians recently out of art school, had hatched the project with Constancia during her East Coast stay. When she invited them to make her apartment their Mexico City base, the couple drove down in their beat-up Chevy. Too busy to participate in the picture-taking expedition, Constancia suggested that a Spanish refugee named María serve as their interpreter and guide.

With Laura behind the wheel, the trio's jalopy swirled up dust on country roads leading to the remote schools, workshops, factories, and fiestas where Tina arranged for John to document the lives of ordinary Mexicans. For four months, they crisscrossed Mexico, lingering to depict the effects of agrarian reform measures at an *ejido* (cooperative farm) in the north, trekking to the isthmus, where Tina was as enchanted as ever by the way the Tehuanas carried even the smallest of bundles on their heads, and straying south to Chiapas, where they had to rush for cover when the skies cracked with torrential tropical rains. At night, they stayed in a succession of fleabag hotels, and over dinner, Tina would chat pleasantly about Mexico or her family. The Condaxes found her personable, if baffling when she made statements such as, "Well, good night. I'm going to do the following: take a bath." Years later, however, they understood Tina's style in light of the habits of clandestine operatives.

Their travels brought to Tina's mind the *Idols Behind Altars* expedition with Edward fourteen summers earlier. On the shores of Lake Pátzcuaro—where an angry, crazed old woman had once charged Edward's camera—the trio ran afoul of villagers resentful of gringo photographers. In the aftermath of the incident, so eerily reminiscent of her earlier experience, Tina disclosed to her companions that she was not really the refugee María but, rather, the photographer Tina Modotti. When John followed with an offer to lend her his Graflex, she politely and firmly rebuffed him.

She had refused Manuel Alvarez Bravo's proposal of photographic assistance, as well. "[A]t that time," remembered Manuel, "I had a little studio in Ayuntamiento Street, and, one day, all of a sudden, the bell rang. I opened, and it was Tina. Well, it was a very emotional moment...then it passed. We were talking, and one thing impressed me very much. I still remember it very well. I said to her, 'Tina'—she liked the Graflex camera a lot and I had a Graflex—and I said, 'I have a Graflex camera and here is a darkroom.' And then she said, 'No, Manuel, not now…not now.' She said this very sadly, very sadly she said, 'Not now.'" She never reappeared at Manuel's studio.

Not only was equipment pressed upon her, but paying clients also stepped forward. Her friend Cuban designer Clara Porset, who had married Xavier Guerrero, brought a message from would-be patrons, who proposed to pay any price she set for a series of photographs. "Tina listened to me with that same old luminous smile," Clara said. "But she went back to her typewriter to finish a piece of work—one of those she was always doing, to help and defend some oppressed and suffering people. And she never spoke to me again about that offer that they made to her."

Tina's demurrals probably stemmed from her realization that she lacked some dimension—which might be called freedom of spirit, self-confidence, or audacity—required to make photographs of the caliber she expected from herself. She was also daunted by her artistic reputation, enhanced by word that "according to the famous film director Eisenstein, [in photography] she was the best." Ignoring a yearning to take pictures, Tina willfully turned her back upon photography. Having once sacrificed art to life, she now sacrificed the joys of creativity to the integrity of her oeuvre. Susan Sontag's statement that "the choice of permanent silence doesn't negate [artists'] work" is wholly applicable. "On the contrary," Sontag continues, "it imparts retroactively an added power and authority to what was broken off—disavowal of the work becoming a new source of its validity, a certificate of unchallengeable seriousness."

But Tina's feelings about photography were more ambivalent than her words and actions suggested. That her decision was based in self-denial is evident from her delight in picture taking if circumstances placed it outside the realm of serious photography. When a friend of Yolanda's was visiting from New York, Tina and Vittorio organized a day trip to the country. They also invited Eladia Lozano, a life-loving nineteen-year-old Spanish Communist whom Tina had befriended during the war. As the foursome was preparing to leave the apartment, Eladia recalled, Tina grabbed a straw hat hanging on the wall. "Come, come, put on this hat, I want to see how it looks on you…," she urged Eladia.

Then I put it on, and she said, "We'll take it along because I want to take a series of photographs.".... And then indeed she took [with the visitor's Leica] a series of very beautiful pictures and...she was saying: "Get closer to that rock, put yourself near that tree, look over here, now look over there, now sit down, now stand up." She took lots and lots. Then Carlos said, "You know, María takes very good photographs." Then I said, "Oh, really!" A few days afterward...they imprisoned Carlos...and all his friends had a horrible fright, yes? Because nothing was known of him, and when [the photographs] were developed, María told me they were splendid, but then, out of fear that the police would come to her house and see the photos...it could damage me so she tore up the prints and the negatives. I only know that they told me they had come out very well, but I never saw them.

Walking near Alameda Park one day in March 1941, Vittorio vanished without a trace, and three weeks passed before comrades discovered that he had been locked up in the notorious El Pocito prison. Confined to a pitch-dark cell, filthy with feces and crawling with rats, Vittorio mentally composed his autobiography and crooned "Addìo Lugano Bella" to keep from going crazy. Playing what once would have been Tina's role, Isabel boldly scrambled onto the roof of a nearby building, where she used hand signals to send messages to Vittorio, who peered through a small opening in the wall. Panic-stricken at the idea of police raids, scandal, and deportation, Tina huddled at home, and when Isabel informed her of Vittorio's whereabouts, she trembled uncontrollably. After he was released through the intervention of high-powered friends, Vittorio returned, to find her red-eyed, rail-thin, and disoriented, as if possessed by the demons of the miserable year preceding her expulsion from Mexico.

By now, the twosome had moved once more, to a building facing the General Hospital, in a neighborhood where streets bore the names of distinguished physicians and where medical supply houses, casket makers, and dispensaries of prostheses abounded. On the roof of 137 Dr. Balmis Street, Tina had discovered a fifty-peso-a-month bargain: a dismal, roughcast bungalow, which, Vittorio objected, was something like the cottage of Snow White and one dwarf.

"Well, there are two of us," Tina retorted.

The house's entryway doubled as kitchen, large enough for a counter, sink, cupboards, and the hard-as-a-rock Turkish bed. Beyond was the dining room, where Tina squeezed a table and four chairs, and a bedroom containing a double bed and a primitive shower that sprayed water everywhere. When rain clattered down on the tin roof, the house turned into an unbearable resonance chamber.

As Tina surely realized, it was reckless for a heart patient to reside in a fifth-floor walk-up. Yet the painful ascent of four steep flights seemed unimportant next to the spectacular panoramic view. "But this is not the real house," she would insist, gesturing at the cottage; "look around!" Mexico City was a mosaic extending in every direction; to the south towered the majestic snow-wreathed volcanoes, Ixtaccíhuatl and Popocatépetl.

When Tina's weariness made it impossible to disregard doctor's orders to rest, she began spending long hours on the roof, where she sat surrounded by cords of drying laundry and old coffee cans planted with geraniums and carnations. She would observe how light and color clung to the mountains, which glittered resplendent in the sun and dissolved into soft grayness under distant rainsqualls. The murmur of the streets floated up, and a low wall girding the terrace brought to mind a ship's railing, as if one were drifting around the city. Sometimes Tina read, but often she simply inhaled the sun-warmed air and gave herself over to introspection.

One can imagine how tentatively she picked up and examined the burdens of her mind. Did she realize to what extent her passion was quelled and her confidence eroded? Why had life taken an irrevocable turn toward fear and premature old age? How had her sensitivity, misfortune, lofty ideals, and fierce desire for social change metamorphosed into tormented silence? Probably she was crippled by a frightening inconsonance between the compassionate Tina and the Tina who was complicit with mind-staggering atrocities. Incapable of the wholeness that had once informed her breathless passion for living, she could only with difficulty navigate among her own feelings. Susceptible to bouts of emotional devastation, she must also have experienced the numbing and disintegration familiar to combat veterans.

Refusing to be felled, Tina anticipated her homecoming to a postfascist Italy "with a joy, an emotion, an enthusiasm that sparkled in her good, clear eyes." Meanwhile, she tried to salvage her personal life by acquiring a family. She wrote to her nephew Tullio Cosolo, now a married man of twenty-three and the only Modotti of his generation, to ask if he would please send her his first son to raise. But Tullio's wife, Argia, said no. One day, however, some Mexican Street Car Company workers, with whom Tina was friendly, delivered a trembling bundle wrapped in sheets of newspaper. It contained a longhaired white dog she named Suzi, who became her constant companion. A stray cat, dubbed Kitty, also took up residence on the terrace, and within months, both animals gave birth. Tina mothered and then gave away the litters of puppies and kittens.

In December, she asked an old friend, businessman Fred Davis, for suggestions about jobs and a letter of recommendation. She also apparently let Mary Louis Doherty know that she was interested in obtaining a camera, and Mary tried to make arrangements through Xavier Guerrero. Although she desperately needed more income, Tina's deteriorating health made a full-time job unfeasible. When her young Spanish friend stopped by, she would lament, "Eladia, I feel so *tired.*" Eladia never remembers seeing Tina laugh, though the older woman once playfully offered her a cup of what Tina hinted was tea with milk but which proved to be fiery pulque. Another time, when the two were alone, Eladia innocently queried, "María, did you have another boyfriend before Carlos?" Tina smiled and said, "Yes, but it's not worth talking about. I've already told Carlos."

On New Year's Eve, December 31, 1941, Tina and Vittorio mingled with politicos and artists at the home of Communist poet Pablo Neruda, who was serving as Chilean consul general in Mexico. More outgoing than usual, Tina enjoyed a long tête-à-tête with Anna Maria Montagnana and raised her glass at midnight to Neruda's toast: "There is coming for all of you, comrades and friends, the day of return to your land." Shortly before dawn, she departed with Vittorio and French journalist Simone Téry for a stroll down the Paseo de la Reforma to watch the sunrise from Chapultepec Park. Simone remembered that, as they stepped out of Pablo's house,

> María saw an elderly Mexican sprawling in a doorway. Indifferent, people passed by him, believing him to be drunk. But María approached:

"Why don't you go home?" she asked him. "Your family will be worried."

"I can't," replied the man, "I'm too weak."

Then and there, María went to the General Hospital to ask that they accept the sick man.

"It's not our affair," they answered. "We are not an emergency hospital. Go see the Green Cross."

María telephoned the Green Cross. She was told that there were no beds available. But María was not discouraged. She did not go home to rest until she was assured that the poor man, who surely would have died of cold on the sidewalk, was to be transported to the Green Cross. That old man no doubt never found out that, like so many others, he owed his life to Tina Modotti. He never found out that five days later the cadaver of Tina Modotti arrived in a hired automobile at the General Hospital from where it was also sent to the Green Cross.

On Monday, January 5, Tina visited muralist José Clemente Orozco—squinting through his spectacles and missing half his teeth, but as oracular as ever—then went home to two translations in progress, an essay on French philosopher Denis Diderot and Mario Montagnana's article on Mussolini. But she turned her hand instead to writing a chatty letter to a friend: "I was just at the house of José Clemente Orozco. This great Mexican artist is also a man of great sensitivity.... I nearly, nearly dare to say I am happy that America is also at war against Hitler.... Naturally, this is in jest, but the reality is that I thus feel closer to our great struggle...."

Time grew short, and, leaving the stationery rolled into her typewriter, Tina dressed for a party that evening at the home of Hannes and Lena Meyer. From her wardrobe, minuscule but impeccably clean and well cared for, she selected a black suit, white blouse, and black shoes. She carefully parted, braided, and pinned up her hair in a style she probably thought less matronly than the bun she had worn for years. After she and Vittorio locked the door, only the animals stirred as darkness crept upon the terrace, and the cottage's tin roof glinted in the light of a full moon.

By Vittorio's account, he returned at midnight, and, finding Tina not yet home, buried himself in a book. Around 1:00 A.M., the bell sounded from the downstairs gate, and, assuming that his companion had forgotten her keys, he ran downstairs to let her in. He was startled to see two men, who asked if he was the husband of Tina Modotti.

"Yes, what's happened?"

"Your wife died, and she's now at the Green Cross."

"What! Who died?"

"Your wife Tina Modotti died in the taxi which was taking her home."

Employees of a mortuary associated with the Green Cross, the pair gave Vittorio a ride to the emergency hospital, where, he recalled, "in a poorly lit room lay Tina, all arranged with her black tailored suit, her white blouse, her face serene, eyes closed, half-open mouth which revealed her small teeth, her straight hair parted in the middle. She seemed asleep, as if she were waiting for someone to awaken her to go walking in the moonlight." Vittorio's emotionally flat account of his farewell to Tina reveals only that he stooped to plant a kiss on her face, gave a statement to the police, and went home.

Around 4:00 A.M., he phoned Isabel Carbajal, and Pedro Martínez Cartón, to whom he delegated the task of identifying and claiming the body, and then went into hiding at Constancia's house. As Vittorio suspected, reporters were soon swarming all over 137 Dr. Balmis Street, and Tina's nightmares about mudslinging and recriminations quickly came true. Headlines branded Vittorio a "fanatical agent of the GPU," and articles suggested that Tina had committed suicide, that Mussolini had personally provided her with an Italian passport, that Robo had mysteriously died while traveling with her in a sleeping car, and that she was a fascist spy.

Word of Tina's death circulated swiftly among her friends. When Adelina Zendejas heard the news from Clara Porset just before sunrise, she hastened to Juárez Hospital, where an autopsy was pending. There she found Tina "on the same cement slab, the same one, where Julio Antonio had been. She was nude, completely nude, with her perfect body, that perfect body she had, exquisite, and her face had something peaceful about it, something restful."

The forensic report stated that Tina's aorta and coronary arteries were partially blocked by fatty plaque and that her lungs were filled with fluid. Doctors determined that she died of "generalized visceral congestion [traumatic damage to internal organs]...caused by an organic lesion of the heart," a phrase that implies a chronic ailment. Their findings point to arteriosclerosis—a condition in which artery walls thicken and lose their elasticity—and congestive heart failure—the heart's inability to pump sufficient blood, which can result in a buildup of fluids, causing the lung tissue to become waterlogged. An examination of the stomach cavity revealed no trace of poison. Though further tissue tests were ordered (results of which did not contradict the original conclusions), a judge promptly signed the death certificate of the "housewife" Tina Modotti, married to Carlos Jiménez Contreras.

"TINA MODOTTI'S DEATH EXACTLY RESEMBLES COMMUNIST LIQUIDATIONS," blazoned *La Prensa* on January 8. Tina's longtime friend and admirer Federico Marín, a medical doctor, made inquiries at the hospital and came away with the impression that she had been poisoned. Bertram Wolfe later wrote of Tina's demise that it "was tragic.... According to the report in the Mexican press...revulsion at Commissario Carlos's purge activities in Republican Spain caused her to break with him upon their return to Mexico. He gave her a farewell party, from which she fled alone in a taxi, asking the driver to rush her to a hospital, and died on the way, some said of heart failure, others of poisoning." In New York, the Italian anarcho-syndicalist Carlo Tresca penned a blistering attack upon Vidali: "The latest [crime] attributed to him is that of having murdered his own sweetheart, Tina Modotti, because she knew too much...." Potentially the leader of postwar Italy's non-Communist left, Tresca was gunned down in Manhattan a year later. A suspect in his murder, Vittorio was never located for questioning, and the crime remains unsolved to this day.

Although it is conceivable that her comrades purged Tina because she was disenchanted with communism, no material clues or talebearers have come to light. Accusations are buttressed only by conjecture and circumstantial evidence: Vittorio's disappearance, the climate of assassination and Red-baiting, and the existence, within the NKVD, of a sophisticated medical department that experimented with poisons and drugs capable of making killings resemble natural deaths. Vittorio's memoirs are self-serving enough to avoid mention of his liaison with Isabel (whom he married two months after Tina's death), but his towering ambition makes a freelance killing unlikely, since assassinations on foreign soil were undertaken only on high-level orders from Moscow.

Unless new evidence emerges, one can assume that Tina died of heart disease at an exceptionally young age. Every one of her five siblings suffered from grave cardiac ailments (which would prove fatal to Yolanda, Ben, and Beppo), strongly suggesting a congenital factor. Behavioral patterns are critically important for arteriosclerosis patients. Tina smoked, led a stressful life, and, when she could afford it, ate a cholesterol-rich diet. Her extreme fatigue, wheezing, and painful ankles and feet all signal a heart condition.

In 1948, Ben Modotti delivered to New York's Italian-language Stalinist organ, *L'Unità del Pòpolo,* a statement about his sister's death. He acted at the request of Vidali, livid over a *Time* magazine article implicating him in a rash of murders, including that of "Tiña Modotti, [his] Communist mistress." Ben affirmed, "She was seriously ill with heart disease, and she died from this illness. Whoever says otherwise is a liar. I only tell the truth about my sister; I do not share Vidali's political opinions, but the truth about my sister's death is what I have stated." Yet Mercedes was unaware of the disease. "I never knew she had heart trouble, did you?" she wrote Edward Weston in 1946. "To tell you the truth I was always a bit uneasy about her, but never did I think I would never see her again. *Così è la vita.*"

Tina's viewing took place at La Moderna, a shabby fifth-class funeral parlor on José M. Izazaga Street. Wrapped in a crisp white shroud, she seemed too small for her coffin. The morning of January 7 saw the departure of a motorcade that inched its way through the Mexico City streets toward the vast Pantheon Dolores, where a fifth-class cemetery plot awaited. Vittorio was absent from a big crowd of mourners who gathered beneath a eucalyptus tree amid a profusion of calla lilies, carnations, and roses. A cloth imprinted with the hammer and sickle draped Tina's bier, on top of which stood Edward's portrait of her, made in Los Angeles so many lifetimes ago.

In Communist fashion, committees were quickly established. Cruz Díaz, Adelina Zendejas, Isabel Carbajal, Pedro Martínez Cartón, and ex-Spanish Red Aid leader Luis Zapirain raised funds and published a fifty-two-page biographical essay and collection of homages to Tina from the pens of European émigrés, journalists, photographers, and Communist functionaries. The group also organized a February 23 memorial event, presided over by Leocadia Prestes, at the People's Theater of the Abelardo

Rodríguez Market. Architect Hannes Meyer designed Tina's gravestone, which was decorated with a bas-relief profile portrait and an excerpt from the poem "Tina Modotti Is Dead." Written by Pablo Neruda as an elegy and response to the defilement of Tina and Vittorio, it read, in part:

Perfect your gentle name,
perfect your fragile life

—bees, shadows, fire,
snow, silence and foam combining

with steel and wire and
pollen to make up your firm
and delicate being.

Perhaps the tribute most remarkable, however, in its cathartic power and ability to bring order and meaning to Tina Modotti's journey, was an exhibition of fifty photographs, which opened on March 19 at Mexico City's Galería del Arte Moderno. Borrowed from friends' collections, the images recalled the photographer's emotional fusion with humble people and her exquisitely painful awareness of the beauty and fugaciousness of material life. Among the works was a self-portrait, which Pablo O'Higgins described in a "broken, suffering voice" as "romantic and serene as a lyric poem," a poignant reminder of what Tina called the "tragic conflict between life which continually changes and form which fixes it immutable."

Endnotes

1. FRIULI AND AUSTRIA (1896–1913)

Gianfranco Ellero's meticulously researched books on Modotti's childhood and family, as well as our conversations and correspondence, are primary sources for this chapter. In addition, I have drawn heavily upon the work of Christiane Barckhausen-Canale and of Udine's Comitato Tina Modotti.

All translations are mine unless otherwise indicated.

4 "trying to scoop": Pablo Neruda, *Memoirs*, trans. Hardie St. Martin (Harmondsworth, England: Penguin Books, Ltd., 1978), 255.

4 Chitchat bounces: Vittorio Vidali, *Retrato de mujer: Una Vida con Tina Modotti*, trans. Antonella Fagetti (Puebla, Mexico: Universidad Autónoma de Puebla, 1984), 82–83.

5 "The dramatic circumstances": *Excelsior* (Mexico City, Mexico), 7 January 1942.

5 "Bees, shadows": Pablo Neruda, "Tina Modotti Is Dead," trans. Alastair Reid, cited in Mildred Constantine, *Tina Modotti: A Fragile Life* (San Francisco: Chronicle Books, 1993), 190.

5 "tragic conflict": Letter from Tina Modotti to Edward Weston, 14 November 1926, Edward Weston Archive, Center for Creative Photography, University of Arizona, Tucson.

6 "Of Italy": Tina Modotti, Moscow questionnaire, cited in Gianfranco Ellero, *Tina Modotti in Carinzia e in Friuli* (Pordenone, Italy: Cinemazero, 1996), 132.

7 Molin Nuovo: Archive of Parrocchia del S.S. Redentore, Udine, Italy.

8 The Italianized plural: Ellero, *Tina Modotti in Carinzia e in Friuli*, 83–84.

8 "a pleasant, jolly voice": Letter from Tina Modotti to Rose and Marionne Richey, 3 April 1922, collection of Ruth and LaBrie Ritchie. Unless otherwise indicated, Richey family correspondence and documents used throughout the book are in the Ritchie collection.

8 he could read fluently: Joseph Modotti and household, 1920 U.S. census, U.S. National Archives and Records Administration, Pacific Region, San Bruno, California.

8 severe phlebitis: Ivana Bonelli et al., "Un cappello caduto nell'acqua. Tracce di Tina nella sua terra d'origine," in Comitato Tina Modotti, ed., *Tina Modotti: Una Vita nella storia* (Tavagnacco, Italy: Edizioni Arti Grafiche Friulane, 1995), 70.

9 "the capitalists would be": *L'Operaio*, 29 August 1896, cited in Ellero, *Tina Modotti in Carinzia e in Friuli*, 73.

9 A serious and composed: Libera Sorini cited in Bonelli et al., "Un cappello caduto nell'acqua. Tracce di Tina nella sua terra d'origine," in Comitato Tina Modotti, ed., *Tina Modotti*, 71.

9 a silk embroiderer: Valentina Agostinis, ed., *Tina Modotti: Gli anni luminosi* (Pordenone, Italy: Edizioni Biblioteca dell'Immagine, Cinemazero, 1992), 16.

10 "child of unknown father": Elena Poniatowska's interview with Vittorio Vidali, 16–21 September 1981.

11 "a saint": Author's interview with Ann Walnum, 19 May 1997.

11 "our blessed mother": Vidali, *Retrato de mujer*, 108.

11 notion that the relationship: A possible exception is Mercedes Modotti's cohabitation with Dante Cosolo. Little is known of the intimate relationships of Benvenuto Modotti.

11 "a true fighter": *La Prensa* (Mexico City, Mexico), 14 January 1929.

11 "younger in spirit": Letter from Tina Modotti to Rose and Marionne Richey, 3 April 1922.

11 (sometimes called Carlo): Giuseppe Modotti obituary, *San Francisco Examiner*, 15 March 1922.

11 With the baby born on August 16: According to Modotti's birth certificate, her date of birth is 17 August 1896; her baptismal record states 16 August. On a questionnaire completed in 1932, Tina gave 16 August as her birthday. A false passport that she used in 1939 and an autobiographical sketch prepared by close friends also mention 16 August. Giuseppe Modotti did not register his daughter's birth with civil authorities until 22 August, and Gianfranco Ellero has reasonably suggested that Giuseppe may have misstated the date of birth in order to comply with the city's five-day deadline for registration.

12 the Friulian custom: Christiane Barckhausen-Canale, *Verdad y leyenda de Tina Modotti* (Mexico City: Editorial Diana, 1992), 22.

12 "that religion": Ellero, *Tina Modotti in Carinzia e in Friuli*, 78.

13 In a cycle: Information about Carinthia at the end of the nineteenth century is largely

derived from Vinzenz Jobst, *Arbeitswelt und Alltag* (Klagenfurt, Austria: Kärntner Druck und Verlagsgesellschaft, 1985); *Aus dem Wilajet Kärnten* (Klagenfurt, Austria: Verlag des Slov Katoliško-politič, 1913); and Herbert Stejskal, ed., *Kärnten, Geschichte und Kultur in Bildern und Dokumenten* (Klagenfurt, Austria: Universitätsverlag Carinthia, 1991). My thanks to Wilhelm Wadl for his assistance and for the documents he provided and to Jesco Köller for his translations.

13 Friedrich Brodnig: Modotti apparently mentioned her father's employment in the factory to her companion Vittorio Vidali, giving Vidali the mistaken impression that Giuseppe Modotti had been a carpenter. See Maria Caronia, *Tina Modotti: Fotografa e rivoluzionaria* (Milan: Idea Editions, 1979), 3.

14 Giuseppe was hospitalized: Bonelli et al., "Un cappello caduto nell'acqua. Tracce di Tina nella sua terra d'origine," in Comitato Tina Modotti, ed., *Tina Modotti*, 70.

15 "Your friends": Pittoni cited in Barckhausen-Canale, *Verdad y leyenda de Tina Modotti*, 47.

16 "For long periods": Tina Modotti, Moscow questionnaire.

16 "In Udine": Author's interview with Eladia de los Ríos, 24 September 1997.

16 "does not know": Bonelli et al., "Un cappello caduto nell'acqua. Tracce di Tina nella sua terra d'origine," in Comitato Tina Modotti, ed., *Tina Modotti*, 63.

16 "[S]he went to": *La Prensa*, 14 January 1929.

16 "the most cultivated": Harry Lawton's interview with Peter Krasnow, 6 June 1970, Sadakichi Hartmann Collection, University of California, Riverside.

16 "mediocrity": Elena Poniatowska's interview with Monna Alfau, 24 August 1981.

17 "of Udine": Elena Poniatowska's interview with Fernando Gamboa, 17 July 1981.

17 amusements such as a school holiday: Ellero, *Tina Modotti in Carinzia e in Friuli*, 54–55.

17 Every November: Livio Jacob, "Vera Vergani e Tina Modotti: Due friulane nel cinema muto," *Sot la Nape*, January–June 1996: 25.

17 "Think of these old": Theodore Dreiser, *A Traveler at Forty* (New York: The Century Company, 1923), 403.

18 autochrome color process: My thanks to Gianfranco Ellero for information about Pietro Modotti's introduction to Italy of the autochrome process.

19 if skeins were piling up: Elio Bartolini, *Filande in Friuli* (Udine: Casamassima Editore, 1974), 7.

20 "Our fire and candles": Yolanda Modotti cited in Vidali, *Retrato de mujer*, 75–76.

20 "Misery and hunger": Tina Modotti cited in Vidali, *Retrato de mujer*, 17.

20 Tina took catechism: Ellero, *Tina Modotti in Carinzia e in Friuli*, 56, 91–92.

21 "[no] belief or religion": Letter from Tina Modotti to Rose and Marionne Richey, 28 February 1922.

21 Such nineteenth-century notions: Speaking of the differences between traditional and contemporary concepts of emigration, Dino Cinel makes a similar point. See Dino Cinel, *From Italy to San Francisco: The Immigrant Experience* (Stanford, California: Stanford University Press, 1982), 69.

21 "always expressed the desire": Letter from Tina Modotti to Rose and Marionne Richey, 11 February 1922.

21 "ridiculous": Margaret Hooks, *Tina Modotti: Photographer and Revolutionary* (San Francisco: Pandora, 1993), 14.

21 docked briefly at Naples: Eugene W. Smith, *Passenger Ships of the World, Past and Present* (Boston: George H. Dean Co., 1978), 173.

2. SAN FRANCISCO (1913–1918)

22 Tina first tasted: Margaret Hooks, *Tina Modotti: Photographer and Revolutionary* (San Francisco: Pandora, 1993), 15.

23 Having long been strapped: Robert D'Attilio makes this point in "Appunti per le future biografie di Tina Modotti: La Famiglia Modotti a San Francisco," in Comitato Tina Modotti, ed., *Tina Modotti: Una Vita nella storia* (Tavagnacco, Italy: Edizioni Arti Grafiche Friulane, 1995), 324.

23 "reasons with her uterus": Letter from Benvenuto Modotti to Tina Modotti, 4 October 1928, cited in Christiane Barckhausen-Canale, *Verdad y leyenda de Tina Modotti* (Mexico City: Editorial Diana, 1992), 338.

24 Alice Rohrer: Letter from Emily Edwards to Mildred Constantine, 19 January 1974, The Getty, Research Institute for the History of Art and the Humanities, Los Angeles, California. Edward Weston made a portrait of Rohrer in 1933, and Tina's siblings Yolanda and Ben lived with Rohrer briefly in New York in 1936.

24 "when night comes": Letter from Tina Modotti to Rose and Marionne Richey, 3 April 1922.

24 "[North Beach] is appealing": Clarence Edgar Edwords, *Bohemian San Francisco* (San Francisco: Paul Elder and Company, 1914), 73.

25 "the greatest revelation": Edwin Markham cited in Tom Cole, *A Short History of San Francisco* (San Francisco: Lexikos, 1981), 118.

26 "new-world activities": Author's interview with Alessandro Baccari, Jr., 13 June 1994.

26 "beautiful though eccentric": Lawrence Estavan, comp., Mary A. Burgess, ed., *The Italian Theatre in San Francisco* (1939; reprint, San Bernardino, California: The Borgo Press, 1991), 60.

26 Dabbling in poetry: Author's interview with Alessandro Baccari, Jr., 13 June 1994.

27 "most amusing spectacle": *La Voce del Pòpolo,* 15 July 1916.

27 "Mr. Arturo Godi": Ibid.

28 "We are not going to forget": *L'Italia,* 29 July 1916.

28 Tina presumably touring: *La Voce del Pòpolo,* 2 August 1916.

28 "promising career": Estavan, comp., Burgess, ed., *The Italian Theatre in San Francisco,* 60.

28 Ruddy-faced and ham-handed: Valenti Angelo, *Arts and Books: A Glorious Variety* (Berkeley: Regional Oral History Office, Bancroft Library, University of California, Berkeley, 1980), 49.

28 "Not very tall": Lolo de la Torriente cited in Maria Caronia, *Tina Modotti: Fotografa e rivoluzionaria* (Milan: Idea Editions, 1979), 5.

28 The images take their places: Tina Modotti is known to have posed for Alessandro Baccari, Jean Charlot, Franz Geritz, Johan Hagemeyer, Pablo O'Higgins, Giovanni Battista Portanova, Jane Reece, Roubaix de l'Abrie Richey, Diego Rivera, Arnold Schröder, Walter Frederick Seely, and Edward Weston. An unsigned portrait in the collection of her grandnephew, Bruno Cosolo, is probably by Mahlon Blaine. Leopoldo Méndez and Martín Pineda did the bas-relief portrait on her tombstone.

29 "Just the fact": Letter from Tina Modotti to Edward Weston, December 1925 or January 1926, Edward Weston Archive, Center for Creative Photography, University of Arizona, Tucson.

30 Luigi Poggi: Idwal Jones, "E viva San Francisco," *American Mercury,* October 1927, cited in Estavan, comp., Burgess, ed., *The Italian Theatre in San Francisco,* 63–64; Joseph Modotti and household, 1920 U.S. census, U.S. National Archives and Records Administration, Pacific Region, San Bruno, California.

30 prompter Gennaro Dorso: Author's interview with Alessandro Baccari, Jr., 13 June 1994.

30 "all fire": *L'Italia,* 5 September 1917.

30 "Tina Modotti": Ibid.

31 "a magnificence and a nobility": Nancy Newhall, ed., *The Daybooks of Edward Weston: I. Mexico* (Millerton, New York: Aperture, 1973), xviii.

31 "the fabulous Tina Modotti": Estavan, comp., Burgess, ed., *The Italian Theatre in San Francisco,* 60.

32 "The sad emotions": *L'Italia,* 4 December 1917.

32 a son called Tullio: By most accounts, Tullio never knew his soldier father. In an interview with Gianfranco Ellero, however, Tullio's son, Bruno Cosolo, stated that Dante Cosolo (a companion of Gioconda and, later, of Mercedes Modotti) was not only the child's adoptive father but also his biological father. See Gianfranco Ellero, *Tina Modotti in Carinzia e in Friuli* (Pordenone, Italy: Cinemazero, 1996), 61.

32 Bruno Pagliai: Author's interview with Alessandro Baccari, Jr., 13 June 1994. See Charles Higham, *Princess Merle: The Romantic Life of Merle Oberon* (New York: Coward-McCann, 1983), 219.

33 "tumbled beds": Letter from Roubaix de l'Abrie Richey to Rose and James Richey, 16 October 1912.

33 "Brooks and its aborigines": Letter from Rev. Paul Datin to Roubaix de l'Abrie Richey, 8 August 1910.

33 "very backward": Letter from Roubaix de l'Abrie Richey to Rose and James Richey, 16 October 1912.

33 "I work": Letter from Roubaix de l'Abrie Richey to Marionne Richey, 21 October 1914.

34 "cool, grey city of love": George Sterling, "The Cool, Grey City of Love (San Francisco)," in George Sterling, *Sails and Mirage and Other Poems* (San Francisco: A. M. Robertson, 1921), 93.

34 "the heart": Letter from Roubaix de l'Abrie Richey to Rose Richey, 23 January 1922.

34 "For goodness sake": Letter from Vola Dorée to Roubaix de l'Abrie Richey, 14 April 1914.

34 "He was the best": Letter from Vola Dorée to Marionne Richey, 13 February 1923.

34 "Never give any other": Letter from Roubaix de l'Abrie Richey to Vola Dorée, n.d.

35 "I am glad": Letter from Marionne Richey to Roubaix de l'Abrie Richey, 4 April 1917.

35 "Nothing seems": Letter from Roubaix de l'Abrie Richey to Marionne Richey, 28 March 1918.

35 "the two young people": *L'Italia,* 16 October 1918. Robo worked as an exhibition guard at the Panama-Pacific International Exposition's Palace of Fine Arts.

35 "Facts are not always beautiful": Roubaix de l'Abrie Richey cited in Tina Modotti-

Richey, *The Book of Robo* (Los Angeles, 1923), 10.

36 "one of the most beautiful": *L'Italia,* 7 February 1918.

36 "inspired by the classic face": *L'Italia,* 27 February 1918.

36 "Some newspapers": *L'Italia,* 1 March 1918.

37 That she was modeling unclothed: Author's interview with Alessandro Baccari, Jr., 13 June 1994.

37 "They come nightly": "Nourishing of Artists Nurses Art," *San Francisco Examiner,* n.d.

38 "A truly futuristic thing": Ibid.

38 "oddest genius": Ibid.

39 "If Tina cared": Author's interview with Alessandro Baccari, Jr., 13 June 1994.

39 "simple charm and gentle manners": Modotti-Richey, *The Book of Robo,* 9.

39 Elder's spring lecture series: *L'Italia,* 9 April 1918.

39 "all that was beautiful": Theodore Dreiser cited in Richard Perceval Graves, *The Brothers Powys* (New York: Scribner's, 1983), 146.

40 "kind and passionate daughter": *L'Italia,* 14 February 1918.

40 "full of brio": *L'Italia,* 9 July 1918.

40 "most gracious": *L'Italia,* 3 August 1918.

41 "Tina Modotti": *L'Italia,* 29 August 1918.

41 "person of refinement": Superior Court of the State of California, City and County of San Francisco, vol. no. 3, case no. 91434.

41 "colossal debut": *La Voce del Pòpolo,* 5 September 1918.

3. LOMPOC AND LOS ANGELES (1918–1921)

45 One day in early October: Many details of life in the Richey household in this and subsequent chapters are extracted from documents in the collection of Ruth and LaBrie Ritchie.

46 "I have been looking": Letter from Rose Richey to Roubaix de l'Abrie Richey, 13 April 1916.

47 "Oh, she got mixed up": Author's interview with Ruth Ritchie, 3 May 1998.

47 "In his periods of buoyant enthusiasm": Tina Modotti-Richey, *The Book of Robo* (Los Angeles, 1923), 11.

47–48 *dolce cuore":* Letter from Roubaix de l'Abrie Richey to Tina Modotti, 23 December 1921.

48 their legal bond: Robo's divorce from Vola Dorée became final on 8 September 1919. In the January 1920 U.S. census, Robo and Tina were inadvertently listed twice. Rose Richey, in Los Angeles, declared that the couple was married and that Tina was a U.S. citizen (presumably by her marriage to Robo). In San Francisco, Giuseppe Modotti

claimed both to be unmarried aliens. It is conceivable that Tina and Robo were wed after these dates. If so, they apparently breathed not a word of it to family or friends (who, in any case, believed them to be already married). Moreover, exhaustive searches of records in the states of California and Oregon turn up no trace of matrimony. Art historian Amy Conger has located notes taken by Nancy Newhall, the editor of Edward Weston's Daybooks, which reveal that Tina told Edward the marriage never took place. See Amy Conger, "Tina Modotti and Edward Weston: A Re-evaluation of Their Photography," in Peter C. Bunnell and David Featherstone, eds., *EW: 100: Centennial Essays in Honor of Edward Weston* (Carmel, California: Friends of Photography, 1986), 77 n. 17. The changing emotional tenor of the relationship made marriage less likely with each passing year.

48 "in vain for": *L'Italia,* 16 October 1918.

48 "Will you please": Letter from Marionne Richey to County Clerk's Office, Redwood City, California, 30 March 1932.

48 "We haven't any record": Note from Alma Paganini to Marionne Richey, n.d.

49 "was art that united her": María Luisa Lafita cited in Christiane Barckhausen-Canale, *Verdad y leyenda de Tina Modotti* (Mexico City: Editorial Diana, 1992), 65.

49 "I tell you": Letter from Rose Richey to Roubaix de l'Abrie Richey, 9 January 1918.

49 burdened with debt: Letter from Marionne Richey to Roubaix de l'Abrie Richey, 18 December 1917.

50 "an excellent and notable": *L'Italia,* 16 October 1918.

50 "ancestor, of generations ago": Modotti-Richey, *The Book of Robo,* 9.

50 "a French artist": Prentice Duell, "Textiles and Interior Decoration Department: A Note on Batik," *California Southland* 23 (November 1921): 19.

50 "she had married": Dr. Leo M. Matthias, *Ausflug nach Mexiko,* cited in Barckhausen-Canale, *Verdad y leyenda de Tina Modotti,* 115.

50 Astonishingly, Giuseppe: Joseph Modotti and household, 1920 U.S. census, U.S. National Archives and Records Administration, Pacific Region, San Bruno, California.

50 "When, where": Modotti-Richey, *The Book of Robo,* 9.

50 "We are often ashamed": Roubaix de l'Abrie Richey cited in Modotti-Richey, *The Book of Robo,* 45.

52 "finest structure": Richard Alleman, *The Movie Lover's Guide to Hollywood* (New York: Harper & Row, 1985), 104–105.

52 "Blue Ali Baba": Raymond Chandler, *The*

Lady in the Lake (New York: Vintage Books, 1988), 134.

52 Léon Bakst's…Orientalist costumes: *San Francisco Examiner,* 26 December 1915.

52 annual batik exhibition: *Los Angeles Times,* 17 November 1918.

52 process was complex and tedious: The process is described in Inger McCabe Elliott, *Batik: Fabled Cloth of Java* (New York: Clarkson N. Potter, 1984), 50–59.

53 "notable batiks": *Los Angeles Times,* 30 October 1921.

53 "exotic qualities": Rafael Vera de Córdova, "Photographs as True Art," *El Universal Ilustrado,* 23 March 1922, reprinted in Beaumont Newhall and Amy Conger, eds., *Edward Weston Omnibus: A Critical Anthology* (Salt Lake City: Peregrine Smith, 1984), 16.

53 "Robo was a tremendous influence": Author's interview with Alessandro Baccari, Jr., 13 June 1994.

53 "wonderful love": Letter from Tina Modotti to Rose and Marionne Richey, 11 February 1922.

53 "filled with his wonderful love": Letter from Tina Modotti to Roy Rosen, [19?] March 1922, cited in Sarah M. Lowe, *Tina Modotti: Photographs* (New York: Harry N. Abrams, 1995), 20.

54 "music, mime": Kevin Starr, *Inventing the Dream: California Through the Progressive Era* (New York and Oxford, England: Oxford University Press, 1985), 88. Sarah M. Lowe first unearthed evidence of Modotti's connection to *The Mission Play.*

54 "lo! hark!": Starr, *Inventing the Dream,* 87.

54 "vague and terrible beauty": Modotti-Richey, *The Book of Robo,* 11.

54 vacationing from the demands: Karen S. Chambers, "Jane Reece: A Photographer's View of the Artist," M.A. thesis, University of Cincinnati, 23.

54 *Madame de Richey:* Another photograph of Tina in this outfit exists as a signed publicity still, suggesting that it was her costume for a movie role. Reece's photographs may have been taken at the former Edendale studio of the Selig Polyscope Company, whose Allesandro Street entrance was modeled after the Mission San Gabriel. See Kalon C. Lahue, ed., *Motion Picture Pioneer: The Selig Polyscope Company* (Cranbury, New Jersey: A. S. Barnes and Co., 1973), 197. For a time, Selig Polyscope held the exclusive right to film at California missions.

54 "Indeed the Idols": *Rubáiyát of Omar Khayyám,* ed. Louis Untermeyer (New York: Random House, 1947), Stanza 93.

55 London Salon: The Dayton Art Institute, *The Soul Unbound: The Photographs of Jane Reece* (Dayton: The Dayton Art Institute, 1997), 37.

55 "posed by": Ibid.

55 "head of an old man": Letter from Tina Modotti to Edward Weston, 18 September 1928, Edward Weston Archive, Center for Creative Photography, University of Arizona, Tucson.

55 "terrible thing": Ibid.

55 "I have not finished": Letter from Roubaix de l'Abrie Richey to Marionne Richey, 21 October 1914. Nothing suggests that his habits later changed.

55 lavishly illustrated catalog: My thanks to Gianfranco Ellero for showing me this publication to which Tina Modotti-Richey affixed her name. It was recently discovered in a used book shop in Trieste, Italy.

56 "…today the concept": Walter Kaufmann, ed. and trans., *The Portable Nietzsche* (New York: Viking Press, 1968), 446.

57 "recall[ing] medieval Florence": Duell, "Textiles and Interior Decoration Department," 19.

57 "soft amber duskiness": Letter from Emmeline Brady to Tina Modotti and Rose and Marionne Richey, 25 May 1922.

57 "nuns of the perpetual adoration": Letter from Tina Modotti to Betty Brandner, n.d., Edward Weston Misc. Collection, Center for Creative Photography.

58 *Gale's Magazine:* Christiane Barckhausen-Canale discovered evidence of Robo's connection with *Gale's.* We don't know how or if Richey and Gale met. Perhaps they had "slacker"—i.e., draft evader—connections, for in 1917 Robo ducked military service through some type of chicanery.

58 "Then the failures": Modotti-Richey, *The Book of Robo,* 12.

59 Myrtle Stedman: Myrtle Stedman clipping file, Academy of Motion Picture Arts and Sciences, Beverly Hills, California. Stedman's first husband, Marshall Stedman, continued his career with the Chicago Opera Company. In November 1922, in Chicago, Edward Weston heard Stedman perform *Aïda* and noted in his *Daybooks,* "Aunt Em took me to the Chicago Opera Co.… Once I got a slight thrill from a duet between Raisa and Marshall.…" Curiously, there was another Myrto in Edward Weston's life. This was Dorothea Childs, a good friend of Tina and Robo in the early 1920s, who later changed her name to Myrto Childe and renewed her friendship with Weston in the 1930s. See Nancy Newhall, ed., *The Daybooks of Edward Weston: II. California* (Millerton, New York: Aperture, 1973), 134.

59 "Myrto is red": Roubaix de l'Abrie Richey cited in Modotti-Richey, *The Book of Robo,* 59.

59 "dear, precious friend": Letter from Tina Modotti to Rose and Marionne Richey, 21 February 1922.

59 *Variety's* words: *Variety,* obituary of Walter Frederick Seely, 22 July 1959.

60 Anita Stewart biographical information is drawn from Diana Altman, *Hollywood East* (New York: Birch Lane Press, 1992); DeWitt Bodeen, *From Hollywood: The Careers of 15 Great American Stars* (Cranbury, New Jersey: A. S. Barnes and Co., 1976); Gary Carey, *All the Stars in Heaven* (New York: E. P. Dutton, 1981); Charles Higham, *Merchant of Dreams: Louis B. Mayer, M.G.M., and the Secret Hollywood* (New York: Donald I. Fine, 1993); Anthony Slide, *Early American Cinema* (Metuchen, New Jersey, and London: The Scarecrow Press, 1994); and Anita Stewart clipping file, Academy of Motion Picture Arts and Sciences.

60 wore nothing more than a sheer veil: Germán List Arzubide, "Mi Amiga Tina Modotti," *Excelsior* (Mexico City), 24 March 1993.

60 "bunched against her neck": Adela Rogers-St. John, "A Pair of Queens," n.p., n.d., Anita Stewart clipping file, Academy of Motion Picture Arts and Sciences.

60 handed down to Tina: Letter from Tina Modotti to Rose and Marionne Richey, 12 February 1922.

61 "A bad film": *Harrison's Reports,* 4 December 1920.

62 "sleek and sinuous": *The Moving Picture World,* 30 October 1920.

62 "had a good laugh": Nancy Newhall, ed., *The Daybooks of Edward Weston: I. Mexico* (Millerton, New York: Aperture, 1973), 56.

62 "Life's unconscious cruelty": Modotti-Richey, *The Book of Robo,* 10.

63 "These Mexicans": Letter from Tina Modotti to Rose and Marionne Richey, 6 February 1922.

63 "Rodion": Antonio Saborit, *Una mujer sin país: Las Cartas de Tina Modotti a Edward Weston, 1921–1931* (Mexico City: Cal y Arena, 1992), 14.

63 "pour[ed] out tears": José Vasconcelos, *Ulises criollo: La Vida del autor escrito por el mismo* (Mexico City: Ediciones Bota, 1935), cited in Bertram D. Wolfe, *The Fabulous Life of Diego Rivera* (New York: Stein and Day, 1969), 193.

63 "Last night I": Letter from Emile Scolari to Marionne Richey, 19 January 1921.

64 "[I]ntense, dreamy": Letter from Ricardo Gómez Robelo to Edward Weston, 19 February 1922, Edward Weston Archive, Center for Creative Photography.

64 "well-read, worldly wise": Newhall, ed., *The Daybooks of Edward Weston: II. California,* 209.

65 "tough, tough baby": Harry Lawton's interview with Roy Rosen, n.d., Sadakichi Hartmann Collection, University of California, Riverside.

65 "Toltec ballet": *Los Angeles Times,* 23 June 1920.

65 "I yearn so eagerly": Letter from Ramiel McGehee to Betty Brandner, n.d., Edward Weston Misc. Collection, Center for Creative Photography.

65 "I, at Tina's": Newhall, ed., *The Daybooks of Edward Weston: II. California,* 154.

4. LOS ANGELES AND MEXICO CITY (1921–1922)

67 "such a happy": Letter from Tina Modotti to Rose and Marionne Richey, 23 March 1922.

67 "The Ford is": Roubaix de l'Abrie Richey, "The Ford Psalm," n.d., collection of Ruth and LaBrie Ritchie.

68 "Once more I have": Letter from Tina Modotti to Edward Weston, c. 25 April 1921, copied into Edward Weston's *Daybook,* Edward Weston Archive, Center for Creative Photography, University of Arizona, Tucson.

69 "Before everything else": Letter from Tina Modotti to Johan Hagemeyer, 21 August 1921, Weston-Hagemeyer Collection, Center for Creative Photography.

69 "precious afternoon": Letter from Tina Modotti to Edward Weston, 16 September 1921, Weston-Hagemeyer Collection, Center for Creative Photography.

69 Johan Hagemeyer: My account of Johan Hagemeyer draws upon Richard Lorenz, "Johan Hagemeyer: A Lifetime of Camera Portraits," *The Archive* 16 (June 1982), Center for Creative Photography.

69 "Life has been": Letter from Edward Weston to Johan Hagemeyer, 18 April 1921, Weston-Hagemeyer Collection, Center for Creative Photography.

70 "Nina": Giovanni Battista Pergolesi, "Nina," *Italian Songs of the Classical Period* (New York: G. Schirmer, 1904).

70 "I have written you": Letter from Tina Modotti to Johan Hagemeyer, 17 September 1921, Weston-Hagemeyer Collection, Center for Creative Photography.

71 "There are innumerable": Roubaix de l'Abrie Richey cited in Tina Modotti-Richey, *The Book of Robo* (Los Angeles, 1923), 12.

71 "the beauty and the charm": Ibid., 13.

71 "the curse of": Ibid., 10.

72 "T goes to Mexico": Letter from Edward Weston to Johan Hagemeyer, n.d., Weston-

Hagemeyer Collection, Center for Creative Photography.

72 "a modest, provincial": Harry Lawton's interview with Peter Krasnow, 6 June 1970, Sadakichi Hartmann Collection, University of California, Riverside.

72 Tom Sawyer: Ben Maddow, *Edward Weston: His Life* (New York: Aperture, 1989), 47.

72 "And then what joy!": Edward Weston cited ibid., 58.

73 "tough, 'insufferable'": Ben Maddow, "Venus Beheaded: Weston and His Women," *New York,* 24 February 1975, 49.

73 "gave you her heart": Nancy Newhall, ed., *The Daybooks of Edward Weston: I. Mexico* (Millerton, New York: Aperture, 1973), xvi.

73 "the first important": Ibid., 145.

73 "sophisticated, magnificent": Harry Lawton's interview with Peter Krasnow.

73 "the most terrible": Letter from Ricardo Gómez Robelo to Edward Weston, 19 September [1922?], Edward Weston Archive, Center for Creative Photography.

73 "drift[s] of jonquils": Letter from Margrethe Mather to Edward Weston, n.d., Edward Weston Archive, Center for Creative Photography.

74 "Feeling his way": Harry Lawton's interview with Peter Krasnow.

74 "an intentional disregard": Modotti-Richey, *The Book of Robo,* 12.

74 "Oh, I hope": Letter from Tina Modotti to Johan Hagemeyer, 17 September 1921, Weston-Hagemeyer Collection, Center for Creative Photography.

74 She kept a print: Mildred Constantine, *Tina Modotti: A Fragile Life* (San Francisco: Chronicle Books, 1993), 47.

75 post office box: In late 1922 or early 1923, Tina would make a submission to a literary journal using, as her return address, Post Office Box 852, Los Angeles. The original is in the collection of the Beinecke Rare Book and Manuscript Library, Yale University Library, New Haven, Connecticut.

76 "small, lone studio": Prentice Duell, "Textiles and Interior Decoration Department: A Note on Batik," *California Southland* 23 (November 1921): 19.

76 "There are only": Letter from Tina Modotti to Johan Hagemeyer, 17 September 1921, Weston-Hagemeyer Collection, Center for Creative Photography.

76 "O slow and sad": Roubaix de l'Abrie Richey, n.d., collection of Ruth and LaBrie Ritchie.

76 "Tina is wine red": Roubaix de l'Abrie Richey cited in Modotti-Richey, *The Book of Robo,* 59.

76 "Tina has to run around": Letter from Marionne Richey to Roubaix de l'Abrie Richey, 6 January 1922.

77 "We had been looking": Letter from Rose Richey to Roubaix de l'Abrie Richey, 24 December 1921.

77 "Everyone carries a cane": Letter from Roubaix de l'Abrie Richey to Tina Modotti, 16 December 1921.

77 "a silver bracelet": Letter from Rose Richey to Roubaix de l'Abrie Richey, 24 December 1921.

78 "wonderful and beautiful city": Letter from Roubaix de l'Abrie Richey to Tina Modotti, 17 December 1921.

78 "Boys driving turkeys": Letter from Roubaix de l'Abrie Richey to Tina Modotti, 23 December 1921.

79 "I thought of you": Letter from Roubaix de l'Abrie Richey to Tina Modotti, 29 December 1921.

79 "Tina received": Letter from Rose Richey to Roubaix de l'Abrie Richey, 4 January 1922.

79 "It is the greatest": Letter from Roubaix de l'Abrie Richey to Tina Modotti, 20 December 1921.

79 "palatial mansion": Ibid.

79 "never tasted anything better": Ibid.

80 "a dirty, crumbling": Letter from Roubaix de l'Abrie Richey to Tina Modotti, 23 December 1921.

80 "I am planning": Letter from Roubaix de l'Abrie Richey to Marionne Richey, 22 January 1922.

80 "remain [in Mexico]": Letter from Roubaix de l'Abrie Richey to Rose Richey, 28 January 1922.

80 "take orders": Letter from Roubaix de l'Abrie Richey to Tina Modotti, 17 December 1921.

81 "girl with the topaz eyes": Pauline Frederick clipping file, Academy of Motion Picture Arts and Sciences, Beverly Hills, California.

81 "comeback in motion pictures": *Variety,* 16 December 1921.

81 "they are willing": Letter from Roubaix de l'Abrie Richey to Tina Modotti, 17 December 1921.

81 "I am always thinking": Letter from Roubaix de l'Abrie Richey to Tina Modotti, 22 December 1921.

81 "I am always thinking about": Letter from Roubaix de l'Abrie Richey to Tina Modotti, 23 December 1921.

81 "And how are": Letter from Roubaix de l'Abrie Richey to Tina Modotti, 1 January 1922.

82 "It has been": Letter from Roubaix de l'Abrie Richey to Rose Richey, 3 January 1922.

82 "A letter from you": Letter from Roubaix de

l'Abrie Richey to Tina Modotti, 7 January 1922.

82 "Tell Tina": Letter from Roubaix de l'Abrie Richey to Rose Richey, 22 January 1922.

83 "So great": Letter from Roubaix de l'Abrie Richey to Tina Modotti, 19 January 1922.

83 "artists' paradise": Letter from Roubaix de l'Abrie Richey to Edward Weston, 23 December 1921, Edward Weston Archive, Center for Creative Photography.

83 "[Tina and Edward]": Letter from Rose Richey to Roubaix de l'Abrie Richey, 1 January 1922.

83 "is anxious too": Letter from Marionne Richey to Roubaix de l'Abrie Richey, 16 January 1922.

83 "All day I was": Letter from Roubaix de l'Abrie Richey to Marionne Richey, 26 January 1922.

83 "Of course I shall be": Letter from Roubaix de l'Abrie Richey to Rose Richey, 23 January 1922.

83 "I can hardly wait": Letter from Roubaix de l'Abrie Richey to Marionne Richey, 30 January 1922.

84 "I intend to go": Letter from Beppo Modotti to Roubaix de l'Abrie Richey, 19 January 1922.

84 "Tina will no doubt": Letter from Roubaix de l'Abrie Richey to Marionne Richey, 26 January 1922.

84 "used to laugh": Newhall, ed., *The Daybooks of Edward Weston: I. Mexico,* 67.

85 "Edward: with tenderness": Letter from Tina Modotti to Edward Weston, 27 January 1922, Edward Weston Archive, Center for Creative Photography.

85 "Spank little Tina": Letter from Roubaix de l'Abrie Richey to Marionne Richey, 30 January 1922.

85 "HAVE SMALLPOX": Telegram from Roubaix de l'Abrie Richey to Tina Modotti, 3 February 1922.

86 "RECEIVED TELEGRAM": Letter from Tina Modotti to Rose Richey, 3 February 1922.

86 "By now you": Letter from Tina Modotti to Rose and Marionne Richey, 3 February 1922.

86 "I am sitting": Letter from Tina Modotti to Rose and Marionne Richey, 5 February 1922.

86 "You can imagine": Letter from Tina Modotti to Rose and Marionne Richey, 8 February 1922.

87 "I hope you": Letter from Tina Modotti to Rose and Marionne Richey, 9 February 1922.

88 "My poor dear": Letter from Tina Modotti to Rose and Marionne Richey, 11 February 1922.

88 *"My very dear":* Letter from Tina Modotti to Rose and Marionne Richey, 11 February 1922.

5. MEXICO CITY AND LOS ANGELES (1922–1923)

90 "I thought my heart": Letter from Tina Modotti to Rose and Marionne Richey, 14 February 1922.

90 "I am up here": Ibid.

91 "I walk the streets": Letter from Tina Modotti to Roy Rosen, [19?] March 1922, cited in Sarah M. Lowe, *Tina Modotti: Photographs* (New York: Harry N. Abrams, 1995), 20.

91 "Is it not strange": Letter from Tina Modotti to Rose and Marionne Richey, 11 February 1922.

92 "useless and unnecessary": Ibid.

92 "Truly, I feel": Ibid.

92 "impossible for me": Letter from Tina Modotti to Rose and Marionne Richey, 28 February 1922.

92 "many from": Letter from Tina Modotti to Rose and Marionne Richey, 17 February 1922.

92 "I worry so": Letter from Tina Modotti to Rose and Marionne Richey, 22 February 1922.

93 "I have never": Letter from Vola Dorée to Rose and Marionne Richey, 9 March 1922.

93 "Perhaps [Tina]": Letter from Roubaix de l'Abrie Richey to Rose Richey, 28 January 1922.

94 "...don't you feel": Letter from Tina Modotti to Rose and Marionne Richey, 11 February 1922.

94 "SHALL KEEP": Telegram from Tina Modotti to Rose and Marionne Richey, 22 February 1922.

94 "Your telegram": Letter from Tina Modotti to Rose and Marionne Richey, 22 February 1922.

94–95 "Well—in the first": Letter from Tina Modotti to Rose and Marionne Richey, 25 February 1922.

95 "Now I know why": Letter from Tina Modotti to Rose and Marionne Richey, 28 February 1922.

95 "It is useless": Letter from Tina Modotti to Rose and Marionne Richey, 1 March 1922.

95 "could have gotten": Letter from Tina Modotti to Rose and Marionne Richey, 7 March 1922.

95 "[Y]ou surely know": Letter from Tina Modotti to Rose and Marionne Richey, 6 March 1922.

95 "EXHIBIT OPENED": Telegram from Tina Modotti to Rose and Marionne Richey, 10 March 1922.

95 "slim, elegant": Elena Poniatowska's interview with Guadalupe Marín, n.d.

96 "trembl[ed] with emotion": Rafael Vera de Córdova, "Photographs as True Art," *El Universal Ilustrado*, 23 March 1922, reprinted in Beaumont Newhall and Amy Conger, eds., *Edward Weston Omnibus: A Critical Anthology* (Salt Lake City: Peregrine Smith, 1984), 13–16.

96 settling of accounts: Christiane Barckhausen-Canale makes this point in *Verdad y leyenda de Tina Modotti* (Mexico City: Editorial Diana, 1992), 78.

96 "La Perlotti": José Vasconcelos cited in Bertram D. Wolfe, *The Fabulous Life of Diego Rivera* (New York: Stein and Day, 1969), 193–194.

97 "Robelo rented": Letter from Tina Modotti to Rose and Marionne Richey, 21 February 1922.

97 "Yesterday—Sunday": Letter from Tina Modotti to Rose and Marionne Richey, 13 March 1922.

98 "I hardly ever go": Letter from Tina Modotti to Rose and Marionne Richey, 8 March 1922.

98 "So it is still raining": Letter from Tina Modotti to Rose and Marionne Richey, 28 February 1928.

98 "People here": Letter from Tina Modotti to Rose and Marionne Richey, 13 March 1922.

99 "I have felt": Letter from Tina Modotti to Rose and Marionne Richey, 7 March 1922.

99 "No doubt": Letter from Tina Modotti to Rose and Marionne Richey, 19 March 1922.

100 "I found my family": Letter from Tina Modotti to Rose and Marionne Richey, 3 April 1922.

101 "Oh! How bitter": Letter from Tina Modotti to Roy Rosen, [19?] March 1922, cited in Lowe, *Tina Modotti,* 20.

101 "I feel that": Letter from Tina Modotti to Johan Hagemeyer, 7 April 1922, Weston-Hagemeyer Collection, Center for Creative Photography, University of Arizona, Tucson.

102 "[T]enderness—pity": Letter from Edward Weston to Marionne Richey, 11 February 1922.

102 "Thank Myrto": Letter from Tina Modotti to Rose and Marionne Richey, 11 February 1922.

102 "Mr. Weston has": Letter from Tina Modotti to Rose and Marionne Richey, 28 February 1922.

102 "[A]lready many": Tina Modotti cited in Amy Conger, "Tina Modotti and Edward Weston: A Re-evaluation of Their Photography," in Peter C. Bunnell and David Featherstone, eds., *EW: 100: Centennial Essays*

in Honor of Edward Weston (Carmel, California: Friends of Photography, 1986), 67.

102 "How can I ever": Letter from Tina Modotti to Roy Rosen, [19?] March 1922, cited in Lowe, *Tina Modotti,* 20.

103 "Sunday night": Letter from Emmeline Brady to Tina Modotti, Rose Richey, and Marionne Richey, 25 May 1922.

103 "Rain on the low": R. W. Borough, "Art, Love and Death: Widow Must Sell Batiks," *Los Angeles Examiner,* 12 May 1922.

104 "And one wonders!": Tina Modotti-Richey, *The Book of Robo* (Los Angeles, 1923), 13.

104 "at a moment": Vittorio Vidali, *Retrato de mujer: Una Vida con Tina Modotti* (Puebla, Mexico: Universidad Autónoma de Puebla, 1984), 19.

104 "Plenipotentiary": *The Dial* 74 (May 1923): 474.

105 "is now living": Ibid., n.p.

105 photographic portraiture: Therese Thau Heyman, "Modernist Photography and the Group f.64," in Paul J. Karlstrom, ed., *On the Edge of America: California Modernist Art, 1900–1950* (Berkeley and Los Angeles: University of California Press, 1996), 259.

105 "the problem of": Letter from Tina Modotti to Edward Weston, 7 July 1925, Edward Weston Archive, Center for Creative Photography.

106 "You don't know": Letter from Tina Modotti to Edward Weston, c. 8 January 1928, Edward Weston Archive, Center for Creative Photography.

106 "[realizing] more fully": Letter from Edward Weston to Johan Hagemeyer, 23 February 1922, Weston-Hagemeyer Collection, Center for Creative Photography.

106 opening a portrait studio: Ben Maddow, *Edward Weston: His Life* (New York: Aperture, 1989), 89.

107 "I looked out": Letter from Tina Modotti to Edward Weston, October 1922, cited in Maddow, *Edward Weston,* 89.

107 "Have you heard": Letter from Tina Modotti to Johan Hagemeyer, 17 October 1922, Johan Hagemeyer Archive, Center for Creative Photography.

108 much-anticipated exhibition: Thomas F. Walsh, *Katherine Anne Porter and Mexico: The Illusion of Eden* (Austin: University of Texas Press, 1992), 57–61; Joan Givner, *Katherine Anne Porter: A Life* (New York: Simon and Schuster, 1982), 165–167.

109 "What would I do": Letter from Edward Weston to Ramiel McGehee, 28 December 1922, Edward Weston Archive, Center for Creative Photography.

109 "We leave for": Letter from Edward Weston to Johan Hagemeyer, 11 January 1923,

Weston-Hagemeyer Collection, Center for Creative Photography.

109 "a joke to": Nancy Newhall, ed., *The Day-books of Edward Weston: I. Mexico* (Millerton, New York: Aperture, 1973), 13.

109 "fine friendship": Letter from Edward Weston to Flora Weston, 1 September 1923, Edward Weston Archive, Center for Creative Photography.

109 "a hostage to": Maddow, *Edward Weston,* 94.

109 "trial marriage": Letter from Edward Weston to Johan Hagemeyer, 15 November 1924, Weston-Hagemeyer Collection, Center for Creative Photography.

109 fibroid tumors: Margaret Hooks, *Tina Modotti: Photographer and Revolutionary* (San Francisco: Pandora, 1993), 205.

109 "not to have a baby": Letter from Tina Modotti to Rose and Marionne Richey, 11 February 1922.

110 "I would like": Vidali, *Retrato de mujer,* 19.

110 "Will you come": Newhall, ed., *The Daybooks of Edward Weston: I. Mexico,* 18.

110 "hidden love": Walter Kaufmann, trans. and ed., *The Portable Nietzsche* (New York: Viking Press, 1968), 228.

110 "spent many vivid hours": Newhall, ed., *The Daybooks of Edward Weston: I. Mexico,* 10.

110 "April 14": Johan Hagemeyer diary, Johan Hagemeyer Archive, Center for Creative Photography.

111 Mexican freighter reeked: Hooks, *Tina Modotti,* 65.

6. Mexico City (1923–1924)

Many of Tina Modotti's photographs have not yet been definitively dated. Thus, the photographic chronology in this book is, in part, conjectural.

115 "regeneration and exaltation": This phrase is José Vasconcelos's.

116 "A moment of": Nancy Newhall, ed., *The Daybooks of Edward Weston: I. Mexico* (Millerton, New York: Aperture, 1973), 75–76.

116 "like so many": Letter from Roubaix de l'Abrie Richey to Tina Modotti, 1 January 1922.

117 elegant sprays of calla lilies: Gianfranco Ellero, "Stilemi nativi nella fotografia di Tina Modotti," *Quaderni della FACE* 81 (July–December 1992): 24.

117 "feel Mexican": *El Universal Ilustrado,* 27 September 1923, Edward Weston Archive, Center for Creative Photography, University of Arizona, Tucson.

117 "humane [and]…genuine": Vittorio Vidali, *Retrato de mujer: Una Vida con Tina Modotti* (Puebla, Mexico: Universidad Autónoma de Puebla, 1984), 18.

117 "her eyes full": Bertram D. Wolfe, *The Fabulous Life of Diego Rivera* (New York: Stein and Day, 1969), 192.

118 "a sort of sweet-oil": Anita Brenner cited in Susannah Joel Glusker, *Anita Brenner: A Mind of Her Own* (Austin: University of Texas Press, 1998), 123.

119 "…[C]louds!": Newhall, ed., *The Daybooks of Edward Weston: I. Mexico,* 21.

119 "The clouds are": Inscription on photograph sent from Tina Modotti to Rose Richey, n.d., private collection.

120 "eighteen amber beads": Newhall, ed., *The Daybooks of Edward Weston: I. Mexico,* 16.

120 "Caught in the act": Inscription on photograph sent from Tina Modotti to Rose Richey, n.d., private collection.

121 "O, that is only": Newhall, ed., *The Daybooks of Edward Weston: I. Mexico,* 68.

121 "Long life": Guest register, Edward Weston Archive, Center for Creative Photography.

121 "Photography begins": Exhibition announcement, Edward Weston Archive, Center for Creative Photography.

121 "the very substance": Newhall, ed., *The Daybooks of Edward Weston: I. Mexico,* 55.

121 "The business of a work": William Mortensen, "Venus and Vulcan," *Camera Craft,* May 1934, 206, cited in Therese Thau Heyman, "Modernist Photography and the Group f.64," in Paul J. Karlstrom, ed., *On the Edge of America: California Modernist Art, 1900–1950* (Berkeley and Los Angeles: University of California Press, 1996), 245.

122 "full of half-baked": Newhall, ed., *The Daybooks of Edward Weston: I. Mexico,* 32.

123 "a strictly normal": John Charlot, *Jean Charlot: A Retrospective* (Honolulu: The University of Hawai'i Art Gallery, 1990), 46. Jean Charlot used these words in speaking of the painter Paul Cézanne. John Charlot believes they apply equally to his father, Jean Charlot.

123 "[W]e were looking": Mildred Constantine's interview with Anita Brenner, n.d., The Getty, Research Institute for the History of Art and the Humanities, Los Angeles, California.

123 "[W]e were all poor": Elena Poniatowska's interview with Carlos Orozco Romero, n.d.

124 "capable of great": Monna Sala cited in Christiane Barckhausen-Canale, *Verdad y leyenda de Tina Modotti* (Mexico City: Editorial Diana, 1992), 96–97.

124 "really screw[ed] up": Manuel Alvarez Bravo cited by Doris Heyden in Hooks, *Tina Modotti,* 155.

125 "Mazatlán": Inscriptions on photographs sent from Tina Modotti to Rose Richey, n.d., private collection.

125 "See?": Letter from Tina Modotti to Johan Hagemeyer, 27 February 1924, Weston-Hagemeyer Collection, Center for Creative Photography.

126 discerned eroticism: Letter from Tina Modotti to Edward Weston, 26 June 1927, Edward Weston Archive, Center for Creative Photography.

126 "white massed purity": Carleton Beals, "Tina Modotti," *Creative Art* 4 (February 1929): xlviii.

126 "a projection of": Sarah M. Lowe, *Tina Modotti: Photographs* (New York: Harry N. Abrams, 1995), 24.

126 "the last rose": Pablo Neruda, "Tina Modotti Is Dead," in *Residence on Earth*, trans. Donald D. Walsh (New York: New Directions Books, 1973), 325.

127 "Tina and I": Letter from Edward Weston to Johan Hagemeyer, 27 February 1924, Weston-Hagemeyer Collection, Center for Creative Photography.

127 "because of grave conditions": Newhall, ed., *The Daybooks of Edward Weston: I. Mexico*, 42.

127 "workers in paints": Anita Brenner, *Idols Behind Altars: The Story of the Mexican Spirit* (Boston: Beacon Press, 1970), 249.

128 "an amusing contrast": Newhall, ed., *The Daybooks of Edward Weston: I. Mexico*, 43.

128 Most likely: Felipe Teixidor believed that Modotti and Hernández Galván were romantically involved. Numerous references to Hernández Galván appear in Weston's *Daybooks* between December 1923 and March 1924.

128 "accustomed to certain things": Anita Brenner diary, 2 December 1925, cited in Glusker, *Anita Brenner*, 42.

128 On one memorable occasion: Carleton Beals, "Tina Modotti: Communist Agent," unpublished typescript, Carleton Beals Archive, Boston University, Boston, Massachusetts.

128 "citizen artists": D. Anthony White, *Siqueiros* (Encino, California: Floricanto Press, 1994), 55.

129 as Comintern members: Ibid., 88.

129 "We certainly have been": Letter from Edward Weston to Flora Weston, 29 March 1924, Edward Weston Archive, Center for Creative Photography.

129 "a veritable bed sheet": Wolfe, *The Fabulous Life of Diego Rivera*, 153.

129 "those horrible frescoes": Brenner, *Idols Behind Altars*, 258.

129 "new walls": Alicia Azuela, "*El Machete* and *Frente a Frente*, Art Committed to Social Justice in Mexico," *Art Journal* 52 (Spring 1993): 83.

130 "his hearty embrace": Newhall, ed., *The Daybooks of Edward Weston: I. Mexico*, 98.

131 Her first published photograph: *El Universal Ilustrado*, 19 July 1924.

132 "She is very happy": Newhall, ed., *The Daybooks of Edward Weston: I. Mexico*, 69.

132 "We have been married": Ibid., 87–88.

132 "Next time": Ibid., 22.

133 "...in case she": Letter from Tina Modotti to Edward Weston, December 1925 or January 1926, Edward Weston Archive, Center for Creative Photography.

133 Felipe Teixidor later remembered: Margaret Hooks, *Tina Modotti: Photographer and Revolutionary* (San Francisco: Pandora, 1993), 98.

133 "not infrequent": Ben Maddow, *Edward Weston: His Life* (New York: Aperture, 1989), 118.

133 "For weeks it hung": Ibid., 119.

133 "[S]heer aesthetic form": Nancy Newhall, ed., *The Daybooks of Edward Weston: II. California* (Millerton, New York: Aperture, 1973), 32.

134 "She called me": Ben Maddow, "Venus Beheaded: Weston and His Women," *New York*, 24 February 1975: 50.

134 "The scandal exploded": Tina Modotti cited in Vidali, *Retrato de mujer*, 18.

135 "To a motorcycle": *El Universal Ilustrado*, 27 September 1923.

136 "a gentle abstract": Letter from Tina Modotti to Edward Weston, 29 December 1924, Edward Weston Archive, Center for Creative Photography.

136 "Send a telegram": Elena Poniatowska's interview with Lulu Quintanilla, n.d.

137 "nothing by comparison": Newhall, ed., *The Daybooks of Edward Weston: I. Mexico*, 101.

137 "[accept] all": Tina Modotti, "On Photography," *Mexican Folkways* 5, no. 4 (October–December 1929): 196–198. Reprinted in *Frida Kahlo and Tina Modotti* (London: Whitechapel Art Gallery, 1982), 28.

137 "Tina and I": Letter from Edward Weston to Johan Hagemeyer, postmarked 13 October 1924, Weston-Hagemeyer Collection, Center for Creative Photography.

138 "[Modotti was]": Mildred Constantine's interview with Anita Brenner, n.d., The Getty, Research Institute for the History of Art and the Humanities, Los Angeles, California.

138 "more abstract": Diego Rivera, "Edward Weston and Tina Modotti," *Mexican Folkways* 2, no. 1 (April/May 1926): 16–17. Reprinted in *Frida Kahlo and Tina Modotti* (London: Whitechapel Art Gallery, 1982), 29.

138 "the Emperor of Photography": *El Sol* (Guadalajara), 5 September 1925.

138 only a sprinkling were women: According to

art historian Eli Bartra, the 1900 census counted four female photographers in Mexico City. Before Tina Modotti, the best known was Natalia Baquedano Hurtado (1872–1936). See Eli Bartra, "Women and Portraiture in Mexico," *History of Photography* 20 (Autumn 1996): 220–225.

138 "I shall write": Letter from Edward Weston to Johan Hagemeyer, 15 November 1924, Weston-Hagemeyer Collection, Center for Creative Photography.

139 swashbuckler film: Released in 1923 by Metro Picture Corporation and presented in Mexico City that July, *Scaramouche* starred the Mexican actor Ramon Novarro, dubbed "the New Valentino." Novarro's character, André Moreau, is a dashing aristocrat as well as an actor who plays the buffoonish Scaramouche, a cowardly braggart in commedia dell'arte tradition and a character not unlike the Stenterello of Modotti's theater days. A story of honor, love, and revenge, *Scaramouche* is set against the backdrop of the impending French Revolution.

139 "...Edward Edward": Letter from Tina Modotti to Edward Weston, 27 December 1924, Edward Weston Archive, Center for Creative Photography. Around this time, Tina made a will in which she left her belongings to Edward and expressed a desire to be cremated.

7. MEXICO CITY (1925–1926)

140 "such a night!": Nancy Newhall, ed., *The Daybooks of Edward Weston: I. Mexico* (Millerton, New York: Aperture, 1973), 117–118.

141 "The fog sweeps": Ibid., 118.

141 "How relieved": Letter from Tina Modotti to Edward Weston, 30 December 1924, Edward Weston Archive, Center for Creative Photography, University of Arizona, Tucson.

142 "I may be": Letter from Tina Modotti to Edward Weston, 2 April 1925, Edward Weston Archive, Center for Creative Photography.

142 "I have not been": Letter from Tina Modotti to Edward Weston, 7 July 1925, Edward Weston Archive, Center for Creative Photography.

143 More insidiously: In dedicating a portrait to a friend, Tina once used the phrase "sacred fire" in a manner suggesting a meaning of "exhilarating fervor for life and love." Modotti's deprecating references to her photography appear in letters written to Edward Weston between 1925 and 1928, in the Edward Weston Archive, Center for Creative Photography.

143–44 "this precious work": Letter from Tina Modotti to Edward Weston, 8 January 1928, Edward Weston Archive, Center for Creative Photography.

144 "[I am an antifascist]": *La Prensa,* 14 January 1929.

144 "My life is": Tina Modotti cited by Agueda Serna Morales in an interview by Christiane Barckhausen-Canale, n.d.

145 "The lungs of Russia": Manuel Maples Arce, "Urbe, Super-poema Bolchevique en Cinco Cantos," 1924, cited in Jean Franco, *The Modern Culture of Latin America: Society and the Artist* (New York: Frederick A. Praeger, 1967), 141.

146 Tina's short speech: Margaret Hooks, *Tina Modotti: Photographer and Revolutionary* (San Francisco: Pandora, 1993), 110.

147 "truly extraordinary graciousness": Elena Poniatowska's interview with Rafael Carrillo, 26 May 1981.

147 With the painter Amado de la Cueva: This account of Siqueiros's activities in Guadalajara is largely drawn from D. Anthony White, *Siqueiros* (Encino, California: Floricanto Press, 1994), 101–104.

148 "a silk blouse": *El Sol,* 25 August 1925, Edward Weston Archive, Center for Creative Photography.

148 "a darn good looking kid": Mercedes Modotti travel diary.

149 "I have been sitting": Newhall, ed., *The Daybooks of Edward Weston: I. Mexico,* 126.

149 "Tina insisted": Ibid., 129.

149 "parade of suitors": Nancy Newhall, ed., *The Daybooks of Edward Weston: II. California* (Millerton, New York: Aperture, 1973), 154.

149 "with sadness": Tina Modotti cited in Vittorio Vidali, *Retrato de mujer: Una Vida con Tina Modotti* (Puebla, Mexico: Universidad Autónoma de Puebla, 1984), 18.

150 For the Estridentista: This idea has been expressed by Sarah M. Lowe in *Tina Modotti, Photographs* (New York: Harry N. Abrams, 1995), 28–29.

151 "Here is Tina": Elena Poniatowska's interview with Pablo O'Higgins, 16 October 1980.

151 "she impressed me": Mildred Constantine, *Tina Modotti: A Fragile Life* (San Francisco: Chronicle Books, 1993), 70.

151 "crazy about Tina": María Jesús O'Higgins cited in Elena Poniatowska, "¿Por qué Tina Modotti?" in Comitato Tina Modotti, ed., *Tina Modotti: Una Vita nella storia* (Tavagnacco, Italy: Edizioni Arti Grafiche Friulane, 1995), 28.

151 "knew [Tina] intimately": Letter from Martha Dodd Stern to Mildred Constantine, 23 December 1974, Martha Dodd Stern

Papers, Library of Congress. Cited in Lowe, *Tina Modotti,* 149.

152 "immense longing": Inaugural Act of the National School of Agriculture, Chapingo, Mexico, 1923.

152 "strict and silent devotion": Ibid.

153 "worthy of anyone's": Newhall, ed., *The Daybooks of Edward Weston: I. Mexico,* 137.

153 "the Sistine Chapel": Carleton Beals, *Glass Houses* (Philadelphia: Lippincott, 1938), 181.

153 "In memory of": Mercedes Modotti travel diary, 1 December 1925.

153 "an immense palm": John A. Britton, *Carleton Beals: A Radical Journalist in Latin America* (Albuquerque: University of New Mexico Press, 1987), 33.

154 "Dear sister": Mercedes Modotti travel diary, 1 December 1925.

154 Down Union Street: As always with the Modotti sisters, Yolanda's romance had taken a tortuous course. In 1924, Guido discovered that Yolanda was planning to vacation with friends on Catalina Island. "I don't know how my friend found out the truth," Yolanda wrote Marionne Richey, "and he got quite mad at me, for the lie I told him and for what I was going to do. The only way he would forgive me was to marry him and spend our vacation together as he intended to do. We have been engaged two years now, long enough for me to know that he will be a good husband. So I made up my mind to get married. I was rather disappointed to give up my trip to Catalina Island, but it was [easier] than to give him up." (Yolanda Modotti to Marionne Richey, postmarked 5 June 1924.) Yolanda later informed friends that her father had forced her to marry Gabrielli in order to obtain U.S. citizenship, though Guido was not naturalized until 1928, after the couple's divorce.

154 "You know what": Letter from Tina Modotti to Edward Weston, 23 January 1926, Edward Weston Archive, Center for Creative Photography.

155 "No detailed comments": Ibid.

155 "wooden expression": Letter from Tina Modotti to Edward Weston, 25 January 1926, Edward Weston Archive, Center for Creative Photography.

155 "[T]he other photographer": Ibid.

155 "things...very chaotic": Ibid.

155 Closer to home: Information about Modotti's relationship with Consuelo Kanaga is drawn from Lowe, *Tina Modotti,* 30, and Barbara Head Millstein and Sarah M. Lowe, *Consuelo Kanaga: An American Photographer* (Seattle, Washington: University of Washington Press, 1992), 125.

156 "I am going": Letter from Tina Modotti to Edward Weston, 23 January 1926, Edward Weston Archive, Center for Creative Photography.

156 "I have been": Letter from Tina Modotti to Edward Weston, 9 February 1926, Edward Weston Archive, Center for Creative Photography.

158 "spiritual inventory": Book jacket, *Idols Behind Altars* (Boston: Beacon Press, 1970).

158 "Have you read": Letter from Tina Modotti to Rose and Marionne Richey, 12 July 1926.

159 "the greasy hands": Newhall, ed., *The Daybooks of Edward Weston: I. Mexico,* 174–175.

160 "willingness to [see]": Frank Tannenbaum, *Peace by Revolution: An Interpretation of Mexico* (New York: Columbia University Press, 1933), 181–182.

160 "[W]e are quite": Letter from Edward Weston to Anita Brenner, 23 July 1926, cited in Amy Conger, *Edward Weston in Mexico: 1923–1926* (Albuquerque: University of New Mexico Press, 1983), 55.

161 "Tina gave a horrified": Newhall, ed., *The Daybooks of Edward Weston: I. Mexico,* 178.

161 "Rain fell every day": Ibid., 186.

161 "The miners sing": Ibid., 185.

161 "Weston *fini!*": Author's interview with Susannah Joel Glusker, 4 January 1996.

162 "More kisses and embraces": Newhall, ed., *The Daybooks of Edward Weston: I. Mexico,* 196.

162 "Srta. Tina": Amy Conger, "Tina Modotti: A Methodology, a Proposal, and a Lost Love Letter," in Comitato Tina Modotti, ed., *Tina Modotti,* 296. My account of this episode is based on Conger's research and interpretation.

163 "man's comprehensiveness": Walter Kaufmann, ed. and trans., *The Portable Nietzsche* (New York: Viking Press, 1968), 445.

163 "...I want to write": Letter from Tina Modotti to Edward Weston, 14 November 1926, Edward Weston Archive, Center for Creative Photography.

163 *"What thou lovest"*: The Center for Creative Photography's *The Archive* notes, "In an edition of *Modern American and British Poetry,* edited by Louis Untermeyer, which Weston and Modotti might have seen, Ezra Pound's Canto LXXXI is printed on page 172." Amy Stark, ed., "The Letters from Tina Modotti to Edward Weston," *The Archive* 22 (January 1986): 45n.

8. MEXICO CITY (1927–1928)

165 "Her studio was": Letter from Emily Edwards to Mildred Constantine, 19 January 1974, The Getty, Research Institute for the

History of Art and the Humanities, Los Angeles, California.

165 "Lately I have been": Letter from Tina Modotti to Edward Weston, 22 March 1927, Edward Weston Archive, Center for Creative Photography, University of Arizona, Tucson.

165 refusing to accept a centavo: Elena Poniatowska's interview with Máximo Pacheco, n.d.

165–66 The Orozcos and "black betrayal": Anita Brenner diary, 20 October 1927, cited in Susannah Glusker, "Anita Brenner: A Mind of Her Own" (Ph.D. dissertation, The Union Institute, 1995), 94.

166 "avalanche of work," *very good now,*" and "undertaken too much": Letter from Tina Modotti to Edward Weston, 4 June 1927, Edward Weston Archive, Center for Creative Photography.

167 "rather mixed up": Letter from Tina Modotti to Albert Bender, 17 November 1927, Albert Bender Collection, Special Collections, Mills College, Oakland, California.

167 Fernández Ledesma told: Elena Poniatowska's interview with Gabriel Fernández Ledesma, 20 May 1981.

167 "One eats spicy meals": Letter from John Dos Passos to Germaine Lucas-Championnière, 30 December 1926, cited in Townsend Ludington, *John Dos Passos: A Twentieth-Century Odyssey* (New York: E. P. Dutton, 1980), 250.

168 her own *tertulias:* Author's interview with Ella Wolfe, 13 November 1997.

168 "a woman of the": Elena Poniatowska's interview with Adelina Zendejas, 27 August 1981.

168 "I am always": Letter from Tina Modotti to Edward Weston, 4 June 1927, Edward Weston Archive, Center for Creative Photography.

168 "work she had to undertake": *La Prensa,* 14 January 1929.

168 "She was vital": Elena Poniatowska's interview with Juan de la Cabada, 19 October 1980.

168 "At that time": Manuel Alvarez Bravo cited in Frederick Kaufman, "An Essay of Memories," *Aperture* 147 (Spring 1997): 10.

168 "I suffered much": Tina Modotti cited in Vittorio Vidali, *Retrato de mujer: Una Vida con Tina Modotti* (Puebla, Mexico: Universidad Autónoma de Puebla, 1984), 18.

168 "To keep in contact": Letter from Tina Modotti to Edward Weston, 22 March 1927, Edward Weston Archive, Center for Creative Photography.

168 "Oh Edward": Letter from Tina Modotti to Edward Weston, 5 April 1929, Edward

Weston Archive, Center for Creative Photography.

169 "Tina dear": Letter from Edward Weston to Tina Modotti, 11 January 1928, cited in Christiane Barckhausen-Canale, *Verdad y leyenda de Tina Modotti* (Mexico City: Editorial Diana, 1992), insert between pages 176 and 177.

169 At Chapingo: Glusker, *Anita Brenner,* 92.

169 "In the middle": Bertram D. Wolfe, *The Fabulous Life of Diego Rivera* (New York: Stein and Day, 1969), 192.

169 "Tina is": Susannah Joel Glusker, *Anita Brenner: A Mind of Her Own* (Austin: University of Texas Press, 1998), 69.

170 "immortal portraits": Letter from Tina Modotti to Edward Weston, 25 December 1925 or January 1926, Edward Weston Archive, Center for Creative Photography.

171 "as I never before": Letter from Tina Modotti to Xavier Guerrero, cited in *Excelsior,* 16 January 1929.

171 "a nature pitched finer": Jean Charlot cited in Alma M. Reed, *The Mexican Muralists* (New York: Crown, 1960), 91.

171 "helped her to understand": Rafael Carrillo cited in Barckhausen-Canale, *Verdad y leyenda de Tina Modotti,* 128.

171 "too vague": Nancy Newhall, ed., *The Daybooks of Edward Weston: II. California* (Millerton, New York: Aperture, 1973), 5.

171 "I did get": John Dos Passos, *The Best Times: An Informal Memoir* (New York: New American Library, 1966), 171.

172 "the roots of": Xavier Guerrero, "A Mexican Painter," trans. Tina Modotti, *New Masses,* May 1927: 18. The photographs are among those Tina gave to Vocio.

172 "You were the one": Letter from Tina Modotti to Xavier Guerrero, cited in *Excelsior,* 16 January 1929.

172 "big, bright, sad": Mildred Constantine's interview with Fernando Gamboa, 20 January 1974.

173 "mystic radicalism": Anita Brenner diary, 1927, cited in Margaret Hooks, *Tina Modotti: Photographer and Revolutionary* (San Francisco: Pandora, 1993), 133.

174 "paying deserved attention": Renato Molina Enríquez, "Obras de Tina Modotti," *Forma* 4 (1927): 30.

174 "They pulled Panchita": Elena Poniatowska's interview with Gabriel Fernández Ledesma, 20 May 1981.

175 "Tina goes hard": Letter from Jean Charlot to Edward Weston, 15 August 1927, Edward Weston Archive, Center for Creative Photography.

175 "My God Edward": Letter from Tina Modotti to Edward Weston, 25 June 1927,

Edward Weston Archive, Center for Creative Photography.

176 "They were so": Letter from Emily Edwards to Mildred Constantine, 19 January 1974, The Getty, Research Institute for the History of Art and the Humanities.

177 "It is such" and "She is busy": Letter from Rose Richey to Marionne Richey, 30 July 1927.

177 "never [pretended]": Elena Poniatowska's interview with Pablo O'Higgins, 16 October 1980.

178 "in middle-class circles": Tina Modotti cited in Vidali, *Retrato de mujer,* 42.

179 "to simplify": Anita Brenner diary, 1927, cited in Hooks, *Tina Modotti,* 133.

179 "We spoke of": Vittorio Vidali, unpublished typescript cited in Barckhausen-Canale, *Verdad y leyenda de Tina Modotti,* 134.

180 "As you see": Ibid., 135.

180 "What is done": Walter Kaufmann, ed. and trans., *The Portable Nietzsche* (New York: Viking Press, 1968), 444.

180 "Well, this is": Elena Poniatowska's interview with Vittorio Vidali, 16–21 September 1981.

181 "a very reserved woman": Ibid.

181 P.O. Box: S.U.S.I. Archive, Berlin.

181 "family portraits": Jean Charlot cited in Mildred Constantine, *Tina Modotti: A Fragile Life* (San Francisco: Chronicle Books, 1993), 104.

181 "debasement and diminution": Marti Casanovas, "Las fotos de Tina Modotti: El anecdotismo revolucionario," *¡30-30!,* 10 July 1928: 4–5. Reprinted in *Frida Kahlo and Tina Modotti* (London: Whitechapel Art Gallery, 1982), 32. Casanovas was arguing the opposite viewpoint.

181 "...you little liar": Letter from Benvenuto Modotti to Tina Modotti, 18 October 1928, cited in Barckhausen-Canale, *Verdad y leyenda de Tina Modotti,* 341.

182 "Miss Modotti triumphed": *El Universal Ilustrado,* 23 August 1928, cited in José Antonio Rodríguez, "La Mirada de la Ruptura," *La Mirada de la Ruptura* (Mexico City: Consejo Nacional para la Cultura y las Artes, Instituto Nacional de Bellas Artes, Museo Estudio Diego Rivera, and Centro de la Imagen, 1994), 68. Rodríguez underscores the differences between the work of Modotti and Alvarez Bravo and that of other participating photographers.

182 "Gee, I wish": Letter from Tina Modotti to Edward Weston, 18 September 1928, Edward Weston Archive, Center for Creative Photography.

182 "a trace": Susan Sontag, *On Photography* (New York: Dell, 1977), 154.

183 "two Italians": Telegram from the Italian Ministry of Foreign Relations to the Ministry of the Interior, 3 July 1928, cited in Barckhausen-Canale, *Verdad y leyenda de Tina Modotti,* 138.

183 One late spring evening: My account of the meeting of Tina Modotti and Julio Antonio Mella is drawn from Mildred Constantine's interview with Rosendo Gómez Lorenzo, 25 January 1974, The Getty, Research Institute for the History of Art and the Humanities.

184 "the Adonis": Elena Poniatowska's interview with Adelina Zendejas, 27 August 1981.

184 "young, beautiful and insolent": Pablo de la Torriente Brau, *Ahora* 1934. Reprinted in *Revolución,* 15 January 1962.

186 "I'm sorry about": Letter from Xavier Guerrero to Tina Modotti, 24 June 1928, Instituto de Historia del Movimiento Comunista y de la Revolución Socialista de Cuba, cited in Barckhausen-Canale, *Verdad y leyenda de Tina Modotti,* 141.

186 "clear and inevitable": Letter from Tina Modotti to Xavier Guerrero, 15 September 1928, cited in *Excelsior,* 16 January 1929.

186 "My dear Tinísima": Letter from Julio Antonio Mella to Tina Modotti 11 September 1928, cited ibid.

187 "There is no doubt": Letter from Tina Modotti to Xavier Guerrero, 15 September 1928, cited ibid.

9. MEXICO CITY (1928–1929)

189 "We were very happy": Tina Modotti cited in *La Prensa,* 14 January 1929.

189 When she found the apartment empty: Adelina Zendejas cited in Adys Cupull, *Julio Antonio Mella en los mexicanos* (Mexico City: Ediciones El Caballito, 1983), 27.

189 "little mother": Letter from Julio Antonio Mella to Tina Modotti, 11 September 1928, cited in *Excelsior,* 16 January 1929.

189 "that back": Ibid.

190 she had photographed his erect penis: Amy Conger and Elena Poniatowska, *Compañeras de México: Women Photograph Women* (University Art Gallery: University of California, Riverside, 1990), 46.

190 With his pal Juan de la Cabada: Elena Poniatowska's interview with Juan de la Cabada, 19 October 1980.

191 But to see her palling: Hayden Herrera, *Frida: A Biography of Frida Kahlo* (New York: Harper & Row, 1983), 79, 86–89.

191 "Easy to sketch": Jean Charlot, foreword to José Clemente Orozco, *The Artist in New York: Letters to Jean Charlot and Unpublished Writings, 1925–1929* (Austin: University of Texas Press, 1974), 18.

192 "...I feel the genius": Letter from Tina Mo-dotti to Edward Weston, 18 September 1928, Edward Weston Archive, Center for Creative Photography, University of Arizona, Tucson.

192 Nonetheless, they broke ground: John Mraz makes this point in "From Positivism to Populism: Toward a History of Photojour-nalism in Mexico," *Afterimage* 18, no. 5 (January 1991), 8.

192 "propaganda pictures": Letter from Tina Modotti to Edward Weston, 23 May 1930, Edward Weston Archive, Center for Creative Photography.

192 Labeled, with bitter irony: These three photographs appeared in *El Machete* on 1 September 1928, 8 September 1928, and 23 June 1928, respectively.

193 "Carbó, *La Semana*": *El Universal*, 15 January 1929.

194 "exercised great vigilance": Pablo O'Higgins cited in Elena Poniatowska's interview with Vittorio Vidali, 16–21 September 1981.

195 "I didn't even think": *La Prensa*, 12 January 1929.

196 "If the price is": Christiane Barckhausen-Canale, *Verdad y leyenda de Tina Modotti* (Mexico City: Editorial Diana, 1992), 158.

196 "life was slipping": Carleton Beals, "Julio Antonio Mella," typescript dated 11 January 1929, Carleton Beals Archive, Boston University, Boston, Massachusetts.

197 "tropical jungle": Letter from Julio Antonio Mella to Tina Modotti, 11 September 1929, cited in *El Universal*, 16 January 1929.

197 Diego made sketches: Bertram D. Wolfe, *The Fabulous Life of Diego Rivera* (New York: Stein and Day, 1969), 231.

197 By early morning: My account of the aftermath of the murder of Julio Antonio Mella is drawn principally from accounts which appeared in the Mexico City newspapers *El Universal*, *Excelsior*, and *La Prensa* between 11 and 17 January 1929.

198 "trying to get rid": *La Prensa*, 12 January 1929.

198 "love nest": Ibid.

198 "For me, Julio Antonio": Tina Modotti cited in *Excelsior*, 14 January 1929.

198 "A woman of steel": *Excelsior*, 14 January 1929.

199 "the owner of": Carleton Beals, *The Great Circle: Further Adventures in Free-Lancing* (Philadelphia: J. B. Lippincott Company, 1940), 217.

199 "The interesting Italian": *El Universal*, 12 January 1929.

199 "lights her match": *Excelsior*, 16 January 1929.

199 "incorrigible innocent": Vittorio Vidali, *Retrato de mujer: Una Vida con Tina Modotti*

(Puebla, Mexico: Universidad Autónoma de Puebla, 1984), 13.

199–200 "the truth would": Tina Modotti cited in *La Prensa*, 12 January 1929.

200 "It's a lie": Ibid.

202 Three witnesses to the crime: Quotations in this exchange are from newspaper articles which appeared in *Excelsior*, *El Universal*, and *La Prensa* on 13 January 1929.

204 "shook noticeably": *La Prensa*, 13 January 1929.

204 "Photographic study": *El Universal*, 14 January 1929.

205 "TINA MODOTTI COMPANION": Telegram from Adolfo Roldán to Emilio Portes Gil, 12 January 1929, Fondo Presidentes, Archivo General de la Nación, Mexico City.

205 "What kind of country": Diego Rivera cited in *Excelsior*, 15 January 1929.

205 "I have not said": Tina Modotti cited in *El Universal*, 14 January 1929.

206 "...*Excelsior* is": *Excelsior*, 17 January 1929.

207 "discover in [Tina]": *Excelsior*, 16 January 1929.

207 "Tina Modotti, romantic": *El Universal*, 16 January 1929.

207 "deep secrets of her past": Ibid.

207 "Did you not": *Excelsior*, 16 January 1929.

210 "What happened": *El Universal*, 17 January 1929.

211 "amorous, egotist": Anita Brenner diary, 28 January 1929, cited in Susannah Joel Glusker, "Anita Brenner: A Mind of Her Own" (Ph.D. dissertation, The Union Institute, 1995), 94. Such was the judgment of Anita Brenner, living in New York, after reading the Mexican press. She continues: "One answer to the innumerable and stupid questions [asked during the investigation] is Tina in a coup....Asked if she loved Xavier, or if she had loved him greatly, she said, *'sí, en su época...'* ["yes, in his time"]."

211 "deprive Mella": *Excelsior*, 17 January 1929.

211 "This photograph was taken": *La Prensa*, 21 January 1929.

10. MEXICO CITY (1929–1930)

213 "a symbol around": Ione Robinson, *A Wall to Paint On* (New York: E. P. Dutton and Company, 1946), 92.

213 "so much suffering": Letter from Tina Modotti to Edward Weston, 5 April 1929, Edward Weston Archive, Center for Creative Photography, University of Arizona, Tucson.

214 "In Mella": Tina Modotti cited in Bertram D. Wolfe, *The Fabulous Life of Diego Rivera* (New York: Stein and Day, 1969), 232.

215 "You KNOW": Letter from Julio Antonio Mella to Tina Modotti, 11 September 1928, cited in *Excelsior,* 16 January 1929.

215 "Always remember, comrade": Pino Cacucci, *I fuochi, le ombre, il silenzio* (Bologna: Agalev Edizioni, 1988), 18. "Mella...[was]": Victor Alba, *Esquema histórico del comunismo en Iberoamerica* (Mexico City: Ediciones Occidentales, 1960), 61.

A full account of issues surrounding the assassination of Julio Antonio Mella lies outside the scope of this book. Evidence of Mella's Trotskyism includes his gift to a friend of a copy of Trotsky's *Opposition Bulletin* inscribed "with the goal of rearming Communism," his editorship of the short-lived magazine *El Tren blindado* (*The Armoured Train*), the name of which evokes Trotsky's agitprop railway car, and comments by Mexican Communist party secretary general Rafael Carrillo in a letter to Bertram and Ella Wolfe. For more ample discussion of this issue and of Mella's relationship with colleagues, see, for example, Olivia Gall, *Trotsky en México* (Mexico City: Ediciones Era, 1991); Alejandro Gálvez Cancino, "L'auto-absolution de Vidali et la mort de Mella," *Cahiers Léon Trotsky* 26 (June 1986); Arnoldo Martínez Verdugo, *Historia del comunismo en México* (Mexico City: Enlace/Grijalbo, 1987); and Hugh Thomas, *Cuba: The Pursuit of Freedom* (New York: Harper & Row, 1971).

K. S. Karol suggests that Mella had also been briefly expelled from the Cuban Communist party, which opposed his hunger strike as a breach of discipline. See K. S. Karol, *Guerrillas in Power: The Course of the Cuban Revolution* (New York: Hill & Wang, 1970), 65–66.

In 1925, rumors circulated in Moscow that Stalin forced Red Army commander Mikhail Frunze, who sympathized with Trotsky, to submit to a fatal operation. Regarding evidence of executions ordered before the terror, see Serge Schmemann, "Soviet Archives Offering a Partly Open, Clouded Window Onto the Past," *New York Times,* 26 April 1995.

Juan Vivès claims that his information concerning Mella's assassination cannot be verified in Cuban Communist Party archives because Fabio Grobart, the former head of Soviet secret services in the Americas, destroyed compromising documents pertaining to the period 1927–1959. Vivès's sources include the personal archives of Cuban politician Raúl Roa, ex-Cuban Communist party chief Juan Marinello, and Marinello's secretary, Juan Andreu. See Juan

Vivès, *Les Maîtres de Cuba* (Paris: Editions Robert Laffont, 1981), 62–63.

216 "Frankly": *La Prensa,* 14 January 1929.

216 *Excelsior* chimed in: *Excelsior,* 14 January 1929.

216 "she was pictured": Carleton Beals, "The Strange Death of Julio Antonio Mella," unpublished typescript, n.d., 2. Carleton Beals Archive, Boston University, Boston, Massachusetts.

216 "[W]hat of her now?": Susannah Joel Glusker, *Anita Brenner: A Mind of Her Own* (Austin: University of Texas Press, 1998), 69.

216 "the tragedy of my soul": Letter from Tina Modotti to Edward Weston, 5 April 1929, Edward Weston Archive, Center for Creative Photography.

217 "However the self": Robert Jay Lifton, *The Protean Self: Human Resilience in an Age of Fragmentation* (New York: Basic Books, 1993), 168. Lifton's work contributed greatly to my thinking about Tina Modotti's personality.

217 "I saw dear Tina": Letter from Monna Alfau to Edward Weston, 2 March 1929, Edward Weston Archive, Center for Creative Photography.

217 "Tina has sacrificed": Letter from Monna Alfau to Edward Weston, 18 September 1929, Edward Weston Archive, Center for Creative Photography.

217 "I am living": Letter from Tina Modotti to Edward Weston, 5 April 1929, Edward Weston Archive, Center for Creative Photography.

218 "where [artists]": Kenneth Rexroth, *An Autobiographical Novel* (Garden City, New York: Doubleday, 1966), 344.

218 "when I saw Tina": Robinson, *A Wall to Paint On,* 85–86.

219 photograph probably posed on Tina's roof: Mariana Figarella Mota made this observation in "Edward Weston y Tina Modotti en México. Su inserción dentro de las estrategias estéticas del arte post-revolucionario" (master's thesis, Universidad Nacional Autónoma de México), 166.

219 "The pictures Tina": Letter from Lee Simonson to Carleton Beals, 27 October 1928, Carleton Beals Archive, Boston University.

219 "she has depicted": Carleton Beals, "Tina Modotti," *Creative Art* 4, no. 2 (February 1929): xlviii.

220 "Tina has been": Robinson, *A Wall to Paint On,* 102.

220 "like a nun": Ibid., 86.

220 "a small party": Ibid., 98.

223 "I am sending": Letter from Tina Modotti to Edward Weston, 17 September 1929,

Edward Weston Archive, Center for Creative Photography.

223 "a perfect snapshot": Beals, "Tina Modotti," xlix.

224 "a kind of castle": Vittorio Vidali, *Retrato de mujer: Una Vida con Tina Modotti* (Puebla, Mexico: Universidad Autónoma de Puebla, 1984), 58.

224 "Only twenty": Letter from Tina Modotti to Edward Weston, 4 July 1929, Edward Weston Archive, Center for Creative Photography.

225 "She liked that book": Elena Poniatowska's interview with Manuel Alvarez Bravo, 12 September 1981.

225 "made a good atmosphere": Hayden Herrera, *Frida: A Biography of Frida Kahlo* (New York: Harper & Row, 1983), 100.

225 "But the most startling": Letter from Tina Modotti to Edward Weston, 17 September 1929, Center for Creative Photography.

226 "I, Diego": Baltasar Dromundo cited in Herrera, *Frida Kahlo,* 102.

226 "He will be considered": Letter from Tina Modotti to Edward Weston, 17 September 1929, Center for Creative Photography.

226 She consigned photographs: Advertisement in *New Masses,* October 1929.

226 "I believe that Agfa": "Boletín mensual de información fotográfica editado por el Departamento Fototécnico de Fábricas unidas," Agfa, August 1929, The Getty, Research Institute for the History of Art and the Humanities, Los Angeles, California.

227 she chatted to a German: Christiane Barckhausen-Canale, *Verdad y leyenda de Tina Modotti* (Mexico City: Editorial Diana, 1992), 179.

227 "test myself anew": Glusker, *Anita Brenner,* 108.

227 "I look upon": Letter from Tina Modotti to Anita Brenner, 9 October 1929, cited in Susannah Glusker, "Anita Brenner: A Mind of Her Own" (Ph.D. dissertation, The Union Institute, 1995), 160.

227 Tina also occupied herself: Udine's noted puppet theater, centered on the adventures of the stock character Facanape Salmistreli, may have piqued Tina's interest in marionettes. In 1940, the impresario Vittorio Podrecca successfully brought Friulian puppetry to Broadway as "Theatre of the Piccoli."

228 "I am thinking": Letter from Tina Modotti to Edward Weston, 17 September 1929, Edward Weston Archive, Center for Creative Photography.

228 "a photographer, nothing": Tina Modotti,

"On Photography," *Mexican Folkways* 5, no. 4 (October–December 1929), 196–198.

229 "perfect platinum prints": Carleton Beals, "Tina Modotti," xlix.

229 A typographers' group: *Tina Modotti* (1942), 5. Vittorio Vidali's memoir of his life with Tina transposes these incidents to the time of her death.

229 "the typewriter you have": Letter from Julio Antonio Mella to Tina Modotti, 11 September 1928, cited in *Excelsior,* 16 January 1929.

229 "Many have fallen": Julio Antonio Mella, "El cuarto aniversario de la Universidad Popular José Martí," cited in Erasmo Dumpierre, *Julio Antonio Mella biografía* (Havana: Secretaria de trabajo ideológico, Comisión Nacional de Historia, 1975), 78.

230 "sending her flowers": Rosa Rodríguez cited in Margaret Hooks, *Tina Modotti: Photographer and Revolutionary* (San Francisco: Pandora, 1993), 192.

230 "Baltasar": Tina Modotti cited in Barckhausen-Canale, *Verdad y leyenda de Tina Modotti,* 173.

230 "like my native land": Elena Poniatowska's interview with Baltasar Dromundo, 12 June (no year date).

230 Like all Comintern parties: Harvey Klehr, John Earl Haynes, and Fridrikh Igorevich Firsov, *The Secret World of American Communism* (New Haven and London: Yale University Press, 1995), 21.

231 "calumnies, hates": Vittorio Vidali, *Retrato de mujer,* 13.

231 "a difficult and stupid": Elena Poniatowska's interview with Pablo O'Higgins, 16 October 1980.

231 Tina also made regular calls: Teresa Gurza's interview with Julio Rosovski, CEMOS, Mexico City, cited in Hooks, *Tina Modotti,* 195.

231 A small, dark, nervous man: Vittorio Vidali, unpublished typescript, cited in Barckhausen-Canale, *Verdad y leyenda de Tina Modotti,* 174.

231 "And what does Tina wish": Vittorio Vidali cited ibid., 175.

232 the notorious general Eulogio Ortiz: Carleton Beals, unpublished typescript, 29 December 1929, Carleton Beals Archive, Boston University.

232 "medicine or anything": Thomas F. Walsh's interview with Mary Louis Doherty, c. 1982, Thomas F. Walsh Papers, Special Collections, University of Maryland at College Park.

232 "little barred skylight": Letter from Tina Modotti to Edward Weston, 25 February

1930, Edward Weston Archive, Center for Creative Photography.

232 "...I am strictly": Letter from Tina Modotti to Beatrice Siskind, 17 February 1930, Fondo Presidentes, Archivo General de la Nación, Mexico City.

233 "What doesn't kill me": Letter from Tina Modotti to Edward Weston, 25 February 1930, Edward Weston Archive, Center for Creative Photography.

233 "vile yellow press": Ibid.

233 "swallowed with": Ibid.

233 "...who would have thought": Letter from Tina Modotti to Edward Weston, 9 March 1930, Edward Weston Archive, Center for Creative Photography.

233 "was delighted": Thomas F. Walsh's interview with Mary Louis Doherty.

233 "Tina's leaving": Letter from Mary Louis Doherty to Edward Weston, 15 May 1930, Edward Weston Archive, Center for Creative Photography.

233 "Tina was putting herself": Ibid.

234 "very simple": Lola Alvarez Bravo, *Recuento fotográfico* (Mexico City: Editorial Penélope, 1982), 97.

234 "so different": Ibid., 97–98.

234 "I'm leaving": Ibid., 98.

234 "a very powerful": Elena Poniatowska's interview with Manuel Alvarez Bravo.

235 "a kind of a haze": Letter from Tina Modotti to Edward Weston, 25 February 1930, Edward Weston Archive, Center for Creative Photography.

235 She was traveling on an Italian passport: Tina's U.S. passport, fraudulently secured by Robo in January 1922, would have been valid for two years and renewable for a total of no more than five. Telephone interview with Donald Beck, U.S. State Department, 2 April 1998.

235 "But who is this idiot": Elena Poniatowska's interview with Vittorio Vidali, 16–21 September 1981.

235 "the strange feeling": Letter from Tina Modotti to Edward Weston, 9 March 1930, Edward Weston Archive, Center for Creative Photography.

235 "The worst of": Ibid.

236 Vittorio, meanwhile: Elena Poniatowska's interview with Vittorio Vidali.

236 "internationally famous": *New Orleans Times-Picayune,* 6 March 1930.

11. Berlin and Moscow (1930–1932)

239 "Who knows": Tina Modotti cited in Vittorio Vidali, *Retrato de mujer: Una Vida con Tina Modotti* (Puebla, Mexico: Universidad Autónoma de Puebla, 1984), 20.

239 "dangerous Communist": Ibid.

240 "Tina is elegant": Ibid., 21.

240 "most useful to": Letter from Tina Modotti to Edward Weston, 14 April 1930, Edward Weston Archive, Center for Creative Photography, University of Arizona, Tucson.

240 "Tina is silent": Vidali, *Retrato de mujer,* 22.

240 "Dear, lovely Tina": Nancy Newhall, ed., *The Daybooks of Edward Weston: II. California* (Millerton, New York: Aperture, 1973), 143.

241 "the strain": Letter from Tina Modotti to Edward Weston, 14 April 1930, Edward Weston Archive, Center for Creative Photography.

241 "[H]ow can I": Ibid.

242 "Have I told": Letter from Tina Modotti to Edward Weston, 23 May 1930, Edward Weston Archive, Center for Creative Photography.

243 "I still think": Ibid.

243 "Besides a smaller camera": Ibid.

244 "crap" and "nasty, cold": Ibid.

244 "this damned light": Letter from Tina Modotti to Edward Weston, 28 May 1930, Edward Weston Archive, Center for Creative Photography.

244 "I have enough": Ibid.

244 "Well, there is nothing": Letter from Tina Modotti to Edward Weston, 23 May 1930, Edward Weston Archive, Center for Creative Photography.

244 "must solve my own": Ibid.

244 "kindness...like": Ibid.

244 Pleasant, slender, and dark-eyed: Letter and photographs from Walter and Monica Heilig to author, 8 May 1998. I am most grateful to the Heiligs for their assistance.

245 "Even the type": Letter from Tina Modotti to Edward Weston, 23 May 1930, Edward Weston Archive, Center for Creative Photography.

245 Virendranath Chattopadhyaya: Janice R. MacKinnon and Stephen R. MacKinnon, *Agnes Smedley: The Life and Times of an American Radical* (Berkeley and Los Angeles: University of California Press, 1988), 70.

245 "the willies": Mildred Constantine's interview with Anita Brenner, n.d., The Getty, Research Institute for the History of Art and the Humanities, Los Angeles, California.

245 explained that her Red Aid work: Christiane Barckhausen-Canale, *Verdad y leyenda de Tina Modotti* (Mexico City: Editorial Diana, 1992), 232.

245 How that translated: Both Carleton Beals

and Mary Louis Doherty were aware of the trip to Spain. See Carleton Beals, "Tina Modotti: Communist Agent," unpublished typescript, 5, Carleton Beals Collection, Boston University, Boston, Massachusetts; and Thomas F. Walsh's interview with Mary Louis Doherty, c. 1982, Thomas F. Walsh Papers, Special Collections, University of Maryland at College Park.

246 Ibero-American Exposition: A roster of participating photographers appears in *Sevilla Exposición Ibero Americana catálogo oficial* (Barcelona: Joaquín Horta, 1929). The set of postcards sent to the Richeys is in the collection of Ruth and LaBrie Ritchie.

246 "delicious" person: From an interview with Lotte Jacobi in *Tina Modotti*, a film by Marie Bardischewski and Ursula Jeshel, Berlin, 1982.

247 "every person who": Egon Erwin Kisch, *Tina Modotti* (1942), 31.

247 "dangerous Communist": Barckhausen-Canale, *Verdad y leyenda de Tina Modotti*, 224.

247 "I have felt": Letter from Tina Modotti to Edward Weston, 23 May 1930, Edward Weston Archive, Center for Creative Photography.

247 They were ignorant: Gianfranco Ellero has unearthed a document in Udine city records listing Gioconda's profession as prostitute. Italian police records also mention her prostitution. See Gianfranco Ellero, *Tina Modotti in Carinzia e in Friuli* (Pordenone, Italy: Cinemazero, 1996), 60.

247 Several times, in years to come: Mario Montagnana, *Tina Modotti* (1942), 47.

247 "Are you crazy?" Vidali, *Retrato de mujer*, 23.

248 "have the capacity": Winifred Gallagher, *The Power of Place: How Our Surroundings Shape Our Thoughts, Emotions, and Actions* (New York: Poseidon Press, 1993), 96.

248 "a large, almost Oriental": Letter from Vittorio Vidali to Nino Capraro, 10 September 1927, Nino Capraro Papers, Immigration History Research Center, University of Minnesota, St. Paul.

248 "millions of children": Ella Winter, *And Not to Yield* (New York: Harcourt, Brace & World, 1965), 149.

249 "He didn't want": Vidali, *Retrato de mujer*, 25.

250 "...Tina was literally": Luis Checchini cited in Barckhausen-Canale, *Verdad y leyenda de Tina Modotti*, 243.

250 "with...the greatest": Tina Modotti cited ibid., 173.

250 "Tina felt": Vidali, *Retrato de mujer*, 28.

250 At 9:30 each morning: Much of the information concerning Tina's experiences at MOPR and life in Moscow derive from my interviews with Angelo Masutti, 27 January

and 2 February 1998, and I am most grateful to him. The research of Christiane Barckhausen-Canale was also very useful. See also Vittorio Vidali, *Diary of the Twentieth Congress of the Communist Party of the Soviet Union* (Westport, Connecticut: Lawrence Hill & Company, 1984), 91, 133.

251 "put into her head": Conchita Ruíz Funes's interview with Vittorio Vidali, Archivo de la Palabra, Mexico City.

251 "always the same": Author's interview with Angelo Masutti, 2 February 1998.

252 "I heard from Tina": Letter from Frances Toor to Joseph Freeman, 12 November 1931, Joseph Freeman Papers, Hoover Institution Archive, Stanford University, Stanford, California.

252 "festivities organized": Vidali, *Retrato de mujer*, 28.

252 "my husband": Moscow questionnaire, 1932, reproduced in Ellero, *Tina Modotti in Carinzia e in Friuli*, 132.

253 "for political reasons": Author's interview with Angelo Masutti, 27 January 1998.

253 "inner radiance": Vivian Gornick, *The Romance of American Communism* (New York: Basic Books, 1977), 13.

253 "was a woman": María Luisa Lafita cited in Christiane Barckhausen-Canale's interview with Elena Poniatowska, n.d.

253 "Everything that is done": Robert Conquest, *The Great Terror* (New York and Oxford, England: Oxford University Press, 1990), 115.

253 "This is a mighty beast": Anthony Ehrenpreis cited in Gornick, *The Romance of American Communism*, 241.

254 "I have been living": Letter from Tina Modotti to Edward Weston, 12 January 1931, Edward Weston Archive, Center for Creative Photography.

254 "Tina has cut": Letter from Edward Weston to Miriam Lerner, n.d., Miriam Lerner Papers, Bancroft Library, University of California at Berkeley.

254 "Well, Angelo": Author's interview with Angelo Masutti, 27 January 1998.

255 "He will be seventeen": Memorandum in the collection of Angelo Masutti.

255 "She was not often": Author's interview with Angelo Masutti, 2 February 1998.

256 In March: Barckhausen-Canale, *Verdad y leyenda de Tina Modotti*, 254.

256 "truly the ideal type": Vidali, *Retrato de mujer*, 29.

256 "making them disappear": Tina Modotti, "Report about My Arrest and Expulsion," 1933.

257 "fascistic-military": Tina Modotti, *5,000,000 Widows, 10,000,000 Orphans: Women! Do You*

Want That Again? (La Jolla, California: Parentheses Writing Series, 1996), 8, 9, 20.

257 "Black Shirt and Red Scarf": My thanks to Christiane Barckhausen-Canale for making this story available to me and translating it.

259 "Nothing is more": Tina Modotti, "Photography as a Weapon for Agitprop for Use by International Red Aid," *AIZ* 3 (1932). Reproduced in *Tina Modotti Exhibition,* the Italian Cultural Institute, London, n.d.

259 In contrast, *AIZ* never: *Camera as Weapon: Worker Photography Between the Wars* (San Diego: Museum of Photographic Arts, 1991), 25.

259 "rescue [a picture]": Walter Benjamin cited in Susan Sontag, *On Photography* (New York: Dell, 1977), 107.

259 first international conference: My account of Red Aid's international congress is drawn from G. Citerne, "Deux mois en Union Soviétique," *La Défense,* 24 March 1933 and 14 April 1933, and from *10 Ans de lutte contre la terreur blanche, le fascisme, la guerre, Congrès Mondial du S.R.I., Moscou, Novembre 1932, Résolutions* (Paris: Editions du S.R.I., 1933).

260 "Inside this vast": G. Citerne, "Deux mois en Union Soviétique," *La Défense,* 14 April 1933.

260 Later, by order: Christiane Barckhausen-Canale, "Aktualität von Tina Modotti," in Comitato Tina Modotti, ed., *Tina Modotti: Una Vita nella storia* (Tavagnacco, Italy: Edizioni Arti Grafiche Friulane, 1995), 57.

12. MOSCOW AND PARIS (1932–1935)

261 "This Italian revolutionary": Pablo Neruda, *Memoirs,* trans. Hardie St. Martin (Harmondsworth, England: Penguin Books, Ltd., 1978), 255.

261 "She seemed less": Lotte Jacobi cited in Christiane Barckhausen-Canale, *Verdad y leyenda de Tina Modotti* (Mexico City: Editorial Diana, 1992), 247.

261 Tina had arrived: Sarah M. Lowe, *Tina Modotti: Photographs* (New York: Harry N. Abrams, 1995), 45.

262 "dangerous, erroneous": Alexander Lavrentiev, *Alexander Rodchenko: Photography 1924–1954* (Edison, New Jersey: Knickerbocker Press, 1996), 25–26; Valery Stigneyev cited in Milton Esterow, "Sergei Gitman's 'Mad Invention,'" *ARTnews* March 1993, 43.

262 "was unhappy": Concha Michel cited in Margaret Hooks, *Tina Modotti: Photographer and Revolutionary* (San Francisco: Pandora, 1993), 220.

262 "I have asked": Letter from Ernestine Evans to Comrade Doletsky, 16 February 1931,

The Getty, Research Institute for the History of Art and the Humanities, Los Angeles, California.

263 British painter Felicia Browne: Herbert Matthews, *Half of Spain Died* (New York: Scribner's, 1973), 193.

263 "I will never write": Rubén Martínez Villena cited by Hugh Thomas, *Cuba: The Pursuit of Freedom* (New York: Harper & Row, 1971), 589.

263 "What kind of times": Bertolt Brecht, "To Those Born Later," in Bertolt Brecht, *Poems 1913–1956* (New York: Methuen, 1976), 318–319. An excerpt of this work appeared in *Camera as Weapon: Worker Photography Between the Wars* (San Diego: Museum of Photographic Arts, 1991).

263 "this, and no other": Pablo O'Higgins cited in Barckhausen-Canale, *Verdad y leyenda de Tina Modotti,* 249.

263 "all art was": Thomas F. Walsh, *Katherine Anne Porter and Mexico: The Illusion of Eden* (Austin: University of Texas Press, 1992), 149. These are O'Higgins's words as recorded by his friend, writer Katherine Anne Porter.

264 "was going to commit": Elena Poniatowska's interview with Pablo O'Higgins, 16 October 1980.

265 "had almost no interest": Vittorio Vidali, *Retrato de mujer: Una Vida con Tina Modotti* (Puebla, Mexico: Universidad Autónoma de Puebla, 1984), 27–28.

265 "...your little trip": Vittorio Vidali, *Missione a Berlino* (Milan: Vangelista Editore, 1978), 100.

266 "This is the beginning": Rudolf Diels, *Lucifer ante Portas* (Stuttgart: Deutsche Verlags-Anstalt, 1950), 194, cited in William L. Shirer, *The Rise and Fall of the Third Reich* (New York: Simon & Schuster, 1966), 192.

267 "a den of espionage": Vidali, *Missione a Berlino,* 103.

267 François Le Bihan: Author's interview with Cécile Rol-Tanguy, 3 February 1998. Anecdotes and quotations about Tina Modotti's life with the Le Bihan family derive from this interview.

269 "The pursuit of man": *Droit d'asile* (Paris: Editions du Secours Rouge International), 19. Red Aid pamphlets and articles were often unsigned or signed with pseudonyms. I am attributing *Droit d'asile* to Tina on the basis of its publication place and date (1934), its subject, and the reference to B. Traven.

269 *"Vive la solidarité":* *MOPR* 3 (March 1934): 7.

270 Contemporary historian: Gordon Brook-Shepherd, *The Austrians: A Thousand-Year Odyssey* (New York: Carroll & Graf, 1997),

281–282. Red Aid accounts are drawn from the European office's *Après notre défaite... Avant notre victoire (les Schutzbundler d'Autriche sur leurs combats de février)*, Défense Edition, 1934, as well as *Avec les familles des combattants viennois de février* and *Les femmes sous la terreur fasciste! Les femmes sur le front de solidarité et du combat!*

271 "Three children": *Après notre défaite...Avant notre victoire*, 31. Signed "P.M."

272 "impossible to struggle": André Marty, *L'Humanité*, 6 February 1934, cited in R. Dan Richardson, *Comintern Army: The International Brigades and the Spanish Civil War* (Lexington, Kentucky: University Press of Kentucky, 1982), 7.

272 As for the Schutzbund rebels: Robert Conquest, *The Great Terror* (New York and Oxford, England: Oxford University Press, 1990), 411.

273 "stay in Paris": Vidali, *Retrato de mujer*, 30.

273 "worse than [wartime]": Elena Poniatowska's interview with María Luisa Lafita, 15 December 1981.

273 In collaboration: Writer Ella Winter and her husband, writer and muckraker Lincoln Steffens, lived in Carmel, California, where they were friendly with Edward Weston.

274 "for urgent and powerful": *La Défense*, 19 October 1934.

274 "more reserved": Conchita Ruíz Funes's interview with Vittorio Vidali, Archivo de la Palabra, Mexico City.

274 "the year in which": Ibid.

274 "When she spoke": Ibid.

274 "I convinced myself": Vidali, *Retrato de mujer*, 31.

274 "A true Bolshevik": Yuri Pyatakov cited in Conquest, *The Great Terror*, 113.

275 "psychologically unacceptable": Nadezhda Krupskaya cited in Pierre Broué, *Trotsky* (Paris: Fayard, 1988), 405.

275 "almost screaming": Vidali, *Missione a Berlino*, 140.

275 "difficult moments": Ibid., 142.

276 "The [Kirov] tragedy": Si-lan Chen Leyda, *Footnote to History* (New York: Dance Horizons, 1984), 198–199.

276 "which was going to show": Ibid., 199.

276 the city's residents, Tina included: Elena Poniatowska's interview with María Luisa Lafita, 15 December 1981.

276 "[Behind] the vigorous": Simone Téry cited in *Tina Modotti* (1942), 26.

276 She pushed through her typewriter: Christiane Barckhausen-Canale, "Aktualität von Tina Modotti," in Comitato Tina Modotti, ed., *Tina Modotti: Una Vita nella storia* (Tavagnacco, Italy: Edizioni Arti Grafiche Friulane, 1995), 59.

277 "a special watchfulness": Vidali, *Retrato de mujer*, 32.

277 Years later, Vittorio: Conchita Ruíz Funes's interview with Vittorio Vidali, Archivo de la Palabra, Mexico City.

277 "more than one use": Author's telephone interview with Steve Higgins, 13 May 1998.

277 "almost as monumental": Jay Leyda cited in Mildred Constantine, *Tina Modotti: A Fragile Life* (San Francisco: Chronicle Books, 1993), 173.

277–78 Raised in Dayton, Ohio: Author's telephone interview with Martha Foley, 16 April 1998.

278 "Her work in the Russian cinema": Lawrence Estavan, comp., Mary A. Burgess, ed., *The Italian Theatre in San Francisco* (1939; reprint, San Bernardino, California: The Borgo Press, 1991), n.p.

278 "Angelo": The postcard is in the collection of Angelo Masutti. Pavlenko may instead refer to Oleg Pavlenko, Leyda's best friend and classmate. See Jay Leyda, *Kino: A History of the Russian and Soviet Film* (Princeton, New Jersey: Princeton University Press, 1983), 368.

278 "Tina is in": Letter from Mercedes Modotti to Rose Richey, 1 December 1935.

279 "I was so glad": Letter from Tina Modotti to Rose and Marionne Richey, 24 December 1935.

280 "that the Soviet": Vidali, *Retrato de mujer*, 32.

280 "the tropical Mussolini": Erasmo Dumpierre, *Julio Antonio Mella biografía* (Havana: Secretaria de trabajo ideológico, Comisión Nacional de Historia, 1975), 106.

281 "[I am an antifascist]": Tina Modotti, cited in *La Prensa*, 14 January 1929.

281 "If I were convinced": Anna Louisa Strong cited in Paul Willen, "Anna Louisa Goes Home Again," *The Reporter*, 7 April 1955, Hoover Institution Archives, Stanford University, Stanford, California.

281 "the law of passion": Vivian Gornick, *The Romance of American Communism* (New York: Basic Books, 1977), 15.

282 "...the veil present": Vidali, *Retrato de mujer*, 31–32.

282 "liked making love": Ibid., 57.

282 "I was madly": Elena Poniatowska's interview with Agueda Serna Morales, n.d.

282 After he struck out: Author's interview with Cécile Rol-Tanguy, 3 February 1998.

13. SPAIN (1936–1939)

286 *"Oggi in Spagna"*: Hugh Thomas, *The Spanish Civil War* (Harmondsworth, England: Penguin Books, Ltd., 1986), 453.

286 "was not, for her": Agueda Serna Morales

cited in Christiane Barckhausen-Canale, *Verdad y leyenda de Tina Modotti* (Mexico City: Editorial Diana, 1992), 300.

287 "it will completely": Agueda Serna Morales cited in Christiane Barckhausen-Canale's interview with Elena Poniatowska, n.d.

287 "the servant": Elena Poniatowska's interview with Vittorio Vidali, 16–21 September 1981.

287 "she spoke slowly": Enrique Castro Delgado, *Hombres made in Moscow* (Mexico City: self-published, 1968), 293.

287 "Live dangerously": Letter from Mercedes Modotti to Tina Modotti, 1 April 1939, cited in Gianfranco Ellero, *Tina Modotti in Carinzia e in Friuli* (Pordenone, Italy: Cine-mazero, 1996), 129.

287 "Tina was always": Conchita Ruíz Funes's interview with Vittorio Vidali, Archivo de la Palabra, Mexico City.

287 "If something had to be": Elena Poniatowska's interview with María Luisa Lafita, 15 December 1981.

288 "I met María": Francisco Galán, *Tina Modotti* (1942), 19.

288 "dreamed of a Spain": Mary Bingham de Urquidi, "Mercy in Madrid," unpublished typescript, 69. Fredericka Martin Papers, Brandeis University, Waltham, Massachusetts.

288 "called to a woman": Ibid., 65.

289 "Women of Madrid!": Dan Kurzman, *Miracle of November: Madrid's Epic Stand, 1936* (New York: G. P. Putnam's Sons, 1980), 214.

290 "never forget": Simone Téry, *Tina Modotti* (1942), 26.

290 "We saved many": Elena Poniatowska's interview with María Luisa Lafita, December 1981.

291 "organizing the sanitary service": Conchita Ruíz Funes's interview with Vittorio Vidali, Archivo de la Palabra, Mexico City.

291 "She was modest": Elena Poniatowska's interview with Manuel Fernández Colino, n.d.

291 "would pass by": Elena Poniatowska's interview with Flor Cernuda, n.d.

292 "shared because this": Elena Poniatowska's interview with María Luisa Lafita, 15 December 1981.

292 "brusque, heavy-drinking": Castro Delgado, *Hombres made in Moscow*, 293.

292 "one of the great": Herbert L. Matthews, *Half of Spain Died* (New York: Scribner's, 1973), 95.

293 "María was capable": Elena Poniatowska's interview with Flor Cernuda, n.d.

293 "And once": Ibid.

293 "Madrid is...": Kurzman, *Miracle of November*, 18.

294 "We give the guarantee": R. Dan Richard-

son, *Comintern Army: The International Brigades and the Spanish Civil War* (Lexington, Kentucky: University Press of Kentucky, 1982), 47.

294 "in a prison": Matthews, *Half of Spain Died*, 120.

294 A letter from Hemingway: Norberto Fuentes, *Hemingway in Cuba* (Secaucus, New Jersey: L. Stuart, 1984), 156.

294 "I have been": Tina Modotti cited in Barckhausen-Canale, *Verdad y leyenda de Tina Modotti*, 297.

295 The same batch: Ellero, *Tina Modotti in Carinzia e in Friuli*, 124–126.

295 "There is always": Letter from Mercedes Modotti to Marionne Richey, 2 March 1938.

295 "My mother died": Tina Modotti cited in Vittorio Vidali, *Retrato de mujer: Una Vida con Tina Modotti* (Puebla, Mexico: Universidad Autónoma de Puebla, 1984), 37.

295 "Dear sister": Letter from Tina Modotti to Mercedes Modotti, December 1936, cited in Barckhausen-Canale, *Verdad y leyenda de Tina Modotti*, 298.

296 "Until the time": Tina Modotti cited in *La Défense*, n.d. See Barckhausen-Canale, *Verdad y leyenda de Tina Modotti*, 282.

297 "the most terrible": Norman Bethune cited in *New York Herald-Tribune*, 18 February 1937.

297 "to carry blood-banks": Unpublished typescript, n.d., Fredericka Martin Papers, Brandeis University.

297 "Old Testament exodus": T. C. Worsley, "Malaga Has Fallen," in Murray A. Sperber, *And I Remember Spain* (New York: Macmillan, 1974), 274.

298 "an extraordinary woman": Vidali, *Retrato de mujer*, 40.

298 "Our car was besieged": Norman Bethune cited in Roderick Stewart, *Bethune* (Toronto: New Press, 1973), 100–101.

298 "Truly an atrocious experience": Tina Modotti cited in Vidali, *Retrato de mujer*, 39–40.

298–99 "lovely, very well-groomed": Constance Kyle cited in Margaret Hooks, *Tina Modotti: Photographer and Revolutionary* (San Francisco: Pandora, 1993), 230.

299 "very well kept up": Elena Poniatowska's interview with María Luisa Lafita, 15 December 1981.

299 "She was not": Elena Poniatowska's interview with Juan de la Cabada, 19 October 1980.

299 Vittorio recounted: Vidali, *Retrato de mujer*, 36.

299 "With my wife": Pino Caccuci, *I fuochi, le ombre, il silenzio* (Bologna: Agalev Edizioni, 1988), 84–85.

300 "In Catalonia": *Pravda*, 17 December 1936,

cited in Dorothy Gallagher, *All the Right Ene-mies: The Life and Murder of Carlo Tresca* (New Brunswick, New Jersey, and London: Rutgers University Press, 1988), 153.

300 "one of the main": Jesús Hernández, *La Grande Trahison* (Paris: Fasquelle Editeurs, 1953), 105–106.

301 "heard very bad": Elena Poniatowska's interview with Fernando Gamboa, 21 July 1981.

301 "*checkas* [Soviet-style interrogation squads] at Albacete": Matthews, *Half of Spain Died*, 110.

301 In his encyclopedic history: Andreu Castells, *Las brigadas internacionales de la guerra de España* (Espulques de Llobregat/Barcelona: Editorial Ariel, 1974), 225, 459.

302 "Dear Comrades": I am extremely grateful to Brazilian historian Dainis Karepovs for sharing his research with me. Karepovs worked with microfilmed documents in the Communist International collection at the Edgard Leuenroth Archive, University of Campinas (UNICAMP), Brazil. He presented his findings on the Besouchet case as a paper to the XIX National History Symposium, Belo Horizonte, Brazil, 21–25 July 1997. See Dainis Karepovs, "O 'Caso Besouchet' ou o Lado Brasileiro dos 'Processos de Moscou' Pelo Mundo."

Regarding the identity of "Jack," Karepovs suggests that he may be the Jack (mentioned in the memoirs of Charlotte Haldane) who worked at the International Brigades' Paris recruitment center. Among the papers of Yolanda Modotti Magrini, now in the collection of Ann Walnum, are two references to another Jack. A February 1943 note from Anthony Fusco to Yolanda speaks of Jack's recent stay at Ben Modotti's New York City apartment (during a period when Vittorio Vidali may have been in the city masterminding the assassination of Italian anarcho-socialist Carlo Tresca). A telegram from Jack to Yolanda, dated 6 February 1965 and written in English sprinkled with Italian, mentions possible visits to Yolanda and Ben Modotti. It is plausible that Jack was one of Vittorio Vidali's many aliases.

304 "All are young": Tina Modotti cited in Vidali, *Retrato de mujer*, 43.

305 "You should have shot": Philippe Cheron, "Tina Staliníssima," in *Vuelta* 82 (September 1983): 47.

305 "all my minutes": Letter from Tina Modotti to Mercedes Modotti, December 1936, cited in Ellero, *Tina Modotti in Carinzia e in Friuli*, 128.

305 "*Night has come*": Antonio Machado, "Meditation," in Alan S. Trueblood, trans., *Antonio*

Machado: Selected Poems (Cambridge, Massachusetts, and London: Harvard University Press, 1982), 263.

305 "The organization of the aid": Vidali, *Retrato de mujer*, 45.

306 "when I awakened": Ibid., 46.

306 For Tina's work: Elena Poniatowska's interview with Manuel Fernández Colino, n.d.

307 "of her we can say": Secours populaire pamphlet, cited in Barckhausen-Canale, *Verdad y leyenda de Tina Modotti*, 301.

307 Their words notwithstanding: James Martin Ryle, "International Red Aid: A Case Study of a Communist Front Organization" (master's thesis, Emory University, 1962), 88; Vittorio Vidali, *Diary of the Twentieth Congress of the Communist Party of the Soviet Union*, trans. Nell Amter Cattonar and A.M. Elliot (Westport, Connecticut: Lawrence Hill & Company, 1984), 17.

307 "It's not fair": Tina Modotti cited in Vidali, *Retrato de mujer*, 45–46.

308 "there, to my surprise": Mildred Constantine, *Tina Modotti: A Fragile Life* (San Francisco: Chronicle Books, 1993), 179–181.

309 "*And when the day*": Antonio Machado, "Portrait," in Trueblood, trans., *Antonio Machado*, 101.

309 Claude later remembered: Author's interview with Claude Willard, 9 April 1992.

309 "You're anxious": Vittorio Vidali, *La Caduta della repùbblica* (Milan: Vangelista, 1979), 108–109.

310 Days later: Ibid., 116–118.

310 Hotel St-Pierre: Elena Poniatowska's interview with Fernando Gamboa, 21 July 1981.

310 The sea was heavy: Author's telephone interview with Bill Windberg, 9 April 1993. The *Queen Mary* belonged to the Cunard White Star Line, which was offering passengers on its RMS *Ausonia* an entertainment program including "Latin-American and Spanish Songs by The 'Julio Mella' Trio." Cunard White Star Entertainment Programme, 16 December 1938, Niebyl-Proctor Library and Archives, Berkeley, California.

14. MEXICO CITY (1939–1942)

312 "Doesn't María": Elena Poniatowska's interview with Adelina Zendejas, 27 August 1981.

313 "That's all": Elena Poniatowska's interview with Monna Alfau, 24 August 1981.

313 Objections to: Lois Elwyn Smith, *Mexico and the Spanish Republicans* (Berkeley and Los Angeles: University of California Press, 1955), 244.

313 "veterans of the Fifth": Ralph de Toledano, *Lament for a Generation* (New York: Farrar, Straus and Cudahy, 1960), 49.

314 Leonid Eitingon: Robert Conquest, *The Great Terror* (New York and Oxford, England: Oxford University Press, 1990), 416.

315 "[W]hat [Spanish poet Antonio] Machado": Elena Poniatowska's interview with Adelina Zendejas, 27 August 1981.

315 Leni Kroul: Author's interview with Leni Kroul, 16 February 1998.

316 New York: During the Spanish Civil War, Tina once claimed to have lived in Brooklyn, New York, a statement she probably would have made only if familiar with the city. Alessandro Baccari, Jr., asserts that, during the 1910s, Tina spent several weeks in New York City, where she worked as a photographic model for his father. Her uncles Angelo and Francesco Modotti were then living in the area. It is also possible that Tina had traveled to New York during the 1920s or 1930s on a Party mission.

317 Manuel Fernández Colino: Christiane Barckhausen-Canale, *Verdad y leyenda de Tina Modotti* (Mexico City: Editorial Diana, 1992), 320.

317 "from Roberto's country": Letter from Mercedes Modotti to Tina Modotti, 1 April 1939, cited in Gianfranco Ellero, *Tina Modotti in Carinzia e in Friuli* (Pordenone, Italy: Cinemazero, 1996), 129. The name Roberto apparently refers to the photographer Roberto Turnbull, whom Mercedes may have met when he visited Los Angeles in 1922.

318 *"Addìo!"*: Benvenuto Modotti, "Come morì Tina Modotti," *L'Unità del Pòpolo* (New York), 13 November 1948.

318 "already very much": Elena Poniatowska's interview with Lya Cardoza y Aragón, 13 January 1982.

318 "our big family": Letter from Tina Modotti to Leni Kroul, 16 April 1940. My thanks to Christiane Barckhausen-Canale for making this letter available to me.

318 "Out of fear": Jesús Hernández, *La Grande Trahison* (Paris: Fasquelle Editeurs, 1953), 10.

318 When it came time: Official Party membership was not a sine qua non of commitment to communism. One of Mexico's most orthodox Stalinists, David Alfaro Siqueiros, was officially banned from the Communist party between 1929 or 1930 and 1946.

319 "But how can we": Vittorio Vidali, *Retrato de mujer: Una Vida con Tina Modotti* (Puebla, Mexico: Universidad Autónoma de Puebla, 1984), 53–54.

319 The cold light of political reality: My account of the congress draws upon Lois Elwyn Smith, *Mexico and the Spanish Republi-*

cans (Berkeley and Los Angeles: University of California Press, 1955), 250–251.

319 a position that, some believed: Margaret Hooks, *Tina Modotti: Photographer and Revolutionary* (San Francisco: Pandora, 1993), 240–241.

319 Social scientists: Adam Hochschild, *The Unquiet Ghost: Russians Remember Stalin* (New York: Viking Penguin, 1994), 58–59.

319 Vittorio was acting as an intermediary: Dorothy Gallagher, *All the Right Enemies: The Life and Murder of Carlo Tresca* (New Brunswick, New Jersey, and London: Rutgers University Press, 1988), 169. An unpublished typescript in the Anita Brenner archives apparently presents evidence that Tina served as a liaison between Germany and the Soviet Union. See Susannah Joel Glusker, *Anita Brenner: A Mind of Her Own* (Austin: University of Texas Press, 1998), 173.

320 "a tact": Elena Poniatowska's interview with Eladia de los Ríos, 12 August 1981.

320 Friends remember: Author's telephone interview with Laura and John Condax, 24 August 1998.

320 "the old lady": Elena Poniatowska's interview with Adelina Zendejas, 27 August 1981.

320 "They're not the same": Tina Modotti cited in Vidali, *Retrato de mujer*, 54.

320 "Your private secretary": Tina Modotti cited in Barckhausen-Canale, *Verdad y leyenda de Tina Modotti*, 323.

321 "because I didn't": Elena Poniatowska's interview with Adelina Zendejas, 27 August 1981.

321 "beautiful letter": Conchita Ruíz Funes's interview with Vittorio Vidali, Archivo de la Palabra, Mexico City.

321 "I called Tina": Author's interview with Leni Kroul, 16 February 1998.

322 "She still bore": Mildred Constantine's interview with Rosendo Gómez Lorenzo, 25 January 1974, The Getty, Research Institute for the History of Art and the Humanities, Los Angeles, California.

322 "very bad": Elena Poniatowska's interview with Fernando Gamboa, 21 July 1981.

322 "You traipsed": Author's interview with Leni Kroul, 16 February 1998.

322 "harder than the devil": Elena Poniatowska's interview with Eladia de los Ríos, 12 August 1981.

323 "an adorable person": Letter from Anita Leocadia Prestes to the author, 25 November 1997.

323 "[A]s to the": Letter from Bertram Wolfe to Martin Temple, 5 April 1940, Bertram D. Wolfe Papers, Hoover Institution Archives, Stanford University, Stanford, California.

323 He was later to win promotion: Seymour Freidin, "Is Tito His Next Target?" *New York Herald-Tribune, This Week Magazine,* 5 February 1950.

323 During the weeks leading up: Author's telephone interview with Laura and John Condax, 24 August 1998; Margaret Hooks, "Assignment, Mexico: The Mystery of the Missing Modottis," *Afterimage* 19, no. 4 (November 1991) 10–11.

324 "[A]t that time": Elena Poniatowska's interview with Manuel Alvarez Bravo, 12 September 1981.

325 "Tina listened to me": Clara Porset, *Tina Modotti* (1942), 17.

325 "according to the famous film director": *Hoy* (Mexico City), 17 January 1942.

325 "the choice of": Susan Sontag, "The Aesthetics of Silence," in *A Susan Sontag Reader* (New York: Farrar Straus & Giroux, 1982), 183.

325 "Come, come": Elena Poniatowska's interview with Eladia de los Ríos, 12 August 1981; author's interview with Eladia de los Ríos, 24 September 1997.

326 Vittorio vanished: Vittorio Vidali, *Giornale di bordo* (Milan: Vangelista Editore, 1977), 100.

326 she trembled uncontrollably: Hooks, *Tina Modotti,* 246.

327 "Well, there are two of us": Vidali, *Retrato de mujer,* 55.

327 "But this is not": Ibid.

328 "with a joy": Mario Montagnana, *Tina Modotti* (1942), 47.

328 She wrote to her nephew: Author's interview with Bruno Cosolo, 4 February 1997.

328 "Eladia, I feel": Author's interview with Eladia de los Ríos, 24 September 1997.

328 "María saw": Simone Téry, *Tina Modotti,* (1942), 26.

329 "I was just": Tina Modotti cited in *Hoy,* 17 January 1942.

330 "Yes, what's happened?": Vidali, *Retrato de mujer,* 62.

330 "fanatical agent of the GPU": *La Prensa,* 8 January 1942.

330 "on the same cement slab": Elena Poniatowska's interview with Adelina Zendejas, 27 August 1981.

330 The forensic report: Death certificate of Tina Modotti Mondini, no. 156273, 7 January 1942, Registro Civil, Mexico City; *El Nacional,* 7 January 1942; Hooks, *Tina Modotti,* 253.

331 "was tragic": Bertram D. Wolfe, *The Fabulous Life of Diego Rivera* (New York: Stein and Day, 1969), 195.

331 "The latest [crime]": Carlo Tresca quoted in *Il Martello,* 4 May 1942, cited in Gallagher, *All the Right Enemies,* 186. When anti-Stalinist leftists gathered for Tresca's memorial meeting in Mexico City some weeks later, they were attacked by one hundred Communists wielding crowbars and knives, allegedly under the command of Vittorio Vidali.

332 Every one of her five siblings: Joseph Modotti, State of California Certificate of Death no. 0190-057058, State of California, Department of Health Services; Yolanda Magrini, State of California Certificate of Death no. 39119047831, County of Los Angeles; letter from William Stern, City of New York Department of Health, to Mrs. Y. Magrini, 24 February 1963, in the collection of Ann Walnum; author's interview with Bruno Cosolo, 4 February 1997.

332 "Tiña Modotti": "Tito & the Executioner," *Time,* 6 September 1948. Vidali had returned permanently to Italy in 1947. In 1956, he was present at Khrushchev's "secret speech" about the Stalinist terror to the Twentieth Congress of the Soviet Communist Party. Vidali made the implausible claim that the purges were news to him and that he was "speechless, horrified. I thought of those comrades who had died. I seemed to see their faces in front of me and seemed to hear the jokes they used to tell. I remembered them with deep affection. All this is fantastic, atrocious." See Vittorio Vidali, *Diary of the Twentieth Congress of the Communist Party of the Soviet Union,* trans. Nell Amter Cattonar and A. M. Elliot (Westport, Connecticut: Lawrence Hill & Company, 1984), 18.

332 "She was seriously ill": Benvenuto Modotti, "Come mori Tina Modotti," *L'Unità del Pòpolo,* 13 November 1948.

332 "I never knew": Letter from Mercedes Modotti to Edward Weston, 16 March 1946, cited in Ellero, *Tina Modotti in Carinzia e in Friuli,* 48.

333 *"Perfect your gentle":* Pablo Neruda, "Tina Modotti Is Dead," trans. Alastair Reid, cited in Mildred Constantine, *Tina Modotti: A Fragile Life* (San Francisco: Chronicle Books, 1993), 190.

333 "broken, suffering voice": "El Hombre de la Esquina" (Mexico City, n.d.).

333 "tragic conflict": Letter from Tina Modotti to Edward Weston, 14 November 1926, Edward Weston Archive, Center for Creative Photography, University of Arizona, Tucson.

Permissions

The author and publisher gratefully acknowledge the following for permission to reprint previously published and unpublished material:

Excerpts from Christiane Barckhausen-Canale, *Verdad y leyenda de Modotti,* Mexico City: Editorial Diana, copyright © 1992 (reprinted 1998), by permission of Christiane Barckhausen-Canale.

Excerpts from papers of and letters to Carleton Beals by permission of Special Collections, Boston University Libraries, Boston.

Excerpt from "To Those Born Later" by Bertolt Brecht, in *Bertolt Brecht: Poems, 1913–1956,* copyright © 1976 by Methuen Publishing Limited, London.

Quotes from the "Research papers regarding Tina Modotti, 1920–1993" by Mildred Constantine, by permission of Getty Research Institute, Research Library, 900223, Los Angeles, California, and Mildred Constantine.

Excerpts from Thomas F. Walsh's interview with Mary Louis Doherty, c. 1982, by permission of Margaret D. Neal, and Papers of Thomas F. Walsh, Special Collections, University of Maryland Libraries.

Material quoted from Harry Lawton's interviews of Peter Krasnow and Roy Rosen are printed through the courtesy of the Special Collections Library, University of California, Riverside, where they are part of the Sadakichi Hartmann Collection.

Excerpts from "Portrait" and "Meditation" by Antonio Machado, reprinted by permission of the publisher from *Antonio Machado: Selected Poems* by Alan S. True-blood (trans.), Cambridge, Mass.: Harvard University Press, copyright © 1982 by the President and Fellows of Harvard College.

Excerpts from "Tina Modotti Is Dead" by Pablo Neruda, by permission of Alastair Reid (trans.).

Quotes from Elena Poniatowska's interviews by permission of Elena Poniatowska.

Excerpt from "Canto LXXXI" by Ezra Pound, from *The Cantos of Ezra Pound,* copyright © 1948 by Ezra Pound. Reprinted by permission of New Directions Publishing Corporation, New York, and Faber and Faber Ltd., London.

Excerpt from the unpublished English-language manuscript *Mercy in Madrid* by Mary Bingham de Urquidi, by permission of Magdelena Urquidi de Acosta, María Urquidi, and Victor L. Urquidi.

Excerpts from Vittorio Vidali, *Retrato de mujer: Una Vida con Tina Modotti,* Antonella Fagetti (trans.), Puebla, Mexico: Universidad Autónoma de Puebla, copyright © 1984, by permission of Carlos Vidali.

Quotes from Conchita Ruíz Funes's interview with Vittorio Vidali, by permission of Biblioteca Nacional de Antropologia e Historia, and Dirección de Estudios Históricos, I.N.A.H., Mexico City.

Texts by Edward Weston, copyright © 1981 Arizona Board of Regents, Center for Creative Photography.

Excerpts from *The Fabulous Life of Diego Rivera* by Bertram D. Wolfe, 08128-1259-x, copyright © 1969 by Stein and Day, by permission of University Press of America, Lanham, Maryland.

PHOTOGRAPHS

Tina at age four...: Collection of Bruno Cosolo.

Tina, 1923: Photograph by Edward Weston, © 1981 Center for Creative Photography, Arizona Board of Regents.

Tina, 1924: Photograph by Edward Weston, © 1981 Center for Creative Photography, Arizona Board of Regents.

Portrait of Edward Weston with a Camera: New Orleans Museum of Art: Museum purchase, Women's Volunteer Committee Fund.

Tina, Reciting, 1924: Photograph by Edward Weston, © 1981 Center for Creative Photography, Arizona Board of Regents.

Tina Modotti: Charlot Collection, University of Hawai'i at Manoa.

Calla Lilies: Fototeca I.N.A.H., Pachuca, Mexico.

Interior of Church: Page Imageworks: Tony and Merrily Page.

Roses: Private collection. Copy print by Mark Citret.

Telephone Wires, Mexico: The Baltimore Museum of Art: Purchase with exchange funds from the Edward Joseph Gallagher III Memorial Collection; and Partial Gift of George H. Dalsheimer, Baltimore, BMA 1988.474.

Campesinos: Hallmark Photographic Collection, Hallmark Cards, Inc., Kansas City, Missouri.

Xavier Guerrero: Charlot Collection, University of Hawai'i at Manoa.

Hands Resting on Tool: The J. Paul Getty Museum, Los Angeles.

Child in Sombrero: Fototeca I.N.A.H., Pachuca, Mexico.

Mexican Sombrero with Hammer and Sickle: Courtesy of Irwin Mayers.

Julio Antonio Mella: Throckmorton Fine Art, Inc., New York.

Mella's Typewriter or *La Técnica:* Tina Modotti. 1928. Gelatin-silver print, $9^3/_8$ x $7^1/_2$" (23.8 x 19 cm.). The Museum of Modern Art, New York. Anonymous gift. Copy Print © 1999 The Museum of Modern Art, New York.

Inspector Valente Quintana... / With a police officer... / Police searching... / Tina awaits her turn... / Tina at the Tizayuca rally...: Archivo General de la Nación, Mexico City.

Distributing Arms: Throckmorton Fine Art, Inc., New York.

Woman with Flag: Tina Modotti. 1928. Palladium print by Richard Benson, 1982. $9^3/_4$ x $7^{11}/_{16}$" (24.8 x 19.1 cm.). The Museum of Modern Art, New York. Courtesy of Isabel Carbajal Bolandi. Copy Print © 1999 The Museum of Modern Art, New York.

Hands of a Puppeteer: Center for Creative Photography, University of Arizona, Tucson.

Tina's snapshot of Vittorio Vidali... / Tina and Vittorio...: Collection of Angelo Masutti.

Eugen Heilig's photograph of Tina...: Courtesy of Monica and Walter Heilig.

"María" with Spanish Communists...: Collection of Christiane Barckhausen-Canale.

Tina in her coffin: Courtesy of *La Prensa,* Mexico City.

Additional copy photography by Chucke Creative Photography, The Darkroom, and Chris Wisner.

Index